THE SUMMIT

THE SUMMIT

BRETTON WOODS, 1944

J.M. KEYNES AND THE RESHAPING
OF THE GLOBAL ECONOMY

ED CONWAY

PEGASUS BOOKS
NEW YORK LONDON

THE SUMMIT

Pegasus Books LLC
80 Broad Street, 5th Floor
New York, NY 10004

First Pegasus Books hardcover edition February 2015

ISBN: 978-1-60598-681-4

10 9 8 7 8 6 5 4 3 2 1

Printed in the United States of America
Distributed by W. W. Norton & Company, Inc.

For my mother, and in memory of my father

Contents

PART IV: THE LIFE AND DEATH OF BRETTON WOODS

Prologue
Saturday 22 July 1944

It wasn't until dinner was about to be served that the assembled guests realised someone was missing.

The dining hall was already packed with delegates. The majority of them were formally dressed in ties or bow ties, though if you looked closely you'd soon notice the bags under their eyes and the slow gait borne of sleep deprivation. Everyone was exhausted. For three weeks they had been negotiating; by turns remonstrating and revelling with each other in the conference rooms, corridors and bars of the hotel. Most had worked through the nights in a desperate bid to close a deal in time.

And this was it: Bretton Woods' final act. The closing banquet and plenary session where it would be revealed whether the most ambitious economic negotiations in history had been a success.

For it was far from assured, even with only a couple of hours left, that the conference would end in triumph. The Russians were still refusing to sign. They had spent the past weeks stubbornly contesting the terms under which they would participate. Rumour had it that Stalin himself had ordered his representatives to stand firm against the Americans. The uncertainty had cast a shadow over the event: after three weeks of near-twenty-four-hour working days, which in turn had followed months and years of behind-the-scenes preparation, the conference looked as though it would end in discord.

That said, merely getting this far was an achievement in itself. The world's leading economic minds had travelled from every corner of the globe, many of them dodging attack on the way. One delegate had even come straight from a prisoner-of-war camp.

The outcome of the war itself was as yet uncertain: British and American troops had landed in Normandy for Operation Overlord only a few weeks before; in the Pacific, Japan occupied most of the contested territories and had only just lost control of Thailand. Momentum was going the Allies' way but even in a best-case scenario, the conflict would not be over for some time.

Moreover, nothing of the scale and ambition of Bretton Woods had been achieved before. The objective was self-consciously grand: to replace the mangled global monetary system responsible for the Great Depression (and, by extension, for the war) with something that worked. No one had ever successfully modified the international monetary system: instead, it had evolved incrementally – from the early days of mercantilism to the British Empire-dominated gold standard which collapsed in 1914, through to the flimsy system of currencies and rules erected after the Great Depression in the 1930s. All previous efforts to achieve what the delegates were attempting had failed, without exception.

Devising a comprehensive new system of governing the world economy was challenge enough, even before one stopped to consider whether it could actually be implemented. For a spectre hung over the Bretton Woods conference: that of the peace summit in Paris twenty-five years before. There, in the Hall of Mirrors at Versailles, the world's leaders had agreed upon a deal which they thought would secure a lasting peace throughout Europe. In the event, it had merely sown the seeds of the Second World War.

Imposing reparations on Germany had served to fuel resentment both in Berlin and among the French and British, who claimed the largest amounts. Nor did the leaders even countenance trying to tackle the broader economic mess left behind by the collapse of the gold standard. To add to the general discord, the Americans had consigned the League of Nations to irrelevance by refusing to join. They had shown scant regard for the sporadic conferences the League sponsored in the interwar period aimed at repairing the world economy.

Here at Bretton Woods, the task was not merely to design an entirely new set of monetary rules, but to show that, for the first time, the US really would engage. Bretton Woods was to be the litmus test of whether twentieth-century internationalism could really work, clearing the path for the foundation of the United Nations the following year.

That, at least, was the official ambition. But had you asked each delegation what they wanted out of the conference, you would have received a host of conflicting answers. For the US, this was the moment to demonstrate their rise to the status of the world's undisputed superpower. Britain's twin aims were to ensure the survival of as much of the Empire as possible while reducing their enormous wartime debts. The Mexicans were desperate that silver would play a part in the world's new economic system (no prizes for guessing their biggest precious-metal export); the French wanted to be recognised as a sovereign economic state. And the Russians ... well, by the beginning of the final dinner it looked as if they had turned up purely to sabotage the deal.

For many, the best that could be hoped for from this banquet and closing plenary session was that, somehow, Henry Morgenthau, the US Treasury Secretary, could put a positive spin on the quandary. But some members of his delegation had privately conceded that failure to secure Russian involvement would represent a failure of the conference.

Predictably, the row with the Soviets had centred on money – specifically, how much the Russians would contribute to the new system of global economic management. And the mood had soured in the past twenty-four hours as it emerged that, despite their politeness and genuine engagement in the sessions, the Russians were unwilling to budge. To add to the delegates' worries, meanwhile, even the Australians, who had seemed to be in favour of the agreement, hadn't been granted permission by Canberra to sign up, with only an hour to go until that final dinner.

This was as much as most of the delegates knew as they filed into the dining room. Despite the hotel's best efforts to keep numbers manageable, hundreds had turned up that night: bleary-eyed delegates, lobbyists, the local great and the good, journalists and even the odd gatecrasher.

The only people assured of a seat were the big names: the chairmen of the delegations, who had taken their places at the high table – at least, all but one of them.

Not every Allied country was represented at Bretton Woods. President Franklin D. Roosevelt had insisted on involving the 'Big Four' – the US, Britain, the Soviet Union and China – but who should come along with them was up for debate. And as with so much else at Bretton Woods, even this had turned into a battle of influence between the British and the Americans. The British regarded the Latin Americans and the Chinese as entirely craven before the US. The Americans suspected the British had undue influence over the Greeks and Indians. In the end the delegations were whittled down to forty-four, though that was still a few too many for the British, who considered the whole enterprise variously a 'monstrous monkeyhouse', a 'Tower of Babel'.

And there were considerable language issues. Officially at least, the conference language was English, but some of the delegates insisted on speaking in their mother tongue. The chairman of the French delegation, Pierre Mendès France, would happily converse with other delegates in fluent English when they bumped into each other in the corridor, but as soon as the microphones were switched on in the committee rooms, he flipped back into French. Nonetheless, that was one step better than the Russian representative, Mikhail

Stepanov, who couldn't speak a word of English. But what he and his team lacked in linguistic proficiency, they made up for in their superhuman consumption of alcohol. Almost every evening they were to be found in the hotel's underground bar and nightclub knocking back spirits and trying enthusiastically to communicate with their foreign counterparts, until that proved too much effort and they burst into Russian folk songs.

The Soviet delegates' days were even more fraught. They and their interpreters spent half their time straining to understand the complex terms being hammered out in the plenary sessions, and the other half trying desperately to confer with Moscow. As one of the delegates later recalled, 'I could not help feeling that they were struggling between the firing squad on the one hand and the English language on the other.'[1]

Grasp of the English language was less of a problem for 'Daddy' Kung, the head of the Chinese delegation. H.H. Kung (full name K'ung Hsiang-hsi) had studied at Yale, and spent much of his life at various points between the US and China. Eventually, after the Communists overthrew the Nationalist government, he would move back to the US and live out his final days a few hours from Bretton Woods, in upstate New York. One of the conference's biggest characters, literally and figuratively, the rotund, genial fellow was a distant descendant of Confucius, and the richest man in China. An outside observer might reasonably have assumed that his real aim at Bretton Woods was to throw the most lavish parties. Remodelling the world economy, so far as it seemed, was something best left to his advisers, who actually engaged with the negotiations.

For most of the conference, Morgenthau took a similar stance, leaving the grunt work to his deputy Harry Dexter White, who boasted that he scarcely had more than five hours' rest a night for the entire conference. But tonight it was Morgenthau himself – the head of the US delegation and honorary president of the conference – who took centre stage. He had sent round word for the dinner and plenary to be brought forward by half an hour so he could broadcast his final speech live to the nation.

Which is why there were eyebrows raised about that empty seat. All of the other major representatives – including Kung, Stepanov, Mendès France and the Canadian delegation head J.L. Ilsley – were now seated around Morgenthau.

Late on Wednesday, three nights earlier, John Maynard Keynes had been taken ill as he bounded up the stairs after a meeting with Morgenthau. They had been arguing about a relatively minor element of the negotiations – whether or not the Bank for International Settlements should be dismantled – when Keynes had dashed up to his room on the second floor of the hotel. He collapsed shortly afterwards.

It was well known that the head of the British delegation had been in poor health. For more than half a decade he had suffered from bacterial endocarditis, an infection of the heart valves which sapped his energy and left him at risk of heart attacks. He had already suffered a series of attacks, so arrangements at the conference had been geared towards preventing the recurrence of something like this. Rather than flying across the Atlantic he had sailed; he left much of the late night work to his colleagues, and tried to resist the temptation to stay out and socialise.

Even so, his was an arduous schedule: 'The pressure of work here has been quite unbelievable,' he wrote in a letter home.[2] This is unsurprising, given the timeframe within which the conference was attempting to devise an unprecedented set of new rules for international economics. True, the fundamentals of the system had been hammered out in the previous months, but securing agreement on the technical terms with forty-four countries to please was turning out to be a superhuman challenge.

Within a few hours, word of Keynes's collapse had spread downstairs to the bar. Journalists presumed he had suffered a heart attack on his way up that staircase. Reuters reported that he had died. Panic spread through the hotel.

That was Wednesday night; and by the time of the banquet three days later, few had since caught sight of the grand old man of economics. Rumour had it that he was back on his feet, but, then again, there was that empty chair staring ominously at the delegates as they sat and waited for the food to be served.

Perhaps the most important single figure at the conference, J.M. Keynes stood, more than anyone else, for what Bretton Woods was about. He had been there in Paris in 1919; he was the man who predicted with eerie prescience the breakdown of the Versailles Treaty, in his internationally bestselling pamphlet *The Economic Consequences of the Peace*. Hero-worshipped by economists and philosophers around the world, he could scarcely move from one meeting room to another at the conference without being accosted by yet another admirer seeking advice, or pearls of wisdom.

Keynes was a genuine international celebrity, the only household name at Bretton Woods – save perhaps for renowned magician Cardini, who had inexplicably appeared in the hotel bar one night to entertain delegates with his illusions. He was instrumental in the Allied war effort. The Reuters report of his alleged death was celebrated on the front pages in Germany.

And not only was Keynes the chairman of one of the Big Four delegations, he was the joint author of a significant chunk of the Bretton Woods proposals. The symbolism of Keynes's role was not lost on his fellow delegates: here was the man who had foreseen World War Two, leading us towards a settlement which would prevent World War Three.

His collapse had shaken everyone. As one of his colleagues wrote: 'I now feel that it is a race between the exhaustion of his powers and the termination of the conference.'[3]

Keynes's battle wasn't merely with his health. In conference rooms on both sides of the Atlantic, he had also been fighting the

American delegation throughout the negotiations. And in these clashes he had come up against a stubborn opponent in the form of White, a rather obscure fifty-one-year-old from the US Treasury.

White was everything Keynes was not. Where Keynes was six foot six inches tall, White was short and stocky. Keynes was part of the British establishment, a member of the House of Lords; White was a self-made man from the rough side of the tracks in Boston. Keynes was a self-publicist, frequently courting the press when he wasn't writing for it; White was one of those shy fellows who wears a loud tie in an attempt to express his colourful side – he relished his privacy and never wrote a major work, save for his doctoral thesis. Keynes had been a conscientious objector in the First World War; White served in the trenches in France.

They were the odd couple of international economics, and for much of the time their relationship had been rocky, caustic and occasionally aggressive. The pair would shout at each other in meetings, bully each other in an attempt to get their way and, afterwards, abuse their rival to their friends.

And yet, despite their differences, this odd couple also had much in common. Both were irreverent outsiders. Both were brilliant. Both rubbed their colleagues up the wrong way; President Roosevelt and British Prime Minister Winston Churchill had respectively appointed White and Keynes out of necessity rather than choice. Because none of their colleagues really knew how to deal with them, both were given rather vague positions and unusual autonomy – something which would later destroy White's career. And, to a level almost unheard of today, despite being unelected advisers, both overshadowed the finance ministers they were officially serving.

And what they had come up with together was a blueprint for a world economy that looked as if it might just work. However, the Bretton Woods system would face discredit from the very beginning if the meeting was to end in the kind of discord the Russians were threatening.

The view from the great windows of the dining hall was as majestic as ever. As the diners took their seats, the room was suddenly flooded with light. As if answering to some almighty cue, the clouds that had hung over the summit of Mount Washington throughout the day suddenly lifted. Pale evening light glinted off the peak. If you had cast your eyes down from the top of the mountain, into the valley that enclosed Bretton Woods, you would have spotted the serene fairways of the golf course, the flags fluttering on the greens and then, close enough that you could hear it, the brook that ran by the hotel itself.

The delegates sat down to see whether they really were about to make history.

The phrase 'history in the making' is bandied around so often that it has lost most of its potency. But when the delegates turned up to the Mount Washington Hotel in the summer of 1944 they were under no delusions that that was precisely what they were doing.

Their task was breathtakingly ambitious: nothing less than to repair the world economy by fashioning a system whereby countries could trade with each other without the threat of financial and economic crises like the ones which had punctuated the 1920s and 1930s. On their shoulders was the responsibility of ensuring that their countrymen would never again face either mass unemployment or economic deprivation, both of which might lead them back to war against each other. The system they created is regarded by many economists as a remarkable success. Indeed the very name 'Bretton Woods' is now used as political and economic shorthand for something very simple: real economic recovery.

Only a handful of the men and women who travelled up to New Hampshire that summer were widely known outside their bureaucracies. There were no heads of state – though no fewer than seven delegates would go on to be presidents and prime ministers of their respective countries. They were, as far as the public was concerned, anonymous technicians and negotiators. What was more, neither of the two lead players in the drama, White and Keynes, was in charge of his country's finance department. Keynes wasn't even a paid official.

Though journalists walked the corridors of the Mount Washington alongside them, and though there were occasional intrusions from domestic politics, the delegates were granted remarkable freedom simply to get on with things. With the press and public fixated on the V1 attacks and the Normandy landings, whereby Allied troops were embarking on the campaign to reclaim mainland Europe, Keynes and White managed to work under the radar. The two representatives had a unique degree of independence to create a blueprint for running the world economy.

They were helped by the fact that, then as now, the workings of the international monetary system are rarely front-page news until they go horribly wrong. However, the rules and agreements on how exchange rates interact, how money flows from one country to another and how central banks set interest rates are the very bedrock of how our economies function. Ever since the first civilisations began trading with each other millennia ago, swapping coins for goods, there has been an international monetary system. And while other economic issues – unemployment, incomes, the behaviour of bankers and businessmen – have always hogged the headlines, their root causes can often be traced back to the behaviour of the system.

It had been thus in the early twentieth century, when the gold standard frayed, triggering an economic chain reaction (hyper-inflation in Austria and Germany, European financial collapse, trade wars and so on) that culminated in the Great Depression and the Second World War. It was thus in 2008 and thereafter, when imbalances between countries in surplus and those in deficit (whether America v. China or Germany v. Greece) caused build-ups of debt which in turn contributed both to a global financial crisis and to the near-collapse of the euro.

Today's global monetary apparatus, with its floating exchange rates and free movement of money across borders, may feel like an inevitable part of the economic furniture. Not only is it relatively young, its very existence is a consequence of a series of accidents, of crises and of short-term political decisions that turned permanent.

This book is, in one sense, an economic history of the past century. Over that period, the characters in these pages changed the international monetary system beyond recognition, and changed our lives in the process. But Bretton Woods sits at its very centre for a simple reason — and not merely because it happened midway through the twentieth century.

The system mapped out by the delegates to the Mount Washington in those three weeks in 1944 permitted the longest period of stability and economic growth in history. Its protagonists laid the firm foundations the global economy had been missing since the collapse of the gold standard in 1914. The institutions these men and women created — the International Monetary Fund and World Bank — are as important today as they were upon their creation.

For a brief period of a couple of decades after the conference, the world economy grew at a faster rate than either under the gold standard or in the more recent, modern era between the late 1970s and 2008. The incidence of financial crises was lower than ever before. Fewer banks failed. Imbalances (in other words trade surpluses and deficits) were smaller. Over the same period, inflation was low and the income gap between the rich and the poor remained narrow.

There is no such thing as a perfect economic system; but, based on its performance, many economists still argue that Bretton Woods was as close as the global economy has ever come to it. Others maintain that stability and economic health during this period was due to other factors – that the system behaved very differently from how the men and women meeting at the Mount Washington anticipated; some argue that Bretton Woods merely stored up problems that exploded in its wake.

Whatever you believe, however – and, this being economics, there will never be a definitive answer – Bretton Woods remains the only time countries ever came together to remould the world's monetary system. And for a tantalising couple of decades, it seemed to work.

But while the IMF and the World Bank live on, the actual system they oversaw, the rules hammered out in 1944 to lay down how different nations should interact economically, is long dead. In 1971, his country's finances straining under the cost of the Vietnam War, Richard Nixon hammered the final nail into Bretton Woods' coffin. The system had been under strain for some time, but when the President ended the link between the US dollar and gold the international monetary system was changed for ever. From that moment, the value of a country's banknotes was linked not to a reference point – be it gold, silver or even the international currency called 'bancor' which Keynes tried and failed to create at Bretton Woods – but to pure trust. Some would nickname this system Bretton Woods II, but in reality it was drastically different from its predecessor.

Since 1971 we have been living in an era of what is called fiat money, where a currency's value depends on the trust investors have in its issuer. To some economists, this is as it should be – many are grateful that there are no longer universal controls on the flow of money from one country to another, as there were for much of the post-war period.

But, expedient and economically elegant though it might have seemed to rid the world of Bretton Woods, there are more troubling correlations since its demise. After 1971, the gap between rich and poor started to widen abruptly. The world has become ever more dominated by the financial industry. The imbalances between debtor and creditor countries have ballooned to unprecedented levels. Economic life has been punctuated with spells of high inflation and sporadic financial crises. Little surprise that, for many politicians at least, Bretton Woods stands for a return to a more ordered world, where there are clearly defined rules about how countries interact with each other economically. It stands for a moment when economists finally took control of a chaotic financial system and wrung some sense into it. No wonder so many politicians want another such agreement – however futile and misguided such an aspiration may be.

Easy as it is to cast Bretton Woods as a symbol of an economic Nirvana, the reality was rather messier. The agreements that emerged were far from perfect. They bore the scars of a difficult birth. There were clauses inserted to please certain countries, others omitted to prevent delegates from storming out. The three weeks delegates spent in New Hampshire in July 1944 were remarkable not for their order and predictability but for their chaos, epitomised by the uncertainty evident as the conference entered its final hours.

Indeed, as delegates made their weary way home from the US, more than a few had serious misgivings about the way the conference ended, and about whether the agreement would ever be fully implemented. And indeed, the system that was eventually created would function quite differently from the templates drawn up by White and Keynes.

It is the aim of this book to describe what really happened in those remarkable twenty-two days – and, of course, the months and years of surrounding meetings and behind-the-scenes debates that are equally intriguing.

For some reason, while it remains one of economics' few household names, Bretton Woods is frequently ignored in accounts of the period. It is not altogether difficult to understand why: it is all too

easy to dismiss international monetary economics as esoteric and
irrelevant – rather than, as it is, the gel that bonds countries
together. Moreover, most of the delegates responsible continue to
be obscure figures who might at best feature in passing in economic
histories or biographies.

It is remarkable that, seventy years on, there is still so much left
to be discovered about Bretton Woods. There have been a number
of books about the conference, from Richard Gardner's 1956
Sterling–Dollar Diplomacy to Benn Steil's 2013 *Battle of Bretton
Woods*, and yet all of them have tended to focus far more on the
economics than the sheer human drama of what happened at
the Mount Washington. They have tended to draw on a relatively
narrow series of sources and have focused almost exclusively on the
struggle between Britain and the United States. Astonishingly,
despite the significant role played by Russia in the conference, since
the opening of the former Soviet archives to researchers in the
wake of the ending of the Cold War, no one had even consulted
the key Finance Ministry files on the Soviet part in Bretton
Woods until the writing of this book. Even among the British
and American delegates, many personal recollections, diaries and
accounts of the conference are published here for the first time.

In broader works about the Second World War Bretton Woods
is usually ignored in favour of the summits at Yalta and Potsdam,
its legacy overshadowed by the Marshall Plan. This is greatly to
underplay its significance.

It is not merely that Bretton Woods was the first major deal
struck in the attempt to construct the post-war world; nor indeed
that alongside the Marshall Plan it helped foster the reconstruction
of Europe and the phoenix-like revival of Japan. It is not even that
the deal was the first substantive move towards the multilateral
post-war world, where countries come together to talk in international institutions. It is not just the intriguing geopolitics, with
Russia yet to construct a coherent international economic policy, or

the surprising level of influence wielded by China, Brazil and India, countries that would not impose themselves again on the global stage for several more decades. It is not only that it provides a glimpse of what US–Soviet co-operation might have looked like, were it not for the onset of the Cold War a couple of years later. It is not just the fact that this marked the moment the United States officially took on the mantle of global economic superpower. Nor, finally, is it merely that the issues grappled with in New Hampshire still haunt the world economy today.

It is also something far simpler: Bretton Woods is a gripping tale.

Few today remember the conference's nail-biting climax. Few recall that during those three weeks of discussions (and indeed in the months that followed), bankers from New York took outrageous steps to try to destroy the agreement. Few remember that the original seed for what became Bretton Woods came not from Britain or America, but from Nazi Germany.

In the end, the final deal was also, in large part, a reflection of the characters who vied to create it: Morgenthau, determined to uproot London as the financial centre of the world and put New York in its rightful place; Keynes, eager to prevent Britain from sinking into obscurity; Stepanov, desperate not to disappoint Joseph Stalin and his foreign commissar Molotov; the Mexican delegation, intent on advocating the role of silver in the new monetary system; and White: brilliant, inscrutable, and carrying with him a secret which would later send shockwaves through Washington. That they could forge something out of such chaos and such divergent demands is a story that deserves to be remembered.

J.K. Galbraith, the Harvard economist and one of Keynes's greatest disciples, once said wistfully that 'there can be few fields of human endeavour in which history counts for so little as in the world of finance.'[4] That wilful forgetfulness was at least partly responsible, in the twenty-first century, for the greatest banking crisis and deepest economic slump in post-war history.

Understanding what really happened at Bretton Woods, and in particular the system's flaws, might in some part explain why its life was so short, and why we have ended up where we are today.

When one looks back at the conversations at the Mount Washington, what is most striking is how easily many of them might apply today: how to try to address the problems of indebted countries, how to restrain the financial sector without sacrificing growth. Their references to the Victorian gold standard might sound dated at first – after all, it came to an end precisely a century before this book's publication, upon the outbreak of the First World War – but consider this: many of the same problems that afflicted its members are now suffered by those in the Eurozone. They are bound into an international monetary system in which they cannot adjust their exchange rates, cannot independently set their monetary policy and cannot (except in direst emergency) impose controls on the flow of money in and out of their borders. The cast and crew might be different but the script is disarmingly familiar.

What makes Bretton Woods unique is that it was the one occasion when people set out to do something about the problems in the international economy. As former Bank of England Governor Mervyn King put it, 'what there was [at Bretton Woods] was a plan to deal with this problem. What we've got now is everyone running away from the problem and not having any plan to deal with it … where we are now is the problem, not a solution.'[5]

The plan adopted in 1944 was hardly perfect. Indeed, even today there are some who argue that the negotiators chose the wrong plan; that had they followed a subtly different path the system would never have collapsed. Such conclusions will be for the reader to make – as indeed will be the question of White's real motives in dealing with the Russians.

The following pages will document how the collapse of the gold standard and the race to implement something in its place inspired White and Keynes to create something entirely new at Bretton

Woods. They will document the inextricably linked story of Britain's fall from economic dominance, up to its moment of greatest humiliation, sparked by the conditions of the Anglo-American war loan in 1947.

But more than this, at its heart, *The Summit* is a human story. It is the story of an unlikely friendship between two men, forged in an unlikely setting amidst a carnival of characters, and of their scheme to prevent yet more bloodshed by reshaping the world's economy.

A word, finally, on the book's title. None of the delegates to Bretton Woods called the meeting a 'summit'. For them it was always a 'parley' or 'conference'. Indeed, it was not until 1950 that Churchill gave the word its modern definition as a meeting of international leaders – strictly speaking, political leaders rather than technicians. All the same, few could claim that Bretton Woods was not a summit of another kind – the very highest point of modern international economic diplomacy.

However, the book is so named not merely for this, but also for the very mountain which gave the hotel its name. None of the guests could leave the conference without remarking on the sight of Mount Washington, the highest peak on the east coast of the United States. It was in the shadow of this peak that the men and women negotiated the future of the world economy in 1944. And, although the very top of the mountain was, more often than not, obscured, once or twice during the three weeks of the conference, the clouds lifted and exposed the summit to the world.

Plan of the Mount Washington Hotel as it was in 1944

Ground floor

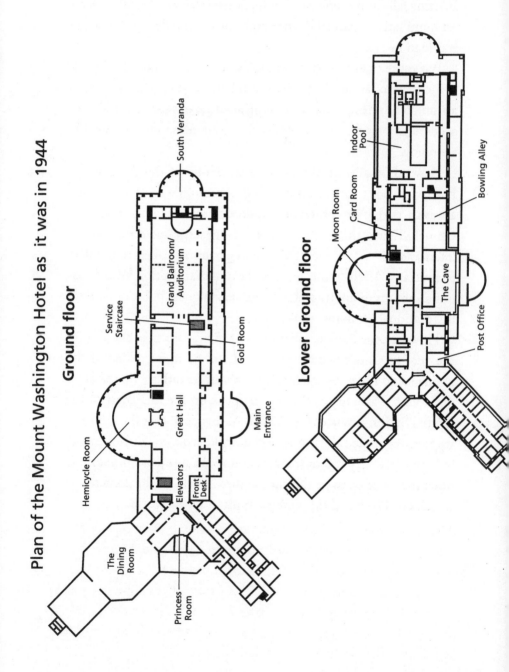

South Veranda

Grand Ballroom/
Auditorium

Service
Staircase

Gold Room

Great Hall

Main
Entrance

Hemicycle Room

Elevators

Front
Desk

The
Dining
Room

Princess
Room

Lower Ground floor

Moon Room

Card Room

Indoor
Pool

Bowling Alley

The Cave

Post Office

CHAPTER ONE

The Mount Washington

It seems a place of dreams, enchanted, legendary.

Boston Globe, 4 June 1944

Look at me, gentlemen ... for I am the poor fool who built all
this!

Joseph Stickney[1]

It is a quirk of history that the most famous place in economics
doesn't exist on a map. Were you to run your finger down an official list of the towns and villages of New Hampshire, you wouldn't
find Bretton Woods. Technically speaking, there is no such town.
This is no accident: Bretton Woods disappeared from the register
more than a century before the conference that made it famous.

Early efforts to settle this lush valley deep in the north of New
Hampshire were not successful. Despite giving away twenty-five
thousand acres to relatives and cronies in 1772, colonial governor
John Wentworth struggled to persuade anyone to visit. In a desperate bid to encourage the wealthier end of his family to pile in,
he rather shamelessly named it after Bretton Hall, near Wakefield
in Yorkshire, the home of his cousin, Sir Thomas Wentworth. It
didn't work; Sir Thomas never made the journey.

He wasn't the only one. Bretton Woods was hardly the most compelling investment for a prospective plantation owner. Penned in on all sides by the White Mountains, it lay a three-week hike from civilisation. The only way to get there faster was to be winched through one of the 'notches', small openings in the mountain ridge which connected the valley to the rest of the world – and even then the journey took seven days.[2] The soil was decent, but as early explorers discovered, even once you managed to reach it, in the winter you had to contend not merely with a temperature tens of degrees below freezing but the threat of death by avalanche or bear attack.

And all that was before a more pressing issue for the average eighteenth-century investor: the impending war of independence.

So Bretton Woods sat there, empty save for the black bears and the odd moose, for almost a century, when at last settlers built a route up through the foothills to the valley. A road was laid down, then a railway, and the people and politicians of New Hampshire finally discovered this cradle in the heart of the White Mountains.

In 1832, as soon as enough voters were living there, the state legislature dispensed with the old colonial name and rechristened the settlement Carroll, after one of the signatories of the Declaration of Independence, John Carroll. And if it weren't for nineteenth-century coal tycoon Joseph Stickney the name Bretton Woods would probably have been forgotten for ever.

Stickney was the man who built the Mount Washington Hotel, and for some reason he exhumed the old name when he incorporated his enterprise. So was born the Bretton Woods Company and, when the hotel was finished, he gave the same name to the railroad station, post office and express office. When the delegates arrived there in 1944, the name Bretton Woods was at the head of each letter they sent home. As with so much else about the summit, even the name was up for grabs.

It might seem irregular that a hotel owner could single-handedly overturn the state legislature's decisions, but, then again, Stickney was no ordinary magnate, just as the Mount Washington was no ordinary hotel.

What is perhaps most striking about the Mount Washington Hotel is that, for such an enormous building, it is strangely unobtrusive. Unlike other grand hotels, which announce their presence from afar, you tend to catch sight of the Mount Washington only at the last minute. After ascending the foothills of the White Mountains, travelling for hours along roads or railways (even today, no one flies there) and threading through one of those notches in the Presidential Mountain Range, you will finally reach the green bowl that contains it. Even then, you still need to snake along the valley floor for another mile or so until suddenly a turret pokes over the treetops on your left and there it is: all 234 rooms of it.

The first point of conversation is the size. The second is the fact that this enormous, hulking structure is made of wood – it remains the biggest wooden building in New England. Perhaps that's what enables it to be both simultaneously huge and inconspicuous, as if the neighbouring forests have come to tolerate their occupant and decided to cohabit amicably.

The driveway loops around strategically from the nearby railway station, a circuitous route designed to afford the best possible views of the hotel as you arrive. Whether by this stage you've concluded it is a great red-roofed white elephant or a fitting testament to America's Gilded Age, you can hardly deny that it's impressive.

That said, it would be going rather too far to call the building beautiful. Some have tried: Stickney himself considered it a 'great Palazzo'. He hired up-and-coming architect Charles Alling Gifford and shipped in more than 250 Italian artisans to work on its timber frame and plastering. He would reference the French and Spanish Renaissances as he whisked guests around the building.

In reality it's more like an enormous, grounded ocean liner, which is perhaps fitting, since the hotel shared at least one model of chandelier with the *Titanic*, and the wraparound veranda, a quarter of a mile in length, feels eerily like the deck of a great sea vessel. And, like a cruise liner, this mammoth structure was purpose-built to be almost entirely self-sufficient. It had its own post office in the basement. A stock ticker was installed with a direct link to Wall Street. The whole place was equipped not merely with electricity throughout but its own coal-fired power station, installed by Thomas Edison himself (just one of the favours Stickney called in during construction).

There were tennis courts, squash courts, heated swimming pools, Turkish baths, boot and gun rooms, a furrier and card rooms for the wives, a bowling alley for the kids, a billiard room for the evening – not to mention bars and restaurants with food and drink of a quality and variety you could rarely find outside the big cities. Even the most demanding New York industrialist or financier could scarcely find an excuse to leave the premises for the duration of his holiday. Unless, that is, he wanted to take the cog railway up Mount Washington itself. But, given the summit was renowned for having the 'worst weather in the world', many guests didn't bother.

The inside was an odd combination of Old World and New. The Great Hall into which guests were first ushered combined 23-foot ceilings and lavish decoration in the style of Versailles with a rustic New Hampshire stone fireplace and moose's head. The stained-glass windows and panels were designed by Tiffany & Co. of New York – some of them by the son of the founder, Louis Comfort Tiffany.

Guests were outnumbered, sometimes two to one, by regiments of staff, and even behind the scenes little expense was spared. There was a water-powered elevator and a printing plant for the hotel's menus; a fleet of coaches and cars to ferry guests around; an orchestra and choir (part time); and chauffeurs (full time).

But then this was the Gilded Age. Extravagant demonstrations of opulence and grandeur were precisely the point. Stickney's creation wasn't the only grand hotel of the era, but it was intended to be the grandest. Wooden it may have been, but unlike many of its rivals, it had a steel frame which meant it was built to last. Other luxury hotels charged $5 a room. Stickney charged $20.

The inflated prices did little to deter the great families of America from visiting. The Vanderbilts and Rockefellers, retinue in tow, would rent an entire wing of the hotel for the summer, to escape the heat of New York or Boston.

At that time, heading north was about the only way to enjoy the summer in some degree of propriety. New York's public baths were full to bursting, and a couple of weeks before the Mount Washington Hotel opened seven people had died in the city because of the heat.* Even as late as the 1940s, air conditioning was not ubiquitous in the big cities, so the Mount Washington was still able to lure tourists with the promise of cool mountain air, fresh sunny days and pleasant nights.

And it was at least partly for its climate that the Mount Washington was chosen as the location of the United Nations Monetary and Financial Conference. After years of work on the articles that would eventually make up the Bretton Woods agreement, by the spring of 1944 it had become clear that the deal would have to be sealed by late July, so there would be something for Franklin D. Roosevelt to unveil at the Democratic Convention later that month.

As far as John Maynard Keynes was concerned, the idea of heading to the sticky eastern seaboard in mid-summer was tantamount to suicide. Although hardly in old age (he had just turned sixty) he was in poor health, having come down some years earlier with a

---

*As it happened, in that very same month the Mount Washington was completed, a young engineer in Brooklyn, Willis Carrier, came up with the germ of the idea for air conditioning, but it would take some decades before it was widely available. Marsha E. Ackermann, *Cool Comfort: America's Romance with Air-Conditioning*, Smithsonian Books, 2002.

throat infection which by turn became a life-threatening heart disease. Subacute bacterial endocarditis can be treated relatively simply with antibiotics these days, but back then even Harley Street's finest doctors could do little to cure him. Despite a series of ever more bizarre and tortuous treatments with eccentric Hungarian physician Janos Plesch, Keynes suspected another major heart attack might be his last.

Although he and his colleagues were hard at work that summer – not merely on the question of exchange rates, but on the suite of government bills that would eventually create Britain's welfare state – Keynes spent an inordinate amount of time trying to ensure the conference wasn't held in the sweltering heat of New York or Washington. Having endured a 'horrible' July in the capital three years earlier, negotiating Lend-Lease – American wartime financial support for Britain* – he raised the issue with Harry Dexter White, who was heading up the US negotiating team. 'For God's sake,' he wrote, 'do not take us to Washington in July, which should surely be a most unfriendly act. We were hoping, you will remember, that the next round [of talks] would be here. If that is impossible, then at least you must arrange for some pleasant resort in the Rocky Mountains, if you are going to keep your flock in a reasonably good temper.'†[3]

There was never any serious question of holding such seminal discussions in Britain, so Henry Morgenthau, the US Treasury Secretary, told White: 'Have it in Maine or New Hampshire, some place up in the mountains there.'[4]

---

*On 2 July 1941 Keynes wrote to Sir Horace Wilson: 'I certainly didn't expect to find myself still in Washington in July! The weather is horrible – nearly 100 this afternoon (the thermometer was still over 90 at half past nine yesterday evening) and very humid.' JMK XXIII, p.149.

†Keynes also raised the matter with Sir Wilfred Eady at the Treasury, telling him: 'If the conference is to come off shortly and not to be postponed until September, I would urge that it is very advisable that it should certainly not be later in June than the date suggested. Otherwise we shall be running straight into tropical weather. Even as it is, it will be frightfully hot.' National Archives, Kew, T247/28.

As it happened, New Hampshire was a useful choice from another perspective. President Roosevelt needed to be able to sell whatever deal came out of the conference to a sceptical Congress. That, after all, was what Woodrow Wilson had failed to do with the League of Nations in 1919. This meant currying favour with the Republicans, and as chance would have it there was one influential Republican member of the Banking and Currency Committee who, for reasons of his own, wanted to host the conference in his state. Despite being an isolationist and sceptic about America's role in international economics, Senator Charles Tobey of New Hampshire was facing re-election; he sorely needed to further raise his profile ahead of November.

There were a number of big hotels in New Hampshire, but most were in a sorry state of repair, the Mount Washington included. The hotel's fortunes had faded along with those of so many of its patrons. Stickney had died barely a year after it opened. His widow Carolyn (Princess Carolyn, as she liked to be called – her second husband was a French aristocrat) remained the figurehead for some years afterwards, but after her death the hotel's grandeur diminished under a series of unenthusiastic owners.

For the past two years the place had been left to the mercy of the New Hampshire winter. Heavy snow, falling from the six-storey-high towers, had torn holes in the roofs, exposing the ballroom and the porches to the elements. The furniture was damp, mostly ruined; some of the lavish paintwork and fittings had rotted away while the wallpaper had peeled from the walls in long strips. The wood was irreparably warped and the plumbing and electrics had corroded. The forest threatened to engulf the hotel with its leaves and branches.

The Depression and the war were already serving to kill off many of the great hotels of New England, and the Mount Washington would most probably have gone the same way had it not been abruptly resuscitated by the conference. Quite how it gained the commission remains something of a mystery. What we do know is that a wealthy Bostonian, David Stoneman, was awarded $300,000 to hold the conference shortly after buying the run-down palazzo. As one gossip columnist remarked at the time, 'this canny Yank is the only US citizen who wound up ahead of the game after Bretton Woods.'[5]

His competitors would later complain that Stoneman had benefited from a White House tip-off. It's a neat conspiracy theory, but it is far more likely that the hotel was chosen for its size, its direct rail access from Washington and New York and the security of its setting, which allowed the National Guard to construct a cordon around the entire valley. Moreover, both Morgenthau and White had faced the humiliation of being turned away from New England hotels in the past because they were Jewish. That was unlikely to be an issue at the Mount Washington, seeing as Stoneman was also a Jew.

The proprietor, a lawyer and venture capitalist whose main family business was movies and movie theatres (he had helped finance D.W. Griffith's 1915 masterpiece *The Birth of a Nation*[*6]), stayed in the hotel throughout. Sporting his trademark white linen suit, he was often to be seen striding grandly down the corridors, inspecting the rooms and the staff, and attempting to bring some order to the chaos.

But with barely a fortnight left until the conference was due to begin, the hotel was in no state to welcome even a few guests – let alone the hundreds it would need to accommodate that July. Entire sections were uninhabitable. Even as the head engineer boasted to a visiting reporter from the *Boston Globe* that 'it will all fit together like the pieces of a picture puzzle', a sudden torrent of water burst through the ceiling of the hotel lobby.[7]

And so, much to Stoneman's relief, in stepped the federal

---

*This also may help explain why the movie's central family is called Stoneman.

government. Washington sent up 150 soldiers, along with some German prisoners of war. The roof was fixed and a new plumbing system installed (somehow nationwide copper rationing regulations were overridden). New telephone lines were laid down, old furniture was thrown out and replaced. According to locals, you can still find items of pre-1944 Mount Washington furniture in homes throughout the valley.*

At the very end, each of the workers was given fifty gallons of white paint and told: 'If it doesn't move, paint it.' And so they went methodically through the hotel, painting everything. The mahogany doors, the brass sidelights, the carefully made fixtures – even the hand-crafted Tiffany windows were doused with a stark coat of white paint. By the time Stoneman's staff realised that the finest decorations of his hotel were being desecrated, most of the ground floor, including the grand ballroom where the plenary sessions would be held, had been painted over in white. Even today you can find the odd speck of white paint on some of the hotel's doors and fittings – a reminder of that desperate bid to smarten up the place before the delegates arrived.

Ahead of the conference, the Americans had invited the Britons and fourteen other hand-picked delegations to the Claridge Hotel in Atlantic City for a week of pre-drafting. They had then taken a special train up to the Mount Washington. As was to be the pattern over the course of the following fortnight, even on board the delegates continued drafting, their work punctuated only by frequent strong drinks and the odd nap. The Cubans brought cigars, much to the gratification of the American delegation.

The train, which was given express treatment, with every signal operator ordered to allow it right of way, arrived one hour early.[8] The bleary-eyed delegates were ejected onto an empty platform in

---

*Many of the old pieces of furniture were left lying around, leaving enterprising locals to come in and pick up anything they fancied.

the middle of nowhere. After a while, military buses arrived to start ferrying them to the hotel, which was still in complete chaos. 'Everything is in a state of glorious confusion,' wrote Lionel Robbins, a member of the British delegation. 'When we arrived half the rooms were not yet ready, and it was rumoured, and I believe it is true, that it had only proved possible to open the hotel in time by calling in the aid of the military.'

The new plumbing system wasn't yet fully operational; the new guests discovered to their disgust that some of the taps produced a sludgy dark liquid.[9] That the administration had shipped in a thousand cases of Coca-Cola (rationed at the time)[10] didn't entirely compensate. Keynes's wife Lydia wrote that 'the whole of the hotel was out of order ... so the taps run all day, the windows do not close or open, the pipes mend and unmend and no-one can get anywhere.'

There was, more importantly, a shortage of the essentials required for an international summit. While just about enough chairs were laid out in the conference rooms, there were too few stenographers to fill them – one of the reasons why, to the eternal frustration of economic historians, there survive only fragmentary transcripts of the proceedings at Bretton Woods.

The hotel administrators sourced fifteen local boy scouts to help run errands.[11] Over the course of the following three weeks they would become one of the conference's more touching fixtures: as the delegates took it in turns to hector each other, the scouts would faithfully ferry microphones from one to another and back again.

A delegate from the American team complained that 'the service was very poor and inadequate'. Assistant Secretary of State Dean Acheson, having been tipped off about the likelihood of chaos, stayed instead 'in a comfortable inn at nearby Crawford Notch. The transportation problem was solved by appropriate attention to the military police assigned to guard our privacy and well-being.' The disarray proved too much for the hotel manager. A story went around that he had locked himself in his office with a case of whiskey and was refusing to open the door.

One of the most problematic unanswered questions was how the hotel would accommodate more than seven hundred delegates – let alone their entourages and the travelling press pack. When you added up all the visitors, this meant well over three thousand people would be in attendance. This was in a hotel with only 234 rooms. Some of the delegations simply decided to stay elsewhere – the Chinese and Russians among them.

The brochure that went out before the summit claimed that for just $11 a day delegates would be entitled to the 'American plan' – a shared room with a bath, or a single room, all meals included.[12] And some were relatively fortunate. Keynes was given one of the best suites in the hotel, a four-windowed set of rooms overlooking the golf links and the Ammonoosuc River. Nonetheless when Lady Keynes, one of the greats of the Ballets Russes, caught sight of the room she started to 'scream [and] cry' with disappointment.[13]

Others were less blessed. In the event, so numerous were the delegates that many ended up sleeping in linen closets and corridors – although, given that the negotiations and drafting sessions would go on through the night, that was less of an issue than it might sound.

Inevitably, as night fell that first evening, most of the delegates found their way downstairs to the bar, which rapidly became one of the focal points of the conference. The nightclub in the bowels of the hotel had had many incarnations over the years. Originally it was used as a garage, then for squash courts. When prohibition came it was set up as the secret hotel bar. Guests would drink teacups of liquor smuggled in from the Canadian border barely sixty miles north. If they spotted Feds approaching on the driveway, the liquor would be replaced with real tea and the barmen would start playing squash for their teetotal 'spectators'.

That first night, the bar was crammed with delegates from all over the world – Colombians, Poles, Liberians, Chinese, Ethiopians, Russians, Filipinos, Icelanders, Iraqis – quite possibly the most cosmopolitan gathering ever seen in that part of New England. And as they drank, sang and exchanged stories, David Stoneman meandered in a daze among them, as if he had decided to give in to the chaos. To top it all off, now that his hotel manager had disappeared, word had gone around that the US Treasury had taken it upon itself to send down to Washington for a replacement.

As the diarist from *The New Yorker* put it: 'It was only then that he realized what he was in for. A gentleman who was watching Mr Stoneman at the moment has told us that his normally pink face went bright and alarmingly red and that not only did he seem to crumple suddenly but that his immaculate white linen suit did, too. From that day on, he wandered about the hotel a shaken man, possibly praying that his select family trade would hear as little as possible about the strange goings on in Bretton Woods.'[14]

Although they came from all corners of the earth, many of the delegates were great friends, having met plenty of times before as their respective countries negotiated wartime loans and struggled to keep their financial systems afloat. They had confronted each other over negotiating tables and made up later in conference barrooms. Now, at Bretton Woods, they were in for a longer and more significant set of discussions than they had ever experienced.

If downstairs was a rowdy but rather inspiring picture of twentieth-century international progressiveness, upstairs the atmosphere was more rarefied – perhaps mildly imperial. A couple of flights above, in suite 219, Keynes was hosting a small private dinner to commemorate the five-hundredth anniversary of the concordat between King's College, Cambridge and New College, Oxford. As someone whose entire life had been associated with King's, the fact that he was more than three thousand miles away would not stand in the way of the great economist's commemoration of the event. Nor would the fact that only a handful of delegates had actually been to either Oxford or Cambridge – let alone to the colleges in question. Happily, his fellow delegate, Robbins, was an alumnus of New College. The other five guests came courtesy of abstruse college connections: Nigel Ronald had been at Winchester, established in the fourteenth century by William of Wykeham, founder also of New College; Dean Acheson and Oscar Cox of the US delegation had attended Yale, which also had a concordat with King's; H.H. Kung of the Chinese delegation had an honorary Yale degree; and Dennis Robertson, with whom Keynes had worked on the early stages of his magnum opus, the *General Theory*, was invited too.

The dinner, it soon transpired, was largely an excuse for Keynes to order some of the hotel's finest wines, 'overcoming the near anarchy in the kitchen and wine cellar',[15] and to do what he did best: hold court to a small room of admirers.

Contrary to appearances, Keynes was not the most eager socialite. Never happier than when he was drafting agreements, he preferred intimate gatherings to hob-nobbing – a tutorial-style atmosphere and a couch or bed near at hand in case he was overcome by exhaustion. This had been a problem in previous visits to the US, where he complained, 'what overwhelms one … is the enormous amount of work, or semi-work, which one has to do at meal times.'[16]

At the Mount Washington, Keynes had been forbidden by Lydia from going down to the bar – and for the most part he was to obey. Nonetheless, he had been looking forward to the small anniversary dinner for weeks, 'as excitedly as a schoolboy'.[17] He gave a brief speech extolling the virtues of universities as institutions which pass down knowledge from generation to generation 'in all our countries, the centre and core of much that is most precious in the world's civilisation … It was all very *pianissimo*, as befitting the occasion, but his emotion when he spoke of our debt to the past was truly moving.'[18]

*

Up there in the cool mountains of New Hampshire, in a suite replete with fine wines, surrounded by men gathered from the three corners of the world, it was possible, for a moment, to forget the fact that the world was still at war. However, on the other side of the Atlantic, the fighting in Normandy and beyond had intensified. Since D-Day twenty-five days earlier, almost one in ten of the 630,000 American, British and Canadian troops who had landed had been reported killed, injured or missing, while the war in the Pacific raged as fiercely as ever. Every day Bob Brand, one of the British delegates, woke up fearing that he would learn that something terrible had befallen his son Jim, who was fighting in France.

London was facing a second, more sinister Blitz courtesy of Hitler's V1s, up to a hundred of which were now raining down on the city every day – indeed, the previous day forty-eight people had been killed when one of them exploded just outside the Air Ministry on Aldwych. The so-called Doodlebugs had ushered in a new age of terror. They were arbitrary killing machines. Launched towards London from bases in northern France, they fell from the sky with their 1800lb payload whenever they ran out of fuel. All you would hear was the approaching, ominous buzz of the primitive pulse-jet engine; then, when it suddenly cut out, the best you could do was take cover and hope you weren't in its path.

And it wasn't merely London which had been terrorised by the unmanned bombs. They were the main topic of conversation in the US at the time of Bretton Woods, with residents of the eastern seaboard terrified that they too would become a target. On the very week the delegations arrived in the US, Willy Ley, the Weapons Editor of New York newspaper *PM*, had been wheeled out to reassure Americans that the Germans would be incapable of constructing a 'robot bomb' capable of traversing the Atlantic and destroying the Big Apple.

Naturally, then, much of the conversation between the Bretton Woods delegates concerned the horrors of war. Most had sons and brothers fighting in Europe or the Pacific. Many knew first hand from the First World War the horror and indignity of such conflict. After drinks were drunk, whether in private dinners or down below in the bar, in a morbid way it was talk of these horrors – 'atrocity stories', as one attendee called them[19] – that united the delegates.

Even here, there was a machismo hierarchy of sorts. As countries which had fought tooth and nail against the Axis powers, and had seen war intrude on their doorsteps, the British and the Russians considered themselves to be in top spot. During one earlier conference a Russian delegate (or rather his interpreter) had taken Robbins aside and whispered: 'here in America they do not know what war is.' Nonetheless, it was the Americans who were now pivotal to the fighting in Europe, not merely bankrolling the war effort but providing the lion's share of men for the Normandy landings. They might not have had to face war on their home soil, but they were now fighting and dying in their thousands.

At the bottom of the pyramid of wartime pride were the French. At this stage, Henri Giraud and Charles de Gaulle's Comité had still to be fully recognised as a government as opposed to a wartime administrative body. Its delegates at Bretton Woods would expend about as much effort trying, behind the scenes, to ensure that they were referred to as 'France' as they would on the actual economic negotiations. It led one of the delegates to conclude that, inevitably, they are 'suffering from a very bad case of inferiority complex, because of what they have gone through'.[20]

However, there was a common enemy and a common cause. In the end, it fell to Tobey, the New Hampshire Senator who had been drafted in to bulk up the Republican head-count, to deliver this message as the summit got under way. With the delegates set to begin their detailed negotiations a couple of days later, on the eve of Independence Day, he stood up to address the conference.

The delegates, most of them more accustomed to technical terminology than to full-blooded American political rhetoric, could hardly have prepared themselves for such an address. In a voice that boomed so noisily through the microphone that the chandeliers in the hotel's great ballroom shook, the senator berated the critics of Bretton Woods, 'some of these around the perimeter of this Conference'. The event, he continued, his voice growing ever louder, his eyes focused on the press corps at the back of the room, had a noble cause. It was for 'the man in the foxhole', under enemy fire.

Then, his fists pumping, his arms raised and his voice rising to a crescendo, Tobey's oratory elevated to the poetic, the religious:

On us is a grave responsibility. To us is given a high privilege. God, the Father of all, give us understanding and a vision of the needs of men today, of the fundamental truth that, whatever our nationality or creed, we are brothers under the skin.

As we confer together here today, amidst the eternal hills, inspired by the sublime beauty around us, and as the shadows of passing clouds above leave their impress for a moment on the slopes of yonder mountains, may the contemplation of the tragic sufferings and sacrifices of every nation bind us together in brotherly love and in a spirit of consecration to the great opportunity which is ours to displace doubt and cynicism with hope and confidence.

Two thousand years ago Christ was hanged on a cross, a spear thrust in his side, nails driven through his hands, a crown of thorns pressed upon his brow, and a cup of vinegar placed to his lips.

He died that men might be saved, and be, in truth, free. There are nations represented here today who, too, have had their sides pierced and a crown of thorns pressed upon them by the sufferings of war. They fight with and for us and we with and for them.

If cooperation can weld the United Nations together in solid phalanx against our enemies in war, surely we shall join together to achieve the vital objective of this Conference, meeting the world's needs for the rehabilitation of a war-torn world.

...I call upon each of you to place your hand with mine upon the lever of the spirit and aspirations that called this Conference into being, and by our united cooperation to lift the level of our age, that its blessings may be passed on to generations yet unborn. Gentlemen, we must not, we cannot, we dare not fail. The hopes and aspirations of the common people of each of our countries rest in us.

It was a speech that had to be heard to be believed, one delegate would later write.[21] The hall erupted in applause, and though some of the delegates had to stifle cynical smirks, even the British were caught up in the excitement. 'Eloquence of this particular brand of emotional verbosity cannot have been heard on our side of the Atlantic for the last quarter of a century,' Robbins wrote in his diary. When he descended from the stage Tobey told his fellow delegates that he was ready to 'lay down his life' for the conference.[22] Keynes dwelt, approvingly, on the point Tobey had made repeatedly throughout his speech: delegates should transcend their political differences in order to seal this agreement in New Hampshire.*

But what Keynes and most of his fellow delegates were unaware of was that this anti-political speech was made primarily for political purposes. Tobey had sidled up to his American colleague from the State Department, Dean Acheson, a little earlier. Given how tough a job he was facing to secure the Republican nomination ahead of the elections, he told Acheson, who reported: 'If he could make the Independence Day address, he would receive most gratifying publicity throughout the state.'[23] As Keynes remarked later, after meeting Senator Tobey, 'What a strange country!'[24]

The incident underlined the collision of interests throughout the conference. When economic historians write about Bretton Woods

---

*Not all of the British reaction was positive. In a handwritten note scrawled on a copy of the speech mailed back home, the Bank of England's man wrote simply: 'Almost everything is wrong with this.' Bank of England Archives, OV38/9.

today they do so as if it were hermetically sealed, a sterile Petri dish in which economists and technicians constructed the world economy of the future. In reality, the three weeks of 'considered negotiations' at the Mount Washington Hotel were tense, chaotic and fractious. They could hardly have been otherwise given the nature of the main protagonists: two men determined to use the conference to safeguard their own economies; a duo whose fight with each other had begun years ago, and whose determination to redraw the economic map could be traced all the way back to 1918.

PART I

COLLAPSE

CHAPTER TWO

The Bitter Peace
1918–1919

You'd really be amused by the amazing complications of
psychology and personality and intrigue which make such
magnificent sport of the impending catastrophe of Europe.

John Maynard Keynes to Vanessa Bell, March 1919[1]

And think ye that building shall endure,
Which shelters the noble and crushes the poor?

From James Russell Lowell, *A Parable*

As winter closed in on the year 1918 and the First World War
limped to its conclusion, Harry Dexter White and John Maynard
Keynes would both find themselves in France.

They were comparatively young men back then – one in his
twenties, the other in his thirties – and neither had yet made a lasting impression on the world. Even so, the contrast between the two
men who would go on to remould the global economic system was
already plain to see.

At thirty-five, Keynes was one of his generation's finest economists. And while his hair was beginning to recede, there
nonetheless remained something youthful about his appearance –
though by all accounts you had to be there in person to feel it. Far

taller than most of his peers, he would bound, long-legged, into and out of rooms. He wasn't exactly handsome (indeed, he spent much of his life ashamed of his appearance – his thick lips especially) but there was a certain magnetism to him, particularly, according to one friend, those 'piercing, brilliant and dark eyes, surmounted by long lashes and thickly luxuriant eyebrows'.[2]

Even at that relatively early age, he had already been made a Companion of the Order of the Bath for services to the country's economy during the war. Like most other members of the Bloomsbury set he was a conscientious objector,* but despite refusing to put on uniform and fight for his country he was now in France on official business. Three years earlier he had been drafted into the Treasury; this tour of France and Belgium was nominally a survey of the extent of war damage. But as far as he was concerned, it was also a sign that his time trapped in the Treasury was drawing to an all-too-welcome close.

His life until then had been more or less everything his parents might have expected: if not a member of the high aristocracy, Keynes was nonetheless of upper-middle-class stock. His father, John Neville Keynes, was a well-respected lecturer in moral sciences at Cambridge; his mother, Florence Ada Keynes, a social reformer and, later on, a local politician. But even these two intellectuals had been outshone by their young son almost from the beginning. A blistering few years at Eton and King's College, Cambridge, had been followed by a spell as a clerk in the India Office, and then a lectureship in economics at King's. Soon after the beginning of the war he was drafted back into government service in the Treasury.

For a naïve young man from a prosperous academic family, who had spent most of his adult life in and out of offices, country estates and sumptuous Georgian townhouses in London, the sight that

---

*Or a variety thereof. His biographers vary as to the precise nature of his objection. Certainly, he refused to fight.

greeted him on the continent would leave an indelible impression: 'The completeness of the destruction was evident,' he wrote. 'For mile after mile nothing was left. No building was habitable and no field fit for the plough. The sameness was also striking. One devastated area was exactly like another – a heap of rubble, a morass of shellholes, a tangle of wire.'

Together with George Theunis, a Belgian official, he toured the empty battlefields, the 'blasted grandeur' of old Europe laid waste before them. Particularly disturbing was the field at Ypres, where almost exactly a year before hundreds of thousands of British soldiers, along with hundreds of thousands of Germans (the exact numbers are still disputed), were slaughtered in a hail of gunfire and clouds of mustard gas.

'In that desolate and ghostly spot,' he wrote, 'the natural colour and humours of the landscape and the climate seemed designed to express to the traveller the memories of the ground. A visitor to the salient early in November 1918, when a few German bodies still added a touch of realism and human error, and the great struggle was not yet certainly ended, could feel there, as nowhere else, the present outrage of war.'[3]

The damage wrought by the war was not merely physical and emotional. The events of 1914 brought to an end a period of economic growth and stability that many thought would endure in perpetuity. As Keynes would write in the opening lines of his 1919 masterpiece *The Economic Consequences of the Peace*, the preceding years had offered a quality of life that seemed to have disappeared for ever:

The inhabitant of London could order by telephone, sipping his morning tea in bed, the various products of the whole earth, in such quantity as he might see fit, and reasonably expect their early delivery upon his doorstep ... He could secure forthwith, if he wished it, cheap and comfortable means of transit to any country or climate without passport or other formality ... But, most important of all, he regarded this state of affairs as normal, certain, and permanent, except in the direction of further improvement, and any deviation from it as aberrant, scandalous, and avoidable.[4]

Though the term had yet to find common currency, it had been the first (and in many senses still the greatest) age of globalisation. As has been the case countless times ahead of a great crisis, the consensus was that politics had become irrelevant – all that mattered were the actions of financiers. As has been the case countless times since, such assumptions were proved gravely wrong.

The golden age ended so abruptly that, even four years later, most economists were still coming to terms with its loss. An assassin's bullet had sparked a political and then financial chain reaction which closed stock markets in country after country; within a few days it was all but impossible to transmit money across borders. With short-term finance suddenly unavailable the simplest functions of everyday commercial life could no longer take place. In London, the financial centre of the world, foreigners suddenly found themselves unable to pay bills, in turn compromising the brokers and banks which transacted with them; the money lent out by banks to the stock exchange and discount market threatened to go bad. For Keynes and his family, a significant amount of whose assets were plugged into the system, it was a financial disaster.

What underlay this catastrophe – though no one, Keynes included, would appreciate the scale of it for some years to come – was a malfunction in the international monetary system. The gold standard – the agreement by which most of the world's trading nations would fix the value of their currencies to the precious metal, and indeed commit to swapping their currencies for a set weight of gold – was disintegrating. As their sources of international funding dried up, that summer London banks started refusing to hand their customers gold in exchange for currency – so-called specie payments. Queues formed outside the Bank of England as people attempted to swap their paper money for gold. The London Stock Exchange closed for the first time in a century and a half of continuous operation. It was, a Bank of England official wrote almost one hundred years later, 'truly a credit crunch'.[5]

Like most economists, Keynes's first reaction was to attempt to turn back the clock. He argued that Britain should do everything it could to restart the specie mechanism and get the gold standard working again – ironic, given that he would later become one of the most renowned proponents of its abolition. He still believed it might be possible to return to that pre-war golden era of globalisation. As far as he or anyone else could conceive, the alternative – a world of floating exchange rates and with London displaced from the centre of the financial network – was a chaos to be avoided at all costs.

In part this is because he believed, again like many others, that the war was likely to be over by the end of 1914. The conventional wisdom – made famous by writer Norman Angell in his 1910 bestseller *The Great Illusion* – was that prolonged military conflict was futile given how significant were the economic, trade and financial ties between nations. Keynes believed this meant a major war was nigh-on impossible; he could hardly have been more wrong. The mistake would leave a scar. He would devote much of the rest of his life to contemplating how apparently stable economic systems could implode, such that even tried-and-tested remedies would no longer work.

The war had raged on for four more years, each bringing with it horrors more outrageous than the last. One by one, a sequence of Keynes's friends lost their lives in the mud of Flanders and the Somme; gossipy letters he sent off to the front would be returned with the word 'killed' scrawled on them. A generation of undergraduates at Cambridge, where he still spent much of his time, would be obliterated; he watched as men who survived came home crippled, their lungs permanently damaged by poison gas.

But it was not until his visit to the Western Front in October 1918 that he would come face-to-face with the battlefields where so many had fallen. A quarter of a century later, Keynes would think back to this tour as he resolved to help create the new international institutions which would be able to help provide for countries torn apart by war and devastation.

The conflict was all but over, the new German government having called for an armistice based on President Woodrow Wilson's Fourteen Points, his framework for a post-war world based on democracy, self-determination and a League of Nations to bind countries together. From Keynes's perspective this wasn't merely a relief for the sake of the country and for humanity – it meant his arduous duties at the Treasury might soon come to an end. As he and Theunis inspected the ruined towns and fields of northern France, the young officials joked about which of them would find his way out of government service the sooner.

But there was work to be done before that. Keynes had been selected to begin work on the negotiations on post-war settlement with Germany and her allies which would take place the following year. The experience would mark his coming of age as a public figure: by the end of 1919 he would have become a household name.

In a US army camp some way back from the front, First Lieutenant Harry Dexter White had just celebrated his twenty-sixth birthday. Now that he was closer to thirty than twenty, perhaps, he hoped, people might finally stop mistaking him for a kid. Maybe it was his height – a mere five foot six inches (which made him a whole foot shorter than Keynes) – or maybe his genial, round face. Probably it was both; either way, everyone assumed he was barely out of high school. This was no laughing matter: as an army officer, he had men to command. Some months earlier he had grown a thin moustache, which at least added one or two years to his apparent age. He would wear it until the day he died.

It wasn't the first time White had taken steps to stand out from the crowd. Born plain, simple Harry White in the more down-trodden end of Boston, he had added the 'Dexter' to his name at the start of high school to differentiate himself from the eighteen other Harry Whites in the phone book. It was the name of his best friend.*

But despite his efforts to distinguish himself, at this stage one would hardly have picked White out as potentially one of the most influential reformers of the international economy. First, and most obviously, he wasn't even a professional economist. Unlike many of the others who were applying for admission to the officers' train-ing camp at Plattsburg, New York, he had no degree, having dropped out of college. His academic record before that was hit-and-miss.

There were fleeting moments of brilliance: he had graduated from Everett High School in three years rather than the normal four for his course; at college he managed to pull off a 99 per cent mark in a course on military history; his schoolmates would later describe him as the 'youngest, smartest and one of the smallest – a retiring boy, but witty'.[6] But there was also plain mediocrity: his high school grades weren't spectacular; he flunked two of the admissions exams for college and had to retake them; and he dropped out after only one semester at Massachusetts Agricultural College.

White was hardly a dunce, but schoolwork took second place behind the demands of the family business. His father Joseph White (who had changed his name from the Weit he was born

*White's sister says White was told by his teacher to add 'a middle name for the sake of identification'. He chose the name of a 'little gentile boy', Dexter, who lived next door and was his best friend. R. Bruce Craig, *Treasonable Doubt: The Harry Dexter White Spy Case*, Lawrence, 2004, p.285.

with) owned a hardware store that had expanded to four branches around Boston and each of his seven children was expected to help out. So by February 1912 Harry was back working in the store. His brother Nathan said that 'family affairs required his return home.'[7]

And, were it not for two significant events in his twenty-fifth year, that might well have been where he stayed. The first of those events was the American declaration of war in April 1917. Even at the start of the year, it was by no means a foregone conclusion that President Wilson would drag his country into the conflict. Though most Americans' sympathies lay with the Allies, that January the President had still been calling for a 'peace without victory', and Britain's plight was looking grim. Some months earlier London had suffered its worst financial crisis of the war after the US Federal Reserve urged American lenders to cut back their credit towards foreign borrowers. The hope was that by starving the Allies of money they could bring the war to a quicker end.

As the cash drained out of Britain, the country's membership of the gold standard looked imperilled. By early 1917 gold was leaving London so quickly that even J.P. Morgan, Britain's chosen (and controversial) New York banker, looked powerless to stem the tide. In retrospect, this was only the first in a series of episodes during the twentieth century where the Bank of England would do everything it could to try to maintain the pound's membership of a fixed currency system. Had Germany not launched unrestricted submarine warfare in February, the likelihood is that the war would indeed have ended by negotiation that year. But a series of U-boat attacks on American ships precipitated the United States' entry into the war by April. Within months, Britain abandoned the peg on sterling – its first major break with the gold standard. As is almost always the case when a country takes such a significant economic step, it was intended as a temporary measure. As is almost always the case, this proved optimistic.

Not that such details mattered all that much to Harry Dexter White. Six days after the US declared war, he volunteered for service. That 99 per cent mark in military history helped him qualify as an officer in the 302nd Infantry Regiment. However, there was a significant complication: he had just fallen in love.

The girl was Anne Terry, a twenty-two-year-old local student. The two of them had plenty in common: both were Jewish, both were from the same part of town, and both were quietly but most certainly ambitious. Terry was born in Russia, emigrating to America with her parents as a child; White's parents had come over from Lithuania, also part of the Tsarist Empire, some decades previously. The couple were married at Boston's Temple Israel on 22 February 1918.

It was a significant watershed for Harry White: from that moment forward his primary loyalty was no longer solely towards his family and his father's stores. He and Anne (who later became a children's writer) would be almost inseparable for the rest of their lives; they would study together, write together and entertain together – including a host of controversial guests from abroad in the years to come.

Shortly after the pair were married White was deployed to France. Few American volunteers were aware of the full horrors of the war the Europeans had been waging for the previous three and a half years. Unfortunately for the young men of the day, this just so happened to be a point when technology had made it considerably easier to defend than attack: one side could hole itself up in a trench and repel its opponents with hideous efficiency using artillery and machine guns. The cost in human lives of each assault on enemy territory was inordinate and inhuman compared with previous conflicts. Average life expectancy for British officers deployed to the front line was a mere six weeks. And, thanks to advances in medicine, more than 80 per cent of those injured on the battlefield were returned to duty.

Few of White's or Keynes's generation were not left in some way scarred by the ordeal. A number of those who would later attend Bretton Woods had served in the trenches; Lionel Robbins of the British delegation was wounded by a German sniper. White himself, however, was fortunate. According to military records, neither of the two regiments he served in saw combat during the war, and, most likely, he spent his time in military and training camps. However, whether it was the proximity to danger, the sight of injured men and contact with those who had seen the horrors of the trenches, or indeed the taste of a career away from his father's hardware stores, the experience would leave him a changed man.

The Great War might also be said to have changed Keynes's outlook, though in his case that had a rather different meaning. His elevation to work in the upper rungs of government, advising a sequence of Chancellors of the Exchequer, had brought with it entry to some of London's most exclusive circles. Whenever the economist wasn't in the Treasury in 1918, he spent his time in a whirlwind of society suppers and soirees. As millions of British, German and American soldiers were fighting for their lives on the other side of the Channel, Keynes still managed to enjoy the high life.

Some nights he spent cavorting in clubs in Soho, others dining with politicians, society hostesses and the occasional royal. There were the Asquiths and the McKennas, a Romanian prince and the Princess of Monaco – not to mention the ever-present Bloomsbury set, the intellectual, literary and artistic group into which he had fallen at Cambridge. Though even Bloomsbury was growing alarmed by Maynard's excitement at this new world, and his penchant for namedropping.

On one occasion he was overheard telling his parlourmaid, Jessie, 'I'm going to dine tonight with the Duke of Connaught. Isn't that grand?' – 'Yes sir, that is grand,' she replied. David Garnett's subsequent diary entry recorded the general sense of revulsion among the Bloomsburyites:

> Nessa [Vanessa Bell] suggests that Maynard is now possibly so far on the downhill path that nothing will save him. Harry [Norton] thinks it is not at all simple – That M. is aware of many of his habits being disgusting to other people – such as helping himself with his own spoon or fork instead of passing his plate, and persists in doing them because it flatters him that people like him so much they don't mind what he does ... General conclusions were that Maynard has a lot of low blood in him – [John Sheppard] says from his nonconformist snobbish ancestry ... Duncan [Grant] has been asked to give him a lecture.[8]

At times, it was difficult to tell whether Keynes's baffling bad habits were really evidence of low birth or were merely intended to provoke. A few years later his friend and fellow Bloomsbury member Lytton Strachey would tell how, on a walk back through fields to King's College with 'Pozzo',* Keynes suddenly said he needed to urinate, 'and did so, walking all the time in the most extraordinary way with legs apart, though there were people all about'. Strachey engaged the same prickly prurience he was to become famous for in his writing, recounting how Keynes declared: '"Oh, it's alright, it's alright, one can't be seen, as long as one keeps walking." He looked like a monstrosity of a gardener with an inefficient watering-pot.'[9]

Up until this point, Keynes's eccentricities had been indulged by his Bloomsbury friends. On one occasion while staying together in Sussex they allowed Keynes to change all the clocks so that they

*The nickname Bloomsbury gave him was intended, depending on who you ask, either to refer to an untrustworthy Corsican diplomat, Carlo Andrea Pozzo di Borgo (1764–1842), or to conjure up the image of a sewer – probably the latter. Either way, Keynes hated it.

were one hour ahead of London time. As with many of Keynes's other gambits, it was half-joke and half-statement. Bloomsbury had refused to abide by mainstream Edwardian cultural, moral and social mores – why should it abide by everyone else's conception of time either? For those less charmed by Keynes's intellectual japery, however, it was yet another example of his astonishing arrogance. Not to mention the fact that it soon sent half the house (particularly the cook) into mad confusion.[10]

By 1918 relations with Bloomsbury were starting to fray. For much of the past decade, Keynes had essentially bankrolled many of its members, putting them up in various houses around that district of London and taking charge of their investments, but now the mood had cooled. Perhaps it was war, perhaps the approach of middle age, but Bloomsbury – old Bloomsbury at least – was unravelling.

Although for many of the set life went on more or less as normal – the London salons, the parties at Garsington, the Tudor country home of Lady Ottoline Morrell – there was no pretending that things had not changed. If there was one overarching theme among the ideas promulgated by the Bloomsbury group it was the notion sown by the Cambridge philosopher G.E. Moore – that art and beauty should be considered an absolute good. But the Great War was as ugly a conflict as one could imagine – an affront both to individual liberty (Strachey would campaign against conscription) and to aesthetic and psychological harmony. The return from the front of shell-shocked soldiers such as Siegfried Sassoon (who stayed for a period at Garsington) further pierced the bubble.

Bloomsbury's reactions to the war were varied. Duncan Grant began by supporting military action, while Keynes was positively enthusiastic about serving the government by working in the Treasury. Most of the rest of the set was aghast. Friendship should come first; after all, as another prominent member of the group, E.M. Forster, put it some years later, 'if I had to choose between betraying my country and betraying my friend, I hope I should have the guts to betray my country'.[11] While most of Bloomsbury attempted to ignore the war as best they could, Keynes not only engaged with it, but seemed positively to thrive on helping his government wage it. For the first, but not the last, time he was drawn into the corridors of power. Jejune the inhabitants of Whitehall may have been by Bloomsbury standards, but there was nonetheless something seductive about being on first-name terms with the Prime Minister, of shaping the government's plans, of grasping the reins rather than sniffing disapprovingly from the sidelines.

However, for his Bloomsbury colleagues it was the ultimate betrayal. At one dinner at Gordon Square in 1916, Strachey placed on Keynes's plate 'the conscientious objector's equivalent of a white feather' – a newspaper report of a militaristic speech by one of Maynard's Treasury colleagues, along with a note: 'Dear Maynard, Why are you still at the Treasury? Yours, Lytton.'[12]

The slights were painful, but not so much as to shame Keynes out of government service. From 1915 until 1919 he worked in Whitehall, determining Britain's economic policy, gaining influence and gradually shaping his thoughts on the future of the international economy. For a young man whose previous experience of government had been a lackadaisical few years in the India Office, it was thoroughly stimulating.

America's entry into the war in 1917 also changed his job overnight. For the first few years of war his main concern had been attempting to anticipate the next financial crisis – and to discern when Britain might run out of money with which to fight. By his own account, things got hairy: in September 1915 he had prepared a memorandum for the Chancellor, Reginald McKenna, warning that Britain would struggle to survive beyond the following March. The advice infuriated David Lloyd George, then Minister of Munitions, who would write in his war memoirs that Keynes was 'much too mercurial and impulsive a counsellor for a great emergency. He dashed at conclusions with acrobatic ease. It made things no better that he rushed into opposite conclusions with the same agility.' Lloyd George added that when that deadline arrived, 'we still bought greater quantities than ever of food, raw material and munitions from abroad and were paying for them and our credit was still high' – words akin to those used by many modern-day Keynesians when berating those who warn them of the dangers of over-spending and over-borrowing.[13]

Keynes would clash with Lloyd George repeatedly in the ensuing years, his natural enthusiasm for his job jarring with his distaste when his master's aims were transparently political rather than straight-forwardly noble. 'I work for a government I despise for ends I think criminal,' he had written to Duncan Grant some months previously.[14] The real souring was to come in the months after the war, however.

When America declared war, suddenly Britain's priorities shifted. Running out of money was no longer an immediate prospect – instead, the objective became to ensure America remained happy enough to keep pumping in its financial support. And so, for the first time, Keynes was sent on a diplomatic mission to the United States – in this case to negotiate American loans and arrange the purchase of some Canadian wheat. He was not a great success, in diplomatic terms, at least. With the Americans he made a 'terrible impression for his rudeness',[15] and even the British ambassador, Sir Cecil Spring-Rice, was taken aback.

'He was really too offensive for words and I shall have to take measures,' Spring-Rice wrote to his wife. 'He is also a Don and the combination is not pleasing. He is also a young man of talent and I presume the rule for such nowadays is to show his immense superiority by crushing the contemptible insignificance of the unworthy outside. He does it hard.'[16]

Time would do little to soften Keynes's hard edges, and he would elicit similar complaints from his American partners ahead of Bretton Woods. He was an aggressive debater, frequently destroying and occasionally humiliating his opponents at the slightest provocation – though his barbs were invariably aimed at the powerful and the pompous; with students and the young, he was remarkably patient. It was a technique honed in the classrooms of Eton and tutorials at Cambridge: an uncompromising, brutal mode of argument that would rarely concede that the other party might be in the slightest bit right. 'Keynes's intellect,' wrote the philosopher Bertrand Russell, 'was the sharpest and clearest that I have ever known. When I argued with him, I felt that I took my life in my hands, and I seldom emerged without feeling something of a fool.'[17]

It made Keynes a fearsome debating opponent, but frequently had disastrous consequences when unleashed in the brittle cauldron of transatlantic diplomacy. It didn't help his cause that he was often just plain wrong.

Revolting as many would find these characteristics, they were nonetheless a potent weapon. Keynes's intellect was combined with a capacity for (often brutal) persuasion and an awareness that even a good argument might be a losing one if not transmitted correctly. Half the battle, he came to realise, was not merely coming up with policies, but getting them implemented, which also meant explaining them in terms others could understand. And so, while Keynes is remembered today as an economist, he would never have found fame and gained influence unless he had also doubled as a writer and journalist – one of the twentieth century's greatest.

However, Keynes's caustic nature caused occasional rifts – even with his closest friends. Even leaving aside their differences over the rights and wrongs of wartime service, his relationship with Bloomsbury was frequently tested when the filthy subject of money intruded. Rather like Britain as a whole in that era, Bloomsbury had managed thus far to float along on the illusion of prosperity, without necessarily having the cash on hand to back up its lofty aspirations. The lives of leisure led by most of the set, the salons, the parties and the servants, were expensive. And though most of the set's members had inherited at least some money, it was far from enough to fund their extravagant lifestyles.

In much the same way as he had confronted his country's impending penury, Keynes approached the reality of his Bloomsbury friends' financial infirmity with a certain brusqueness. A few years earlier he had moved into 46 Gordon Square, Clive and Vanessa Bell's London townhouse, but by 1918 the couple were living with painter Duncan Grant in Charleston, their country home in East Sussex. A month before his visit to France in 1918, Keynes engineered what was effectively a reverse takeover of the property, renewing the lease in his name rather than that of Clive Bell – a move which infuriated Bell, who had assumed he could hang on to his rooms there for his occasional visits into town to visit his mistress. To add insult to injury, Keynes also moved Clive's bed into his own bedroom and left Clive with one that felt 'more like the seat of a third-class railway carriage'. Having tried and failed to persuade Keynes to return his bed, Bell waited until he was away on war business before retrieving it himself. Keynes returned home to find the uncomfortable bed back in his room, accompanied by a letter from Bell. 'As you appear to fuck less than I do it may serve well enough,' it said.[18]

In fact, Keynes's sex life had so far been quite eventful. Like his Bloomsbury counterparts he had experimented with both homosexual and heterosexual relationships – although many more of the former than the latter. Unlike Bloomsbury, but very like Keynes, he used to keep a statistical record of his conquests: names, numbers and a coded notation of what they got up to. The tables, still stored among his personal papers at King's College, Cambridge, make for surreal reading: they include The Sculptor of Florence, The French Conscript, The Clergyman, The Irish Nobleman of the Whitechapel Baths and, ominously, The Blackmailer.[19]

His early partners – Duncan Grant and Lytton Strachey – had been replaced by a stream of other men, interspersed with the occasional woman. So it is little surprise that when he first met Lydia Lopokova, star of Diaghilev's Ballets Russes company, he was more interested in her male ballet partner than the prima ballerina.

It happened in October, just before he left for France, at a party given by the Sitwells in Chelsea. Lopokova was already an international sensation. Born into a poor family in St Petersburg, her father the chief usher at the Alexandrinsky Theatre, she and all her siblings became ballet dancers – though none so successful as Lydia. Not long after joining the Ballets Russes – the phenomenally successful company which revitalised ballet with modern, expressive adaptations – she left for the United States, where she became a renowned society figure. By 1918 she had been engaged twice, married once, and had had an on–off affair with Igor Stravinsky.

Keynes had seen her earlier in the month but deemed her 'poor', remarking to a friend: 'She is a rotten dancer – she has such a stiff bottom.'[20] Nonetheless, at the Sitwells' party Lydia was charming, 'making us pinch her legs to see how strong she was – which we did very shyly'. It also turned out that her ballet partner, Stanislas Idzikovsky, who had looked so impressive on stage, was in person 'the most ridiculous little creature you ever saw'. Said Lydia: 'I don't like dancing with him … It is not nice to dance with something only up to your breasts and I am always afraid he will drop me.'[21]

She and Keynes would remain in contact from that day forward – though for the time being their hearts were elsewhere. Anyway, there were more important issues at hand. The war was about to end. Shortly after Keynes's tour of the French battlefields he was officially appointed head of the economic section of Britain's mission to the 1919 Paris peace conference.

When Harry Dexter White returned to America in 1919 he found it much the same as when he left. True, if you looked close enough there was yet more evidence of economic progress: the skylines of

New York and Chicago were rising ever faster, the two cities locked in a vertical race for the crown of world's tallest building. But that progress was, for the moment, imperceptible. What was more obvious to him was that while the country was fast becoming wealthier, the increases in income were not shared out equally.

Large swathes of American cities remained trapped in squalor. In Beacon Hill, where White had grown up, the wealthy establishment lived in grand apartment buildings and houses a mere stone's throw from areas of extreme deprivation, overpopulated tenement blocks and putrid shacks. The Spanish influenza epidemic, which had arrived in the United States via Boston the previous year, was killing hundreds of thousands, including many in the North End of the city where White had volunteered before the war. The neighbourhood was reeling, too, from what became known as the Boston Molasses Disaster, when a large storage tank exploded, unleashing a giant wave of molasses which killed 21 and injured 150.

Even as Wall Street was booming, heading towards the bubble that would define the era, there was scant evidence of prosperity in the centre of Boston. Indeed, much of the rest of the country was mired in permanent poverty. So stark were such contrasts that they had helped inspire the rise of a political movement – the Progressives, who in this pre-Depression, pre-New Deal era campaigned for social reform, as well as the imposition of limits on laissez-faire capitalism.

In the meantime, those without jobs or family networks had to rely on other sources of support, such as the settlement houses, where the most needy – often but not always immigrants – could go for food, shelter, basic healthcare and classes to make them more employable. These were typically found in the deprived parts of big cities like Boston and New York, and had originally been modelled after Toynbee Hall in London.

As a schoolboy, White had volunteered in a number of settlement houses, as well as devoting his Sundays (the only day free from school or work at the shop) to teaching boys at the Home for Jewish Children at Dorchester.[22] Having been demobilised from the army in February 1919 he was drawn back towards the cause of social justice. He worked for a few months in the family store, but it was clear almost immediately that he did not want to be there. According to his brother Nathan, 'life in the army had changed his outlook.'[23] Later that year he cut the cord for good, taking up the directorship of an orphan asylum for the children of American Expeditionary Force servicemen killed in the war. This job was followed by promotion to director of New York's Corner House – one of the city's bigger settlement houses.

It was a similar path to that chosen by many young, idealistic Americans of the era, akin to the voluntary service many youngsters take before or after university today. Some of the leading authors of the New Deal, such as Harry Hopkins and White's future employer Henry Morgenthau Jr, would undergo similar rites of passage in their younger years, spending time in the houses, following in the footsteps of Jacob Riis, writer of *How the Other Half Lives*. It was in these years that the idea of an American welfare state was formed, though it would take the financial chaos of the Wall Street Crash a decade later, and the depression that followed, to forge it properly.

Such imbalances are common hallmarks of an emerging economy – evidence of 'growing pains' as it develops a middle class – and indeed these decades marked America's coming of age as a superpower. In pure economic terms (at least as measured by gross domestic product – GDP – per capita) the United States had already overtaken Britain to become the world's biggest economy a few decades before in the 1890s, but even in 1914 it was still a bit-player on the international stage. At the start of the Great War, the dollar was quoted in fewer financial centres than relative minnows like the Italian lira or Austrian schilling.[24] London, on the other hand, was the world's undisputed financial hub, responsible for almost half the world's exported capital, financing most of the flows of international trade and housing the majority of the insurance industry.

The war changed that: in its desperation to fund the war effort, Britain would have to liquidate 15 per cent of its overseas investments, an enormous instant reduction in its international wealth. The US, meanwhile, was alone in both having the capacity to extend credit to its allies in Europe and retaining a stable currency. In stark contrast to the pound, which was devalued against gold in the latter stages of the war, the dollar kept its value, giving traders and financiers the stability they depended on when transacting international business. Over time, this experience would become ingrained in the respective countries' national psyches: whereas Britons associated the gold standard with economic pain and strife, Americans associated it with their rise to economic potency.

It was during the war that America became, in Barry Eichengreen's words, 'factory and grainery to the world'.[25] Exporting billions of dollars of goods, it turned its current account deficit into the surplus that would become the dominant force at Bretton Woods a quarter of a century later.

Not that this would endear the British or other borrowers to the Americans. During the war, Lord Eustace Percy wrote that 'our job is ... to keep sentiment in America so sweet that it will lend us practically unlimited money'.[26] By the end of the war the European Allies owed the American government over $7 billion, and half that again to banks such as J.P. Morgan. In the wake of the war, when the Europeans struggled to repay those American debts, relations would turn sour, tempering US generosity in the Second World War.

If the Great War was the moment the Britons first realised that, when it came to money, America would from now on be calling the shots, the 1920s were when participants in financial markets finally recognised the reality of the newly redrawn economic league table.

As historian David Kynaston put it, 'the baton, which London had once assumed from Amsterdam, now passed to New York.'[27] Halfway through the decade the dollar had displaced sterling as the dominant international unit. It had taken barely more than ten years since its arrival on the world stage.

However, the fact that the world's dominant currency was now the dollar rather than the pound sterling did not necessarily mean that all the financial activity had to leave the City of London – at least as far as its traders were concerned. The demise of the gold standard had ushered in an unfamiliar new world of floating exchange rates. For exporters with overseas customers this was a threat; for the brokers and jobbers of the Square Mile it was a golden opportunity.

'With the unpegging of the world's exchanges in March 1919,' wrote H.W. Phillips, 'there started one of the largest businesses the world has seen. A veritable orgy of dealing took place, and every centre seemed to be besieging London on long-distance calls.'[28] One of the men at the end of these telephones, George Bolton, a dealer at Société Générale, would later go on to represent Britain at Bretton Woods. So quickly and enthusiastically did the City seize on the new business of foreign exchange that it soon became one of the biggest and most lucrative activities in the City. And although the United States would frequently attempt to challenge London's supremacy in this financial business, it remains the dominant player even today.

For the moment, though, these financial and economic shifts had little impact on White. Come 1922, with his thirtieth birthday approaching, he was still in charge of the Corner House. If anything, the enormous structural shifts America was undergoing only served to make his job harder. The gap in incomes between Wall Street and those who came in and out of the settlement house was getting ever wider, and White was powerless to do much about it. It was around now that he realised that without further qualifications he stood little chance of making a lasting difference. So he applied to take a degree in government at Columbia University as a mature student. He was successful. After three terms he moved across to Stanford University on the West Coast, switching, too, to economics. He would later remark that he had 'realized that most governmental problems are economic, so I stayed with economics'.[29]

Finally, at the age of thirty-one, living with his wife in a small property near San Francisco, White started to hit his intellectual stride. His degree in economics 'with great distinction' came in late 1924, followed by a master's degree the next year. The small, smart boy from Boston was now, said those with whom he studied, a confident, assertive, stand-out student, one who would think nothing of arguing with his professors in class (a characteristic he shared with Keynes, who had spent much of his time at Eton and Cambridge berating his tutors). White declared confidently that his next step would be to take his Ph.D. at Harvard.

This was also the moment White made his first notable foray into politics. His choice of champion is intriguing. In early 1924 he wrote, on behalf of himself and other mature students, a letter urging Senator Robert La Follette to stand in that year's presidential election. 'Fighting Bob' was one of the most radical candidates to stand for that office: he opposed big corporations, he proposed nationalising the railroads and electric utilities, he supported the strengthening of labour laws and opposed war. So far on the fringes were his policies that the only party to offer him an official platform was the Communists. However, he stood independently, on behalf of the progressive movement. Although he eventually won five million votes, making him one of the most successful third-party candidates in history, he nonetheless came in third behind Calvin Coolidge and Democrat John W. Davis.

However, he had left a lasting impression on the United States, and on the young Harry Dexter White. Not for the last time, the economist showed himself ready and willing to stand up for what he believed in, and to support a political cause, however unfashionable. In his letter to the senator, White had declared: 'At no time has our country been more in need of a leader, and ... at no time since Lincoln's has there been a man more fitted to lead than you.'[30]

No sooner had Keynes returned home from the 'blasted grandeur' of France and Belgium in November 1918 than he was set to work on the terms of the coming peace treaty.

It was clear from the very beginning that the process would be tortuous. On the one hand, this was the grand opportunity to put Europe right, to cure the benighted continent of its bellicose ways – something the Congress of Vienna in 1815 had never achieved. It was a chance to enshrine an international body to prevent worldwide conflicts ever happening again; the moment, too, to make self-determination more than an abstract noun in a textbook. For Woodrow Wilson it was the opportunity to implement a peace in accordance with his beloved Fourteen Points.*

The reality Keynes discovered upon his arrival in Paris early in 1919 was different: a hissing snakepit of politicians, all with competing political objectives. The French and Italians wanted to carve up chunks of Austria and Germany between themselves. France's Prime Minister Clemenceau wanted to recoup the billions of dollars' worth of costs France had sustained during the war. Most of the British electorate wanted the same thing, and Lloyd George was keen to secure re-election. Britain wanted to arrange the peace quickly before America became too influential, while America wanted to ensure the Europeans would pay their debts. Most of the American population wanted nothing more to do with this distant European war, and Congress was lukewarm about the Fourteen Points.

*Liberal Europeans, too, were extremely enthusiastic about Wilson's Fourteen Points and the promise of a League of Nations. Indeed, the Fabians commissioned a detailed study into the matter by Keynes's Bloomsbury acolyte Leonard Woolf.

It was from somewhere in between Wilson's idealism and Lloyd George's brutal pragmatism that the muddle of Versailles emerged. 'What do you want me to do?' quipped Clemenceau at one point of his two fellow leaders. 'I find myself between Jesus Christ on one side and Napoleon Bonaparte on the other.' Wilson considered Lloyd George 'to have no principles whatever of his own ... he reacted according to the advice of the last person who had talked with him: that expediency was his sole guiding star.'[31] It didn't help that Europe was facing economic turmoil. The sanctions imposed by the Allies against Germany during the war stayed in place. Living standards across the continent continued to fall, trade remained stagnant in the face of blockades. Although the armistice had been signed, it was a very strange kind of peace, with troops still mobilised throughout mainland Europe in the absence of clarity over the settlement. The gold standard was still in ruins – in the latest sign of its decay, Britain had abandoned its currency peg with France, bringing to an end a century of stability – and resentment stalked the corridors of the Parisian hotels where the negotiations were to take place.

While Keynes boasted to his mother, 'I have been put in principal charge of financial matters for the Peace Conference,'[32] the reality was more prosaic: he was given responsibility for attempting to ensure the economic revival of the continent. In Paris in 1919 this came a distant third to the main political aims of carving up Europe and attempting to impose reparations on Germany.

Even before his tour of the battlefields the previous November, Keynes had attempted to erect an academic deterrent against such efforts, issuing a memorandum warning the Prime Minister that any money demanded of Germany should be based on her capacity to pay, rather than on the amount aggrieved parties felt they were due. Keynes had calculated this at roughly £3 billion, based on Germany's remaining gold reserves, securities and inventories, and her prospects for exports in the coming years. This was £1 billion shy of what he and the Treasury estimated the Allies could reasonably claim in compensation for war costs, but far smaller than the sums demanded by others. The Australian Prime Minister, Billy Hughes, was claiming £25 billion, a preposterous figure which was nonetheless supported by Lord Cunliffe, the former governor of the Bank of England (who had never quite seen eye-to-eye with Keynes), and Lord Sumner, the two official UK advisers on reparations. Keynes would nickname them the 'Heavenly Twins'.

Keynes succeeded in influencing the Treasury submission on the matter, which concluded that 'If Germany is to be "milked", she must not first of all be ruined.' But such words were less potent than those uttered by Sir Eric Geddes, the First Lord of the Admiralty, who said: 'The Germans, if this Government is returned, are going to pay every penny; they are going to be squeezed as a lemon is squeezed – until the pips squeak. My only doubt is not whether we can squeeze hard enough, but whether there is enough juice.'[33]

And it was the election of December 1918 that sealed it: one of the planks of Lloyd George's campaign was to seek the 'fullest indemnity from Germany'. When the conference began the following month, the question of Germany's capacity to pay was a secondary consideration behind the demand for retribution from the war's victors – something Georges Clemenceau heartily agreed with. Into the quagmire strode Woodrow Wilson, who made an unprecedented personal visit to Paris, hoping that this gesture alone would influence his European counterparts into agreeing a just peace. As it was, he would soon become bogged down in the negotiations and remain stuck in Paris for most of the six months it took to get the treaty signed. His ambitious and earnest programme for remoulding international diplomacy, the Fourteen Points, was frequently treated with the kind of disdain he rarely encountered back home ('God had only ten,' joked Clemenceau).

Within a few months it was clear to Keynes that his ideas had fallen on fallow ground. Lloyd George, with whom his relationship had been difficult ever since they first encountered each other in 1916, was less than receptive; so was Clemenceau. Keynes held out hope that Wilson would come to his aid, but the President had little time for the economist's suggestion that America write off the war debts it was owed in order to put Europe back on its feet. Nor did Wilson put up much resistance to Lloyd George or Clemenceau when it came to reparations.

It was a double failure as far as Keynes was concerned: so much attention was paid to reparations that the question of economic reconstruction fell by the wayside. The most important issue of all, in retrospect – how to rebuild the international monetary system – wasn't even on the table. The experience would reinforce his determination twenty-five years later to ensure that neither mistake was made at Bretton Woods.

For Keynes, the most sympathetic characters during the 1919 negotiations were the Germans, their plight embodied in the person of Dr Carl Melchior, a banker and spokesman for the nation. He made such an impression that Keynes would later make him the subject of his most sensitive work, the posthumously published 'Dr Melchior: A Defeated Enemy'. The real opposition, Keynes soon discovered during that thankless and increasingly exhausting spring in Paris, was not the Germans but his own colleagues and the various different camps set up by the Allies throughout the city.

The British, four hundred officials in total from the UK and its Dominions, took over the Hotel Majestic, a fraying, once-great hotel on the Avenue Kléber near the Arc de Triomphe. Paranoid about the possibility of French spies, Scotland Yard packed the hotel full of officers. The entire existing staff was turfed out and replaced with British-appointed chefs, porters and valets – which, according to British diplomat Harold Nicolson, meant the food was of the slightly dowdy 'Anglo-Swiss variety'.[34]

The cast list was extraordinary: T.E. Lawrence (of Arabia) was present alongside Emir Feisal of Saudi Arabia; playwright Jean Cocteau and novelist Marcel Proust floated in and out of the lobby. If you visited the kitchens you might have spotted a very young Ho Chi Minh, the future revolutionary leader of Vietnam, washing dishes. As time wore on, with the conference taking far longer than anyone had envisaged, the strain started to show, not merely on the participants but just as noticeably on the city itself, which had hardly found time to draw breath since the war had officially ended. The rooms in which the meetings took place started off freezing and draughty but by the time summer arrived were overwhelmingly sweaty. There were bedbug infestations and plumbing disasters.[35]

Even after three months, the Allies could not agree a figure for reparations. It had to be somewhere between the faintly ridiculous French claim of £25 billion and the American ceiling of £5 billion (the British were, at that stage, in the middle at £11 billion). In the event, they agreed to disagree, omitting a specific amount from the treaty itself and leaving the issue hanging uncomfortably over Germany for years to come. The notion that reparations should be commensurate with the country's capacity to pay had been ignored. Even Lloyd George was by this stage harbouring sincere regrets about the punishment about to be meted out, warning his fellow leaders that 'You may strip Germany of her colonies, reduce her armaments to a mere police force and her navy to that of a fifth-rate power; all the same in the end if she feels that she has been unjustly treated in the peace of 1919 she will find means of exacting retribution from her conquerors.'[36] But he did nothing to reverse the treaty's course.

Particularly egregious, so far as ordinary Germans were concerned, was Article 231, which attributed all the guilt for the war to Germany; even the British Foreign Secretary Arthur Balfour acknowledged that an 'awkward case' could be made in Germany's favour on this point. The clause was especially galling given that, in the words of Margaret Macmillan, 'as a result of the armistice terms, the great majority of Germans never experienced their country's defeat at first hand.'[37]

As far as Keynes was concerned, 'The Peace is outrageous and impossible and can bring nothing but misfortune.' In a letter to Duncan Grant in May, he wrote: 'Certainly if I were in the Germans' place I'd die rather than sign such a Peace.' By this stage he was 'utterly worn out, partly by incessant work and partly by depression at the evil round me'. The only consolation was that the weather had improved – though that was scant recompense for the implosion of Europe. 'Here I could cry all day for rage and vexation,' he wrote. 'The world can't be quite as bad as it looks from the Majestic.'[38]

Keynes was far from alone in his condemnation of the negotiations. His views were shared by his South African counterpart Jan Smuts and by Herbert Hoover, who would be US President a decade later. 'We agreed that it was terrible,' wrote Hoover,[39] who had masterminded the relief programme for Belgium and was spearheading the efficiency movement back home.*

By the time the Germans signed the Treaty of Versailles the following month, Keynes had absolved himself of the disaster, handing in his notice and leaving for London. 'I can do no more good here,' he wrote to Lloyd George. 'I've gone on hoping even through these last dreadful weeks that you'd find some way to make of the Treaty a just and expedient document. But now it's apparently too late. The battle is lost. I leave the twins to gloat over the devastation of Europe.'[40]

However, he wasn't quite finished with the subject. Before the

---

*Hoover's name at this stage was literally synonymous with cost-cutting: thanks to his strenuous efforts during the war, the word 'Hooverize', meaning to economise, had entered the lexicon. A decade and a half later his name would become synonymous with the Great Depression: Hoovervilles were the names of shanty towns constructed by the homeless in the 1930s.

end of that month, he was sitting down at his desk at Charleston, spilling his resentment and anger over the events in Paris on to paper. In the coming months he would produce sixty thousand words – a fluent, brilliant exposition of the problems with the treaty, accompanied by unforgiving pen portraits of the three men responsible for it. The resulting book, *The Economic Consequences of the Peace*, is still in many senses Keynes's masterpiece – not merely for its analysis of what went wrong in Paris, but for the literary flair and individualism with which it was written. Keynes was self-consciously writing for as wide an audience as possible. There may have been economics in there – and indeed the odd table of figures – but the purpose was to underline how simple was the economics, and by extension how neglectful were the politicians to ignore it.

The treaty, he wrote, was a 'Carthaginian Peace', akin to Rome's brutal treatment of Carthage, which after the Third Punic War was destroyed and its surviving inhabitants sold into slavery: 'My purpose in this book is to show that the Carthaginian Peace is not practically right or possible. Although the school of thought from which it springs is aware of the economic factor, it overlooks, nevertheless, the deeper economic tendencies which are to govern the future.' The result, in Robert Skidelsky's words, is 'a personal statement unique in twentieth-century literature. Keynes was staking the claim of the economist to be Prince. All other forms of rule were bankrupt.'[41] It was the first great popular work to attempt to depict international military affairs through an economic rather than a political prism.

Clemenceau was portrayed as a wily old man duping the naïve American President, who had arrived hopelessly unprepared for the circus of negotiations in Paris: 'the President had thought out nothing; when it came to practice his ideas were nebulous and incomplete. He had no plan, no scheme, no constructive ideas whatever for clothing with the flesh of life the commandments which he had thundered from the White House.' It was a cardinal error of conference-going: as a result the negotiations started from the basis of a French or British draft, putting Wilson in the perpetual position of 'obstruction, criticism, and negation'. It was a strategy mistake the Americans would ensure was not to be repeated at Bretton Woods.

Keynes's original draft also contained a withering description of Lloyd George as 'this extraordinary figure of our time, this syren, this goat-footed bard, this half-human visitor to our age from the hag-ridden magic and enchanted woods of Celtic antiquity'. On the advice of Asquith and his mother, he left that passage out, though the remaining descriptions of the Prime Minister watching on 'with six or seven senses not available to ordinary men' and bamboozling the President caused offence all the same. He also allowed a few of his more eccentric obsessions to intrude on the text, including his love of judging people based on the appearance of their hands (a study whose technical term is chirognomy). Wilson's hands, 'though capable and fairly strong, were wanting in sensitiveness and finesse'.[42] Clemenceau's, tantalisingly, were always covered by his grey suede gloves. The acid, witty, occasionally indiscreet portraits – undoubtedly a key element of the book's success – were clearly in part influenced by Keynes's Bloomsbury friend Lytton Strachey's *Eminent Victorians*, which had appeared the previous year.

The depiction of Wilson as a Don Quixote figure caused outrage in America, but that hardly dampened the sales figures: within a year Keynes had sold a hundred thousand copies and (thanks in part to the fact that he had personally negotiated the terms) was a very wealthy man.

But the book did more: it established Keynes as an internationally renowned figure. In much the same way that economists since have periodically laid claim to seeing financial and economic crashes before the rest of the world, Keynes became known as the Cassandra and economic clairvoyant of his era. While some of the more pessimistic predictions in the book did not come to pass (it was clearly written in the very depths of despair for the fate of Europe), events were to bear out many of his warnings over the following years. On reparations, he said: 'I do not believe that any of these tributes will continue to be paid, at the best, for more than a very few years. They do not square with human nature or agree with the spirit of the age.' He warned that unless debts were forgiven various European nations would 'seek their friends in other directions, and any future rupture of peaceable relations will always carry with it the enormous advantage of escaping the payment of external debts'.

There were warnings about the risks of inflation. Keynes quoted Lenin, saying: 'There is no subtler, no surer means of overturning the existing basis of society than to debauch the currency.' And underlying it all was the insight – which is often forgotten even today – that when you are trying to impose debts or reparations on a country you must do so with reference to that country's ability to pay.

The whole experience, in Keynes's mind, was 'one of the most serious acts of political unwisdom for which our statesmen have ever been responsible'. He added: 'To what a different future Europe might have looked forward if either Mr Lloyd George or Mr Wilson had apprehended that the most serious of the problems which claimed their attention were not political or territorial but financial and economic.'

Such insights were to play a considerable part when the Allied leaders began to draw up their plans for reconstruction in the wake of the Second World War. Economic considerations would not be relegated to the sidelines – they would be the foundation for the post-war plans.

Keynes's book was only one element of a broader backlash against the treaty. In the years that followed, the Allies would return again and again to the issue of reparations, gradually revising down the amount demanded from the Germans in the face of the country's economic slide, its spiral into hyperinflation and a lengthy depression.

Wilson finally returned home in summer 1919 to a nation, and more pertinently a Senate, which was lukewarm towards both the treaty and the creation of his League of Nations. The conference had cemented much of the bitterness already brewing in the United States about the country's experience of the war. Some fifty thousand American soldiers had been sacrificed in the mud of northern Europe for what was, at heart, someone else's war – and now almost all the Europeans (on both sides) were planning to repudiate their debts. It went beyond ingratitude – and many Congressmen would spend the following years attempting to write into law whatever safeguards they could to prevent the United States from either lending belligerents like Britain money or, for that matter, sending their boys back into battle.

Despite the general feeling in his country, Wilson ploughed on with his crusade to secure the two-thirds majority necessary to pass the treaty. But even winning the Nobel Peace Prize did little to help (in fact, in some quarters this European award probably undermined his cause). Late in the summer he embarked on a nationwide speaking tour to try to sway the public mood, but he collapsed halfway through with a severe stroke that effectively ended his active period in office. Shortly afterwards there was an opportunity to pass a treaty with reservations, that would at least have allowed America to join the League of Nations, but Wilson rejected the compromise. Some said that the stroke had changed his personality; it certainly seems to have undermined his ability to engage with the debate. Either way, the United States never joined the League, leaving the enterprise doomed from the very start.

Paris had only served to confirm US suspicions about the double-crossing Europeans. Moreover, the experience underlined the fact that the British, in particular, seemed hell-bent on squeezing as much extra money as possible out of Washington. Before Bretton Woods, Bernard Baruch of the 1919 US delegation would warn Henry Morgenthau to watch out for Keynes – who, he claimed, had double-crossed the Americans on the issue at Versailles.

But few were happy – and Keynes's misgivings, if more dramatically and eloquently put than others', were widely shared. Lloyd George's conclusion was perhaps the most prescient. 'We shall have to do the whole thing over again in twenty five years at three times the cost,' he said.[43] He had predicted the date of Bretton Woods almost to the day.

CHAPTER THREE

A Short History of Gold

In the very heart of the City of London, in a network of vast rooms three storeys below ground level, sits one of the world's oldest and largest stockpiles of gold. The Bank of England's vaults are buried so deep beneath the surface that as you walk through them today, the only sounds you can hear are the echo of your own footsteps and, from somewhere beyond the walls, the occasional rumble of a London Underground train as it pulls out of Bank station.

These days the vaults hold over four hundred thousand gold bars, locked away behind reinforced steel walls and a series of giant doors, one of which demands a key three feet long to unlock it. So heavy are the bars (each weighs on average thirteen kilos, or two stones) that there is a rule against stacking too many of them on top of one another, for fear of the floor sinking into the soft London clay on which it is built.

There is something hypnotic about seeing all that gold in front of you – though, as one scientist put it when he caught sight of the hoard, 'it's a bit sad, rather like a mausoleum where the dead gold is sitting waiting for people to remember it.'[1]

And, if you were having a contemplative moment, you might

well ask why it is all there in the first place. Why squirrel so much of one element away from plain sight? The straightforward but not very enlightening answer is that it is valuable – very valuable. Take the oldest bar in the vaults, which was first placed there in 1916. It is worth an astonishing $520,000 (its value was around $7,300 when it arrived, which also tells you something about inflation, but that's another story). Clearly you have to keep such expensive items safely locked away.

But, to probe deeper, why do we append so much value to a simple lump of metal? How and why have we given these ingots and bars such a crucial role in the economic system? It was only in the years following the Great War that economists started sincerely to ask themselves such questions. For most of them – Keynes and White included – it had been an article of faith until then that advanced economies such as the United States and United Kingdom would return to the gold standard. For centuries, gold had been the yardstick against which the world's major currencies were valued, the linchpin in the international monetary system – why should that change?

The years that followed would provide a series of compelling explanations, as one economic disaster followed another, from the hyperinflation of Weimar Germany to Britain's miserable period of general strikes, the collapse of Austria's Credit-Anstalt and the American Depression of the 1930s. Each of these episodes could be traced back in some way to humankind's dysfunctional relationship with gold. The gold vaults in London and, for that matter, beneath the Federal Reserve Bank of New York and the Banque de France in Paris, were at the very epicentre of the crisis in the interwar years.

Not that this was particularly obvious in the years immediately after the Armistice. For many, life returned to normal. Keynes and White left government and military service respectively. Like most of their fellow countrymen they went home to their families, hoping, for a period at least, that the economic system would pick up where it left off in 1914. They were both to discover that that was not to be.

Both would come to the conclusion over the following years that it was not merely greedy bankers and incapable regulators who were to blame for these successive crises – though that wouldn't stop them throwing some criticism their way. The reality was that the entire international economic edifice was built on gold foundations that could no longer support it.

It was in this period that Keynes and White independently came to realise that an entirely new framework was needed if the world were not to slide into a succession of slumps in the following years. Quite what that framework would be was only to emerge after the world had relapsed into another war – a war at least in part caused by the malfunctioning of the gold standard.

The gold standard might never have come into existence were it not for an elementary mathematical mistake made in his old age by Sir Isaac Newton. In 1699, having contributed in innumerable ways to mathematics and physics, the fiftysomething scientist was appointed Master of the Royal Mint. The job was generally regarded as a sinecure where great men could while away the final years of their lives, but Sir Isaac wasn't one to sit back and watch the UK currency system carry on as normal. So he made some changes.

As in most civilisations since the earliest days of recorded history, money in England at the turn of the eighteenth century meant something very specific – a certain weight of precious metal. The pound was so named because, in its infancy, during Anglo-Saxon times, it had represented a pound in weight of sterling silver coins (hence the term pound sterling). Although civilisations since Roman times had sometimes used gold as currency, silver was a far more popular metal for coinage by Newton's time.

Gold, metallurgists soon realised, was too light and malleable for the minting of coins. Conversely, copper coins were too heavy, as the Swedes discovered to their cost when they experimented with a copper standard in the seventeenth century. Citizens tired of having to carry around rectangular copper slabs which were a hundred times the weight of identically valued silver coins.*

Nonetheless there was one constant principle: the concept of money was synonymous with the value of the coin you held in your hand. The system was hardly inviolable: from the earliest days, successive monarchs had periodically debased the coinage, adulterating its precious metal content and attempting to use the extra silver or gold to help fund wars, or provide more lavish banquets. Such efforts often triggered inflation or financial crises, after which there would be a 'cleansing' of the system, and newly denominated coins were issued. The principle that money should be worth the metal it was made from nevertheless proved difficult to shake.

However, tying a currency to a metal meant being vulnerable to any gluts or shortages in the supply of that metal. What you'll pay for a given amount of a commodity clearly depends on how scarce it is. A major discovery of gold or silver (or, for that matter, copper) could cause an unexpected increase in the money supply and hence in inflation. A shortage could mean that without enough precious metal to go around, workers would have to accept pay cuts – regardless of how fast the economy was growing. In the case of gold, the latter was typically more common, particularly given that while household incomes have multiplied many times since the Industrial Revolution, all the gold ever mined will still fit into a cube the size of a tennis court.†

This balancing act was doubly difficult when countries adopted

---

*There were positives, however. Burglars who broke into a house in Viborg and discovered a pile of cash had to leave it behind because they could not carry it. The weight is also said to have encouraged government investment in the road network between Stockholm and the provinces, as tax revenues could not be transported without the use of wagons. For more on this see Eli Heckscher, *An Economic History of Sweden*, Vol. 95, Cambridge, MA, 1954, pp. 88–91.

†Although it should be said the precise amount of mined and unmined gold remains under dispute, given that the precious metal has been in use for thousands of years. Some contend that the conventional estimates under-represent mined gold by a factor of sixteen.

bimetallic currencies, as Britain had by the seventeenth century. Unlike much of the rest of Europe, where silver coins were generally favoured, Britain's coinage was a combination of gold and silver. In order to make such a system sustainable, the metal content of each coin had to be proportionate to its value, and hence to worldwide supply. Get this ratio wrong, and as soon as people realised, they would simply melt down the coins and sell off the undervalued metal to make a profit.

That is precisely what happened when Newton introduced his reforms at the Royal Mint in the eighteenth century. Most of his changes were as sensible and innovative as one might have expected from the great man: coins were to be minted by machines rather than people to make them more uniform; they would be 'milled' at the edges to make them more difficult to counterfeit. But he also selected a new ratio of gold and silver for England's coins. In so doing, he overvalued gold and undervalued silver, and although he recommended that the supplies of the two metals be monitored in case of supply changes, his initial decision stuck. In the years that followed, silver rapidly escaped from the coinage system into the pockets of those canny enough to melt it down, and Britain was left on a de facto gold standard – something that was formalised the following century when silver's status as legal tender was revoked.

Britain's status as a global economic superpower, and London's as the world's financial hub, for almost two centuries after Newton's fateful decision more or less sealed it: gradually other major countries moved from their silver and bimetallic standards on to gold.* However, the process took time: only by 1870 was the gold standard, as it is broadly regarded today, in force – and even then only

---

*There were other factors, among them the glut of silver discovered in the United States in the 1850s, which meant those on bimetallic standards faced the same problem as Britain had in the early eighteenth century. A further incentive was that trade could flow more easily between countries on the same metallic standard, since gold could be swapped for gold.

in a handful of advanced economies: England, Germany, France and the United States. In those countries gold coins circulated as currency (although, as Thomas Sargent and Francois Velde have pointed out, even then there was plenty of 'token' small change which traded for well above its intrinsic value[2]) and while paper money circulated, the central bank was duty bound to keep enough gold in reserve to match its theoretical value.

It was from this period that the majority of monetary gold in the world found its way into vaults such as the Bank of England's, where it would play an essential role in the international monetary system. One problem hadn't gone away – tying a currency to a precious metal was inherently deflationary. The amount of money flowing through an economy was, in theory at least, tied to the amount of gold in central banks' vaults, rather than the capacity of that economy to expand.

But when it came to international trade, the system promised to be self-correcting. When country A had a trade deficit with country B (i.e. it imported more goods from that country than it exported), it would gradually pass its gold reserves on to B. With less gold circulating in country A, its prices would fall (and workers would face pay cuts), while they would rise by a similar amount in country B. This change in prices would encourage country B to start buying more of those cheaper goods from country A, and the system would correct itself – or so went the so-called Price Specie Flow theory developed by eighteenth-century philosopher David Hume.

While the theory gives the impression that the seaways of the period were perpetually clogged with ships transferring gold from one part of the world to another, in practice the precious metal rarely left vaults such as those under Threadneedle Street. Instead, before any such move was necessary, central bankers would pre-emptively raise interest rates to slow their economy, or cut them to speed it up. Those transfers of gold rarely needed to take place. And, anyway, given that most of the vaults, including the Bank of England's, held gold on behalf of their trading partners, in such an eventuality a gold transfer could be accomplished by merely moving a serial number from one column to another in a ledger.

There was no formal agreement enshrining any of the above, but in the clubbable world of central banking at the turn of the twentieth century, that hardly mattered: the bureaucrats followed what Keynes later dubbed 'the rules of the game'. During the decades between 1870 and 1914 there was simply no question that central bankers would maintain the value of their currencies – an assumption which seems all the more blithe given how rife the history books are with examples of monarchs debasing their coinage.

The system seemed, on the surface, to work perfectly. Currencies remained pegged to one another; traders could buy and sell goods from overseas without losing out from currency fluctuations; money flowed between countries with little or no restriction. And at the very centre, Keynes added, was the Bank of England, which by dint of Britain's dominance and London's importance 'could almost have claimed to be the conductor of the international orchestra'.[3]

The result was that, for most of the nineteenth century, wages were more or less static, as was inflation – a notion that seems almost incredible to the modern reader. Under the gold standard, governments did not have the capacity to print money to evade a crisis – nor did they have the capacity to do so to adjust to a growing population, or a higher rate of economic productivity. But then policymakers had less cause to fear an irate public, given that the franchise was limited primarily to men of property – this being before the labour and union movements took root.

Workers who suffered pay cuts as the quantity of gold in the Bank of England's vaults decreased had little democratic outlet for complaint; though when populist political movements did crop up, they were frequently focused on abolishing the gold standard. Gold became the primary political issue in the United States, where workers suffered deflation (both of prices and wages) of a fifth between 1870 and 1890. Following fierce lobbying by the silver industry (lobbying which would continue at the Bretton Woods conference), there were repeated attempts to convert to formal bimetallism, or even to replace gold with silver. Indeed, the rallying cry of William Jennings Bryant, the Democratic candidate for President in 1896, was: 'You shall not crucify mankind upon a cross of gold.' So deeply entrenched was popular revulsion to the system that it is thought by some that *The Wonderful Wizard of Oz*, L. Frank Baum's 1900 children's book which was later adapted into a film, was an allegory about the economic system, where the yellow brick road stands for the gold standard and the name Oz for the ounces in which gold was measured.

But as was repeatedly the case throughout the gold standard's short life, it was saved by happenstance. A series of big gold discoveries in this period injected a slug of extra cash into the global economic system, and the silver rebellion died away.

Indeed, the more one examines the gold standard of the nineteenth century, the clearer it is that it survived in large part because of a sequence of anomalies and accidents. Along with the lucky run of gold discoveries was the fact that the period from 1871 to 1913 was one of almost unprecedented peace in Europe.

Moreover, in reality central banks never slavishly followed the gold standard's strictures, allowing considerably more money to circulate around their economies. In 1913, for instance, there was around $5 billion worth of currency in households' and businesses' hands throughout Britain, backed up by only $800 million worth of gold. The Bank of England, and other central banks, relied on their neighbours' faith that, in extremis, they could squeeze the money supply if called upon to prove the value of their currency. Finally, although there were repeated financial crises throughout the period, none was of sufficient size to topple the monetary system altogether.

This last point was significant, since it would eventually come back to haunt the world between the wars. The gold standard was simply not equipped to accommodate the banking system which had developed by then. Under what became known as fractional reserve banking – the system of finance that prevails to this day – banks were allowed to issue credit (in other words lend cash) without necessarily holding that money in their balance sheets. As with the central banks and their gold holdings, such a system worked very well provided that everyone retained their faith in the system, and did not attempt to extract full payment of their cash holdings at the same time. When they did, private banks (which, unlike central banks, couldn't make good by simply reducing the amount of cash flowing around the economy) faced the prospect of a depositor run, and sudden collapse.

Fractional reserve banking enabled the expansion of credit that helped finance the latter stages of the Industrial Revolution, but it also left the central bank with a problem. So much credit had the banks extended that were one of them to fail, it would have far-reaching implications for the entire economic system – something that became clear with the collapse of the firm Overend and Gurney in 1866. The accepted lesson from this mid-Victorian financial crisis was that the Bank of England should provide cash to help tide troubled banks through any such event (unless they really were bust). What was less well appreciated, however, was that the Bank of England might not have enough money to do so, since the contents of its vaults were its gold reserves. It was an early rendition of the too-big-to-fail dilemma which has plagued today's global financial system.

And in 1890, just such a crisis took place, when London merchant bank Baring Brothers faced collapse after losing money it had lent to Argentina. The bank was only saved after the Bank of England borrowed £3 million of gold from the Bank of France and was pledged a further £1.5 million by the state bank in

Russia. Again, the clubbable world of central banking came to the rescue.

The reality was that the gold standard was a flawed system for organising economic relations between nations. But this inconvenient truth would take many years to sink in. Had the gold standard collapsed of its own accord – as it almost certainly would have done, given time – the world might have been spared the Depression. It might have moved to a monetary system akin to Bretton Woods or floating currencies far sooner, rather than the mutated version of the standard that was cobbled together in the 1920s.

However, in the event the system's collapse was directly attributed to the Great War. As peace broke out, the world's politicians could see no alternative but to return to gold. Others were less sure. For one American schoolboy, the system's flaws were patent even earlier. Twelve-year-old Eddie Bernstein was fixated with two French gold coins his father owned – but it wasn't their shininess that fascinated him. In 1916 his father had taken them into the bank and was given nineteen cents for each one. 'But at that time, my father explained to me, French francs weren't really worth nineteen cents apiece,' he later remembered. 'But the gold coins were.'

In Hans Christian Andersen's tale, it took a child's innocent question to expose the fact that the Emperor had no clothes. The young schoolboy's point – that the link between money and the value of the coinage itself had been ruptured – was similarly powerful. Nonetheless, over the following decades the world would drag itself into deep depression in an effort to re-establish the monetary system. Eddie Bernstein would grow up to be one of the economists who helped create a new economic system at Bretton Woods almost three decades later.

CHAPTER FOUR

Economic Consequences

1920–1939

They had a chance after the war that no generation has ever had. There was a whole civilisation to be saved and remade – and all they seem to do is to play the fool.

Evelyn Waugh, *Vile Bodies*

You are all a lost generation.

Gertrude Stein to Ernest Hemingway

For all but the Bright Young Things of Evelyn Waugh's *Vile Bodies*, the Twenties were a miserable decade in Britain. No sooner had the country come to terms with the tragedy of the Great War than there was a dreadful slump. The gap between haves and have-nots widened. Unemployment, which had been below 3 per cent of the working population before the war, shot up to 11 per cent – the highest rate since statistical records began in the mid-nineteenth century. Though they weren't to realise it, the British people were about to undergo the biggest failed economic experiment in their history.

For the man who saw it all coming, on the other hand, life wasn't half bad. By 1920, Keynes was settling back into private life as Britain's most influential economist. Though he had finally escaped the clutches of the Treasury and was now teaching at King's College again, he was still sought out by the Chancellor, Austen Chamberlain – and by many others too. Governments around the world came calling: Keynes was the only person to provide advice on reparations for both Britain and Germany, where his book would enshrine him as a figure of great affection, even into the Second World War.

For most of the 1920s Keynes made his living as a journalist and writer – a public intellectual, to use a modern epithet. It meant that by the time he started producing the heavier theoretical works that established his economic credibility in the 1930s (*A Treatise on Money*, the *General Theory*), he was already a household name. Having also, thanks to *The Economic Consequences of the Peace*, become quite wealthy – though he had not inherited vast sums, as had many of his Bloomsbury friends, royalties from the book meant suddenly he had an annual income of over £5000, equivalent to around £150,000 or $250,000 today – he almost immediately put the money to work.

While writing *The Economic Consequences of the Peace*, Keynes had begun placing bets on currencies – buying dollars and selling German marks. Currencies were, for the first time, rising and falling against each other. For businesses used to the exchange rate stability of the gold standard, this was a terrifying, destabilising prospect. But for Keynes, it was the money-making opportunity of a lifetime. With his friend Oswald 'Foxy' Falk, another tall, privileged old Treasury hand who had been in Paris with him in 1919 and was now in charge of City stockbroker Buckmaster and Moore, he created a syndicate to invest on behalf of friends and family. Its first few months were promising: early bets on a fall in sterling paid off, as did similar 'short' positions on the lira and franc, but after five months the market moved against it. Keynes was forced to liquidate his investments and was left owing almost £20,000 to his nearest and dearest.

Characteristically, he refused to give up, scraping together what money he could from book deals and journalism and reinvesting it. Somehow, he managed to end up not merely solvent, but with the syndicate in profit. It was a sign of things to come: Keynes would actively speculate on currencies, shares and commodities for much of the rest of his life – mostly when lying in bed at the start of each day. He became chairman of the National Mutual Life Assurance Company in 1921 and, as bursar at King's, took charge of the college's finances. For fusty old fellows used to investing their sums in government debt or railway shares, the arrival of this eccentric chap, intent on putting his money into the most bizarre enterprises, was a shock to the system. On one occasion, when a commodity investment failed to pay off before the contract was due for delivery, he even estimated the capacity of King's College Chapel in case he needed to use it as a grain storage facility.[1]

Nonetheless, he made more money than he lost. By 1945, the King's endowment was to be about twelve times bigger than when he first started managing it in earnest in 1920. His personal fortune was prone to wild fluctuations, doubling after his first disaster in the early 1920s, then crashing back to earth again in the Wall Street Crash of 1929, before swelling again in the 1930s.

Keynes's attitude was that the profits from his investments ought not to be hoarded, but should instead be spent on as many 'civilised' pastimes as possible. Under the influence of artist friends Duncan Grant and Vanessa Bell he invested in modern art, snapping up works by Picasso, Seurat and Matisse. One night, on the way back from Paris, Keynes strode into Charleston, proudly informing Vanessa and Duncan that he had left a Cézanne in a haystack.[2]

He continued to grow his library of rare books over the 1920s and 1930s, planning to amass 'a really comprehensive collection to illustrate the history of thought', including some of the writings of Sir Isaac Newton.[3] Much of the rest of the money he spent on lavish holidays for his friends and family, and on his other favourite pastime: the ballet. He had been an avid visitor to Covent Garden and the Coliseum for years, but friends noticed towards the end of 1921 that he was spending even more time there than usual. The explanation was the dancer whose legs he had been allowed to squeeze back in 1918, before setting off for Paris.

Keynes had remained in touch with Lydia Lopokova after that first meeting, and although he continued to pursue relationships with men in the following years, he grew increasingly fond of her. By December 1921 he would confess to Lytton Strachey: 'I'm entangled – a dreadful business – and barely fit to speak to.'[4]

His Bloomsbury friends were disturbed by the affair: it wasn't merely that Keynes was consorting with a woman – after all, many of the Bloomsbury men gave up homosexuality in their thirties – it was just, well, *her*. She could speak English (in a strict sense at least), but every sentence was littered with malapropisms and solecisms. Moreover, her life thus far had been punctuated with scandal. Not only was she married (to Randolfo Barocchi, the Diaghilev ballet company's business manager), she had carried on some notorious affairs. In 1919 she had disappeared amid rumours of a nervous breakdown, with newspaper hoardings proclaiming: 'Famous Ballerina Vanishes'. Eighteen months later she reappeared, now separated from Barocchi (a bigamist, it transpired), and soon enough was back on stage – this very public soap opera reinforcing her reputation as one of ballet's most intriguing stars.

Appearing on stage she would sometimes remain oblivious as various items of her costume became unbuttoned or fell off. But for Keynes – and the general public, who could not get enough of her – the sloppiness was part of the attraction. Soon enough he was smitten, his infatuation sealed by Lydia's performance in *The Sleeping Princess*, Diaghilev's lavish Christmas 1921 adaptation of Tchaikovsky's ballet *The Sleeping Beauty*. The show was a flop, cancelled before the end of its run, but Keynes nonetheless sat there night after night, watching his lover from the half-empty stalls. Malcolm MacDonald, who would later spend time with the couple in Canada in the wake of Bretton Woods, recalled Lydia on stage: 'Her small, slim, lithe figure poised on tiptoe in an elegant white ballet dress, with her face lit by the inspiration of dance, seemed angelic.

'In fact, Maynard Keynes was courting her. If I had known this at the time, I would perhaps have dropped something rather crushing on his head from my lofty seat in the gallery.'[5]

It would take some time for Lydia's divorce to come through, but over the coming months and years the pair would become inseparable, exchanging a stream of love letters, before eventually marrying in 1925. The letters underline their very real and physical attraction to each other, as well as betraying something of Lydia's charming, occasionally poetic mangling of the English language. 'I lick you tenderly', ends one, 'I warm my lips to yours, they feel very red' another. In one of them, Lydia signs off: 'I gobble you my dear Maynard. I am not like you talented in idea put into words [*sic*], I express myself better in impulses to you … I re-gobble you.' Keynes responded: 'I want to be foxed and gobbled abundantly.'[6]

For Keynes, who had spent most of his life deeply ashamed of his appearance, the arrival of this sensual, loving woman was a watershed: finally he was able to consign his physical insecurities to the past. The only regret, as time wore on, was their failure to have children. They tried, but Lydia miscarried in 1927. One day many years later, while observing a bare tree in the grounds of Tilton, the Sussex house he and Lydia had bought once married, he remarked, 'Barren fig tree; Baron Keynes.'[7]

As the 1920s went on, Keynes settled into domestic life with Lydia and, gradually, started to lose touch with his Bloomsbury circle. A summer holiday all together in a grand house in Dorset in 1923 was the clincher. At one point, Lydia threw her sanitary towel in the empty fire grate, sparking a magnificent row among the Bloomsbury set. For all his brilliance, even Keynes himself was occasionally revolting. Virginia Woolf wrote: 'Maynard is grown very gross & stout, especially when he wraps his leopard spotted dressing gown tight around his knees and stands in front of the fire … He has a queer swollen eel like look, not very pleasant. But his eyes are remarkable, & as I truly said when he gave me some pages of his new book to read, the process of mind there displayed is as far ahead of me as Shakespeare's.'[8] The estrangement was cemented – at least for Vanessa Bell and Duncan Grant – when Lydia moved into Gordon Square and promptly whitewashed the frescoes they had painted on the walls. Sacrilege, as far as Bloomsbury was concerned.

Keynes's influence at the Treasury started to wane, too, as those with whom he had worked during the war moved on, though his interest in the way they were running the economy was as deep, and as critical, as ever. In the years that followed the war, the Treasury and Bank had presided over a brief economic boom, provoked in part to lessen the pain of demobilisation, as soldiers came home from war. Interest rates, which no longer needed to be set in accordance with the gold standard, were kept low, and soon enough inflation started to creep higher. In 1920, the Bank of England yanked up interest rates to 7 per cent. The objective was not merely to pierce the economic bubble: it was to bring down prices so that Britain could rejoin the gold standard – that was the cross-party political objective, as recommended by the former governor of the Bank, and Keynes's adversary from Paris, Lord Cunliffe.

It did not take long for Keynes to sense that this arrangement was perverse. In order to bring the pound back down to its former gold standard value of $4.86, the Bank of England had to suck money out of the economy, so that the amount of paper currency flowing around Britain would no longer be out of line with the amount of gold in its vaults. This in turn entailed wage cuts and economic austerity of a sort rarely before experienced in the country. The falls in salaries and living standards so fuelled public outrage that a newly unionised worker class soon took to the streets. A series of protests culminated eventually in the 1926 General Strike, where the army was called in to protect businesses from picketing workers.

The notion that this misery was in any way linked to the gold standard took some time to sink in. Since it was assumed that the standard had collapsed because of the war, rather than due to its own inherent problems, it felt logical to reconstruct it after the fighting ceased. Indeed, many hoped not merely that it would be reconstituted but that it might now be extended to the more 'primitive' economies where it had never previously taken root. So-called 'money doctors', such as Edwin Kemmerer of Princeton University, were sent around the world proselytising for the gold standard – in much the same way that the International Monetary Fund would preach economic reform in the developing world during the 1980s and 1990s.

But while the enthusiasm for gold was, if anything, greater after the war than before it, the standard that would emerge during the 1930s was unmistakably different from the one that preceded the war. Whereas the pre-war gold standard had been dominated by Britain, this new version had only one indisputable star – with unexpected consequences.

Unlike everyone else, the United States had never left the standard in the first place. During the war, gold had flooded into the country, pushing up prices nationwide. Watching the bars arriving in his vaults at the Federal Reserve Bank of New York, Governor Benjamin Strong decided to take action, contracting the amount of cash in the system, in spite of all that extra money. It was a flagrant abandonment of the gold standard, though in his case to protect against inflation, rather than the deflation that was being experienced everywhere else – equivalent, Keynes wrote, to 'burying in the vaults of Washington what the miners of the Rand have laboriously brought to the surface'.[9]

To Keynes, at least, the preposterousness of the system was plain to see: America subverting the gold standard in order to protect its economy; Britain slavishly slashing living standards in an effort to rejoin it; the rest of Europe in turmoil. What had happened was a perversion of what gold actually stood for: it was not a god, or something to be worshipped; it was merely a medium of exchange. After all, he said, 'Money is only important for what it will procure.'[10] Over the course of 1922 and 1923 he wrote a series of essays in the *Manchester Guardian*, which would later be collected and published as *A Tract on Monetary Reform*. This was the book Virginia Woolf had read when she likened Keynes's mind to Shakespeare's.

The problem with the gold standard, Keynes wrote, was that it meant central bankers were duty-bound to set domestic borrowing costs not in accordance with the state of their own economies but in order to obey its rules. To follow those rules would result in crippling deflation in the poorer, European economies and destabilising inflation in the United States. It was no wonder, he added, that Ben Strong had been forced to take action. But that could not disguise the hypocrisy of pretending to adhere to the gold standard while, in reality, doing anything but. The consequence, he wrote, was that 'a dollar standard was set up on the pedestal of the Golden Calf ... This is the way by which a rich country is able to combine new wisdom with old prejudice.'[11]

Though the recent years of floating exchange rates had provided a profitable sideline for speculation, Keynes still could not conceive of currencies being unfixed permanently. The veil had not yet lifted on the early twentieth-century economic mind – it simply did not occur to Keynes, or indeed anyone else, that such a system might be feasible. However, if currencies were to be fixed, he said, they should not be fixed to a lump of metal. 'In truth,' he concluded, 'the gold standard is already a barbarous relic.'[12]

However, the *Tract* was more than a book about gold. In that work, for the first time, Keynes started to voice the kinds of economic opinions that would later become features of the movement known as 'Keynesianism'.

One precept was that a country should set its own economic policy first and foremost for domestic reasons, rather than because of how much gold was in its vaults. Another was that deflation was to be avoided at all costs. This was not to say that inflation was always a positive phenomenon; but, he said, deflation was, at that point in time, 'more injurious' than inflation.[13] The other precepts that would become integral to Keynesianism – the need for government investment, for instance – would come later, but the fundamental principles of his economic policy were already forming, and were finding voice in the frequent articles he wrote for newspapers and magazines. (Indeed, during Keynes's life, so much of his output appeared in the media, rather than in textbooks, that the term 'Keynesian' was already in parlance before the publication of the *General Theory*.)

It was the *Tract* that first introduced the world to such notions – the most striking being that economic decisions should not ignore the immediate future: the pain and economic cost associated with wage cuts this year might not outweigh the benefits in the following years. 'In the long run we are all dead,' he wrote in the *Tract* – arguably his most famous aphorism.[14]

However, the book could do little to prevent the 'barbarous relic' of which he had written once again becoming the dominant force in international economic policymaking. After a long period of economic depression and deflation, Britain eventually managed to cut domestic prices and strengthen the value of the pound. In 1925, Winston Churchill, then Chancellor, formally took Britain back into the gold standard at pre-war parity. At a private dinner shortly before his decision, Keynes urged him not to go ahead, but either there was a personality clash or his persuasiveness failed him. Keynes did not let Churchill forget it, dashing out a furious pamphlet ('The Economic Consequences of Mr Churchill') and ribbing him for the decision repeatedly thereafter. Churchill would later admit it was the greatest mistake of his life.*

Though nine years his junior, Harry Dexter White was starting to show his age as much as Keynes by 1924. His hairline was receding; he was filling out. His voice had deepened and he had a more confident air about him. The diminutive thirtysomething from Boston was finally looking like an adult. The difference was that, for the time being, he was still a college undergraduate.

While Keynes spent the 1920s cementing his reputation, establishing himself as the world's foremost proponent of government stimulus, White spent the decade catching up. After breezing through Stanford he secured, as he had confidently predicted the previous year, a place in graduate school at Harvard. And finally life started to speed up – which was just as well, because White was a man in a hurry. He was obviously intelligent, his classmates recalled, even compared with the rest of a highly competitive intake – but he also had a tendency to take himself a little too seriously. Perhaps it came of being an outsider. Though he had been born only a few miles away on the other side of the Charles River, White did not find Harvard a welcoming place. It was a WASPish New England enclave where Jewish students found it particularly hard to progress, let alone gain a professorship or tenure. All too often White's genial, jokey side would give way to bitterness. Every so often he would lash out – particularly when classmates teased him or, God forbid, his wife.[15]

Nonetheless, it was a happier time. There in Boston, White and his wife had two daughters. Like the rest of the United States, the city was thriving. As the 1920s progressed, America's economy continued to expand. With gold still pouring into the country as

---

*The pamphlet had to be renamed for its American audience, most of whom had never heard of this obscure British politician. Its eventual title in the United States was 'The Economic Consequences of Sterling Parity'.

the rest of the world remained mired in various degrees of turmoil, a bubble in asset prices was slowly being inflated. But bubbles are not obvious to everyone until they burst, as this one would in dramatic circumstances in 1929. So, for the time being, White started to focus his time and analysis on Europe, which was still grappling with the costs of the war, and the challenge of returning to the gold standard.

Those in France and Germany who thought the loss of almost four million soldiers between them was the worst of it were now coming to terms with the miserable peace settlement laid down in 1919. The two would spend most of the decade locked in a bitter diplomatic struggle over reparations, which only served to exacerbate the bigger economic disaster facing both of them. As each had sought to finance a catastrophically expensive war, they had engaged their printing presses. The amount of money flowing around the economy had tripled in France and quadrupled in Germany; their gold stocks, meanwhile, had diminished.

To add to France's woes, America was demanding repayment of her war debt, if not in full, then at ninety cents in the dollar – a sum that would have bankrupted France overnight. Her cause was not helped when Britain agreed to pay back 80 per cent, and promptly put even more pressure on France and Germany to repay their own British war debts and reparations. As Keynes had predicted in 1919, Europe started to tear itself apart in its desperate scrabble for cash. Between 1924 and 1929 the Allies squeezed almost $2 billion in reparations out of Germany. About $1 billion of it passed straight to the United States to pay off war debts and interest.

The irony was not lost on the residents of London, Paris and Berlin. Much as they might despise each other, there was a common scapegoat: 'Shylock', as the United States would find itself branded. The Americans, for their part, could hardly believe that the entire continent was determined to default, and resented them for merely trying to ensure the rightful repayment of their debts. It would take until 1926 for France to settle its war debts at a mere forty cents in the dollar – but by then there were bigger matters to worry about.

Given the expansion of their money supplies during the war, both France and Germany faced a massive inflationary threat in the immediate aftermath of the conflict. France, perhaps informed by the institutional memory of the Assignat hyperinflation during the Revolution, immediately clamped down on the money supply, gradually bringing its double-digit inflation under control. Germany took the opposite course, continuing to expand the money supply in a desperate bid to keep up its reparations payments. The result was the most notorious case of hyperinflation in history. Between August and November 1923 the amount of marks a dollar could buy was catapulted from 620,000 to 630 billion (630,000,000,000). It triggered an economic collapse which was reversed only after economist Hjalmar Schacht, who was brought in to head the central bank, cancelled the currency and forcibly put the country back on the gold standard.

France, on the other hand, waited. Unlike Britain, which slashed wages and yoked itself to the gold standard once more, France devalued the franc until it reached a point where rejoining might give it a competitive advantage. From an economist's perspective it was an intriguing case. In theory, at least, the country had given itself far more economic breathing space than any of its neighbours, while slashing its war debt repayments. The reality was messier. Throughout the early 1920s it repeatedly fell victim to onslaughts of speculation, as investors desperately attempted to pull money out of the country. Successive governments fell – five of them between 1919 and 1923 – and none managed to bring the public finances under control.

As was the case throughout Europe, a newly re-energised public was demanding not merely democracy but fresh systems of welfare

as recompense for what they had suffered over the previous decade.
That in turn increased the pressure on politicians to spend more –
in spite of their debts. The easiest solution for the politicians was to
turn back again on the familiar enemy.

In 1923, new French Prime Minister Raymond Poincaré sent
troops into the Ruhr, the industrial heartland of Germany. The
Americans intervened, dispatching banker Charles Dawes to negotiate a compromise. He cut the value of reparations to around 1 per
cent of Germany's economy. Even so, France's crisis persisted as
speculators continued to take money out of the country. In early
1925 the dollar bought nineteen francs; by July the following year
it could buy forty-one. The ordeal was held up by economists as a
blunt reminder of the damage that could occur under floating
exchange rates.

All of which might go some way to explaining why White
decided to write his Ph.D. thesis on the stricken country. But rather
than concentrate on its gorier recent economic history, he focused
on its more distant experience as a member of the gold standard in
the prelude to the war. In 1928 he returned to France for the first
time since he had served there. The country had barely recovered
from its recent economic distress and, perhaps unsurprisingly,
White's efforts to dig out the relevant accounts and statistics from
its pre-war finances were not entirely successful. His resulting
thesis, *The French International Accounts 1880–1913*, was therefore
a rather odd hybrid – one half a patchy balance sheet for pre-war
France, the other an analysis of how well the French economy had
fared during this period. But while much of the book reads like an
elegy for a bygone era in international relations, it occasionally hints
at a more progressive outlook. Keynes is cited a number of times,
as is Frank Taussig, White's supervisor at Harvard. Perhaps most
intriguing is White's statement that 'the orthodox attitude toward
unrestricted capital exports is open to criticism; the assumption that
the capital exports benefit both the country and the world at large

is not unassailable ... some measure of intelligent control of the volume and direction of foreign investments is desirable.'[16]

It was an early alarm bell about the damage that could be wrought by so-called 'hot money' – the flows of untrammelled cash poured into and pulled out of troubled countries by investors – something that would later be a central focus at Bretton Woods. The thesis was well received, going on to win the David A. Wells prize for the best piece of economic research in 1931–2, and was published by the university press. But it already felt out of date. By 1932 America's boom had turned to deep depression. The investment bubble, fuelled in part by the flow of gold into the country throughout the 1920s, had ended with the Wall Street Crash of 1929. Everyone had assumed that the share price slump would soon be reversed – that employment levels would rebound. They were wrong: year after year the country's economic condition deteriorated.

It was unlike anything anyone had witnessed before. American industrial production fell by 48 per cent between 1929 and 1932; unemployment reached 25 per cent of the US workforce. A sequence of banks collapsed, but the strictures of the gold standard made rescuing them difficult. The attitude of the day, anyway, was more in tune with President Hoover's Treasury Secretary Andrew Mellon, who urged him to 'liquidate labor, liquidate stocks, liquidate farmers, liquidate real estate ... it will purge the rottenness out of the system.'

White disagreed. Together with classmate Lauchlin Currie (with whom he would eventually work in Washington) and another student he wrote a memorandum suggesting what the President should be doing: writing off debts, funding public works projects and pumping cash into the economy – the kinds of remedies Keynes had been calling for in the press for years.

Even at the age of forty, White was still desperate to make a difference – to be noticed. But that wasn't going to happen at Harvard. It was patently obvious that however well he was regarded, he was unlikely to be promoted to faculty, so that year he left for a professorship at Lawrence College, in Appleton, Wisconsin. But life in the Midwest did nothing to dull his impatience; and though Franklin D. Roosevelt had come into office blazing a trail for economic reform, clamping down on the banks, forcibly removing the United States from the gold standard, White felt he had not gone far enough.

'The path, I suspect, may lie in the direction of centralized control over foreign exchanges and trade,' he wrote to Professor Taussig at Harvard. 'I have been spending the spring and summer reading and thinking about the problem but my opinion is as yet unsettled. I am also learning Russian in the hope that I may get a fellowship which would enable me to spend a year chiefly in Russia. There I should like to study intensively the technique of planning at the Institute of Economic Investigation of Gosplan.'[17] His curiosity was hardly out of place in those days, when many economics students wanted to understand how an alternative economic system worked in practice. Though in the years after the war, such an attitude would be presented in a very different light.

However, the following summer, White received the call-up he had been waiting for: a letter from Jacob Viner, a Chicago economics professor and adviser to Treasury Secretary Henry Morgenthau, inviting him to Washington to help with a temporary project. Almost immediately White telegraphed his reply: 'Will be very glad to come to work with you.' The summer project turned into a permanent job at the Treasury. He might have been late to the party once again, missing out on Roosevelt's first hundred days, but at least he was finally where he wanted to be. He was forty-two.

For someone who came to politics so late in life, White would display a tenacious grasp of the greasy pole in the years that followed. His rise within the Treasury at Pennsylvania Avenue was remarkably rapid. Within weeks of his arrival in Washington, he and his wife had befriended Morgenthau's secretary and gatekeeper Henrietta Klotz (she and Anne were instantly 'very, very good friends').[18] Like a true Washington insider, White was studiously civil to anyone in a position to help him advance – and brutally rude to those who could not. It was said he learned how to use flattery to his advantage when he worked on the shop floor of his father's store. 'You can't pile it on too thick,' he once told a colleague.[19]

To Morgenthau he was the ultimate right-hand man: someone to whom he could relate – they were both Jewish, both doting husbands, both sensitive to slights and insults, with particularly keen moral compasses – and, unlike most economists, he dispensed his wisdom without being patronising. For others, White was to be both feared and despised: a 'stinker ... a nasty, self-centred triple-barrelled son-of-a-bitch,' according to one colleague; 'One of the most stubborn individuals I have ever known,' in the words of another.[20]

Somehow, over his decade or so in the Treasury, White managed to keep those two instincts just about in check – though it was a precarious balancing act. By the time he left he had so many enemies that a grisly downfall became almost inevitable. And very occasionally the foul-mouthed side of his personality would intrude on his official duties. Years later a colleague told of one such moment in a meeting in Morgenthau's office, after White attempted to dispute some analysis presented by one of his Treasury rivals. 'Oh Harry,' said the Treasury Secretary, 'you always think that if it isn't done by your shop, it isn't any good.'

White blurted out: 'Shit.'

His colleague, Eddie Bernstein, recounted what followed: 'The Secretary, who was a very prim man, said, "Harry, if you can't talk decently, you'd better leave the room." So White went out of the room and I stayed behind. I then explained to the Secretary our point of view. After the meeting, I went out to see White to report what had happened. He was weeping.

'White had a short temper, and he was easily upset by the

Secretary of the Treasury because he depended for his influence on his close relationship with the Secretary.'[21]

Indeed, for the vast majority of his time at the Treasury, White was not even officially a civil servant; he was appointed on an ad hoc basis to various roles all the way through to 1945. Around him, he gathered a close-knit group of friends and advisers – Bernstein was one, alongside his Harvard classmate Lauchlin Currie, William Ludwig Ullmann, Frank Coe and Sol Adler. And he hugged Morgenthau as tightly as he could.

There was a fitting symmetry here: Morgenthau's own position and influence were a product of his personal connection with the President. The pair had grown up on neighbouring farms in Hyde Park, New York. Morgenthau and his wife Elly had become close to Franklin and Eleanor Roosevelt in the 1920s, when the future President was recovering from polio. Morgenthau knew substantially less about finance and economics than he did about farming, but that mattered far less to Roosevelt than his complete and unquestioning loyalty. For those at the more rarefied State Department, the fact that the future of the world economy was in the hands of someone whose main qualification was his aptitude for cultivating apple orchards was frankly horrifying – particularly given the state of the international monetary system.

By 1935 the gold standard was all but dead. Only a few random economies – Lithuania, the Netherlands and, most notably, France – were still officially converting their currencies into the precious metal. Tempting though it was to blame it all on the Wall Street Crash (and there is no doubt it didn't help), the real low point had been the summer of 1931, when Austria's oldest and largest bank, Credit-Anstalt, collapsed. The bank (actually a rolled-up conglomerate of several other failing institutions) was both too big to fail and too big to bail – its liabilities being greater than the Austrian government budget. Since, as a member of the gold standard, the country could not afford to effect a rescue on its own, it looked elsewhere for help, but even the newly created Bank for International Settlements (BIS) was unable to assist. The country was swiftly forced to abandon membership of the gold standard, whereupon currency speculators started to look for other weak links. The biggest and most obvious was Britain.

Britain had stuck with the gold standard for six miserable years after Churchill's decision to rejoin in 1925. But far from improving matters, this seemed to make them progressively worse. The mistake, it soon became clear, had been to rejoin at the pre-war parity: doing so meant the pound was overvalued, which in turn forced British producers to slash their prices and wages in a vain attempt to attract overseas buyers. It hadn't helped that the French had devalued the franc so far that they easily outcompeted their British rivals on price, which in turn drained British gold out of London and into Paris as importers spent cash on goods that were made in France. And so the vicious cycle intensified.

In September 1931, as the Bank of England sought to defend the pound and the Treasury attempted to balance its books, Whitehall launched the latest in a series of austerity drives. Pay for public sector workers, including those in the military, was slashed. It was the final straw. When officers on a number of ships in the British Atlantic Fleet docked in Invergordon began to issue orders, a group of sailors refused to follow them. Bemoaning the wage cuts, they carried out only essential duties. Some massed on deck; a piano was brought up and they began to sing and cheer. It hardly looked like treason, but then again strikes by the military were unheard of. The Invergordon Mutiny, as it came to be known, sent shudders through the economic establishment, and caused markets to plunge yet further.

Britain had reached the limits of how much extra pain could be imposed. In truth, cuts of a similar degree – both to the government's budget and the stock of money flowing around the economy – had been achieved before. But between 1914 and 1931, something had changed: the rise of the franchise and of labour movements meant that the austerity that was a routine part of membership of the gold standard was no longer politically palatable.

In the weeks that followed, Britain and most other European nations formally ended their membership of the gold standard, ditching the legal requirement for the central bank to swap banknotes for gold if requested. The news was received with horror in the United States. As far as financiers were concerned this was yet another default on war debt. In the ensuing two years there was much brow-beating on both sides of the Atlantic until, in 1933, the London World Economic Conference was held, with the intention of setting out a roadmap to a new gold standard.

But the conference's grand aims were punctured when the newly inaugurated US President, Franklin D. Roosevelt, dismissed the meeting as representing the 'old fetishes of so-called international bankers'. The United States, he added, 'seeks the kind of dollar which a generation hence will have the same purchasing and debt-paying power as the dollar value we hope to obtain in the near future'.[22]

His pledge could hardly have been more ironic: that very year Roosevelt would preside over a sequence of dollar devaluations, intended to compete with those the Europeans had carried out since 1931. He issued an executive order 'nationalizing' gold – meaning all gold in private hands had to be turned over to the Federal Reserve, with the owners paid the statutory price of $20.67 an ounce, rather than the $29.62 that was the metal's market valuation.

With America's abandonment, the gold standard was finally over – though in reality, what had been in place over the previous decade had been a farce from the very beginning. Even when all the European countries were back 'on gold' in the late 1920s, gold coins had never been in circulation anywhere except America. In an effort to safeguard the stocks in its vaults, the Bank of England had started to impose ever more spurious restraints on who could withdraw it and when. Indeed, so low had gold supplies fallen that most European central banks were forced to improvise, treating foreign currency and securities as a kind of quasi-gold on their balance sheets – hence the fact that this period is often referred to as the 'gold exchange standard'.

And who could blame them? In contrast with the late Victorian period, worldwide supplies of gold were barely increasing, while the amount of money needed to sustain the economy was growing exponentially. It was like trying to balance an inverted pyramid on the head of a shrinking pin.

Now that the gold standard was officially defunct, there was little to stop politicians from trying to squeeze their exchange rates up or (more frequently) down in order to make their exports artificially cheaper. And that is what followed, with countries around the world competitively devaluing their currencies in a race to the bottom. Eventually Britain and the United States would set up official bodies – the Exchange Equalisation Account and Exchange Stabilization Fund respectively – to intervene in foreign exchange markets and determine their currency value. In the meantime, Roosevelt used a primitive scheme to set the value of the dollar where he wanted it – which meant as low against the pound as possible.

This laid the ground for one of the more surreal episodes in the history of monetary policymaking. Each morning Roosevelt would merrily set the dollar's gold value from bed over his eggs and coffee, apparently plucking numbers out of thin air. On one occasion he suggested raising the price by twenty-one cents. 'It's a lucky number,' he said with a laugh, 'because it's three times seven.'[23]

The only thing more unsettling than the details of the policy, recommended to Roosevelt by economists who were 'notoriously inept',[24] was that it was – temporarily – successful.* As the dollar weakened, the cost of borrowing and investing across the United

*Dean Acheson, then acting Treasury Secretary, was vehemently against the policy. Roosevelt fired him, although he would later resurface at the State Department.

States fell and the economy started to bounce back from the depths of the Depression. By 1934 the dollar price of an ounce of gold had risen from its gold standard value of $20.67 to an arbitrary level of $35. It would remain there for the next four decades.

But domestic success could hardly obscure the fact that this was a preposterous mutation of the gold standard – or, as Keynes called it, 'the gold standard on the booze'.[25] And with no international agreement on the level of exchange rates, there was nothing to stop every country following suit, sparking a worldwide struggle as each nation attempted to cut the value of its currency beneath those of its neighbours.

The flip side of this monetary battle was a trade war. Without international agreement on the level of currencies, countries resorted to imposing crude limits on the amount and price of goods entering and leaving their shores. America imposed the Smoot–Hawley tariff of 1930; Britain constructed the sterling zone, freeing trade and capital flows within the Empire while erecting barriers to keep out everyone else. Imperial Preference, as it was called, would cause transatlantic economic relations to sour even further.

Harry Dexter White had been drafted into the Treasury to research precisely this problem: it was patent that the world's monetary system had imploded, but no one wanted to step forward to rebuild it. In 1935, White had his first big break. Cordell Hull of the State Department had attempted to intervene, sending out a memorandum to American embassies early that year suggesting that the US should aim to stabilise the dollar–sterling exchange rate. Morgenthau was furious at this flagrant attempt to butt in on his turf and White was dispatched to London as a 'special agent' of the Treasury.

Though he had joined the department less than a year previously, White already seemed quite at home in his new role as an emissary. His British hosts, desperate to squeeze what details they could from him about Roosevelt's economic policies, entertained him lavishly, inviting him out for lunches and dinners, taking him to the theatre. 'Almost all of them asked me to call again, some of them being quite pressing in their invitations,' he reported. Perhaps predictably, given the tensions between State Department and Treasury, relations with his contact at the US Embassy were frosty ('He was skeptical of my success'), but charming them would do him few favours anyway.

It was also his first chance to meet John Maynard Keynes in person. How well their meeting went is not clear from White's rather dry account. The fact that Keynes made no note of it is a clue as to how significant he considered it. By then, he was regarded as the most influential voice on the economy in the United States – arguably even more so than he was in England.

So long and so eloquently had he argued for the kinds of radical economic projects the Roosevelt administration had put in place – from closing the banks and ditching the gold standard to spending public funds on large-scale investment projects – that many thought him their author. But while there is little doubt that his writings influenced those around Roosevelt, including White, the truth is that Keynes himself had struggled to gain traction with the White House. As was to be the case again and again, his chief undoing was his demeanour.

An open letter he had written to Roosevelt was considered arrogant and patronising; in one section he lectured the President on the kind of tone to adopt in conversations with businessmen ('Treat them (even the big ones), not as wolves or tigers, but as domestic animals by nature').[26] His encounters with other American policymakers were little better. On a visit in 1934, seeing an American economist carefully cleaning his hands with a single towel from a folded pile in the bathroom, Keynes threw the whole pile on the floor, declaring proudly that this was a far better way to stimulate employment than his American friend's.[27]

He had met the President but their encounter was polite and brisk. And, as ever, Keynes was less fixated by Roosevelt's policies than his hands, which, much like Woodrow Wilson's, were 'Firm and fairly strong, but not clever or with finesse, shortish round nails like those at the end of a business-man's fingers'.[28] Roosevelt later remarked to a colleague that Keynes 'left a whole rigmarole of figures. He must be a mathematician rather than a political economist.'[29] There is no evidence that the meeting did anything to change the course of American economic policy. After all, Roosevelt was so inscrutable that even the oddballs who wanted a return to a silver standard believed he was quietly rooting for them.

Nor was there much evidence that American economic policy had changed in the wake of Keynes's visit – something for which he blamed the convoluted American political system. Whatever the solution for Britain and America's dysfunctional relationship with gold, he told White, it seemed that anything the administration decided upon 'might be overruled by Congress ... He thought the way out might be by British, French and American Treasury co-operation which did not involve any Congressional, or Parliamentary action,' White wrote.[30]

For White, if the British visit proved anything, it was that by now no one seriously expected to return to the gold standard. 'Most of the business men I talked with thought that there would be no advantage in having sterling fixed to gold. They feared a repetition of the events following 1925. They have come to believe that the lack of prosperity from 1925 to 1931 in England was caused chiefly by a return to the gold standard.' Nor, for that matter, did anyone really care. 'On the whole, it was surprising to find so little concern – almost a complete lack of interest – in exchange problems, gold standard, and the like, among the business men.'

The best that could be hoped for, said banker Bob Brand and economist Lionel Robbins, was some sort of agreement between the United States and Britain on currencies. They may have been right, but by the time it did eventually arrive, it was too late.

*

A nagging doubt occupied Keynes's mind as the 1930s drew on: he may have established a reputation as an economic prophet, but what if his ideas were never to be put into practice? In the preface to *Essays in Persuasion* in 1931, he had described his writings as 'the croakings of a Cassandra who could never influence the course of events in time'.[31] He became determined to produce a series of works which might actually achieve that. And with economic and political storm clouds gathering over the English Channel, he was running out of time.

Germany's story had the air of Shakespearean tragedy. Having rescued itself from hyperinflation, the country looked, for a period, to be set for recovery. Foreign investment flooded in (particularly from the United States) and unemployment started, gradually, to fall – though any surpluses generated went straight into reparations.

Then came the Wall Street Crash of 1929, and the flow of American investment suddenly dried up. The economy slid into recession once again. The collapse of Credit-Anstalt in neighbouring Austria two years later worsened the recession, as any remaining investors abandoned Germany's banking sector.* The recession deepened but Chancellor Heinrich Brüning, still paranoid about the possibility of reigniting inflation, refused to countenance lower interest rates, imposing deflation on the country as if it were still within the gold standard.

As unemployment remained stubbornly high, Brüning was turfed out of office in May 1932. The following month Britain and France finally forgave Germany all reparations. It was a hollow victory: the country was exhausted. After a decade and a half of economic misery, every mainstream political movement had been

---

*They did so despite the fact that Germany's banking sector was relatively isolated from Austria's – a common investment mistake. Investors were accused of a similar sin in the Asian crisis of the late 1990s, when they abandoned Far East assets en masse – including those that were perfectly healthy.

discredited. In the elections that summer, the Nazi Party won 230 seats, becoming the largest party in the Reichstag.

Meanwhile, in Britain, Oswald Mosley's British Union of Fascists was growing in popularity – while the Communist movement had installed itself in university campuses from Cambridge to London. As often happens during a prolonged depression, people turned in their desperation to extremist political movements.

Keynes's frustration was that mainstream economic theory – the kind taught by his Cambridge idol Alfred Marshall, author of the first great economics textbook – had no compelling explanation for the persistent species of slump that had afflicted Britain, the United States and elsewhere. And it was in response to this failing that in 1936 he published his *General Theory of Employment, Interest and Money*, the product of more than half a decade of thought, research and writing.

The book's ambition was manifest in its very title, an allusion to Einstein's General Theory of Relativity. He wanted nothing less than to recast and overhaul the entire classical economic model. 'I believe myself to be writing a book on economic theory,' he wrote to George Bernard Shaw, 'which will largely revolutionise – not, I suppose, at once but in the course of the next ten years – the way that the world thinks about economic problems.' However, he added, 'When my new theory has been duly assimilated and mixed with politics and feelings and passions, I can't predict what the final upshot will be in its effects on action and affairs.'[32]

At its heart, the book was inspired by – and to a large extent was about – the Great Depression. Classical economics had argued that employment would be determined by the cost of labour – and that the market was self-adjusting, with supply creating its own demand. In practice, Keynes said, that simply didn't hold true. In the real world, what mattered was how much money consumers, businesses and investors were willing to spend. During the Depression, people had done precisely the opposite of what, according to classical economics, they were expected to do, hoarding their money – in bank accounts, under mattresses, wherever. So the *General Theory* set out to devise a set of models and rules to accommodate such behaviour.

The kernel of the idea had in fact come from his brilliant Cambridge colleague Dennis Robertson – though in the course of their research, the pair fell out. Not until Bretton Woods would they work together in earnest again – and even then with not altogether happy consequences.

Though some were unconvinced, the *General Theory* was highly influential from its very publication. For those who advocated that governments should spend more in order to attain full employment, it contained the germs of policy, pointing out that when all others in an economy were reluctant to spend, the government could and should step in. Particularly striking was one passage in Book Three:

> If the Treasury were to fill old bottles with banknotes, bury them at suitable depths in disused coalmines which are then filled up to the surface with town rubbish, and leave it to private enter-prise on well-tried principles of *laissez-faire* to dig the notes up again ... there need be no more unemployment and, with the help of the repercussions, the real income of the community, and its capital wealth also, would probably become a good deal greater than it actually is. It would, indeed, be more sensible to build houses and the like; but if there are political and practical difficulties in the way of this, the above would be better than nothing.[33]

Provocative as they undoubtedly were, such sentiments were hardly alien to anyone who had read Keynes since the mid-1920s. Indeed, in a radio broadcast in the early 1930s he had provocatively asked: 'why not pull down the whole of South London from Westminster to Greenwich ... Would that employ men? Why, of course it would! Is it better that the men should stand idle and miserable, drawing the dole? Of course it is not.'*[34]

The difference was that the *General Theory* provided the statistical and economic machinery to justify such policies. With the help of another Cambridge colleague, Richard Kahn, Keynes came up with the notion of the 'multiplier' – the factor by which a certain amount of government (or private sector) spending could multiply into growth across the economy.

In academic circles, the book was a roaring success. In Cambridge, it quickly enshrined itself as the Bible of undergraduate economics, spreading to influence economic teaching in universities throughout the world. It was popular, too, in Germany, where Keynes's preface pointed out that its ideas 'can be much easier adapted to the conditions of a totalitarian state'.[35] In retrospect, that was an unfortunate phrase. Nonetheless, Hitler had for years been carrying out what is today often seen as a bastardised form of Keynesianism, embarking on massive public works projects in a bid to reduce unemployment.

The *General Theory* also found fertile ground in the White House, where Keynes had hitherto been regarded as something of a nuisance. Harry Hopkins of the Federal Surplus Relief Administration and Marriner Eccles of the Federal Reserve urged the President to ditch his balanced-budget policy, though Morgenthau remained unconvinced.

In France, home of Jean-Baptiste Say, the nineteenth-century economist whose famous law was that 'supply creates its own demand', the reception was more hostile. Keynes was, after all, debunking Say's law altogether. But then again the French had never seen eye-to-eye with Keynes. Over the past two decades, while he had led a crusade against the gold standard, France had

---

*The broadcast sparked a flurry of criticism in the newspapers, which Keynes characteristically enjoyed. 'Never such publicity in my life,' he wrote to Lydia.

remained faithful to gold, building up the second-biggest stash of the stuff after America. As the world tumbled into depression in the 1930s and everyone else abandoned the gold standard, France clung desperately on to the wreckage until the very end. Only in 1936 did it cut the link, finally emerging from recession shortly afterwards.

As 1937 dawned it did look, finally, as if every element of Keynes's life was lining up on his side. The economic revolution he had promised seemed to be taking root. His speculative fortunes, having recovered from their lows following the Wall Street Crash, had never been greater. He had found love and happiness. He had set up the Arts Theatre in Cambridge and, better still, had managed to persuade W.H. Auden to give Lydia a part in a play he was writing (though he was unimpressed by Auden's hands: 'his finger nails are eaten to the bones with dirt and wet, one of the worst cases ever, like a preparatory schoolboy').[36] With all the components of his life purring away perfectly, perhaps it was inevitable that something would fail him. In the event, it turned out to be his body.

Keynes had never been the healthiest individual. In 1931 he had suffered a nasty attack of pleurisy; he had experienced chronic tooth problems and occasional sudden spells of breathlessness, though each time he had been struck down he soon recovered his health. But almost as soon as the *General Theory* was published, he suffered a string of maladies: influenza, shortages of breath, weakness that consigned him to bed. Over Christmas he was afflicted again and by January 1937 he felt his 'breathing muscles were so wonky ... that I only just managed a walk'.[37] He presumed it was rheumatism. He didn't realise that his heart was giving way.

Winter turned to spring, and plaudits for the *General Theory* continued to stream in, but still his health worsened. Finally, in May, he suffered a series of spasms and collapsed with what was probably a heart attack. It left the usually energetic Keynes, who would habitually bound up and down flights of stairs, unable even

to crawl upstairs to his bedroom. He and Lydia consulted a succession of doctors, who offered a succession of diagnoses: some said
it was pseudo-angina, others a form of tonsillitis; the eventual ver-
·dict was subacute bacterial endocarditis – an infection of the valves.
of his heart.

All told, Keynes was to spend the best part of two years in his
sick bed – three months of it at Ruthin Castle, a sanatorium in
north Wales, the rest at Tilton. It was not the only blow to occur
during 1937. The American economy slumped back into recession
and Wall Street plunged. In the space of one year, Keynes's fortune,
most of which was in shares, shrank by two-thirds. The trauma did
not help his recovery. In November 1937, following yet another
downwards lurch in prices, Lydia, who had by then become
Keynes's full-time nurse, wrote in her medical notes, 'Slump fatal
for health.'[38] Another preoccupation that dented his health was the
rise of a re-energised and aggressive Germany under Hitler: Keynes
felt convinced that there would not be another war, but as 1937
became 1938, he started to question his faith.

It was not until Keynes encountered the eccentric Hungarian
physician Janos Plesch in early 1939 that he came anywhere close
to recovery. Plesch, who had moved to London from Berlin after
the Nazi takeover in 1933, was a remarkable character who seemed
to have treated everyone, including Albert Einstein and George
Bernard Shaw, along with half the aristocracy of England and
Germany. Rather like Keynes when it came to the economy,
Plesch's instinct was to throw every kind of remedy at a patient.
Very shortly he had Keynes on opium pills, injections and a salt-
free diet; he prescribed three-hour sessions of ice packs on his chest;
he even jumped up and down on him as he lay in bed. So gruesome
was the experience, and so gleeful was Plesch as he meted out such
treatment, that Lydia nicknamed him 'The Ogre'. In among these
remedies, he put Keynes on a course of Prontosil – a strange red dye
extract which was barely out of the laboratories in Germany, but

which had shown promising anti-bacterial results in mice. At first it made Keynes so ill he could hardly stand up but, astonishingly, barely a week later he felt almost completely cured for the first time since his initial attack. It seemed like a miracle; in fact, Prontosil was an early precursor to antibiotics in these days before penicillin.

Plesch was 'something between a genius and a quack',[39] said Keynes, adding that 'it was he, and he alone, that brought me back into active life'.[40] However, while he was able to return to work – to teaching at Cambridge, to writing and debating – his heart disease would continue to plague him for the rest of his life. Lydia would devote herself entirely to looking after him, charting his progress and discreetly monitoring his health throughout. 'I used to be the prima ballerina,' she would joke, 'but now I'm just the second fiddle.'[41]

On 21 March 1939 the chief cashier at the Bank of England received an unexpected request from the Bank for International Settlements in Basel, Switzerland. The message asked the bank to transfer about £5.6 million in gold from its No. 2 account to its No. 17 account.

This was, on the face of it, a routine request. Though the BIS had ostensibly been set up nine years earlier as an institution to manage Germany's reparations payments, central bankers in general, and the Bank of England's governor Montagu Norman in particular, had soon started to treat it as a club for their international business. Not only was it a forum for them to meet secretly, it also took on the role of custodian, looking after its members' gold reserves in a network of vaults around the world. The advantage was that gold could be transferred discreetly from one country to another with the flick of a pen; plus your reserves were entrusted to an institution which could be relied on to look after them safely. Or so went the theory.

Shortly after the bank received the order, the chief cashier had a dreadful thought. He was 'fairly sure that the No. 2 Account was a Czech National Bank Account and [the Bank] believed, although they were not sure at the time, that No. 17 was a Reichsbank'. Was this what they suspected it to be?

Four days earlier Hitler had stood up in Prague Castle. Czechoslovakia was now occupied by the Nazis. It didn't take a forensic accountant to join up the dots: he was immediately stripping the country of its gold. The invasion of Czechoslovakia was not only about *Lebensraum* – the Nazi ideology of territorial expansion – it was aimed at shoring up Germany's creaking finances. In January of 1939 the Führer had received a memorandum from the board of the Reichsbank, led by Hjalmar Schacht, the man who conquered hyperinflation. His manic spending on the military threatened to cause the 'national financial structure' to collapse. 'It is our duty to warn against this assault on the currency.'[42] Hitler fired Schacht soon afterwards.

Now he was attempting to modify Germany's balance of payments in his favour, at the barrel of a gun. He had sent armed officers into the Czech National Bank and ordered them to make the request. It was processed by the hapless BIS president, Wim Beyen, and sent through to London. It was within Beyen's and the Bank of England's rights to refuse, or at least delay, the transfer, but that would have meant allowing politics to intrude into the cosy world of central banking. Barely raising his eyebrows, Norman decided unilaterally to put it straight into action. The BIS was an institution he had helped create; 'it would be wrong and dangerous for the future of the BIS ... to attempt for political reasons to influence decisions of the President of the BIS.'[43]

The gold was transferred that same day, and a further small amount the following day. The Nazis subsequently disposed of the entire stash – nearly two thousand gold bars in total – in Belgium, Holland and London. The governor avoided answering the Treasury's demands to know what had happened to the gold, and then authorised a further transfer in June.

Unsurprisingly, when it emerged what had happened, there was a major scandal. How could the government reasonably expect people to enlist when it was 'so butter-fingered that six million pounds of gold can be transferred to the Nazi government', asked Churchill. Labour MP George Strauss called it 'the rape of Czechoslovakia'.[44]

For those who thought the Bank for International Settlements might be the institution to help reconstruct the international economy, it was also a wake-up call. Three years before, in 1936, the United States, Britain and France had finally put the worst of their currency battles behind them, signing the Tripartite Pact and fixing their exchange rates. There had been hopes that a permanent new international monetary system might soon follow, perhaps administered by the BIS itself.

But now the BIS and Bank of England had been accessories to theft – theft, moreover, whose proceeds would subsequently finance weapons to be used against the citizens of London and Paris. So infuriated were Morgenthau and White that they vowed to sideline the shadowy international institution once and for all.

In the meantime, the world was creeping closer, once again, to war. Two decades of economic turmoil, and a botched peace settlement after the Great War, had fuelled the rise of extremism throughout Europe. It was already clear even to those who had supported the Munich agreement the previous September, in which Neville Chamberlain gave Hitler the right to occupy the Sudetenland, that appeasement had been a tremendous mistake – something that would haunt the world for years.

'Do you remember the chap who in 1931 shrugged his shoulders when Japan invaded Manchuria,' White would write some years later. '[The chap who] repeated the shrugging in 1938 when Italy and Germany sent their troops to Spain and again when Germany marched into Czechoslovakia? He's the chap, you remember, who, when Germany attacked Poland, muttered "Aw, let 'em stew in their own juice. What business is it of ours if they want to kill each other off.'"[45] Such an attitude, he wrote, simply wouldn't do any more. America and its allies would have to learn from the sequence of disasters over the preceding decades. Totalitarianism could not be allowed to rise and – just as importantly – they should never allow the world's economy to give it space to breathe again.

PART II

MAKING PLANS

CHAPTER FIVE

Lunatic Proposals

1940–1941

Britain's broke; it's your money we want.

Lord Lothian to American journalists

After what I have gone through for two and a half years for them to send a person over here to put me in a position as though I wasn't trying to do everything I can, I say it is a damn outrage.

Henry Morgenthau

It is occasionally forgotten that the first nation to put forward a formal plan to remould the international monetary system after the Second World War was not America or Britain, but Germany. In July 1940, Hitler's economics minister, Walther Funk, stood up in front of an audience of journalists and unveiled the German plan for a financial 'New Order' stretching across a putative Nazi world.

Funk, a squat, bald fellow with a penchant for cognac and young men, had been plucked from his perch as a financial reporter a few years earlier after impressing Joseph Goebbels with his ideas for turning Germany into Europe's industrial powerhouse. His economic vision for the Third Reich, on the other hand, was mostly inherited from his predecessor Hjalmar Schacht.

Tempting as it was to dismiss this as the ravings of a deranged alcoholic, his scheme was surprisingly sophisticated: currencies would be fixed to one another and payments channelled through a central clearing office in Berlin. Gold would be rendered more or less irrelevant, and trade with countries outside the system (the United States for instance) would have to balance, with exports matching imports. The plan was a worrying development from the Allied perspective. Until then, it had been relatively easy to dismiss the Nazis' economic policies as medieval nonsense, grounded on protectionism and bilateralism. This was of a different order of refinement.*

The propaganda threat was not lost on Harold Nicolson, official censor at the Ministry of Information. Nicolson, a politician who would in later days become more famous for his unconventional open marriage with Vita Sackville-West, realised that unless Britain was able to respond, Germany, already looking invincible in mainland Europe, could also lay claim to possessing the most comprehensive post-war economic plan. So in November he sent Keynes an account of Funk's plan and asked him to discredit it. Rather predictably, the attempt to force Keynes to sing from a pre-agreed song sheet backfired.

'In my opinion about three quarters of the passages quoted from the German broadcasts would be quite excellent if the name of Great Britain were substituted for Germany or the Axis as the case may be,' he wrote back. 'If Funk's plan is taken at face value, it is excellent and just what we ourselves should be thinking of doing.'[1]

Indeed, with its emasculation of gold, its controls on capital and its aspiration to balance surpluses and deficits on current accounts in the future, the Funk plan was in many senses the inspiration for

---

*Indeed, squint a little and you can see an early blueprint for the future economic shape of today's European Union.

the proposals Keynes himself and – to a lesser extent – White would later put forward. Certainly, it was only at this moment, and thanks to the Nazi plan for their New Order, that Keynes and his Whitehall colleagues started to put some structured thought into how to rebuild the international monetary system.

As far as they were concerned, there was no longer any pretence that the world should try, as it had in 1919, to reassemble the pre-war system of rules and regulations (or, to be more accurate, simply to hope it would reassemble itself without any co-ordinated help). No one wanted to return to the world of 1939 – nor were there any recent examples of a system that might work. 'Nothing in the record of the past would make us want to repeat it,' wrote Emanuel Goldenweiser of the US Federal Reserve. 'During the last war we pegged exchanges. Immediately after the conclusion of the war we had a breakdown in exchanges, and then we had a scramble which was primarily a matter of everyone trying to protect his immediate future and "letting the devil take the hindmost".'[2] It was plain, then, that if the world was to avoid a repeat of the 1930s, with all that implied, it would have to impose an entirely new set of international economic rules. No one had ever managed to do that before.

But then, if there was an economic pastime of choice in the late 1930s and early 1940s, it was trying to come up with a plan for a new world order – for the legal and political spheres as much as the economic. While the Nazis were first to the table with a detailed official blueprint, similar work had been going on in finance ministries around the world – and much of it would surface in the run-up to Bretton Woods.

Keynes had been considering the issue on and off since the slow-motion disintegration of the gold standard in the interwar period – particularly when Winston Churchill attempted to rejoin in the 1920s. Similar conversations were being held elsewhere in London among the displaced finance ministries of many of the occupied

European nations – not to mention on the other side of the
Atlantic. In fact, perhaps the most comprehensive single paper on
the problems with the international monetary system (and a set of
potential solutions akin to Bretton Woods) was written during this
period by Estonian League of Nations economist Ragnar Nurkse.
So widespread was the pursuit of a new economic Nirvana that, the
following year, one of Keynes's colleagues would send him a memorandum on an international clearing arrangement drawn up by a
German working as a labourer on his farm – a young Rhodes
scholar called E.F. Schumacher.*

The Funk plan was nonetheless the first catalyst for the process
of negotiation, debate and argument between the Allies that would
lead in due course to Bretton Woods four years later. A few weeks
after Nicolson handed him his propaganda assignment, Keynes circulated within the Treasury his own proposals for an international
monetary system. The plan was, he admitted, a crude adaptation of
the Nazi scheme – though (ironically, given his attitude towards the
precious metal) with a slightly more prominent role for gold.
Countries' currencies would be fixed, their international payments
funnelled through a central office, and those flows of capital
policed.

'I have ... taken the line that what we offer is the same as what
Dr Funk offers, except that we shall do it better and more honestly,'
he wrote. 'This is important. For a proposal to return to the
blessings of 1920–33 will not have much propaganda value.'[3] His
major innovation was to suggest the creation of a European
Reconstruction Fund to rebuild the continent's war-ravaged
economies. The point, he added, was 'to prevent the starvation of
the post-armistice period, the currency disorders throughout
Europe and the wild fluctuations of employment, markets and

---

*Schumacher, later a prominent economist in his own right, would the following
year be drafted in to help William Beveridge with his seminal report on the welfare state.

prices which were the cause of so much misery in the twenty years between the two wars; and we shall see to it that this shall be compatible with the proper liberty of each country over its own economic fortunes.'[4]

What Keynes failed to realise was that, over in Washington DC, Harry Dexter White, the young Jewish economist who had been in London in 1935 asking all sorts of questions about the gold standard, was contemplating an uncannily similar plan. However, the two of them would soon be forced to put their ideas aside: after all, Britain would soon be on what looked like the brink of defeat to Hitler's Third Reich.

So great was the threat of a British defeat in 1940 that, sitting in his office in the US Treasury that summer, White prepared a dossier mapping out the economic implications of such an outcome for America. 'Should Germany succeed in defeating France and England,' he wrote, 'the United States will be confronted with a new situation fraught with grave problems. The problems are so vital that we must be prepared for all eventualities.'*

As he wrote, in early June, France was on the brink of capitulation. In a masterstroke of military planning, Hitler's armies had scythed through the Ardennes Forest, bypassing the supposedly impenetrable Maginot Line, and were en route to Paris. By the end of the month, France would join Holland and Belgium under German occupation. Allied troops were evacuated from Dunkirk, jettisoning many of their weapons and supplies on the beach.

Britain was left in the most vulnerable position so far in the war, fighting a continental battle against Germany almost entirely on its own, with depleted resources. It wasn't only White who feared

---

*Harry Dexter White papers, Box 9, Folder 3. White goes on to map out the consequences, including greater military expenditure, a borrowing programme 'which transcends anything that we have hitherto had to contend with' and the threat of inflation, falls in exports and, of course, the 'ever-present danger of military aggression'.

the imminent possibility of invasion – Joseph Kennedy, the American ambassador in London and father of the future President, had advised President Franklin D. Roosevelt that Britain was doomed.

When Winston Churchill became Prime Minister that year he immediately changed the country's footing to one of total war. Out of the window went the carefully honed financial plans for an affordable conflict (plans honed in part by Keynes himself); instead Britain was to fight the war on a basis of unlimited liability. Rather than eking out its resources and economic reserves for another couple of years, Britain would throw every penny it had at the conflict. The new rate of spending meant it was now due to run out of money by the first half of 1941. As in the Great War, there was only one obvious source of financial support thereafter: the United States.

But while the vast majority of Americans supported the British cause against Hitler, there was little appetite for direct involvement. In September 1940 more than 80 per cent of Americans favoured staying out of the war; only a third wanted their country to provide assistance to help Britain fight Germany.[5] For Roosevelt, desperately sensitive to public opinion, this meant having to move slowly – particularly since he was fighting for an unprecedented third term as President that November. Churchill was dismayed. Even as London was pounded by tons of German bombs in the Blitz that autumn, Roosevelt seemed to rule out stepping in to help. 'I give you one more assurance,' the President told an audience in Boston on 30 October. 'I have said this before, but I shall say it again and again and again: Your boys are not going to be sent into any foreign war.'[6]

Committing troops was one thing; financial assistance was another – but even in that regard there were problems. For one thing, the vast majority of Americans assumed Britain would soon be defeated: would it not be foolhardy to lend them money which

might never be paid back? And even if they did survive, the likelihood of being repaid wasn't necessarily high – after all, the British
had form. Though the City of London might have disputed it on
technical grounds, the truth was that Britain had never paid off
all the money America lent it during the Great War – and
Americans had not forgotten it, a fact that was scarred into the
statute book. The Johnson Act of 1934 prevented the United
States from lending to countries in default on their Great War
debts (of which Britain was one). And then there were the
Neutrality Acts (five of which Roosevelt himself had signed
between 1935 and 1937), which made it illegal to provide arms to
warring nations anyway.

In short, there was a double lock on any help – financial or
otherwise – the United States could provide for Britain in those
early months of the war. Roosevelt would spend the following year
trying to wrestle free of it. First went the Neutrality Acts, which the
President managed to repeal following months of backroom negotiation. The powerful isolationist lobby managed to reinstate a
so-called 'cash and carry' clause which stipulated that if the United
States were to sell arms, it could do so only for cash and only if the
purchaser's own vessels could be used to carry those purchases away.
The 'carry' provision just so happened to play into the hands of
Britain, with its sizeable navy (though it also benefited Japan at the
expense of China). The 'cash' element was more of a problem: the
UK's stocks of dollars were fast diminishing.

The transatlantic tensions that would crop up repeatedly during
the Bretton Woods negotiations now started to show. The British
convinced themselves that the Americans would not be willing to
help. 'It is always best and safest,' said Churchill's predecessor as
Prime Minister, Neville Chamberlain, 'to count on nothing from
the Americans but words.'[7] Churchill was privately certain that
Roosevelt would eventually step in, but the months that followed
would test his conviction.

The Americans, on the other hand, were sure that the British were overstating their parlous financial position. By now their country was the undisputed world economic superpower, but Britain stubbornly clung on to much of its Empire; London was still a major financial centre. So when Lord Lothian, the British ambassador, hit the tarmac in New York in November 1940 and declared to the press, 'Well boys, Britain's broke; it's your money we want,' it seemed to confirm widespread suspicions.

Was Britain really in such dire straits? What had happened to the fruits of its centuries of imperial dominance? Henry Morgenthau pointed out that there were still sizeable British investments in Argentinian railways; there were enormous British holdings in businesses in America; there was Shell Oil, Lever Brothers, Dunlop Tire & Rubber, Brown & Williamson Tobacco and, most prominently of all, American Viscose. Before there was any question of providing financial aid, Morgenthau told the Britons they would have to divest themselves of some of these assets. So, after an arduous series of negotiations, Viscose, the man-made fabric company, was forcibly sold off by its owner Samuel Courtauld for around $50 million: less than half its estimated value.[8]

Between the spring of 1940 and March 1941 Britain disposed of $335 million in securities, and moved $235 million in dollar balances and $2 billion of gold to the United States in exchange for arms, food and supplies.[9] Morgenthau and Roosevelt even joked about the possibility of acquiring the Crown Jewels from the Tower of London or Magna Carta in lieu of payment for aid.[10] Though this was more dark humour than reality, it underlined the economic truism that when a country is deeply indebted and reliant on another for aid, every one of its most prized assets is often soon in play.

It was in these early months of the war that much of Britain's remaining assets were sold, both to pay for the war and, as far as Morgenthau was concerned, to convince American voters that the country was at the absolute limits of financial desperation. Without establishing this there would be no chance of persuading Congress to support further financial help if that proved necessary.

By the end of 1940 it was clear it would be necessary. A loan had been out of the question until after the Presidential elections passed, but early the following month, as Roosevelt took a vacation in the Caribbean to rest and celebrate his re-election, Churchill sent the letter which changed the course of the war.

'The moment approaches,' he wrote, 'when we shall no longer be able to pay cash' for arms and supplies from the Americans. The Treasury now had no choice but to agree. White himself, by then in charge of its international economic wing, had calculated that Britain had an enormous shortfall in comparison with the $5 billion worth of orders it had already placed.

It was then that Roosevelt had his brainwave. He read and re-read Churchill's letter over the following days until it struck him. 'We must find some way to lease or even lend these goods to the British,' he wrote. The idea had, in reality, been germinating for some time: to try to provide financial assistance to the UK without the financial dressing.

Shortly after he returned to Washington, he unveiled the lifeline in a press conference. The details were vague – intentionally so, given that Lend-Lease might fall foul of previous legislation against financial aid. Said the President:

Suppose my neighbor's home catches fire, and I have a length of garden hose four or five hundred feet away. If he can take my garden hose and connect it up with his hydrant, I may help him to put out his fire. Now, what do I do? I don't say to him before that operation, 'Neighbor, my garden hose cost me $15; you have to pay me $15 for it.' What is the transaction that goes on? I don't want $15 – I want my garden hose back after the fire is over. All right. If it goes through the fire all right, intact, without any damage to it, he gives it back to me and thanks me very much for the use of it. But suppose it gets smashed up – holes in it – during the fire; we don't have to have too much formality about it, but I say to him, 'I was glad to lend you that hose; I see I can't use it any more, it's all smashed up.' He says, 'How many feet of it were there?' I tell him, 'There were 150 feet of it.' He says, 'All right, I will replace it.' Now, if I get a nice garden hose back, I am in pretty good shape.

In other words, if you lend certain munitions and get the munitions back at the end of the war, if they are intact you haven't been hurt – you are all right; if they have been damaged or have deteriorated or have been lost completely, it seems to me you come out pretty well if you have them replaced by the fellow to whom you have lent them.

Of course, in reality Lend-Lease was almost precisely what it claimed not to be: financial support. More than half of British deficits during the war would be covered by the agreement (before one even added on its later contribution to Soviet Russia). Roosevelt's masterstroke was in the branding – casting it as an informal deal between neighbours and, as he put it, '[getting] rid of the silly, foolish old dollar sign'. Roosevelt was walking a tightrope, attempting gently to coax a sceptical and fearful American public towards engaging the Nazi threat without alienating them entirely.

Nonetheless, it is clear in retrospect that this was the moment America committed itself to the Second World War. Roosevelt had been edging closer and closer to a formal alliance since the late 1930s, when he first coined the term 'United Nations' to describe those countries fighting against totalitarianism. As historian Ian Kershaw put it, 'Roosevelt's advisers had correctly judged that, following lend-lease, it would ultimately become impossible to stay out of the conflict.' Churchill deemed it a 'point of no return' for the Americans; and though he would spend the following year impatiently waiting for a formal declaration of war, this economic gesture amounted to pretty much the same thing.[11] That, certainly, was how Goebbels and the Wehrmacht perceived it.

However, in characteristic style, having made this bold leap, Roosevelt immediately took a step backwards. Much of the following year he would spend hesitating over the bill's implementation, as it shuffled through Congress and into law. With Britain still in desperate need of war supplies, the dollar sign, far from being eliminated, was looming ever larger. In 1941, a mere 1 per cent of arms used by Britain and its Empire would end up being covered by Lend-Lease.[12] Two days after Roosevelt's press conference, the Treasury cabled its representative in Washington, Sir Frederick Phillips, to ask how long it would take for this new-found American beneficence to kick in; after all, British stocks of gold and dollars were almost entirely spent. 'At the present rate of loss they will only last till about Tuesday next.'[13] That wasn't Britain's only concern. The State Department was already contemplating the long-term implications of Lend-Lease. It was clearly going to be expensive; and they wanted to extract value for their money.

Even at this stage it was by no means assured that Keynes would be the principal British negotiator with the Americans. Though his health was still fragile, he had spent an increasing amount of time since the beginning of the war working in the Treasury for his old friend Sir Richard 'Hoppy' Hopkins, a man who Lionel Robbins described as 'Diminutive in stature, with a general appearance rather like that of an extremely intelligent monkey'.[14] But he had been focused on domestic affairs as much as international; for instance, the department was commissioning preliminary work on the creation of a welfare state. Were it not for a high-explosive German bomb, Keynes might well have become as closely involved with that project as his old friend William Beveridge.

But on the night of 16 April 1941, during one of the heaviest raids of the Blitz, a bomb fell directly on the air raid shelter of a large house in Shortlands, in the suburbs of London. When the wardens sifted through the wreckage they found three bodies – one of them instantly recognisable. Lord Stamp had been trying to protect his wife from the impact when the bomb hit, but they were killed instantly, along with their eldest son.*

Josiah Stamp had been one of Keynes's oldest friends. They had spent many hours debating economic policy during the Depression. Some of their lightly bickering fireside chats were even broadcast by the BBC. Like Keynes, Stamp was by this stage regarded as one of the grand old men of British economics – the difference being that he was indisputably a member of the establishment, having attained the Holy Trinity of British economics: a peerage, a seat on the Court of the Bank of England and a prominent toehold at the Treasury. He had been Chamberlain's chief economic adviser, and although Churchill was now Prime Minister, Stamp was the natural choice for a financial envoy to the Americans – after all, he had worked with them in 1924, negotiating the Dawes Plan which aimed at reviving the German economy and putting right some of the mistakes made at Versailles.†

Keynes, on the other hand, was still considered a maverick. As far as old Treasury hands were concerned he was best consulted on those occasional issues where an alternative (and frequently madcap) idea was desirable. He had helped out from time to time with Nicolson and his propaganda response to Funk's New Order; had produced a few papers about war finance; and had sat on a consultative sub-committee on the special problems arising from war

---

*Rescuers who found Lord Stamp's body in the ruins of his bombed house yesterday saw that he had tried to shield his wife. He was crouching as though to give protection above the camp bed on which his wife lay in their smashed shelter ... There was more than one direct hit on the house.' *The Argus*, Melbourne, Victoria, 17 April 1941.

†Beveridge would later write in Stamp's *Oxford Dictionary of National Biography* entry: 'by this direct hit the Germans did more harm to their chief enemy than they could then have realized. In the difficult economic aftermath of war Stamp would have been an ideal negotiator between Britain and the United States, which he knew so well.'

conditions ('a new super-dud committee at the Treasury', as he called it). He spent some time fighting for the creation of figures on gross domestic product (like most other countries at this period, Britain had a lamentable supply of reliable economic statistics), and set up an informal discussion group with three other middle-aged economists – Beveridge and two fellow Great War veterans, Walter Layton and Arthur Salter (he and Lydia called them 'the Old Dogs').

But following Stamp's death Keynes took his position at the very height of the British economic firmament. He was appointed to Stamp's seat on the Court of the Bank of England, assuming his place on what Hoppy called 'Mount Olympus'.

'Rather appalling, I feel, such respectability!' Keynes wrote to his mother. 'Coming after a fellowship at Eton I feel it is only a matter of time before I become a Bishop or Dean of York.' (As it happened, a couple of years later he would be awarded a hereditary peerage, making him Baron Keynes of Tilton.) Brendan Bracken of the Ministry of Information wrote: 'It will be the sort of surprise that came to Moses when he struck the rock and found water ... I hope that your new Directorate will not interfere with the work you are doing for the Treasury. You are their best stormtrooper.'[15]

And when, two days after Stamp's death, the Chancellor of the Exchequer, Sir Kingsley Wood, decided he needed to send someone to Washington to discuss Lend-Lease, Keynes's was the first name that came to mind. Maynard may well have proven himself during the Great War to be a rather terrible diplomat when it came to the Americans, but then routine diplomacy didn't seem to be working.

The early enthusiasm for Lend-Lease had given way to a sense of dread. Britain was still haemorrhaging cash in order to pay for arms, food and supplies, while the US prevaricated. Even though the bill was pushed through Congress relatively quickly, passing into law in March, the expected bounty of weapons was nowhere to be seen. Part of the problem was Roosevelt's own hesitancy; part was that the State Department had yet to finalise the official treaty agreement to be signed with the British.

The process hadn't been helped by the fact that London was losing faith in Phillips, their economic representative on the ground in DC. Sir Frederick, a blunt, inarticulate but intellectually brilliant civil servant who liked to shut himself into an overheated room and play music at full blast when he needed to concentrate, was entrenched in Washington. Morgenthau – to the astonishment of most of his colleagues, who found Phillips difficult, unfriendly and supercilious – had taken a shine to the balding Briton. 'I like that man,' a colleague once heard the Treasury Secretary say. 'I suspect he's a little slow of speech as I am myself.' This most unlikely couple would sit in apparently comfortable silence with each other for hours on end – something almost everyone found enormously disconcerting. Keynes quipped about Phillips: 'he could be silent in several languages'.[16]

So Keynes flew out to Washington for what would be the first of six missions to the country. Though it was pitched as a low-key visit, the promise of a spot of publicity was too much for Keynes to resist. On his departure he informed the press that he was off on a fact-finding mission about Lend-Lease. After a week-long journey (involving three flights via Lisbon and the Azores) he and Lydia arrived in New York to a storm of flash-bulbs. Shortly afterwards they travelled down to Washington, where they set up base in the grand Mayflower Hotel.

This ostentatious arrival was only the first in a series of episodes which alienated the Americans. Apparently forgetting the lessons of his 1917 visit, Keynes imagined that he could conduct business in Washington in much the same way as he did in London. It was a fatal misconception: in Britain, parliamentary government meant decisions were taken privately by ministers and civil servants; when consensus wasn't reached, the differences could be ironed out over the Cabinet table, or in the library at the Athenaeum. If you knew the right people, you could influence policy as you saw fit.

In the US, on the other hand, the separation of powers between different wings of government – the executive (the White House), legislative (Congress) and judiciary (the Supreme Court) – meant there was no single locus of power. White House support for a policy offered no guarantee that it would pass into law through Congress – even though the Democrats had a majority in both houses. Even the executive itself contained complexities that seemed to pass over Keynes's head. The Treasury Department, for instance, was locked in a war of attrition with the State Department over who should determine international economic policy.

For Keynes, who was accustomed to waltzing into Downing Street and influencing government policy with only a few well-executed conversations, the encounter with this nest of vipers was deeply frustrating. 'To the outsider it looks almost incredibly inefficient,' he wrote. 'One wonders how decisions are ever reached at all. There is no clear hierarchy of authority. The different departments of the Government criticise one another in public and produce rival programmes. There is perpetual internecine warfare between prominent personalities.'[17]

Nor did Keynes's attitude do him any favours. What passed for wit in Britain more often than not came across as insulting and snide in the United States. From Keynes's perspective, on the other hand, many of his American counterparts seemed disturbingly uptight.

Within a few weeks of his arrival in the country, Keynes managed to irritate almost everyone. The British Embassy was put out when he insisted on going in to see the Treasury Secretary alone, without Phillips; the State Department was horrified about his attitude towards Lend-Lease; and Morgenthau was simply infuriated

by everything he did. About the only person who wasn't exasper-
ated by Keynes was Albert Einstein, who received the economist at
home in bed.*

Morgenthau, a taciturn man who was easily offended, figured he
had already gone way beyond what was strictly acceptable in his
support for Britain: indeed, he had agreed $35 million without
Congressional approval, putting him in an invidious position. Now
along came this man, uninvited, apparently expressing not gratitude
but outrage that more hadn't been funnelled Britain's way. The fact
that he came bearing recommendation letters from Ben Cohen of
the State Department and the American ambassador in London,
John Winant, neither of whom Morgenthau trusted, didn't help
matters – nor did his readiness to go above his head to the
President on occasion.

But it was the ingratitude that struck deepest. 'After what I have
gone through for two and a half years for them to send a person
over here to put me in a position as though I wasn't trying to do
everything I can, I say it is a damn outrage,' Morgenthau fumed on
19 June. He had called in his senior advisers, including White and
Jacob Viner, to discuss Keynes's latest solecism, a letter written
home, and copied to Morgenthau, complaining about the lack of
progress in the Lend-Lease negotiations. The letter so irritated
Morgenthau that he summoned Phillips and read it aloud to him
in derisive tones ('Maynard does *not* know this,' Phillips later added
in the cable home).[18]

What made matters worse was that Keynes spent part of his visit

---

*The pair, who had last met in the 1930s before Einstein left for America, had
someone in common: Janos Plesch, The Ogre, who had also treated Einstein.
When Keynes arrived in Princeton, he found that 'The old sage was in bed with
his vast olive corrugated countenance crowned with a white shock of Struwelpeter
hair, and with a big toe protruding from under the counterpane. He was full of
gusto and enthusiasm and urged above everything with all the emphasis he could
command that if, when we are ready, we bomb Germany continuously and without remorse they most certainly will not stand it.' JMK XXIII, p. 113.

attempting to persuade Roosevelt to change his economic policies and invest more, and had let slip his criticisms at a recent soirée in Washington. 'I am sick and tired of publicly holding up the British hands and then they send somebody over here and he goes to a meeting and criticizes the President of the United States for the way he is running this country,' Morgenthau carried on. 'I say that man should go home.'

The outburst was unusual for someone of Morgenthau's generally benign temperament. Ironically enough, given his subsequently prickly relationship with Keynes, it was White who rode to the Briton's defence. 'I … am sorry to see you take that attitude,' he said. 'I think he has tried very, very diligently and very carefully to accomplish his ends. I think he has tried to be careful of everybody's feelings.'[19]

Keynes, for his part, reported that he found Morgenthau tricky – 'almost intolerably tiresome to deal with'. The pair simply couldn't communicate, he added – 'misunderstandings peep out of every corner'.[20] But, as would be the case throughout his dealings with the Americans, he was apparently oblivious of the full extent of the irritation he engendered, perhaps because there were bigger things to worry about.

Britain was in trouble. It needed Lend-Lease to cover existing contracts for essential imports from the US – not to mention being extended to India and its Dominions – not as a luxury but because its cache of dollars and gold reserves was perilously close to exhaustion. However, the Americans remained unconvinced of Britain's situation, suspecting instead that Keynes intended to sabotage the Viscose sale, which was only now being processed. 'I think that they are pushing,' said White, adding, 'I don't think that they are quite in the straits that he makes out that they are.'[21]

The solution to this mutual distrust was simple, if unpleasant for both parties. Morgenthau asked Keynes and his colleagues to come to his office each day to explain what Britain's dollar position was:

how much money it had and what it needed in the way of materials. Then the Americans would decide how much aid they could hand out. '[I want to know] down to the last sou what the British Treasury position is,' said Morgenthau.[22]

If there had been any doubt hitherto about Britain's financial subordination to the United States, these secret daily meetings laid the matter to rest. Over the following weeks they would consider, in exhaustive and occasionally humiliating detail, the kinds of products Britain was about to run short of – everything from weapons and steel to cocoa and wool – and determine which contracts the American army would take over. In many senses, the meetings were an early precursor of the sessions bankrupt countries would later have to submit to under International Monetary Fund programmes. At last, however, progress was being made.

But there was a bigger issue still looming over the negotiations. The Americans wanted something substantive in return for Lend-Lease; Keynes would learn, to his horror, what it was only in the final days of his visit.

So obsessed was the State Department with free trade in those days that its officials openly referred to it in religious terms. You would 'go to mass' and 'tell your beads' each day, praying for cuts in tariffs, removal of trade restrictions and non-discrimination more broadly, as one staffer put it.[23] This was ironic, given how protectionist the United States had been for the vast majority of its existence – but by this stage it was the world's biggest producer. It was seeking destinations for all its goods, whereas Britain, once the world's great proponent of free trade, was now a country in deficit and desperate for some respite from competition. It seemed only a matter of time before the issue broke out into the open.

Though, beyond compensation for damaged equipment, the Americans did not expect money in return for Lend-Lease, Roosevelt had asked Cordell Hull to devise some kind of 'consideration or considerations to be given us by the British in return for the material provided'.[24] Such a consideration was bound to be significant: after all, it would amount to the first meaningful agreement on how economic relations would evolve after the war.

After a few early conversations with Dean Acheson, Keynes had realised that something of the sort was brewing (and that it was likely to impinge on Imperial Preference and other protections) and attempted to pre-empt the matter. In a lunch meeting with the President early on in the visit, he had explained his response to Funk's New Order speech, mapping out Britain's vision for a post-war global economy. Roosevelt sat there with the air of casual indifference he generally displayed when economics came up in conversation. And while Keynes found the President deeply impressive, he realised that 'he does not really care for [economic policy] any more than our own Prime Minister does.'[25]

However, Keynes would not give up – after all, the issue was of crucial importance to Britain. His country would end the war not only deeply indebted but also extremely vulnerable to speculative attack. It was crucial, as far as he was concerned, that the post-war system should afford Britain some degree of protection – both from the threat of a sudden outflow of cash, and from the risk of its exporters being outcompeted by its rivals overseas.

America wasn't the only threat in this regard: Britain had so far been leaning on its Dominions – particularly Egypt and India – to provide the bulk of the wartime materials it so desperately needed to fight in Europe. The upshot was that these countries were left with enormous sterling balances as the proceeds of their exports. While in the long run no one would dispute that they should be allowed to exchange that sterling for other currencies, in the short run Britain needed to keep them handcuffed to its own economy, allowing them to use their sterling only to buy British goods.

If Britain was to avoid financial collapse after the war it would therefore have to impose capital controls, both to prevent the

Dominions swapping sterling for other currencies and to stop any sudden outflows of cash from London. It would also have to safeguard the Imperial Preference system – whose mantra was 'home producers first, Empire producers second, and foreign producers last' – by levying tariffs on imports from outside the Empire.

Keynes pressed the matter again in another meeting with the President in July, by which time he had been in Washington for more than two months. Roosevelt finally said he wanted to draft a short private agreement on Lend-Lease. Much to Keynes's amusement – and Acheson's annoyance – the President asked the Briton to pass the message on to the State Department. Whether this political slight had anything to do with it, the eventual agreement Acheson handed to Keynes just before his departure for London at the end of July had a sting in its tail.

Scanning the document, when Keynes came to Article VII he spluttered in amazement. The clause called for a deal between the US and UK (and, potentially, other countries) aimed at 'mutually advantageous economic relations between them and the betterment of world-wide economic relations' – in other words, an economic pact on the future shape of the global economy. That much was uncontroversial – in fact, it was welcome to Keynes. It was what followed that was disturbing: the deal should 'provide against discrimination in either the United States of America or the United Kingdom against the importation of any product originating in the other country'.

He asked Acheson whether this meant the elimination of Imperial Preference. Acheson said it did – whereupon, he later recalled, Keynes 'burst into a speech such as only he could make', warning that such a commitment was simply impossible.[26]

There is an unwritten rule in economics: however strongly you might believe in trade restrictions, it borders on sacrilege to say so in polite society. Free trade was and is a sacred principle in economics: partly because its benefits were one of the earliest rules laid down by the first economists, Adam Smith and David Ricardo; partly because it was a collapse in trade that lay behind the Depression in the 1930s. And although there are one or two acceptable economic rationales for imposing restrictions on trade, championing them is often foolhardy – nowhere more so than America, where trade restrictions and tariffs had been one of the chief causes of the War of Independence.

And yet that is what Keynes proceeded to do, rebuking the Americans for misunderstanding how important such restrictions would be for the health of the UK economy in the years following the war. Privately, he dubbed Article VII the 'lunatic proposals of Mr Hull'.[27] In a memo to Hull, Harry Hawkins, head of the State Department's treaties division, warned that Keynes intended Britain to follow a 'deliberate policy ... of bilateral and commercial economic arrangements with foreign countries. Although Mr Keynes presumably is not presenting the views of the British Government on questions of basic economic policy, his standing and influence are such that any views he may have are bound to receive consideration in the United Kingdom and hence are of real concern to us here.'[28]

Keynes took the draft agreement back with him to London. It had been an exhausting trip, he wrote to a friend: 'I always regard a visit [to the USA] as in the nature of a serious illness to be followed by a convalescence.'[29] But the stay had at least underlined what had first become clear when Britain received word of Funk's plan for a German New Order. The Allies, who had committed themselves to rebuilding the world's diplomatic institutions in the Atlantic Charter that summer, would have to start by reshaping the world economy. The row over Article VII of the Lend-Lease agreement had underlined the fact that it was not going to be easy.

Once again, however, discussions about the future of the world economic system would soon have to take a back seat. Over the course of the following months, American relations with Japan were to become increasingly strained, as Roosevelt and Morgenthau, advised by White, extended financial support to the Soviet Union. And few could have guessed at what happened next. On the morning of 7 December 1941, hundreds of Japanese fighter-bombers staged a surprise attack on the US naval fleet at Pearl Harbor. Four navy battleships were sunk; 188 aircraft were destroyed; and more than two thousand Americans were killed. The following day the United States declared war on Japan. Roosevelt's careful tightrope walk was over. America was officially at war.

CHAPTER SIX

Bedlam

1941–1944

In Washington Lord Halifax
Once whispered to Lord Keynes:
'It's true they have the money bags
But we have the brains.'

Note found among papers from first
Anglo-American discussions[1]

Being very close to the details of the stabilization plans, as I
have been, has a 'sucking-in' effect on one's mentality; it
becomes difficult to rise above details and look at the picture
as a whole.

Emanuel Goldenweiser[2]

Sunday morning phone calls from the office weren't unheard of in
the White household. Even so, the call that came through from the
Treasury Secretary at 10 a.m. on Sunday 14 December 1941 was
unusual. Shortly after White picked up the receiver Morgenthau
began telling him about the dream he had the previous night. It was
the strangest thing, he said: that after the war there would be a
world with an international currency, and a central fund to admin-
ister it. Was there any economic sense to this? Could White look
into whether such a thing might be possible?[3]

A week before, on the day of the Pearl Harbor attack, Morgenthau had elevated White to his highest position yet, giving him the status of Assistant Secretary (though not the title – White still wasn't even an official civil servant). 'He will be in charge of all foreign affairs for me,' said Morgenthau. 'I want it in one brain, and I want it in Harry White's brain.'⁴ With the United States now formally at war, White was the second most important figure in the Treasury: astonishing given he had entered government service barely more than seven years before.

Quite where the kernel of Morgenthau's international currency idea came from remains a mystery. Perhaps it genuinely was a brain-wave from his sleeping mind, though the Treasury Secretary rarely paid much attention to policymaking – visionary or otherwise. Perhaps it was inspired by something else. After all, the notion of a world currency wasn't exactly new: Roosevelt had been kicking round a similar idea in the Inter-American Debates a few years ear-lier. Keynes had suggested something of the sort in his *Treatise on Money* in 1930 – a supernational body to replace the gold standard, issuing 'Supernational Bank Money' to countries facing balance of payments difficulties. Then again, the probability that Morgenthau had actually read Keynes's *Treatise* – hardly his most user-friendly work – is close to zero.

Either way, this element of the request was a little tricky for White. While he had spent plenty of time contemplating the future of the world's monetary system, which clearly needed repairing after the mess it had been left in, an international currency had never entered the equation. No matter: over the coming fortnight he would put together the first draft of what would become known as the White plan.

Unbeknown to the Americans, the British had already been at work on their own competing vision since September. Work had begun almost as soon as Keynes returned from his long stay in Washington. The last-minute shock of Article VII had been a wake-up call: while ministers had shown little interest in his response to the German New Order blueprint earlier in the year, suddenly it became the talk of the Treasury. 'When I got back here I found that Whitehall was very much more prepared to take a serious interest in post-war problems than before I left with various high up committees being established to think about this,' he wrote to his friend Acheson.[5]

While London had allowed itself to fantasise, briefly, that the United States' entry into the war would change everything – that American troops would soon be on the ground in Europe and that all existing debts would be cancelled – reality soon kicked in. America's military focus would largely remain on the Pacific theatre for months; not until 1942 would American troops enter the war in the West, in North Africa, while its first significant role on the north European front would only come with Operation Overlord in 1944, a few weeks before Bretton Woods itself. Lend-Lease, meanwhile, was to carry on in its pre-agreed form – Hull's 'lunatic proposals' and all. Economic tensions between Britain and America would continue to fester.

As his colleagues in Washington continued to wrestle with the Americans over Article VII, doing what they could to safeguard Imperial Preference, Keynes took himself off to Tilton to write what would become the Keynes plan.

The two plans, which together would form the foundations of what later came to be known as Bretton Woods, would take years to hone and develop. While they would have much in common, there were also key differences – most of them deriving from the contrasting situations of the two sides. Britain was a debtor nation; if it were to win the war, it would be a bankrupt victor, in desperate need of support. The United States was set for world economic domination; White's plan would be designed not merely to secure its rise, but to ensure that the outgoing superpower would be shuffled even further from centre stage.

But both schemes also had a common goal: to replace the

existing mangled monetary system with something that would last – and would not spark another Great Depression, and in turn, another war. It would not do to return to the gold standard, or indeed to the gold exchange standard of the interwar years: both had consigned member countries to deflation, and had deprived them of the opportunity to adapt domestic interest rates to the ups and downs of their own economies. But neither were floating exchange rates much more acceptable: the experience of the 1920s had reinforced the notion that untethered currencies were associated with dangerous flows of 'hot money' and inescapable lurches in exchange rates. Keynes and White would both find themselves aiming for something in the middle.

It would be eighteen months before official negotiations between the Britons and Americans began, by which time each had grown so attached to its respective plan that they would not compromise without a fight.

Keynes's starting point was familiar enough: the gold standard was a dud. It had worked only briefly in the late nineteenth century, and then due to a sequence of happy accidents. It failed because, when countries found themselves with a balance of payments deficit (i.e. its households and companies were borrowing and importing more from the rest of the world than they were lending and exporting), the painful adjustment was 'compulsory for the debtor and voluntary for the creditor'.

His aim, then, was to devise a scheme which made this adjustment equal: where those countries which built up large surpluses by exporting their goods around the world would be just as responsible for reducing these as the debtor countries which imported from them. That Britain had swung from being one of the world's great creditor nations to one of the biggest debtors over the past half-century was not coincidental.

Since reading the coverage of the Nazis' monetary plan the

previous year, Keynes had toyed with adapting the scheme into something more Anglo-Saxon. After all, he wrote, its progenitor, Hjalmar Schacht, had 'stumbled in desperation on something new which had in it the germs of a good technical idea': a system which replaced the exchange of money with the enforced exchange of goods – barter.

The principle was that rather than being entitled to trade with whoever they wanted, and building up stashes of other countries' currency (or indeed gold) in their central bank vaults, countries should enter into bilateral agreements with their trading partners. For every unit of, say, cars or motorbikes Germany exported to Britain, Britain would eventually have to make up that deficit, be it in grain, livestock or pharmaceuticals.

The scheme would, admittedly, demand that each country set up individual agreements with all its trading partners, which screamed protectionism. But on the plus side, it could more or less accommodate the existing sterling area and Imperial Preference, leaving the United States on the outside, looking in (note that this plan was first drawn up months before America entered the war).

This was a particular relief to the Bank of England, for whom the post-war world held two main fears: first, that the sterling area over which it presided might be disbanded; second, that London might lose its position as the world's leading financial centre. Its concerns were well founded: these were precisely the two crowns Morgenthau and White were desperate to dislodge. In talks with the Chinese in the 1930s they had repeatedly urged Beijing to peg its currency, the yuan, to the dollar rather than to sterling; 'the United States is a coming nation and England is a going one,' White had reasoned.[6] Explaining Keynes's proposals to Montagu Norman, executive governor Cameron Cobbold laid out the Bank's main stipulation: 'we should still wish the sterling area to bank and clear in sterling and regard sterling as their link with other currencies'.[7]

However, most of the rest of Whitehall was disturbed by this aspect of Keynes's proposal: not merely because of its German inspiration, but because it would alienate the Americans – it was, after all, almost entirely incompatible with the principles of Article VII. Moreover, there was something not quite right about the notion of replacing money with barter – which, wrote civil servant Sir David Waley, 'having been in abeyance from the Stone Age till 1939, was then re-discovered by Dr Schacht'.[8] Sir Horace Wilson, permanent secretary to the Treasury, summoned up the prospect of Britain only allowing 'a ship to enter Liverpool Docks if we are quite certain that she will at once re-load there with manufactured goods and will go straight back to the port whence she sailed'.[9]

However, the Schachtian plan was actually something of a decoy. The real brainwave was the alternative Keynes presented – his ultimate scheme.

The plan, which became known as the Clearing Union, was certainly novel. Consider a high street bank: it can allow even its indebted customers to borrow money through overdraft facilities – though it charges them for the privilege. Keynes's Clearing Union attempted to apply the same principle to international economic relations. There would be an international central bank, the Clearing Union itself, with its own currency, 'bancor', freely convertible at a fixed rate into all other currencies. Every country would have its own individual account at the Union, denominated in bancor, and countries would use these accounts whenever there was trade between them. If country A was selling bananas to country B, a debit would be made (in bancor) in country B's ledger as those bananas changed hands and a credit posted to country A's account. (Of course, this would all be invisible to the banana-seller, who would trade in local currency; the real action would happen at central bank level.)

Countries with a heavy reliance on imported goods would eventually find themselves with a large overdraft at the Clearing Union – this would be limited to a certain size (a percentage of the country's pre-war trade volumes), and there would be interest charges to try to encourage that country to get back into balance. Should it suffer persistent overdrafts ('deficits'), it would be designated a 'deficiency' country and be allowed to depreciate its currency by a limited amount.

There would also (and this was the unusual element) be similar penalties imposed on those with large credits at the Clearing Union to incentivise them to import more and export less. Bancor was to be given a value in gold, but while one could pay in gold in exchange for bancor, one could not withdraw it by paying in bancor. This was Keynes's *coup de grâce*: slowly but surely, gold would be retired from monetary service.

Unlike a normal bank, the Clearing Union itself would not need any capital to be paid in because, provided it was truly international, its debits would balance out its credits – unless Planet Earth was envisaging a trade deficit with Mars. In fact, Keynes imagined that through its operations the Union would turn a profit, allowing it to finance an international police force and an organisation to provide economic relief and development aid.

Some might well say, Keynes concluded, that 'it is complicated and novel and perhaps Utopian in the sense, not that it is impracticable, but that it assumes a higher degree of understanding, of the spirit of bold innovation, and of international cooperation and trust than it is safe or reasonable to assume. Nevertheless, it is with this scheme that I should approach the United States.'[10]

To say it was radical was an understatement. But then again the Depression and war had left a wreck in place of the international monetary system. 'This complete break with the past offers us an opportunity,' Keynes concluded. 'Things are possible to-day which would have been impossible if they involved the prior disestablishment of a settled system.'

Lionel Robbins, in charge of economic affairs for the Cabinet Office, considered it 'a real release of fresh air in this surcharged and stale atmosphere'.[11] Dennis Robertson, Keynes's great academic foil (also, now, at the Treasury), wrote: 'I sat up last night reading your revised "proposal" with great excitement and a growing hope that the spirit of Burke and Adam Smith is on earth again.'[12] The Bank of England was predictably horrified at anything that would so undermine sterling's role in foreign exchange – but it was in an unhappy minority of one, which is where it would find itself for most of the negotiations.

Perhaps in an effort to bring the Bank onside, Keynes underplayed the novelty of his proposals, saying that they 'lay no claim to originality. They are an attempt to reduce to practical shape certain general ideas belonging to the contemporary climate of economic opinion, which have been given publicity in recent months by writers of several different nationalities. It is difficult to see how any plan can be successful which does not use these general ideas, which are born of the spirit of the age.'[13]

As Keynes and the Treasury worked their way through the first drafts, however, eventually removing the barter option and refining some of the terms, it was obvious which parts the Americans would object to. The creation of an international police force was just one. Bob Brand, the Lazard banker who was now with the Treasury team in Washington, urged Keynes to drop anything that smacked of 'supranational government'.[14] Nor was basing the key institution on a bank likely to go down well, given the Roosevelt administration's dislike of 'money-lenders', warned Waley.[15]

But the most glaring objection would certainly be to the proposed attitude to those overdrafts and credits: the world's leading creditor nation would doubtless be horrified at the prospect of having to pay a fee for the privilege (a suggestion for which there was no precedent in monetary history). 'We are surely a long way,' wrote one colleague, Lucius Thompson-McCausland, 'from a political world in which surplus countries would be content to go on paying taxes forever for the benefit of foreigners.'

'Your argument,' replied Keynes, 'is like saying that if we admit the principle of capital punishment that can only end sooner or later in the entire depopulation of the country.'[16]

It was a surreal period. London was no longer under the torrential bombardment it had suffered between September 1940 and May 1941; the threat of a German invasion had faded, as Hitler took the fateful decision to train his sights on Moscow. Though it was still far from clear that the war would be won, this only served to reinforce the determination among those left in Whitehall to try to create a set of better institutions for the post-war era. For once, it was not shameful to be Utopian. And Keynes's vision was not the only one. In the months that followed, William Beveridge would sketch out his plan for the welfare state in Britain. James Meade and Lionel Robbins – both of whom were to be involved with Keynes in the Bretton Woods preparations – would draw up the seminal White Paper on Employment, promoting full employment in Britain, a policy that would last until the late 1970s. The Treasury – indeed the government as a whole – was unusually well stocked with fine minds, men and women summoned on war business from their posts at universities, in industry and the City of London.

'Social life in London was almost non-existent,' Robbins would write years later. 'Most of us slept in the building; and even when duties were not pressing, we were apt to sit around in the canteens or offices discussing common problems. Yet we were certainly not unhappy or oppressed by the comparative discomfort of our surroundings. My own bedroom, a great privilege, was a more or less bomb-proof cellar through which secret messages scurried in their vacuum tubes like giant rats in the ceilings.'[17]

While the residents of London had by now become accustomed to the rhythms of wartime life, those in Washington DC were only now coming to terms with the fact that their country was at war.

For Harry White that meant wasting no time. No sooner had Morgenthau called him to ask whether his dream about an international currency was possible than he got to work. Sitting at home, in the leafy suburbs north-west of the American capital, he began to draft, all the way through Hanukkah and then Christmas, until he finally delivered his scheme to the Treasury Secretary on 30 December 1941. The resulting document may have lacked some of the razzmatazz of Keynes's Clearing Union, but then White wasn't aiming for Utopia: he was proposing something he fully expected to be implemented. As Keynes would soon learn, there were some things Congress, or the American public, would never accept.

Nonetheless, White's plan was, in its own, less extravagant way, as radical a departure from the past as Keynes's, its ultimate ambition nothing short of preventing a third world war. As the drafting continued he was to add an unusually emotive manifesto:

> There is a desperate need for instruments which will pave the way and make easy a high degree of cooperation and collaboration among the United Nations in economic fields hitherto held too sacrosanct for international action or multilateral sovereignty. A breach must be made and widened in the outmoded and disastrous economic policy of each-country-for-itself-and-the-devil-take-the-weakest. Just as the failure to develop an effective League of Nations has made possible two devastating wars within one generation, so the absence of a high degree of economic collaboration among the leading nations will, during the coming decade, inevitably result in economic warfare that will be but the prelude and instigator of military warfare on an even vaster scale.[18]

In economic terms, there were two distinct objectives: first, to 'stabilise foreign exchange rates'; after all, the beggar-thy-neighbour sequence of competitive devaluations in the 1930s was widely regarded as responsible for the worst of the Depression and the eventual war. Second, to set up an agency charged with rebuilding the world economy after the war.

White would create two distinct organisations to carry out these roles – an Inter-Allied Stabilisation Fund to deal with exchange rates and an Inter-Allied Bank to tackle reconstruction and re-development. Keynes would spend much of the following years sniping over the fact that what White called a fund was really more like a bank, whereas his bank behaved more like a fund. In practice, the Bank ended up as little more than an afterthought until the run-up to the Bretton Woods conference itself; most of White's effort went into the Fund.

And though the Fund was quite different from Keynes's Clearing Union, their objectives were almost identical: to ensure that currencies did not become misaligned with each other, and were a fair representation of what things were worth, rather than being manipulated for political ends, as had happened between the wars. Under White's plan, exchange rates would be fixed according to their gold value (while Keynes wanted to bury the gold standard, White still believed that the precious metal 'is the best medium of international exchange yet devised').[19] Countries would retain caches of gold and other currencies in their central banks with which to trade with each other, but the Fund would step in when countries faced a problem – a shortage of a particular currency which was threatening their ability to trade. In other words, while Keynes's Clearing Union was a central element of the mechanism by which countries traded with each other, handling every foreign exchange transaction, White's Fund existed primarily for emergency lending. Loans of these sorts (and indeed membership of the Fund) would be predicated on each country taking measures to try to bring its economy back to balance, and its currency into line.

There would be a board of directors to oversee these lending operations – though, White added, 'the US should have enough votes to block any decision',[20] and there would be checks to prevent countries withdrawing unlimited amounts of US dollars. By this stage, American economic dominance was already such that the dollar was the only major currency which could be freely converted into gold – so certain protections needed to be built into White's system to ensure other countries could not write themselves a blank cheque by withdrawing dollars.

Then there was the question of that new international currency Morgenthau had requested. White could find no place for it in his earliest drafts; in his later ones the following spring he was altogether set against the idea. 'A "trade dollar" or "Demos" or "Victor" or "what-have-you" unit of currency,' White wrote, referencing some of the ideas for names that had been knocking around the administration, 'would no more help foreign trade than would the adoption of a new flag.' Whether an existing currency could play that role was another question, he added:

> For many decades the British pound sterling was regarded virtually as an international currency unit. But its utility as an international unit of account and also as a common medium of exchange in many international financial and trade transactions rested on the fact that sterling was for a long time most stable in terms of gold value … But when sterling lost its stability in terms of gold, its use as a unit of account rapidly diminished. Only the United States dollar has any chance of serving in that capacity now. However, if an attempt were made to recommend the use of the dollar as the international unit of account, there would unquestionably be some opposition on the part of those countries who, out of reasons of national prestige or anticipated monetary loss, would prefer not to promote a broader use in international use of a currency unit of some other country.[21]

White would later incorporate an international currency into his plans for his Reconstruction and Development Bank – though it was clear from the outset that he had decided against making Unitas (the name the Americans finally set on for a prospective international currency, after the United Nations) an integral part of his monetary plan.

With the help of his right-hand man Eddie Bernstein, he continued drafting and redrafting until, by May 1942, he had an eighty plus-page proposal he considered his 'preliminary draft'. Some of the finer details would change over the coming years, but the two institutions sketched out by White that year are remarkably similar to the International Monetary Fund and International Bank for Reconstruction and Development (the World Bank) which would be created at Bretton Woods two years later.

While the British had hoped to settle the main details of their respective plans in a cosy private session with the Americans, and had with increasing desperation been trying to table talks throughout 1942, White had different ideas. Submitting his proposal to Morgenthau in May, he suggested they call a conference of all the Allied governments to decide on his plan, potentially within months.*

But first things first: there were enemies closer to home that would need to be neutralised. Cordell Hull's State Department would almost certainly object to the Treasury taking responsibility for something so integral to international affairs. No sooner had they seen it than they would try to extinguish it, said Morgenthau. '[Their] idea is to kill it,' he said in a meeting of his lieutenants. 'Because we've got an idea and State hasn't, and they don't want anybody else to have any ideas.'[22]

They had little to fear from Hull himself, who was as ineffectual as he was uncharismatic. One listener who heard him deliver a key

---

*Leaving absolutely nothing to chance, White even drafted speeches to be made by representatives of the various countries there at this meeting. Eric Helleiner, *Forgotten Foundations of Bretton Woods*, Cornell, 2014, p. 105.

speech on the wireless would write, 'One got the impression of an aged and tired old man whistling through a set of false teeth which did not properly fit him.'[23] The bigger threat was posed by his younger, more dynamic, more ambitious lieutenants, like the suave Dean Acheson and the diminutive Leo Pasvolsky.

The State Department was intent on holding informal talks with the British, the Russians and the Chinese – Roosevelt's 'Big Four' – before any grand international conference. That much Morgenthau could agree on – provided the Treasury remained in the driving seat. In the event, White and Morgenthau would find themselves fighting as tense and protracted a battle with their own colleagues from other wings of the administration as they would with the British and the rest of their international allies.

It wasn't until the summer of 1942 that Keynes and White finally had a chance to inspect their rivals' plans. As was usually the case when it came to other people's ideas, Keynes was immediately unimpressed.

'Seldom have I been so much bored and so much interested,' he reported to Phillips, the Treasury's man in Washington, after wading through White's overwritten document.[24] All the same, the plans had a reassuring amount in common. Both envisaged a world of fixed, not floating, exchange rates. Both involved a central co-ordinating organisation to impose discipline on countries running domestic policies which would leave their economies out of step with those exchange rate levels. Both proposed some degree of control over flows of investment ('hot money') around the world. Keynes's main objection was that White's plan was 'in fact not much more than a version of the gold standard, which simply aims at multiplying the effective volume of the gold base'.

What White had missed, Keynes added, was that applying the principle of banking and overdrafts to the global economy, as he had done, would break the link with gold and, if done sensibly, keep a check on imbalances. He was pleasantly surprised, however, to find a generous clause buried in the small print of White's plan which would have solved one of Britain's biggest problems – the build-up of 'blocked balances' of sterling owed to its Dominions – by incorporating them into the Fund, effectively using America's balance sheet to help pay them off. This was a bonus.

A copy of Keynes's plan had also been sent to Washington; he had added the subtitle 'Not Utopia, but Eutopia', alluding to the fact that in Ancient Greek Utopia literally meant 'no place' while Eutopia meant 'good place'. Phillips, perhaps anticipating that this wry Oxbridge-style allusion might only serve to alienate the Americans further, added a covering note to White pointing out that the Keynes plan was designed to 'meet the threat of another world-wide post-war depression'.[25]

As soon as the plan arrived in the Treasury, Bernstein handed it to junior official Gardner Patterson, who promptly 'embraced it heart and soul', producing a memo singing its praises. This intellectual rebellion was instantly quelled. 'I had to tell him we couldn't use his memorandum,' Bernstein would later say. 'We needed a plan which required two things: first, it had to have limited liability on the extension of credit by the United States ... The second fault was that the Keynes Plan did not require much discipline by other countries. Most of the discipline he had in mind was on the United States as a creditor country.'[26]

Using the State Department as a conduit, White and Bernstein peppered the British Treasury with a ream of questions about their proposal. The questions and answers flew back and forth across the Atlantic for months – a face-to-face meeting could wait until these substantive issues were resolved. But as chance would have it, Morgenthau and White were flying to England in October 1942 anyway – primarily to inspect aircraft and equipment and make economic and currency arrangements for the impending North African campaign. The American ambassador, Winant, and his assistant Ernest Penrose suggested some informal talks with the

Treasury over the plan. 'I don't want to talk with anyone except Keynes,' said White.[27]

A meeting was hastily arranged for the pair of them at the American Embassy. For White, whose economic maturity had coincided with a world which was Keynesian, in nature if not in name, it was a significant occasion. 'The happiest moment in the life of Harry White,' recalled one veteran of the negotiations, 'came when he could call Keynes by his first name.'[28]

But there was something that stuck in the throat about fawning on an Englishman. As Bernstein would later testify, White was most certainly 'anti-British'.[29] This time he was coming to the table with almost all the chips on his side. The brief one-off meeting was 'lively and at times somewhat acrimonious but fruitful', reported Penrose. 'There was a substantial area of agreement but there were also sharp differences.' Most of those differences came down to what was and was not politically feasible. There was the Fund's size, which Keynes thought too small in White's plan (he also derided White's insistence that countries should pay an up-front contribution); White explained that Congress would not accept anything else. Keynes said that, in turn, Parliament would not accept White's proposal that countries not be allowed to change their exchange rate without a four-fifths majority vote at the Fund (i.e. an American veto). He 'heatedly' urged White to begin direct negotiations alone with Britain, or possibly with the Dominions and the Soviet Union tacked on. White warned that this would give the impression of an Anglo-Saxon financial 'gang-up'.[30]

The session may have been brief, but it provided enough evidence that their future encounters would be difficult. A dynamic had been established: Keynes remonstrating and demanding changes; White politely (then increasingly impolitely) refusing; and both parties pleading politics.

Realising that they could easily be outflanked by the Americans, the British team called in the Dominions and India to try to drum up external support for the Clearing Union. To the delight of the British the Dominions' representatives were extremely enthusiastic; what Keynes failed to realise was that they would be equally enthusiastic when White showed them his competing plans. When British officials drilled down, it transpired that the Dominions' interest was largely focused on the size of their quotas – in other words what they might be entitled to withdraw – rather than on the structure.

The main exception was Canada, the only other major country to play a significant role in the negotiations. Louis Rasminsky, the young Canadian delegate who would go on to become governor of the Bank of Canada, later recalled the visit as 'one of the great intellectual experiences of my life. Keynes, flanked by Lionel Robbins and Frederick Phillips, was brilliant but not overbearingly so. He created the atmosphere in which everyone present was participating as an equal.'[31]

It was one of Keynes's more surprising qualities: even in those days, having been established for some time as the world's greatest living economist, he was not above engaging with the most junior official. As one colleague put it, 'he was just "Keynes", free to shoot at anybody – anybody, regardless of rank, was free to go to him with his troubles.'[32] Nor did he restrain himself from intervening in the smallest, most irrelevant issue if it piqued his curiosity; in such cases he was often wrong, in which case one could eventually disregard his suggestion once his mind moved on elsewhere.

Following their discussions with the British and, later, the Americans, Rasminsky and his Canadian colleagues would come up with their own alternative plan. It was, 'in characteristic Canadian fashion', a compromise – a beefed-up version of the American plan. In Whitehall the plan was swiftly dubbed 'Off-White', but it did little to influence the eventual outcome. The French also came up with their own bizarre rival proposal. Predictably, it was predicated on gold – the 'international currency of the future' which had been 'consecrated by a mystic thousands of years old'.[33]

If, after his first meeting with White, it was not already plain to Keynes that the Americans had essentially ruled out his Clearing Union scheme, it became increasingly transparent as the lists of technical questions continued to stream in from the State Department. Keynes was suspicious: the tone of discussion, he wrote, 'suggests a very harmless, indeed, almost too harmless an atmosphere'.[34]

Moreover, there was still no date in the diary for more face-to-face talks. In January 1943 the news they had been fearing arrived, via Phillips: neither of Keynes's plans was acceptable to the State Department, which was still intent on consulting with experts from many other countries.[35] All of this, Keynes wrote to his Treasury colleague Sir Wilfred Eady, 'is far from fragrant in my nostrils'. In his exasperation, he speculated that perhaps the Americans themselves might not even favour the White plan; it was repeatedly described as 'unofficial' – maybe it was simply a 'man of straw' for the Britons to exhaust themselves boxing?[36]

For months he waited to hear back from Washington about his latest draft, continuing to ask, in vain, for them to consider putting together a US–UK compromise statement. When the US Treasury confirmed it was publishing the White plan separately and sending it out to Allied governments for consideration, Sir David Waley echoed Keynes's sentiments: 'It will, of course, be very unfortunate, if the impression is created that the rival plans are being put up for auction, but there again we cannot help ourselves.'[37]

Having been kept secret for eighteen months, the two plans were at last published in full in April 1943 after the American scheme was leaked to Paul Einzig of the *Financial News* (the paper would later merge with the *Financial Times*).* The leak was deeply

---

*The leak coincided with disclosures about British security secrets in American newspapers. In a cable to the Treasury, Keynes wrote: 'If we are unable to control the reptiles of our Press how can we expect the Americans to control theirs?' Paul Einzig, *In the Centre of Things*, London, 1960, p. 173.

annoying for the Americans; only a few days beforehand Roosevelt had ordered Morgenthau not to publish the US scheme. 'These things are too early,' he said. 'We haven't begun to win the war.'[38] So infuriated was the Chancellor with the leak that he played with the idea of having Einzig arrested.[39]

Despite having campaigned since the very beginning for an Anglo-American joint plan, Keynes suddenly professed himself delighted that the two schemes were now out in the open. 'If in fact we had managed to reach a compromise behind the scenes, isn't it about ten to one that Congress would have turned it down,' he declared.[40]

In a series of meetings, including informal discussions at the Hot Springs conference in May and private sessions between Bernstein and Robertson, the Americans had emphasised that it was to be the White plan, or no plan.* The Dominions, India and other countries whom Keynes had thought were cheerleaders for his plan seemed now to be reluctant to press the Americans on it.

Now that there was no longer a question of implementing their own plan, the British tactics switched to trying to make White's more generous. This meant trying to increase the size of the Fund (so that troubled countries would have more to draw from); giving members greater control of their interest rates; keeping down the amount of gold members would have to give the Fund as part of their quotas; and trying to create an international currency.

White had, in one of his earlier drafts, inserted a clause that his

---

*The Hot Springs conference in Virginia in May, the first major conference on post-war administration, focused, perhaps surprisingly, on food. When an American official informed Keynes of it he said: 'What you are saying is that your President with his great political insight has decided that the best strategy for post-war reconstruction is to start with vitamins and then by a circuitous route work round to the international balance of payments!' Ernest Penrose, *Economic Planning for the Peace*, Princeton, 1953, p. 120.

Reconstruction and Development Bank should use Unitas, its own unit of account, for issuing loans. American work on the Bank had been largely abandoned by this stage, but the idea of the currency was allowed to linger, and Keynes seized upon it. If the Americans would only 'monetise' Unitas – making it a unit nations could trade with – then perhaps the two plans would at least seem to have been synthesised. Thinking, apparently, that the main obstacle was the name (he liked neither Unitas nor his own bancor), Keynes appealed to the public to come up with a better one, which triggered a flood of letters to the Treasury and to newspapers; among the suggestions were Fint, Proudof, Unibanks, Bit, Poundol and, Keynes's favourite, Orb.[41] Months later, Keynes sent round a note to his Treasury colleagues asking: 'Do you think it is any use to try *unicorn* on Harry? It is, of course, much more picturesque and romantic and would have the advantage of supplying a suitable emblem for the institution's note-paper and hereafter for a note issue, should the course of evolution ever bring them to that.'[42]

By then the issue was already effectively dead, although Keynes continued to raise it until the Bretton Woods conference itself. White would later concede: 'The notion of a new world currency had caught the public imagination. It seemed to have become a symbol of monetary progress, something revolutionary, something important ... We finally decided to drop it because we feared that in the hands of the opposition it might become target for unfair criticism; it would be easy to point to the new currency and declare that some new crack-brained scheme was being concocted.'[43]

However, there was some good news for the British – at least as far as one member of their team was concerned. Buried in later American drafts, Roy Harrod, an Oxford economist working with Keynes, spotted an apparently innocuous clause on 'scarce currencies'. It seemed to address the key British concern that – unlike the Clearing Union, which would have charged them a fee for building up their savings – White's plan did not impose any discipline on creditor nations like the United States. The clause stated that countries would be free to levy tariffs on a country whose currency became scarce. For Harrod, who read the draft on a midnight train from London to Oxford, crowded with sleeping troops, this was a major concession. It would apparently give the British *carte blanche* to impose trade barriers on the US if the world faced another depression.

> As I sat huddled in my corner, I felt an exhilaration such as only comes once or twice in a lifetime. There were the dishevelled soldiers sprawling over one another in sleep; and here was I, tightly pressed into my corner, holding these little flimsy sheets. One had the urge to wake them all up. 'Here, boys, is great news. Here is an offer, which can make things very different for you when the war is over; your lords and masters do not seem to have realised it yet; but they soon will; see for yourselves this paragraph 7; read what it says. I know that you set great store by the Beveridge scheme; but that is only written on a bit of paper; it will all fall to pieces, if this country has a bad slump and trade difficulties. Here is the real thing, because it will save us from a slump and make all those Beveridge plans lastingly possible.' Was I too enthusiastic?

The answer, it must be said, is probably yes. There never was a post-war depression; the clause was (strangely) never considered enormously controversial by the Americans; it would indeed make it into the IMF's Articles of Agreement, but has, to this day, never been triggered.

By the time the British and Americans finally engaged in a proper debate on their plans in the autumn of 1943, the landscape had changed yet again. It was by now becoming clear that the Allies were winning the war in Europe. After a sequence of defeats in

North Africa, Mussolini had fallen from power in Italy. News of
the country's unconditional surrender reached Keynes and his team
of negotiators, including Robbins and Meade, as they sailed across
the Atlantic on the *Queen Mary*. 'This should, I suppose, have been
the highlight of the day,' wrote Meade in his diary, 'but so engrossed
had I become in other affairs of state that the announcement left
me quite unmoved! I suppose I am rather inhuman.'[44]

Soviet troops were forcing the Germans back towards their borders, but Leningrad remained under siege – a cause for major
concern among the Keyneses: Lydia's family was still stuck inside
the benighted city. In the course of their visit to the United States,
her mother would die – though they were not to learn of this until
their return.

As would be the case when they sailed over for Bretton Woods
itself, the delegation intended to use the voyage to prepare their
position. But as the *Queen Mary* zigzagged its way through the
rough seas, most of them were consigned to their cabins with sea-
sickness. Lydia, who had come along with Keynes to attend to his
health (which mainly involved ordering him to lie down and rest),
was 'perfectly charming, fussing over and tending her distinguished
husband, moving about as if in a ballet, and talking and behaving
with the utmost simplicity and without a trace of affectation.'[45]

Keynes himself was on typically wry form, quipping as the team
sat down together on the first morning that 'it looks more like the
last supper than the first breakfast.'[46] As with his Lend-Lease visit,
he anticipated concluding business within a few days. In fact the
trip was to last six weeks.

The official plan was to tackle a range of issues – not only the
monetary talks. Having now committed to Article VII – albeit a
slightly watered-down version – the British were duty-bound to
discuss trade and employment policy as well. But since most of the
participants believed that all such talks would be irrelevant without
a deal on the fundamental foundations of currencies, those other

issues remained on the back burner.* As if to extinguish any
impression that this was a forum for a cosy backroom deal between
Britain and the United States, the talks were dubbed 'preliminary,
informal, non-committal, purely unofficial'.

Remembering his last, disastrous visit, the Americans were
desperate for Keynes to keep a low profile, so the British delegation divided itself into small groups to take the train down to
Washington. As ever, the plan backfired. 'Keynes was in first-class
form,' wrote Meade. 'There was a flow of acid comment on the
American countryside, their air-raid precautions, lack of birds and
the sterility of the land! He and Lydia and Ronald indulged in a
tremendous discussion on modern painting; and the whole journey
was rounded off by Lydia singing the Casse-Noisette music at the
top of her voice and dancing it with her hands. We had been
instructed to slip into Washington unnoticed: as far as the Keynes
party was concerned, I do not think that we attained our objective.'[47]

The imposing US Treasury building, rebuilt and expanded
since the British burnt it and the White House down in 1814,
was to play host to the debates, in which Keynes and White
would repeatedly explode in each other's direction. The British
hope for the talks – which were by now focused entirely on the
White plan, Keynes's scheme having been mothballed some
months previously – was to improve the generosity of the Fund
and ensure the installation of Unitas as a proper currency.

They started promisingly, with friendly private discussions
between White and Keynes, followed by an opening speech from
Keynes which was, in Meade's awestruck rendering, 'absolutely in
the first rank of speechifying. I have never heard him better – more
brilliant, more persuasive, more witty or more truly moving in his
appeal.'[48] One of the Americans whispered to Robbins that 'Berle

*The relevant part of Article VII now stipulated that the UK and US would work
towards 'the elimination of all forms of discriminatory treatment in international
commerce, and to the reduction of tariffs and other trade barriers'.

[of the State Department] and White say that your Baron Keynes sure pees perfume.'[49]

But as the talks went on the delegates became increasingly exhausted and, by turns, ever more irate. 'We are horribly over-worked and the pace is terrific,' Keynes wrote to Eady in the Treasury back home. 'Several meetings every day and not nearly enough time to think out one's own policy or do one's home work; all of which is much aggravated by the fact that I am lunching or dining out at least ten times a week.'[50] Happily, however, the temperature in Washington did not seem to be aggravating his health, and at least he had Lydia constantly alongside him. During dinners she would '[appear] intermittently to massage Lord Keynes's chest at about where the heart would be,' said one fellow diner.[51] And so indulged were the rest of the delegates (who were used to British-style rations rather than American helpings) that after one too many cocktail par-ties James Meade said he detected 'the symptoms of incipient alcohol poisoning' and determined to stick to tomato juice.[52]

It was only after the promising first few meetings that Keynes started to lose his temper. At one stage he called the US plans 'loony'. At another he said that the Americans were planning to make the Fund so intrusive, to make its lending so conditional, that Britain would never draw on it. The man from the Bank of England, Lucius Thompson-McCausland, related what followed: 'An incredulous gasp from the Americans followed by Harry White with "Do you mean that England will never draw on the Fund?" "We should never let ourselves draw on terms like that." This answer from Keynes drew appreciative smiles and applause from Pasvolsky and Berle, the two State Department representatives.'[53]

While the behaviour may have amused some, Keynes's col-leagues were dismayed that his 'ill manners' were waylaying the talks. 'That man is a menace in negotiations,' fumed Meade.[54] White, for his part, gave as good as he got. 'He was often brusque,

even crude, in his meetings with Keynes and the British delegation,'
wrote his colleague Ray Mikesell.[55] To those who opposed him –
including his State Department rivals – White could be sarcastic
and cruel; occasionally it showed during these talks. On one occasion he gave Keynes a draft set of minutes of their conversations
and, having read it, the Briton threw it to the ground in disgust.
'This is intolerable,' he said. 'We had better simply break off
negotiations.'

White replied: 'We will try to produce something which Your
Highness *can* understand.'[56]

The atmosphere was most succinctly illustrated by Meade, who
after yet another day of bickering scribbled in his diary: 'What
absolute Bedlam these discussions are! Keynes and White sit next
each other, each flanked by a long row of his own supporters.
Without any agenda or any prepared idea of what is going to be
discussed they go for each other in a strident duet of discord which
after a crescendo of abuse on either side leads up to a chaotic
adjournment.'

So stressful did White find the encounters with Keynes – under
the eyes of so many of his colleagues – that he became sick at various points through the meetings and had to send his deputy,
Bernstein, in his place.[57] Bernstein was one of those fellows who
prefer to bottle up their emotion than show it.* While White
reacted with fury to Keynes's taunts, Bernstein would answer with
long, technical responses which Keynes likened to the Talmud (ironically, one of Bernstein's ancestors, Samuel Edels, was a distinguished
scholar who wrote a commentary on the Jewish book of law).

---

*A case in point is Bernstein's resignation from the IMF, where he was director
of research, many years later. Having worked for a number of managing directors,
the decision came almost entirely out of the blue. Only later did he confide in a
colleague that it was because he had been unable to read the managing director's
handwriting, and had tired of trying to decipher the scrawls (Rasminsky, informal memoirs). Bernstein himself was rather more frank in his own oral history
some years afterwards (see references *passim*).

Keynes's private comments were even more unpleasant. 'Bernstein is a regular little rabbi, a reader of the Talmud, to Harry's grand political high rabbidom,' he ranted after one encounter. 'The chap knows every rat run in his local ghetto, but it is difficult to persuade him to come out for a walk with us on the high ways of the world.'[58] Though comments such as these were hardly uncommon among the British ruling class of the era (and Keynes showed few traits beyond this of genuinely malicious anti-Semitism), they were enough to embarrass some of the more sensitive members of the British delegation. After one outburst at Bernstein by the British representative, Keynes's faithful fellow scholar Robertson took the American aside and apologised on behalf of his country. Bernstein later said that had Morgenthau known of Keynes's remarks he would have called off the discussions altogether.[59]

At one stage, Keynes pulled White into a meeting room, ostensibly to tell him what he and the rest of the British delegation thought of him. A letter home shows that the feelings were not entirely negative:

> Any reserves we may have about him are a pale reflection of what his colleagues feel. He is over-bearing, a bad colleague, always trying to bounce you, with a harsh rasping voice, aesthetically oppressive in mind and manner; he has not the faintest conception how to behave or observe the rules of civilised intercourse. At the same time, I have a very great respect and even liking for him. In many respects he is the best man here. A very able and devoted public servant, carrying an immense burden of responsibility and initiative, of high integrity and of clear sighted idealistic international purpose, genuinely intending to do his best for the world. Moreover, his over-powering will combined with the fact that he has constructive ideas mean that he does get things done, which few else here do.[60]

Nonetheless, their clashes were worrying, wrote Meade: 'it augurs ill for the future unless these negotiations can somehow or another be got out of the hands of two such prima donnas as White and Keynes. There must be a growing accumulation of exasperation and bad temper as long as it goes on in this way.'[61]

On the bright side, there had at least been some progress. The Americans agreed to raise the total size of the Fund from $5 billion to $10 billion, though countries would have to pay in more gold in exchange; members would be allowed to adjust their currency rate by 10 per cent (Keynes was desperate to secure such flexibility for the Bank of England, guardian of Britain's currency), though any change beyond this would have to be approved by the Fund's board. The latter point highlighted another fundamental difference between the Briton and the American: Keynes wanted most of these decisions to be automatic, based on objective tests; White wanted the Fund's directors to be able to exercise their own discretion.

But Keynes's attempts to create the international currency he wanted were unsuccessful. Bernstein warned that Wall Street's main concern about Unitas being a part of the Fund was that the United States would be tying itself to a 'trick' currency. Keynes, said Bernstein, 'became nasty to me at this meeting ... he said it was just ignorance on my part not to recognize how much better it would be if the White plan were rewritten in his terms'.[62]

There was some sourness, too, about the way the second half of White's plan – the Bank – was structured. White was a 'perfect ass' in the way he approached it, wrote Keynes: the plan seemed to imply that the war-ravaged countries of Europe would be compelled to pay for their own redevelopment relief. An outsider, he added, 'will regard it as the work of a lunatic, or as some sort of bad joke ... Harry admits that without the least wish to dissent. Having put these lunatic robes on his Frankenstein he then proceeds at various stages to introduce jokers, which might actually cause the scheme to work out in practice in a way exactly the opposite of what it appears to be on the surface. How an intelligent and wise man like him can believe that this is the right way to approach a great issue, heaven knows.'[63]

All the same, the meetings had been productive. And when one took a step back, this was clearly a watershed moment in international economics. Every other attempt to set the world back on a healthy course had failed – most notably the London conference of 1933. Now, real economic issues were being hammered out over the table, not by partisan politicians but by some of the world's smartest economists.

Young James Meade, who himself would later become a Nobel laureate, wrote, 'Ten years ago at Oxford I should never have dreamed that an economist could live in such a heaven of practical application of real economic analysis!'[64] And by the end of the six-week marathon of debating and drafting, a spirit of camaraderie had started to grow between the Britons and Americans, 'with almost emotional scenes on parting'.[65]

In the following months, the stream of letters across the Atlantic continued. Some issues remained unresolved: whenever internationally accepted currencies were referred to they were called 'gold-convertible exchange' – what did that mean? The question of the Fund's power to change members' exchange rates remained unanswered. And what about the institution's name? 'International Stabilization Fund' didn't sound right, as far as Keynes was concerned; what about 'International Monetary Union'? White pointed out that Congress would baulk at the word 'Union'. So Keynes suggested 'International Monetary Fund'. White was happy with that. At last, there was something they agreed on.

White had just one problem hanging over him: the Russians. Since the earliest days of the negotiations, he and Morgenthau had been trying to elicit some interest from Moscow in the post-war plans. They had, in fact, repeatedly attempted to convince the Soviet Union to take some part in the various stability agreements they had signed in recent years, including the Tripartite Pact. But the Russians had expressed little curiosity. They had refused to send technicians to discuss the plans in the summer of 1943. Now, as New Year passed and time started to run out before a conference would need officially to be called, Moscow still had not given the go-ahead.

Eventually, technicians were sent in January 1944. They held a series of hasty meetings with White, at which the American described the Fund in terms that would have shocked Keynes: 'the Fund would help maintain the gold standard,'[66] he said – a direct contradiction of how he couched it to the British. But, given that Russia was one of the world's largest and growing gold exporters, it was a description designed to appeal to them.

However, the meetings with the Russians remained terse and tricky – in large part because none of the technicians was given any autonomy. At the very first meeting, the Russian ambassador, Andrei Gromyko, had turned to them and said: 'Remember! You are observers. You are not to give any opinion of any kind.'[67] They also seemed far more interested in securing a post-war loan than in any monetary agreement.

By now the British and Americans had agreed a 'Joint Statement' which would serve as the blueprint to be debated at Bretton Woods. But they were running out of time to get it published and start making plans for a conference. They set a deadline of 21 April – the day Morgenthau was to testify before the Senate on the issue. Given the election later that year, they would have to postpone the conference for twelve months if they could not persuade all the countries involved – including Russia – to agree, and it would be impossible to create anything so ambitious once peacetime and its petty politicking were back in place.

By 20 April there was still no word from the Kremlin. Figuring it was time for a drastic move, White took 'an awful chance' and told Averell Harriman, ambassador in Moscow, to inform the Kremlin that the British had agreed to the statement's publication (they had – but they hadn't yet told the Americans) in the hope that this would push foreign commissar Vyacheslav Molotov into accepting.[68]

Only at the very last minute, with Morgenthau already in the midst of his testimony, did word finally come down from Moscow. The Russians had some objections, Molotov said, but they would 'instruct their experts to associate themselves with Mr Morgenthau's project'.

The conference was on. However, this last-minute ordeal was a sign of things to come. If most of the strain during the preparations for the conference had been between the British and Americans, in the coming months the Russians would add a whole new level of stress. It begged the question: given theirs was a closed economy, functioning on such different lines from the rest of the Western world, why try to move heaven and earth to keep them involved?

For the answer, one must first consider the case of Harry Dexter White.

CHAPTER SEVEN

The Wrong Harry White

One day in the winter of 1944, a large black car with diplomatic plates rolled up outside a small bungalow in north-east Washington DC. The uniformed driver walked up to the door with a heavy package, on which was written: 'Handle carefully. For the Honorable Harry D. White'.

Having accepted the delivery, the man of the house prised open the case with equal measures of curiosity and weariness. Inside were four bottles of liquor, five boxes of Russian cigarettes and a crested, engraved card, which read: 'The Government Purchasing Commission of the Soviet Union in the USA extends season's greetings ...'

'Again!' he exclaimed to his wife.

This was not the first such package to arrive at the house. Over the past four years there had been an almost unremitting stream of gifts and cards from embassies, from the Democratic Party and even from the White House: clearly none of them actually meant for Harry DeNeal White, carpenter and resident of the Washington area. The intended recipient, he realised, was someone who was appearing in the papers with increasing regularity: another Harry D. White, who worked at the Treasury.

But this latest gift was the final straw. Something wasn't quite right about the big black sedan and the chauffeur. Come to think of it, why was one of the leading architects of international capitalism receiving fawning Christmas presents from Communists?

So the wrong Harry White finally picked up the telephone, called the Treasury and asked for his namesake. He read out the message on the card and asked to what address he should forward the parcel. A rasping, staccato voice came on the other end of the line.

Keep half the whiskey and cigarettes, said Harry Dexter White. Send the rest on to me.[1]

Six months before, in the early summer of 1944, White had found himself at the very limits of his capacity. The demands of work were overwhelming: he was liaising with countries from around the world; he was frantically checking through the small print of his plan for Bretton Woods; he was doing everything possible to ensure the conference would go without a hitch. He was also, the Federal Bureau of Investigation would later conclude, passing state secrets to the Soviet Union.

'The strange case of Harry Dexter White', as *Time* magazine called it in a double-barrelled attack on the economist some years later, remains one of the most intriguing, and hotly debated, elements of the Bretton Woods story. It also remains something of a conundrum.

By the time of the conference, the FBI had received at least one – possibly two – separate testimonies that White was involved in an underground Communist ring. It was beginning work on an investigation. What it didn't yet know was that the network's ringmaster was present at the Bretton Woods conference, along with White and a number of his alleged co-conspirators. Nor did it know that White was in direct contact with an alleged agent from NKVD – the predecessor to the KGB – at the Mount Washington Hotel itself during the summit.

The bare bones of the conspiracy were laid out in a top-secret dossier sent by J. Edgar Hoover, the chief of the FBI, to the White House the following year. 'As a result of the bureau's investigative operations,' the report read, 'information has been obtained that a number of persons employed by the Government of the US have been furnishing data and information to persons outside the Federal Government who are in turn transmitting this information to agents of the Soviet government.'[2]

The ringmaster was an economist named Greg Silvermaster. A slight, dark-haired man with a moustache and the trace of a British accent, Silvermaster had spent a peripatetic childhood: born in the Ukraine, educated in British schools in China, he arrived in the United States in 1914. By the early 1930s he had completed a Ph.D. in economics, with a dissertation entitled 'Lenin's Economic Thought Prior to the October Revolution'. He had floated around government for some years, and by the time of the Second World War he was working as an economist in the Agriculture Department and the Board of Economic Warfare. Or at least that was his day job.

At night, working out of the basement of his house in Washington and assisted by his wife Helen, Silvermaster would photograph batches of confidential administration files gleaned from his sources. Then, the FBI dossier continued, he 'turned the exposed but undeveloped film over to a contact ... In the past, it is reported, the contact man made trips to Washington, DC once every two weeks, and would pick up on each occasion an average of 40 rolls of 35mm film.'[3]

A year after Bretton Woods, a defector from the Silvermaster group, Elizabeth Bentley, said that White had been a member of the ring – though she admitted she had never met him. White denied everything. Yes, he had been friends with Silvermaster for ten years or so, but 'If I thought he was a Communist I would not have associated with him,' he later said, adding: 'I think that Mr Silvermaster is a very charming fellow, a good singer.' He had been down to Silvermaster's basement, he admitted, but only to play ping-pong.[4]

But the accusation from Bentley, lover of and courier for her Soviet control, Jacob Golos, had rung a bell in the Bureau: this was not the first time White had been accused of being a spy.

Back in 1942 White had been interviewed by the House of Representatives Un-American Activities Committee amid suspicions that he had been a member of the Washington Committee for Democratic Action – an alleged Communist front organisation. During a tense interview conducted under oath, he 'denied membership of any organization which he had reason to believe might be dominated by the Communist Party or the policies of which were dictated by any foreign government. The great part of the interview,' the FBI file added, 'was the denunciation on the part of White of this type of investigation.' It transpired that his name was not on the group's register; however, his wife's was.[5]

In the spring of 1944, during the final few months before Bretton Woods, the wife of a War Production Board economist named Victor Perlo had written to the FBI accusing her husband and twenty-five others of engaging in espionage. She also forwarded the same accusations to the White House, under a pseudonym. White's name was on the list.[6]*

And then there was Whittaker Chambers. The journalist, writer and self-professed Communist spy had turned up on Assistant Secretary of State Adolph Berle's doorstep on 2 September 1939 with a confession: he had acted as courier for another, earlier spy ring in the 1930s. White, he would later tell the FBI, had been one of its key members.

The problem was that none of these witnesses was particularly

---

*Another identification was made many years later. Soviet agent Vitaliy Pavlov wrote a piece in a Russian intelligence periodical recounting a lunch with White in 1941, shortly before the Pearl Harbor attack, in which he urged White and the administration to take a strong line against Japan.

reliable. Bentley's story contained inconsistencies – what was more, she had a nasty habit of accusing people who were patently innocent. Perlo, meanwhile, had an agenda: she was furious at her husband for divorcing her. And Chambers' story evolved and became ever more elaborate in the telling. Nonetheless, they do provide a picture of White which, if one believes them, casts new light on his work throughout the 1930s and 1940s.

White, said Chambers, was 'not a party member, but a fellow traveller' (in other words a Communist sympathiser): 'He was perfectly willing to meet me secretly; I sometimes had the impression that he enjoyed secrecy for its own sake … He talked endlessly about the "Secretary" [Morgenthau] whose moods were a fair barometer of White's. If White's spirits were up, I knew that the Secretary was smiling. If he was depressed, I knew that the Secretary had had a bad day.'[7] And later:

> I see him sauntering down Connecticut Avenue at night, a slight, furtive figure. I am loitering at the Ordway Theater, where he has insisted (probably out of laziness) that I meet him for the third time in a row. Yet he is nervous at the contact, and idles along, constantly peeping behind him, too conspicuously watchful. He has a book under his arm. His wife has just written a book of Bible stories retold for children, for their two daughters, in fact. She wants Carl [one of Chambers' self-assumed pseudonyms], whose reputation for literacy has reached her, to have a copy. In a dark shady side street beyond Connecticut Avenue, White slips the book under my arm. I still have it.[8]

It was only when Bentley named White, and a cast of other characters including his Harvard classmate Lauch Currie, his colleague Harold Glasser and his assistant on Soviet matters, William Ullman, that Chambers' testimony was suddenly taken seriously. Chambers not only had White's name, he also had two specific pieces of evidence. First, the fact that White had accepted an expensive rug as a thank-you gift. Second, and more compelling, a document Chambers produced some years later on which White had scribbled some notes, detailing various meetings over the course of just over a month – including figures on trade with the Far East and on the Japanese banking system, and details of a Hungarian debt settlement and a diplomatic mission to London. The document, which included some confidential, if hardly top-secret, nuggets, was apparently of the kind White would pass to the Soviets.

All of this detail was compelling – enough in the eyes of some to convict White straight away. In fact the FBI said in a later, revised dossier that it had received evidence from 'a total of thirty sources, the reliability of which had previously been established'.[9] But it was not until the mid-1990s that the most convincing evidence finally arrived in the public domain, with the declassification of five thousand of the Venona files. Venona was a long-running cryptographic project aimed at breaking the code employed in cables sent by the Soviet intelligence agencies throughout the war. Though the cables are often garbled and incomprehensible, they provide further evidence of the existence of an extensive spy network within the administration during this period.

Of the fourteen people identified by Bentley as agents, eleven featured under codenames in the Venona cables. Silvermaster was ROBERT, Bentley was UMNITSA (meaning 'clever girl') and Harry Dexter White was RICHARD or JURIST. According to the cables, White was both a source of information from Silvermaster's network, and, in 1944 and 1945, had face-to-face meetings with NKVD officials. Indeed, the cables seem to confirm that in the prelude to Bretton Woods the Soviet authorities arranged for him to meet directly with its agents, one of whom was codenamed KOL'TSOV.

One cable from the NKVD station in New York back to Moscow, dated 4–5 August 1944, is particularly intriguing:

As regards the techniques of further work with us Jurist [White] said that his wife was ready for any self-sacrifice; he himself did not think about his personal security, but a compromise would lead to a political scandal and the discredit of all supporters of the new course [presumably Roosevelt's New Deal], therefore he would have to be very cautious … Jurist has no suitable apartment for a permanent meeting place; all his friends are family people. Meetings could be held at their houses in such a way that one meeting devolved on each every 4–5 months. He proposed infrequent conversations lasting up to half an hour while driving in his automobile.[10]

In another cable later that year, Silvermaster recounts a conversation in which White's wife Anne mentioned that Harry was considering leaving Washington for a private sector job; he suggested using NKVD funds to help pay for their daughter's education, thus enabling a useful contact to be kept in a senior administration role.

Quite what kind of information White passed to the Soviets remains unclear: the Venona files were primarily concerned with administrative matters rather than intelligence itself. However, it appears to have ranged from White's own territory – international economics and finance – to broader White House diplomatic positions and strategy. On one occasion, White encouraged the Soviets to push for better terms on an American loan he himself was helping the State Department to draw up.

Since the release of the Venona transcripts, further information from the NKVD archives has come to light, courtesy of former agent Alexander Vassiliev. It also confirms the identification of White – though it is more equivocal than it first appears. For instance, it points out that while Moscow did indeed wire over $2000 to help pay for White's daughter's education, the cash ended up with Silvermaster rather than White.

And this, in the end, is the problem in trying to draw any firm conclusions about the case against White – there are gaping lacunae and confounding inconsistencies. For instance, while the Venona transcripts imply that White's wife was an influential figure pushing him towards espionage, Bentley's testimony says explicitly that Anne Terry White 'was not a Communist and disliked his revolutionary activities'.[11] Some of the sources imply that White himself was a Communist – others that he was merely sympathetic to the cause.

Nor does an exhaustive reading of White's own papers – published and unpublished – make matters any plainer. It is clear, from reading his work, that he was politically of the left; clear, too, that he admired many of the characteristics of socialism as well as of capitalism. But there is nothing to suggest that he preferred the Socialist or Communist system over capitalism. Indeed, one document, 'Political Economic Int of Future', which some have construed as a paean to the Russian economy, is in fact a rather rambling exegesis on the differences and similarities between capitalism and socialism. It is not a statement of belief.*

True, White was less dismissive of Communism than Keynes –

---

*See in particular Benn Steil, *The Battle of Bretton Woods*, Princeton, 2013. The document in question is in Box 9/18 of White's papers at Princeton. However, both former IMF historian James Boughton and White biographer R. Bruce Craig have disputed Steil's interpretation, pointing out that the document does not change the existing intellectual picture of White. There are also significant questions over the specific line Steil uses to evidence White's affection for Communism. White concludes his lengthy comparison between capitalism and socialism by saying: 'What then is the cause of the opposition [between the two factions]? The answer would seem clear: it is basically opposition of capitalism to socialism. Those who believe sincerely in the superiority of capitalism over socialism fear Russia as the source of socialist ideology. Russia is the first instance of a socialist economy in action. (The small socialist community experiments have little in common with the Russian economy, interesting case studies though they are, they are too small to be active as a soc. economic system in action).' There then follows another page which adds the line: 'And it works'. However, since this final page is, unlike all the others, unnumbered, one must ask whether it should be construed as a sentence following directly on from the previous paragraph. It may well be a note. Nor is the punctuation entirely clear from White's handwriting. What Steil reads as an exclamation mark might well be a question mark, which significantly changes the tenor: 'And it works?' rather than 'And it works!'

who, having spent time examining the works of Marx, came away cold, writing to George Bernard Shaw that:

> My feelings about *Das Kapital* are the same as my feelings about the Koran. I know that it is historically important and I know that many people, not all of whom are idiots, find it a sort of Rock of Ages and containing inspiration. Yet when I look into it, it is to me inexplicable that it can have this effect. Its dreary, out-of-date, academic controversialising seems so extraordinarily unsuitable as material for the purpose. But then, as I have said, I feel just the same about the Koran. How could either of these books carry fire and sword round half the world? It beats me. Clearly there is some defect in my understanding ... whatever the sociological value of [Marx's *Das Kapital*], I am sure that its contemporary economic value (apart from occasional but inconstructive and discontinuous flashes of insight) is *nil*.[12]

As far as White was concerned, the two economic models could happily co-exist. His futile hope was that if they took the time to think about it, Americans might avoid the temptation to demonise Communism.

Whether you believe White was a spy depends largely on your definition of the word. What White did might be classified as a form of espionage. But as spies go, he was a pretty lousy one. He was reluctant to provide much in the way of detailed information. He seems to have frustrated almost all of his contacts, both American and Russian. He was frequently described as 'nervous', 'reluctant' and 'cowardly'.

One possibility was that White was merely carrying out his own, personal form of diplomacy – unaware that the Soviets were construing this as espionage. Indeed, while some of the sources state that White was fully aware of where his information was being sent, others imply that he was a 'blind' agent – terminology for

being used without his knowledge.[13] Julius Kobyakov, a former
KGB major general who had access to the service's internal files,
most of which have never been publicly released, wrote that

> There was no record that someone had pitched or otherwise
> recruited [White] and set the terms of his cooperation with the
> Soviet intelligence. There was nothing in the way of clandestine
> communications arrangements, etc. White for all practical pur-
> poses might be categorized as a sub-source, which not necessarily
> denigrates the quality and value of the information that was
> attributed to him.
>
> But to categorize an individual as an agent or a spy we need
> to prove that he 'wittingly' cooperated with the 'foreign intelli-
> gence service', and 'fulfilled the tasks', assigned to him. That's
> how the Soviet intelligence defines its agents, and, I believe, that
> American intelligence works along the same lines.[14]

White, Kobyakov concluded, simply didn't know that he was a
Soviet agent. It was a belief shared by Ray Mikesell, White's colleague at the Treasury, who wrote:

> White sought to conduct his own foreign policy independently
> of the State Department. He dealt directly with foreign officials
> in Washington, and members of the Monetary Research staff in
> American embassies in Allied countries, including myself,
> secretly reported directly to White without going through their
> embassies.
>
> White sometimes used the press to promote his policies that
> were in opposition to those of the State Department. On one
> occasion, while I was alone with him in his office, he dictated
> over the phone a long, top-secret State Department statement to
> a reporter ...
>
> Many people have asked me if White was a Communist. I am

convinced that he was not. White believed in free markets and capitalism and devoted his energies to planning for a post-war world with free and non-discriminatory trade and payments. He was, however, quite willing to deal with Communist officials to achieve his objectives.

White and his colleagues, Mikesell concluded, 'simply ran their own foreign ministry'.[15]

That may well be the case. But it would have been extraordinarily naïve of White not to realise the use to which his information might be put. He undoubtedly knew he was secretly providing confidential information to the Soviets that was regarded by Moscow as extremely useful – however he categorised it. In July 1944 Pavel Fitin, the head of NKVD intelligence and the recipient of the Venona cables, hinted that the Soviets were indeed relying on intelligence from White in their preparations for Bretton Woods, saying that the material from the United States 'could turn out to be very useful to the Instance [Stalin and Soviet leaders] and, particularly, for our delegation to the international currency-financial conference that is now taking place in the US'.[16] This apparent reference to the Bretton Woods conference is a sign that material from White and other Treasury sources would be used actively to strengthen the Soviet negotiating position.

While it may be questionable whether the evidence against White would be strong enough to stand up in a court of law,[17] two Senate investigations in the decades since his death have nonetheless concluded that he was indeed a 'Communist sympathizer', in the words of the first,[18] and guilty of 'complicity', in the words of the second.[19]

The most dangerous mistake one can make, however, when assessing White's motivations is to forget the context. It simply was not scandalous – in the way it became in the late 1940s and 1950s – to toy with Communism in the United States during this period.

Many of White's friends and colleagues, including his brother-in-law, were Communists. For the most part this was an intellectual, philosophical choice – not treason.

After all, Russia was an ally. The goriest details of what went on in the Soviet Union under Stalin had not yet come to light. And even though there was enough evidence of Russian brutalism to cause concerns in the West, this did not stop Churchill privately agreeing with Stalin to slice up eastern and southern Europe after the war.[20] Plenty of respected intellectuals who would later become prominent anti-Communists held similar views – indeed the renowned Canadian economist J.K. Galbraith would tell James Meade, while he was in Washington, that 'Russia should be permitted to absorb Poland, the Balkans and the whole of Eastern Europe in order to spread the benefits of Communism'.[21]

Throughout this period, the Roosevelt administration went to extreme lengths to try to normalise relations with the Russians. In 1933 Roosevelt officially recognised the Soviet Union, reversing Woodrow Wilson's decision to refuse recognition following the Bolshevik Revolution in 1917. It was Roosevelt's hope that the two nations might continue to move closer to each other in the following years – sentiments reinforced by occasional reports from Moscow that the country was easing off on hard-line socialism.

Even in 1946 the general opinion in Washington was that 'Stalin has been our best friend.'[22] In other words, there simply was not during this period the stigma attached to dealing with the Soviets that developed over the following years. And, if Mikesell is right, White simply viewed his interactions with the Russians as a means of carrying out broader American foreign policy – without having to go through the odious State Department.

Indeed, it was White's belief – as indeed it was the belief of many throughout the administration – that the priority for the United States, if it was to prevent another war, would be to maintain friendly relations with Russia. He wrote that 'when we speak of the possibility of war there are only two possible major opponents in the foreseeable future, one is the United States and the other is Russia. No major war is possible unless these two are on opposing sides. No major war is possible in the next couple of generations at least with these two countries at peace with each other.' England, he added, 'is not strong enough' to help balance the power.

> The major task that confronts American diplomacy – and the only task that has any real value in the major problems that confront us – is to devise means whereby continued peace and friendly relations can be assured between the United States and Russia. Everything else in the field of international diplomacy pales into insignificance beside this major task. It matters little what our political relationships with England become or what happens in the Balkans or the Far East if the problems between the United States and Russia can be solved.[23]

This paper, written just a short time after the war, best illustrates White's thesis of the future path of the world. It underlines why he took extreme measures to maintain good relations between the United States and Russia. The problem is that he overstepped the mark. It was part of his job to negotiate with Russians; it was acceptable to socialise and fraternise with them. However, it appears White provided at least some information that may have undermined the efforts of his fellow negotiators.

Having said that, there is no evidence that White's Soviet activities undermined the Bretton Woods agreement itself. A few redundant clauses in the final document are the sum total of the legacy of his efforts to integrate Russian demands (which were, anyway, supported by Morgenthau).

In the end, White behaved as he did not because he intended to destabilise capitalism and the United States. He did so because he intended to strengthen both and – most of all – to prevent another war. Achieving that would mean maintaining Russia as an ally, rather than allowing the relationship to degenerate into one of mutual mistrust.

In these pre-Yalta days, there were genuine hopes that, notwithstanding the philosophical and political gulf between them, America and Russia could exist happily side by side in the future. Bretton Woods, as far as White was concerned, was not merely about repairing the international monetary system, it was the first test of whether diplomacy with the Soviets could work. As the weeks drew on in the spring of 1944, he was about to find out how successful that would be.

CHAPTER EIGHT

Snakebite Party

June 1944

I have often had the ambition of doing work on a ship, but this is the first time it has really come off.

John Maynard Keynes[1]

We had breakfast, lunch, and dinner together, smelling oranges again after so many years and wondering at the sight of really white bread.

Wim Beyen[2]

The air raid sirens were still sounding in London on 16 June 1944 when Keynes and Lydia set off for America. The din had started in the early hours and went on for most of the day. 'Most odd,' Keynes wrote to his mother just before leaving Gordon Square.[3] Only later did they discover what had just happened: the first of the flying bombs had hit.

To the untrained eye, they looked like small planes, a blaze of fire spouting from the tail. So when the craft were first spotted swarming over the Channel and dropping suddenly from the sky, people assumed that they were witnessing Luftwaffe pilots meeting their fate at the hands of British anti-aircraft fire.

As night wore on and the first of the strange, buzzing planes exploded on the south and east of London, a more ominous reality sank in: this was Hitler's long-feared 'revenge weapon'. The weekend that Keynes set off for Bretton Woods marked the beginning of London's second Blitz. On Friday morning alone, seventy-three V1s fell on Greater London. The War Cabinet, which a few days earlier had been concentrating on his plans for the conference, was now hearing that fifty people had been killed and four hundred injured – though it was warned that 'later reports would probably show a larger number of casualties.'[4]

Whereas the raids on London four years earlier had at least been somewhat predictable (for one thing, they tended to come at night), the Doodlebugs were more arbitrary, their attacks more protracted. Looking out of the window as he left the capital, Wim Beyen, the Dutch delegate travelling with the British, remarked: 'We saw again the sight, so familiar from the days of the 1940 blitz, of the brave and imperturbable Londoners looking at the sky for signs of this new plague.'[5]

Beyen was one of a number of European delegates who met with the Britons in London before sharing the voyage over. The Foreign Office had given them the unlikely moniker of 'Snakebite party'. While his fellow passengers were primarily concerned with the forthcoming negotiations, Beyen had an additional worry: he had been in charge of the Bank for International Settlements when it transferred the Czech gold to the Reichsbank in 1939 – something Harry Dexter White had repeatedly denounced in the American press. Might he be walking into an ambush?

There was no question of delaying the journey. Though the summit itself wasn't due to begin for another fortnight, Harry White had scheduled a critical pre-drafting session in Atlantic City – and they could not afford to miss it. Even as things stood, they were running late. White and his colleagues would arrive at the Claridge Hotel on the Atlantic City waterfront that very weekend; Keynes and his travelling crew would not disembark in New

York until the following Friday. They had wanted to set off sooner but were delayed by 'regulations imposed by the highest military authorities'.[6] D-day had taken place just ten days earlier; Allied troops, including the first major American deployment in Europe, were now moving slowly inland from the Normandy coastline. Every day the newspapers carried reports of fierce battles between the invading troops and German forces.

Keynes was already a little perturbed about White's plans, which were growing 'curiouser and curiouser'. To judge from the length of the invitation list the British had received a few weeks ago, Bretton Woods was shaping up to be the 'most monstrous monkeyhouse assembled for years'. The influx of delegates from so many nations threatened to complicate the neat plans drawn up over the past few years by the British and Americans. Even more alarmingly, White was considering allowing journalists almost unfettered access to the proceedings. Nothing, Keynes exclaimed, would be confidential.[7]

Given how much ink the two countries had already spilled, Keynes had been assuming that the final conference would be a mere formality – little more than political theatre. The point of the Atlantic City pre-conference, he thought, was for the Britons and Americans (and a small selection of others) to tie up any loose ends. So he was disturbed when the American papers reported that Bretton Woods itself would last for several weeks. 'Unless this is a misprint for several days,' he wrote, 'it is not easy to see how the main monkey-house is going to occupy itself. It would seem probable that acute alcoholic poisoning would set in before the end.'[8] This was hardly hyperbole – after all, the previous year's negotiations in Washington had been so alcoholic that James Meade was eventually forced to forswear cocktails so as to avoid sliding into addiction.

In the event, there was no need to be concerned about the lack of gainful activity – even if the same could not be said for the levels of alcohol consumption.

The hours put in by the Treasury staffs on both sides of the Atlantic over the past year, not to mention the British mission to Washington the previous autumn and the countless cables and letters since, were starting to pay off: White had recently sent out a final draft of the Bretton Woods agreement. For many countries, it was the first time they had seen the details of the most important changes to the global economy in decades. This threatened to make the initial meetings at the conference itself rather awkward.

With Roosevelt facing re-election later that year, White had been set two tasks: first, to ensure a deal was sealed in time for the President's nomination at the Democratic Convention in late July; second, not to give the impression that Bretton Woods would be sewn up before anyone at the official meeting was allowed a word in edgeways.

Of course, the latter objective was more or less incompatible with the former. Trying to negotiate every clause and sub-clause of such a complex agreement with forty-four nations at the table would have been impossible given three years, let alone just under three weeks. But then again, Roosevelt was determined to avoid giving Congress the impression that this radical new plan was being foisted on them without their consultation or involvement. That, after all, had been Woodrow Wilson's mistake after the Versailles Treaty. And White realised that he risked a walk-out of any one of the other countries if they felt they had not been sufficiently involved.

His solution was to try to stitch up most of the economic essentials in advance at Atlantic City, dangling the more controversial issues (largely the question of quotas) in front of the nations as something to fight over at Bretton Woods itself. At least that way all involved would feel they were part of the negotiations – even if this was merely a token role in comparison with the favoured 'Big Four' – in particular the US, whose primacy few doubted. And at least this way the Americans and British could avoid having to air the majority of their grievances in public. Atlantic City gave them a relatively private opportunity to get at each other's throats ahead of the big event itself.

The draft the Americans had sent over was broadly familiar. The general terms of what would eventually become Bretton Woods were starting to emerge from the macro-economic fog.

The mechanisms of the International Monetary Fund were designed to kick in if ever countries found themselves again in a balance of payments crisis such as had happened in the 1930s, when countries in deficit were suddenly unable to borrow and exporting countries failed to find markets for their goods. Rather than leaving the market to its own devices – the laissez-faire strategy discredited in the Depression – the Fund would be able to step in and lend countries money, crucially in whichever currency they most needed. So as to avoid the threat of competitive devaluations, the Fund would also arbitrate whether a country could devalue its exchange rate.

This was a critical innovation. For both Keynes and White the main problem with the gold standard had been its rigidity. Countries' domestic monetary policies had been strapped so tightly to gold that they would routinely have to inflict recessions on their people purely because of the amount of gold in their vaults. Under their new vision, a country might depreciate its currency routinely, and without sparking a crisis of confidence, if it needed to gain a competitive boost and cheapen its exports.

A few weeks earlier, in May, Keynes had attempted to sell this element of the plan to a still-sceptical House of Lords. 'Was it not I, when many of to-day's iconoclasts were still worshippers of the Calf, who wrote that "Gold is a barbarous relic"?'[9] True, many of his original ideas had now been shed. 'And this, by me at least, is to be much regretted,' he said, adding that there was thereby one relief: 'As a result, however, there is no longer any need for a new-fangled international monetary unit. Your Lordships will remember how little any of us liked the names proposed – bancor, unitas, dolphin, bezant, daric and heaven knows what.'[10]

On the bright side, however, the United States had agreed to the so-called 'scarce currency clause' under which it would accept penalties if it allowed the world to run short of dollars. And only the American currency would be tied rigidly to gold, which in its case hardly seemed to matter, given that its gold reserves dwarfed those of any other country.

The quid pro quo was that governments would have the right to restrict the movement of capital from country to country – permanently. To a world which, before the war at least, had been used to the kind of unfettered globalisation so memorably described in those opening lines of *The Economic Consequences of the Peace*, this would take some getting used to. Travellers would be prevented from moving their cash from one country to another; banks would be regulated to prevent them doing likewise. As Keynes acknowledged to the House of Lords, 'What used to be a heresy is now endorsed as orthodox.'[11]

All of this had been agreed, in broad terms at least, by the British and the Americans – though the Americans reserved the right not to police their own capital flows quite so strictly. Even so, when the latest drafts had arrived in London, complete with small print, officials at the Treasury and Bank of England were aghast.

White's plan involved ceding an unprecedented amount of economic sovereignty to the International Monetary Fund. As they read through the draft agreement, the Chancellor, by now Sir John Anderson, and governor realised with horror that White seemed to be suggesting that the Fund would have the right to prevent countries from devaluing their exchange rates. Why should anyone else be allowed to determine the value of sterling? To sign away one's economic sovereignty in that way would be tantamount to treason!

The Bank's new governor, Lord Catto,* was particularly adamant.

---

*The press nicknamed the double act of the governor and Keynes 'Catto and Doggo'.

The sixty-five-year-old Scotsman, described by a colleague as 'one of the smallest men I have ever met', had just succeeded the great Montagu Norman. He was damned if his first act of international economic diplomacy was to be the surrender of the right to control his own currency.[12]

The disagreement brought into focus a real difference in attitude between Britain and the United States. To the Americans, Bretton Woods needed to look as similar as possible to the gold standard: politicians' hands should be tied to prevent them from inflating away their debts. It was essential to avoid the threat of the competitive devaluations that had wreaked such havoc in the 1930s. In addition, they wanted to rid the old system of its English accent.

While the Americans wanted to avoid repeating the 1930s, the British were more worried about the 1920s, their own lowest ebb. For Keynes and his colleagues, the abandonment of gold in 1931 had marked the beginning of the end of their Depression. For them, Bretton Woods should be about ensuring stable world trade – without the rigidity of the gold standard.

Another remaining bone of contention concerned just how the Fund would carry out its role as lender of last resort. Say, for instance, Britain needed to improve its balance of trade: given that it could only devalue sterling by a certain amount while remaining part of the system, it might need some external help from the Fund to tide it over. But, whereas White wanted to make sure such help would be conditional on the borrowing country carrying out certain reforms to return it to health – and wanted to impose 'deterrent charges' on anyone who used the Fund – Keynes disagreed. As far as he was concerned, the Fund should be regarded as a kind of economic health spa. There should be no stigma associated with going to it for help: all countries should be entitled – nay, encouraged – to do so at some point. For White, however, the Fund was Accident and Emergency – countries should only be wheeled in if close to complete economic collapse.

Again, there are prosaic explanations for the difference of opinion. Britain was one of the world's most indebted nations; the US had become the world's most powerful creditor nation. The UK was therefore far more likely to have recourse to the Fund than the US ever would.

To make matters worse, it looked suspiciously as if the Americans intended the headquarters of both the Fund and the Bank to be in Washington. This was unacceptable, said the Foreign Office: it was only fair that one or the other should be in Europe. Over the course of the following weeks, the ministry would pepper the Bretton Woods delegates with demands on this point. One telegram of 2 July read: 'the location of the Fund should be in London, or failing that, elsewhere in Europe, e.g. Amsterdam. Looked at from here, best course would seem to be that you should propose that Bank should be located in USA and Fund in London,' before adding: 'But you will be the best judge of tactics.'

But the real timebomb at the heart of the negotiations was the question of quotas – what level of resources each country should contribute to the Fund. Perhaps counterintuitively, given their straitened finances, most countries were desperate to contribute as much as possible. A larger quota meant more influence when the Fund took decisions in the future; though it is hard not to conclude that the battle over quotas was really just an episode of diplomatic one-upmanship. Russia wanted its quota to be in line with Britain's, China wanted to vie with Russia, India not to have a smaller quota than China. There were skirmishes all the way down the political food chain until one arrived at scraps involving minnows like Greece and Yugoslavia.

The fact was that for most countries, quotas were the only tangible element of the Bretton Woods agreement that they stood a chance of influencing – and the part of the agreement that would be most closely scrutinised by their foreign ministries back home. It was a question of pride. And although all other quotas would be rendered practically irrelevant by America's enormous slug of voting rights, it was to become the most incendiary issue of all – indeed, it remains so to this day.*

To add to the sense of chaos upon Keynes's departure, it soon transpired that even within the British delegation there was a considerable divergence of views on how to take on the Americans – in particular when it came to that controversial question of control over the sterling exchange rate.

Such disputes were dealt with ruthlessly. Cabinet Office economist Lionel Robbins, who was known to oppose any plans to fight the Americans, was excluded by the Treasury from a number of key pre-planning meetings before the ship weighed anchor. By the time he discovered the plot, the vessel had already set sail. He fumed in his diary: 'I greatly doubt the wisdom of reopening the issue at this stage; and if I had been asked for my opinion before setting out, I should have advised in this sense. I am not hopeful, and I am very sorry that the amendment is to be proposed. It is a consolation to know that it has not to be pushed *a l'outrance*' – to the very limits.[13]

It was not the first time Robbins and Keynes had disagreed. Ever since 1929, when William Beveridge plucked him from obscurity and made him the youngest professor at the London School of Economics, or for that matter in the country, Robbins had waged a series of intellectual battles with Keynes. For one thing, he wasn't an enormous fan of what would later be called Keynesianism: he disagreed that the right solution to the Depression was to increase public spending and impose tariffs. In the 1930s he had given Friedrich Hayek a platform at the LSE to lecture on Austrian economics, attempting to challenge Keynes's grip on the British economic establishment. And in the months before the Bretton

---

*At the time of writing, the Fund was in the process of pushing through a revision of its quota scheme, increasing China's share to reflect its growth in recent years. The negotiations took many, many years.

Woods conference he had tentatively wondered whether it might make more sense to allow currencies around the world to float rather than being fixed to one another. Such ideas would not become orthodoxy for another quarter of a century.

A tall, handsome man with a booming voice and, to the bemusement of his students, a tendency to leave disconcertingly long gaps between his sentences, Robbins was happy to play second fiddle to Keynes – in the Bretton Woods negotiations at least. The pair would make yet another odd couple of economics. Unlike Keynes, Robbins had fought in the Great War, being injured by a sniper's bullet. Whereas Keynes shone bright but could be abrasive, sometimes racist or anti-Semitic, Robbins was more subtle, more gentle and less tolerant of chauvinism, and in the late 1930s had tried to find academic positions for German Jewish economists outside Nazi Germany.

Back in Whitehall, some were worried that sending Keynes had been a mistake in the first place. He had hardly endeared himself to American politicians on previous visits. Wall Street treated him with suspicion. The US newspapers cast his Lordship (it was always 'Lord Keynes') as a beguiling genius who had fooled Roosevelt into following his policies and would no doubt dupe the Americans all over again at Bretton Woods.

Moreover, it had not gone unnoticed in the press that whereas some countries were sending their finance ministers and central bank chiefs, Britain had opted instead to send a group of unelected technicians. Strictly speaking, the most senior British official travelling to the US was neither Keynes nor Robbins but Sir Wilfred Eady, a joint second secretary at the Treasury – one rung down from the top of the bureaucracy. Despite Eady's seniority (or perhaps because of it) Keynes had little patience for the lifetime civil servant. 'If I had taken you very young and had had limitless patience,' Keynes once said to him, 'I might have taught you the elements of economics. As it is, I must assume you understand your own art of administration.'[14] Keynes had taken Robbins aside when he learned of Eady's inclusion in the delegation and exclaimed: 'Lionel, I can scarcely bear it.'[15]

Among the other members of the British delegation was Dennis Robertson, the quiet but brilliant economist who had fallen out with Keynes after helping him create the General Theory. Alongside Robertson were Foreign Office official Nigel Ronald, bespectacled Bank of England official George Bolton (who would later represent Britain at the IMF) and legal adviser and rising Foreign Office star Eric Beckett, who would put in longer hours at the conference than anyone else. As is still the case at international conferences today, it was the lawyers who worked the hardest.

The British delegation had sailed rather than flying in part because of Keynes's health, but also to give them an opportunity to thrash out a comprehensive plan to submit to the Americans. Now the pressure was on. They had less than a week to prepare their final response to those disturbing American plans. And that was before one considered the World Bank. The British delegation had hardly begun to contemplate a detailed position on that; they would have to come up with one more or less from scratch.

They did at least have strength in numbers. So many of Europe's displaced governments had decamped to London during the war that they brought with them a motley crew of economists and financiers from around the Allied world. There was René Boël, an occasionally abrasive Belgian aristocrat and industrialist who was advising his country's exiled government. Beyen the Dutchman came highly recommended, notwithstanding his involvement in the Czech gold scandal, but turned out to be rather mischievous. He seemed intent on winding up Boël by disagreeing with almost everything he said. There was the suave governor of Greece's central bank, Kyriakos Varvaressos: an amusing companion, though you couldn't trust him any further than you could throw his six-foot-plus frame – White, for one, considered him 'nothing but a British stooge'.[16] Keynes had a soft spot for Varvaressos, though he also knew from having worked on Britain's wartime loans to Athens that the country had a rather 'relaxed' attitude towards economic discipline. Meanwhile, the head of the Indian delegation was in fact an Englishman: Sir Jeremy Raisman – the finance minister of what was, for the time being, a British colony. And alongside them were delegates from China, Czechoslovakia, Norway, Poland and one man, Lauren Casaday, from the US Embassy in London. Such was the international assortment that boarded the *Queen Mary* to set sail for New York as the air raid sirens blared in London.

For most of the passengers on the 3608-mile Atlantic crossing, the voyage was memorable not for the economic mission on board, but for something far more exciting: the *Queen Mary* carried with her the first batch of German prisoners of war captured in the Normandy landings. The prisoners, who were kept below deck behind barbed-wire barricades, made up more than half of the five thousand passengers. Throughout the crossing, the economists' discussions would be interrupted by threatening orders barked in German over the loudspeakers at the prisoners on board.[17]

Brainwashed by Goebbels' propaganda, the Germans feared for their lives even after their capture. In fact, once in the United States they were surprisingly well treated. At Christmas that year, Eddie Bernstein of the US Treasury even lifted the blocks on financial transfers from Germany to help Hitler to provide a gift of $25 to each of the PoWs.[18]

The 'Grey Ghost', as the ship had been nicknamed following the drab paintjob she had received when converted into a troop carrier earlier in the war, also brought with her 920 military personnel. Hitler had supposedly offered a reward of $250,000 and the Iron Cross to the U-boat that sank the *Queen Mary*, but thanks to her top speed of 28.5 knots and the zigzag routes she plied, she had evaded attack thus far.[19]

On board, the delegates encountered small pleasures the like of which they had rarely seen since the beginning of rationing: oranges, white bread, cheap tobacco – though these would be nothing in comparison with what they were to find in America. They strolled on deck during the hot days, leaning back on anti-aircraft guns in the roasting sun.

In his spare time Keynes read Hayek's newly published book *The Road to Serfdom*, later telling his rival that 'it is a grand book ... You will not expect me to accept quite all the economic dicta in it. But morally and philosophically I find myself in agreement with virtually the whole of it; and not only in agreement with it, but in a deeply moved agreement.'[20] The fact that Keynes could find so much to concur with in what is widely regarded as an anti-Keynesian book might well come as a surprise. Then again, Hayek supported one of Keynes's more controversial proposals: that the war could be paid for in part by a one-off wealth tax (a 'capital levy').

In their cabins on board ship, the delegates listened anxiously to the BBC for reports on how London was faring under the V1 bombardment. They ate and drank together and tried to avoid the boat safety drills each day. But, most of all, they worked.

Holed up in what had been the ship's library, now a bare room containing little more than tables and chairs, they met day after day to draft their proposals. On one day, Keynes found himself working for ten hours straight without a break. In a slightly frantic handwritten note, Bolton wrote: 'I don't think that I have ever worked harder but it is quite impossible to know whether I have had any success.' Keynes wrote to Sir Richard Hopkins of the Treasury: 'I have often had the ambition of doing work on a ship, but this is the first time it has really come off.'

However, it fast became apparent from their meetings that the negotiations over the following month would be far from simple. Suddenly the Britons were bombarded with a slew of unexpected demands from their Allies which threatened to complicate matters even further.

The Belgian, Boël, proved himself a 'pestilent nuisance', trying to insert complex clauses into the draft to discourage countries from using the Fund. Varvaressos took the stand to denounce any suggestion that Greece should have to repay her external debt after the war, betraying a conviction that the primary purpose of the World Bank would be to raise funds to rebuild his country.[21]

Beyen spent much of the voyage trying to provoke both Boël and Keynes. At the first meeting on Saturday night, Bolton complained in his diary, 'Beyen was frankly uninterested and facetious and made no helpful contribution to the discussion.'[22] If there was one thing Beyen was clear on, it was that there should be as small a management team as possible at the Fund, 'say, a General Manager and two managers,' Bolton reported. 'In Beyen's opinion it would be calamitous to have a redundant staff with nothing to do except intrigue and gossip.' Ironically Beyen would later become the Dutch representative on the staff of the IMF, and would help lay the foundations of the European Union and the European Commission, one of the largest bureaucracies in the world.

There was also a problem looming with the Indian delegation – to no one's surprise, the question of the enormous debts Britain owed to its Dominion territories kept cropping up. Raisman declared himself 'shocked and surprised' that Britain was continuing to block the Indians from converting the mountain of sterling they had amassed after lending and exporting so much to Britain during the war. The Cabinet could have laid the issue to rest the previous year had they taken up White's generous offer to subsume the sterling debts into the IMF. Instead they had rejected his suggestion and stubbornly decided to attempt to negotiate away the issue with their Dominions independently.

It meant that Britain would be left facing a debt crisis of enormous proportions after the war. Keynes and his colleagues were to spend the following weeks battling Indian attempts to raise the subject of their blocked sterling balances as part of the Bretton

Woods discussions. As they fought out the issue on board the *Queen Mary*, Eady warned Raisman that if the Indians tried to bring it up at the conference, 'the UK delegation will stonewall and refuse to discuss it'.

Sir Jeremy added that the Indians were furious about the prospect that China would be one of the big players both at Bretton Woods and in the founding of the United Nations, the Fund's political brother, which was also in its early preparatory stages. If India did not get a seat on the board, he added, the delegation would return home and refuse to sign. Although Keynes managed to fob off demands from the Chinese and Polish delegates for a larger quota by telling them that that would have to wait until Bretton Woods itself, it was clear that the delegates were steeling themselves for a battle. With chaos ensuing whenever the Allies met, the British delegation found that the only way to get enough work done was to meet privately in Keynes and Lydia's cabin, before holding broader meetings with the rest of the Allies.

Most of the first few days was spent hammering out a formal objection to Article IV of White's draft – the clause that the Fund would have the final say over the level of a country's currency. 'Particular anxiety is felt in the United Kingdom, and probably also in other countries, as to whether the ultimate independence of the domestic policy of a country from outside dictation is fully safeguarded,' read the British statement.[23] Keynes also queried White's 'idiocy' in using the phrase 'gold-convertible exchange' to describe countries' currencies. After all, that seemed to suggest that this really would be another gold standard. Far preferable was to call currencies 'convertible exchange' – as they could be exchanged for other currencies, if not for gold – though this, too, was hardly ideal.

The problem they were wrestling with was, ultimately, the essence of the Bretton Woods deal: there had to be something at the centre of the system, a unit to which other currencies could be anchored. After the nightmare of the 1930s, neither White nor

Keynes thought it should be gold (not for every country, anyway). It couldn't be a new international currency like bancor or Unitas – that idea had already bitten the dust – but it had to be universally acceptable, credible enough to be used as an effective means of purchase anywhere in the world. Right now there was only one currency that fitted that description: the dollar. However, Keynes was loath to establish an official dollar standard. So their suggestion remained the rather vague 'convertible exchange', and they tried to make progress on more tractable issues.

Gradually, as the ship zigzagged its way across the Atlantic, the travellers drew up a full set of proposals for the Americans. Meanwhile, almost single-handedly, Keynes was writing a detailed proposal for the shape of the World Bank.* Until now, the UK had devoted less attention to this secondary Bretton Woods institution. The Fund, after all, was the big deal – it would monitor how the new world economic order fitted together. But Keynes suddenly found himself possessed with a new-found enthusiasm for the Bank – to the extent that his colleagues started to wonder whether he had forgotten about the Fund entirely.

In part this was owing to the fact that the Fund only did half of the work his original Clearing Union plan would. The Keynes plan had been designed not merely to moderate future exchange rates and international trade balances: it had sought to help finance the reconstruction of Europe after the war. The Bank, Keynes remembered on board the *Queen Mary*, was the missing link that would at least partly help reconcile White's plan with his own proposals.

His main criticism remained the Bank's name: *it* should be called

---

*The embryonic Bank would go through a variety of names before its official birth. At this stage, Keynes was calling it the International Corporation for Reconstruction and Development. Other names in the offing included the International Guarantee and Investment Association and the International Financial Institution for Reconstruction and Development.

the Fund, he said, and the Fund a bank. After all, the Bank's main function was not to lend money itself but to help encourage private investors to invest their money in the war-torn and damaged countries most in need of development. He worked through the nights on a finely polished proposal to present to White and emerged with an elegantly written and persuasive document, which promptly disintegrated as soon as it was held up to closer scrutiny. The problem was that no one on board (Keynes included) was an expert on international finance: they were mostly economists and diplomats, perfectly comfortable negotiating trade deals but less at home with guarantees, bonds and cross-currency loans. At one stage Bolton wrote in his diary:

> No-one except myself knows much about foreign loans and general bonds, and God forbid that I should ever claim to be an expert on a subject like this. K. has already got twice out of his depth on guarantees and how they are made and the currency in which loans are denominated. Beyen sets himself out to pinprick and irritate K. and Eady amiably flaps his hands and expatiates on the moral virtues of this particular crusade. Beckett and I will try to hold the fort but even if we were capable of grasping and exposing all the points, we simply haven't enough time. I can expect no help from the Allies who, in general, have a vested interest in the Bank.*

Still, once Keynes had set himself on a certain course it was notoriously difficult to divert him, even if to do so would be in his best interests.

When the ship reached New York early on the Friday, most of the preparatory work had been done, and the team had produced

---

*Their vested interest being that they expected the Bank to provide much-needed assistance for them as they rebuilt their economies after the war. Bank of England Archives, OV38/8.

a twenty-five-page document of proposals – the 'Boat Draft', as it would come to be known. Manhattan was muggy and misty that morning, Robbins wrote. The skyscrapers emerged from the dawn haze, 'a kaleidoscope of solemn forms, softly changing like dumb music, as we slid through the oily water'.[24]

After the ship made landfall, the party was met by representatives from the British Embassy in Washington. 'Snakebite party arrived', the embassy cabled to the Foreign Office. Bolton scribbled a note to his colleagues back home. He asked after his family in London, and whether the 'secret weapon [was] causing undue anxiety'. And he inserted a note of caution: 'The Fund and the Bank are now hardly recognisable, but whether they are improved is another matter,' he wrote. 'Harry White is obviously going to have a shock.'[25]

CHAPTER NINE

Babel on Wheels

June 1944

What we're doing is whipping the draft into shape.

Harry Dexter White[1]

Atlantic City certainly has to be seen to be believed. Nothing that I have ever seen at home is a patch on it.

Lionel Robbins

Harry Dexter White had already been at Atlantic City for a week and a half. The seaside resort was even hotter and stickier than normal that year – not that he or his colleagues from the American delegation had had much chance to enjoy it.

On the first day of their stay White's fellow technicians had persuaded him to hold a meeting outside on the beach. White, who had not brought swimming trunks, was forced to borrow a pair from one of his junior colleagues. The notion of the bespectacled economist discussing the future of foreign exchange dressed only in a bathing suit caused howls of laughter in Morgenthau's office when the anecdote was later relayed to the Treasury Secretary.[2]

No sooner had White and his technicians arrived in the New Jersey resort than the press started snooping around. The Atlantic City conference was intended to be a secret, but the sudden appearance on the boardwalk of a multitude of awkward-looking economists dressed in suits instantly set alarm bells ringing. 'Has the Bretton Woods Conference Begun?' asked the headline in one newspaper, which speculated that 'For all we can tell, the major decisions may already have been made there … If the Bretton Woods meeting is to be as open as the country has been led to expect, it has got off to a bad start at Atlantic City.'[3] The beachside meetings were cancelled; the rest of the conference took place behind closed doors.

The fact that most of the foreign delegations had been delayed due to the D-Day security lockdown was a stroke of luck; there was plenty to be done on the home front before the circus arrived in town. After all, it was the Americans who had the largest delegation – more than forty-strong before you counted secretaries and assistants. Merely corralling them into a manageable unit would be difficult enough, let alone preventing the more meddlesome ones from tampering with White's well-laid plans.

White's solution was simple: make sure none of the other big fish would actually be present in Atlantic City, so that the real work of the final detailed drafting for Bretton Woods could be done unimpeded. In addition, he ensured that even those in the American delegation knew as little as possible about what was going on.

That wasn't a problem for the Treasury Secretary himself: Morgenthau was usually happy to defer to White when it came to the arduous task of preparing the Bretton Woods agreements. He would spend the two weeks in Washington instead, plotting the forthcoming Presidential election with Roosevelt. Fred Vinson, Morgenthau's second-in-command, was more of a threat: regarded as Morgenthau's natural successor, he was more curious about the details of the negotiations. To White's relief, though, Vinson – a former semi-professional baseball player who had a habit of chewing tobacco through meetings – showed no inclination of heading to Atlantic City.[4]

The thorn in White's side, as ever, was the State Department, which insisted on interfering with the draft plans, negotiating independently with other countries and, most irritatingly of all, constantly demanding updates from the Treasury. White had successfully kept Dean Acheson, the Assistant Secretary of State, away from Atlantic City – though Acheson sent a spy along, in the form of junior official John Parke Young.

Even after neutralising his own countrymen, White would still be faced with the challenge of his biggest nemesis – the one currently en route from London. But Keynes could wait until later: White had a plan for him too. In the meantime he holed himself up in the Claridge Hotel, the twenty-four-storey 'Skyscraper By The Sea', insulated both from the big beasts of Washington and the heat and bustle of the boardwalk, and set to work.

Beside White, as ever, was his redoubtable deputy Edward Bernstein. Along with White and Keynes, Bernstein would be the central character in the drafting of the Bretton Woods proposals. If anyone doubted Bernstein's intellectual brilliance, it was not the man himself. Not only had this self-declared economic genius diagnosed the problems of the gold standard as a twelve-year-old, he had also, at around the same time, read Adam Smith's pioneering masterpiece *The Wealth of Nations* and found that although it was indeed a great book, there were a number of glaring errors ('After all, Adam Smith wasn't perfect, he was just exceptional!').

Bernstein would claim in later years that the majority of what the Treasury Secretary called his plan and what everyone else called the 'White plan' should really have been dubbed the 'Bernstein plan'.[5] And to some extent he had a point: with White in the chairman's seat for most of Bretton Woods itself, it would be left to Bernstein to take on the British and others in the committees and debates.

The first few days at Atlantic City were arduous: fourteen-hour days of dense, interminable drafting sessions. Countless 'i's were dotted and 't's crossed in the original drafts for both the Fund and the Bank. However, the complexity of the plans was not without purpose. International monetary systems such as the gold standard might very easily fall apart if the articles were so straightforward that one side was instantly able to declare them invalid, or insist that they had been breached. The more specific a rule, the more rigid would be the system and the more obvious when a country was falling foul of it. The lesson of history was that Bretton Woods would only survive if its rules (whether on exchange rates, capital movements or terms of aid) were vague enough to accommodate a range of potential crises in the future. This vagueness manifested itself in the draft articles, smeared by the Americans with reams of deathly complex legal terminology.

Keynes nicknamed this legal jargon Cherokee, and would spend the next month moaning that it should be excised. He seemed not to have realised that the complexity was there not simply because of the Americans' obsession with legal terminology, but in an intentional effort to be vague. 'We didn't take the Cherokee out,' Bernstein would later declare proudly. 'It stayed in Cherokee.'[6]

And, mind-numbing though the work was at times, for White it also served as a team-building exercise. By the time the conference itself started in July, the opportunities for the American secretariat to consult with each other would be scarce. Unless drilled in precisely what they (or rather, he) wanted out of Bretton Woods, they risked being challenged by their foreign counterparts. From the Thursday of their arrival until the foreigners came to town, the US team were subtly indoctrinated. Everyone was split into groups representing the key themes relating to the Fund ('Purposes, Policies and Subscriptions'; 'Operations of the Fund'; 'Organisation and Management'; 'Establishment of the Fund'). Complain though they did, no one except White, Bernstein and a few other close advisers was allowed to see a complete draft.

Everyone was, however, encouraged to speak freely, even to challenge White if need be. And the documents that remain from Atlantic City (White asked that no full minutes be kept) show his subordinates did indeed disagree with him.

Some of the foreign delegations arrived the following Monday afternoon, but White insisted that full discussions with other countries should begin only after the British arrived, which was not until the weekend. He was well aware of the potential for chaos if others were to be involved in what were supposed, for the time being, to be consensual technical sessions.

So, by the time the British were picked up from the station the following Friday, 23 June, the Americans had already put the finishing touches on the detailed draft of articles creating the Fund. Save for some extra details and embellishments, the document they produced was still recognisably the same plan that had been sent to London and elsewhere earlier that month. Keynes was about to disrupt these well-laid plans.

In the meantime, however, there was a more pressing domestic issue to deal with. Morgenthau was starting to pry. White had not communicated with his boss for the past week – the ostensible excuse being that it was well below the Treasury Secretary's pay grade to occupy himself with a mere legalistic drafting session. But the day before the British arrived, Morgenthau had called up, joking pointedly that he did not 'know what's going on other than I hear when you're short of bath towels or something like that ...'

The rather awkward exchange that followed was captured by Morgenthau's tape recorder. White protested that he had not made any major decisions, saying that they had been 'whipping the draft into shape'.

'Yeah, but look; Harry, you're leaving me completely high and dry, and all the rest of the American delegates, and then you expect us to come up there and sign on the dotted line, and it won't work. It just won't ...'

'Well, I was going to suggest that …'

'I mean it just won't work. It's very nice, I mean, I know you are working your head off, but …' White tried to interject but Morgenthau, by now clearly agitated, was getting into his swing: 'You're leaving all the rest of us completely high and dry.'

White reluctantly suggested that perhaps some of the other American delegates could come up to Atlantic City – or, less reluctantly, perhaps he could explain the US position to them at Bretton Woods itself, before the negotiations got under way.

'Yeah, but supposing I don't like at all what's been agreed to,' said Morgenthau, 'the point is, if you'd sent me the stuff and kept me posted as you went along, I would know … If I don't read it, it's my own fault, but if I don't have anything from you, then it's your fault.'[7]

By the end of the telephone call White had managed to placate Morgenthau, as he usually could. But it was a significant warning. Until then, he had been able to draft most of the key agreements and articles on his own. Now it was clear, with the big conference itself only a week away, that his colleagues would be breathing down his neck for the foreseeable future.

On Friday evening, even as the secretariat was tapping out White's proposed draft, Keynes brandished the British 'Boat Draft' in front of him.

As Bolton had predicted, White was in for a shock. He cast his eye over the document as he ate dinner with Keynes. The amendments were extensive. One of the secretaries, Alice Bourneuf, reported: 'The British suggestions are extremely complicated. They redefine most of the terms and revise so many of the provisions that it will take long and careful study to figure out what their suggestions amount to.'[8]

This time, White immediately sent Morgenthau a note about the British draft and its 'several troublesome differences'[9] with the

American position. Some of the suggestions could be dismissed immediately – for instance the British proposal that governments should retain flexibility to alter their own exchange rates. 'We think we should not budge one bit,' White wrote. He was similarly sceptical about the proposals to soften the conditions on borrowing from the Fund, adding: 'it looks as though the American delegation will be in for a nasty fight on this matter at the conference.'

More promising was the fact that Keynes had apparently become fixated on the Bank. Until then, most of their discussions and arguments had centred on the Fund – hardly surprising given that it would be the central institution in the redesigned world economy. The Bank had always felt like something of an afterthought – and, reflecting this, the original American drafts on it had become increasingly vague. White had privately assumed that there was no way they would be able to set up both institutions in the limited time allotted them at Bretton Woods the following month.[10] Now, however, out of nowhere, Keynes had revised the draft proposals in trademark flamboyant style. The following afternoon in White's office, he expounded on his vision for the Bank at length. By Robbins' account it was a virtuoso performance:

> Keynes was in his most lucid and persuasive mood; and the effect was irresistible. At such moments, I often find myself thinking that Keynes must be one of the most remarkable men that have ever lived – the quick logic, the birdlike swoop of intuition, the vivid, wide vision, above all the incomparable sense of the fitness of words; all combine to make something several degrees beyond the limit of ordinary human achievement ... The Americans sat entranced as the God-like visitor sang and the golden light played around.[11]

Bolton's account was more prosaic: 'The Americans were all extremely friendly but, on the whole, rather reticent.'[12]

In fact, when it came to the Bank at least, the 'Boat Draft' had more or less coincided with White's own vision. The only real difference was that the British didn't want to have to pay in all their required capital immediately. In theory, that meant the richer countries (specifically the US) would have to absorb any losses the Bank made on its early investments. But then, as one American official said, that was fine: 'There wouldn't be any loss to the investors.'[13]

Keynes, for his part, had decided that the Bank could well be the vehicle used to help reconstruct Europe, without most of the cost falling on the British.* On the *Queen Mary*, Bolton had written: 'It is becoming more and more clear that K. is losing interest in the Fund and is becoming violently enthusiastic regarding the building up of the Bank. It is difficult to visualise what effect this will have on our discussions at Atlantic City and Bretton Woods.'[14]

One effect was to give White carte blanche for his cunning scheme to divert Keynes's attentions during Bretton Woods itself: he had decided to nominate him as chairman of Commission II, charged with deciding the structure of the Bank rather than the Fund (he himself would chair the more important Commission I). But to the surprise of Keynes's colleagues, his proposals seemed to go down extraordinarily well with White – partly, perhaps, because he didn't care as much for the Bank. Either way, the Boat Draft would shape discussion on the Bank for the following weeks, and turn it from a half-considered scheme into a fully fledged institution within the space of a month.

The Fund was another matter entirely. In the following days the British and Americans fought fiercely over the differences highlighted in Keynes's Boat Draft. According to Bolton, White 'in a

---

*The Bank later became associated more with development and with supporting low-income countries regardless of their involvement in the Second World War: this was one of the ways the Americans secured agreement from their Latin American neighbours for the broader Bretton Woods package.

raging heat has bluntly refused to accept any change whatsoever in the exchange and convertibility clauses in which the question of sovereignty arises [in other words, precisely the aspect the UK Treasury and Bank of England were most adamant about]. As expected, he says that the political position makes it impossible for him to retreat any further.' Not for the first or the last time, Keynes threatened to walk out – but soon relented.

He and the rest of the delegates were not helped by a punishing schedule. There was a mind-boggling amount of ground to cover before they left for the conference the following Friday. Each day they churned out 'unbelievable' quantities of paper. After one day of non-stop negotiations, Keynes said his 'system gave ominous signs of conking out'.[15] However, he was at least spared the worst of the New Jersey heat wave thanks to the North Atlantic breeze that came through his and Lydia's tenth-floor window.

The Claridge Hotel, a brickwork beast completed just in time for the complete collapse in demand during the Great Depression, was packed – and not merely with holidaymakers. It so happened that the economists were sharing the hotel with the annual convention of the Homeopathic Institute. The two groups would find themselves mingling awkwardly at certain points in the day. Each morning as the economists took their breakfast, waiters would approach them and joke: 'Are you homeopath or are you monetary?'[16]

Overworked as they were, and still exhausted from the combination of travel and hard graft on the *Queen Mary*, most of the British delegation were allowed Sunday off, and spent the day walking in a daze through the unlikely surroundings of Atlantic City. It was an intoxicating experience. The Europeans, used to a dowdy, ersatz existence of rationing and making-do, had barely recovered from the sight and smell of orange peel on board the *Queen Mary*. Now, in this holiday resort, they encountered a world more gaudy and plentiful than had even existed in Britain before the war. The boardwalk teemed with scantily clad vacationers. There

were hot-dog stands and enormous hoardings advertising Schlitz
beer and Original Sea Taffy; there were fairground rides and stalls.
It was a sensory overload, fine for streetwise Americans but hardly
natural territory for an earnest British economist. Indeed, on a visit
to the Heinz pier one day, Dennis Robertson was on the verge of
swallowing a small plastic gherkin which visitors were given to pin
on their coat lapel, when a colleague spotted him and yanked it
from his mouth just in time.

Atlantic City was by now well into holiday season. All along the
boardwalk, up and down from the Claridge, the beach was packed
with vacationers, whose main worries were of a different variety
from those of the delegates who had recently arrived from war-torn
parts of the world. There were two main talking points at Atlantic
City that summer: who was up and who was down in the latest
yacht race to Absecon Island Yacht Club; and the rash of candid
camera snappers who had converged on the beach to catch youngsters in their swimwear now that the wartime ban on photography
had been lifted. The war came a distant third; the world's monetary
future barely even registered.[17]

The British delegates could be excused for seeming a touch dazed.
With a week to go until the conference itself, they were already
facing a monumental challenge: on the one hand, White and the
Americans were trying to draft them into economic obscurity; on
the other, the Dominion governments were making the reasonable
point that Britain should not use Bretton Woods to free itself of its
wartime debts.

By now it was clear from the economic runes that Britain's days
as an economic superpower were numbered. The Americans had by
far the world's largest economy and there was little doubt that
Bretton Woods would systematically formalise this. Meanwhile,
though the previous year the Cabinet had turned down White's
generous offer to deal with the debts in the process of setting up

Bretton Woods, the colonial powers were determined not to allow the UK to default on the billions of pounds of loans it had been granted during the war. It was an economic pincer movement that would almost certainly leave Britain a far diminished power once the conflict was over. But Keynes was aware that he had at the very least an opportunity to do something to mitigate the decline. For Britain, Bretton Woods would become a form of disaster management rather than economic opportunism.

A useful foil to distract the Indians and Australians from their gripes was the issue of quotas. Although the subject of a country's share of votes on the Fund and Bank boards remained strictly off-limits at Atlantic City, it was about the only matter the foreign delegates talked about behind the scenes. The Australian delegate, Sir Leslie Melville, was particularly furious, according to Bolton. 'What will happen when the 44 nations are let loose to argue about the relative quotas is anyone's guess,' he wrote. 'I would not be at all surprised to see an all-in wrestling match.'

The other issue that would remain undiscussed until Bretton Woods itself was the question of where the Fund and Bank would be located. It was already clear that the Americans were assuming both institutions would be in Washington. White's problem, he would tell the British informally, was that if anything else were to be the case, there was next to no chance that Congress would ratify the Bretton Woods agreement.

Pleading national politics was to become a constant of the negotiations. Agree as they might in private, the officials encountered all sorts of immovable red lines imposed by politicians back home. As Robbins put it, the attitude was that 'We may have to treat each other rough in public – just as men with temperamental wives may have to cut their friends if they encounter one another in mixed society. But here, over a meal, all that is forgotten. Indeed, we are more friends than ever now that you've admitted you, too, are unhappily married.'[18]

While the junior officials liked to blame the politicians for any impasse, Keynes preferred to blame the lawyers – especially when it came to the Americans' incomprehensible resistance to his controversial exchange rate proposals. 'White and Bernstein have been brought over to our point of view,' he wrote to 'Hoppy' Hopkins (rather optimistically, since they were as far from each other's views as they had been for months), 'but they are having the usual trouble which always occurs in this country and is one of the causes of preventing anything sensible being done; that is that they have to consult their lawyers, who are proving difficult. In this lawyer-ridden country even more than elsewhere lawyers seem to be paid to discover ways of making it impossible to do what may prove sensible in future circumstances.'[19]

And while Keynes was thus venting his frustration, White was taking his out on his State Department rivals. Acheson's spy, John Parke Young, kept asking for detailed minutes of the negotiations. At one point, having been cornered by Young, White told him he'd tell his secretary to release the notes of the meetings to him. But when Young later went to collect them, the secretary said: 'Well, he said not to give them to you ... He said that I couldn't give them to you or to anybody.' When told later about this rather odd encounter, Young said that Acheson 'just laughed ... He knew Harry White.'[20]

Acheson did indeed know White: they had clashed plenty of times before. He would later write in his memoirs: 'I have often been so outraged by Harry White's capacity for rudeness in discussion that the charges made against him [of being a Communist spy] would have seemed mild compared to expressions I have used.'[21]

But despite his reputation, White was, for the most part, on genial form in Atlantic City. Keynes, who had been equally ready for a bust-up, instead found his erstwhile nemesis 'wreathed in smiles and amiability, hospitable, benevolent and complacent ... He also seems extremely fit and happy, and inclined to agree with almost anything which is said to him. Heaven grant that it continues but it seems too much to hope for.'[22] Of course, there were to be scrapes, but not quite of the kind that had occurred in their previous encounters. Perhaps it was the fact that there were so many other adversaries to handle; either way, a few days later Keynes was able to write home that 'White has proved an altogether admirable chairman. His kindness to me personally has been extreme.'[23]

The private negotiations continued throughout the week, although the contemporary notes on the later discussions are thinner. It was gradually becoming evident that, save for his suggestions about the Bank and some small-scale changes in wording on the Fund, Keynes's modifications were falling on deaf ears.

The draft documents written by the Americans remained more or less unchanged. There were still, however, one or two other problems yet to be resolved. The question remained of how long countries would have to prepare before joining the Fund (the Americans wanted a finite deadline of three years from the end of the war; the British five years, or perhaps even an indefinite period). There were issues about the phraseology of the articles and whether they implied a country's currency could be directly swapped for gold, or for another currency. And the Mexicans were starting to make their case for silver to be included as a reference for the international monetary system.

It wasn't only the Mexicans who had a taste for silver. Chinese delegate H.H. 'Daddy' Kung was a silver millionaire who could not be ruled out as a supporter of this crackpot scheme – which was all the more reason why he should be handled carefully. Kung was left waiting on the runway for forty minutes after his plane arrived in Washington, provoking yet another row between the State Department and a furious Morgenthau. When the pair held their first press conferences, the questions dealt exclusively with the matter of whether Kung would lobby in favour of a 'silver standard' being instituted after the war.

'Well, you know, gold is very useful,' said Kung. 'I sold a lot of silver to Mr Morgenthau and he sold some gold to me.' Morgenthau interjected: 'Fair exchange!'[24]

As the American technicians continued to work through the finer details of the draft documents, there was little left for the other foreign nations to do, save seethe quietly in the shadows over the quota issue.

In all, seventy-five experts from sixteen countries were present at the Atlantic City talks, plus one or two delegates who somehow managed to inveigle their way into the proceedings. Among this latter category was the Greek delegate Varvaressos, who seemed, to judge from his interjections, not to have absorbed the fact that the Fund was to be used only in emergencies rather than providing a steady stream of cash for his country. 'The Varvaressian Utopia,' observed Robbins, 'is clearly a world in which debtor countries have unlimited facilities for overdrawing and no penalties for default, however flagrant. He is a decorative creature and an entertaining companion, but I am convinced that, despite the high esteem in which he is held in the Treasury, he is fundamentally a bit of a fraud.'[25]

White managed for the most part to sustain the notion that anyone beyond the Americans and, to a lesser degree, the Britons would still have a say in the Bretton Woods agreements after everyone headed up to New Hampshire – although judging from his conversations with Keynes, he didn't necessarily believe it. White 'agrees that we and the Americans should reach as high a degree of agreement behind the scenes as to which of the alternatives we are ready to drop and which we agree in pressing,' Keynes reported back home, although – as would be the case throughout the conference – his cable overstated the degree of camaraderie and co-operation between the British and Americans, which was certainly better than in the previous year's negotiations, but far from perfect. 'Thus to the largest extent possible White and I will have

an agreed text, but on the surface a good many matters may be presented in alternative versions.'[26]

And while the British delegates were without any mail from
London, still desperate to hear from loved ones, the headlines from
Europe were more promising. The RAF and Home Front had now,
one week into Britain's second Blitz, started to devise ways of
defending the city from V1 attacks. Across the Channel, the Allied
battalions were penetrating deeper into Nazi-occupied France.
Harry White's hard work in Atlantic City seemed to be paying off
too. But, he told Morgenthau, it had only amounted to 'softening
up the beach heads for D week at Bretton Woods'.[27]

On Friday evening, the delegations checked out of the Claridge and
boarded a special train up to the Mount Washington Hotel. While
some of the delegates attempted to get some sleep after a long
week, others carried on drafting through the night. At Philadelphia
the Atlantic City carriages were hitched on to the main conference
train from Washington DC. It was at this point that the locomo-
tive really did become the 'Tower of Babel on Wheels', as it soon
became known, each carriage delivering a cacophonous crowd from
the ends of the earth. The main talking point was that the Chinese
government was said to have brought along a staggering forty-
seven delegates.

Economists were not the only cargo on board. As the train thundered towards the conference, one reporter on board 'noticed
unusual activity at the express car, and drew near to look. The pack-
ages men were handling so swiftly yet with such loving care were
cases of liquor – 60 cases of every variety and the choicest brands –
addressed to Bretton Woods, N.H.'[28]

Between Atlantic City and Bretton Woods, the number of attendees would swell from under a hundred to over seven hundred.
Among them was a gaunt, pale-looking member of the Greek
delegation named Alexander Argyropoulos. He had arrived in New

York the previous week, but had skipped the Atlantic City session, with good reason: he had been a prisoner of war for a year. His arrival in New York marked the end of what he would come to call his 'Odyssey', when he was finally reunited with his wife Kaity and daughter Efthalia, who had escaped Greece when it was invaded.[29] But recuperation would have to wait: there was work to be done.

Another member of the Greek delegation was a young economist named Andreas Papandreou. Some years later, in the 1980s and 1990s, he would go on to become Prime Minister of Greece. A couple of decades later his son, George, having been elected to the same position, would be forced to accept the biggest ever bailout extended by the institution his father helped create at Bretton Woods.

Belgium's Baron Boël was joined by Camille Gutt, the man who would eventually become the Fund's first managing director. The head of the French delegation, Pierre Mendès France, would, a decade later, become his country's Prime Minister. For the moment, however, he was running late. He would meet up with the rest of his delegation after the conference had begun.

One of the Indian delegation, Sir Theodore Gregory, had had to fly from Delhi in a transport plane – a three-day journey during which he slept on the floor next to a particularly delicate cargo of unexploded Japanese bombs.

The train also brought with it half of the Soviet delegation – the other half was flying in via Alaska. Among those travelling up from Washington was tall, handsome Nikolai Chechulin. In the official register of Bretton Woods he is listed as the deputy president of the State Bank. However, the FBI later concluded he was also a 'special representative' for the NKVD. His codename was KOL'TSOV, and he was there to make contact with Harry White.[30]

PART III
THE SUMMIT

CHAPTER TEN

Week One

The Quota Wars

For a short space of three weeks we were making a better world by being better people.

Fred Vinson

We are marooned in this most beautiful bowl in the White Mountains completely out of touch with the outside world.

George Bolton[1]

A visitor arriving in the lobby of the Mount Washington Hotel in early July 1944 would have been greeted with an overwhelming spectacle. 'There are meetings going on all the time – all over the place,' wrote one observer. 'Big meetings in which formal speeches are made, medium conferences where the delegates take their coats off and relax a little, and private two-man huddles in the lobby where they raise their voices a bit and shake their fingers at each other. This is mind-power at work.'[2]

That was one way of putting it. Another, wrote George Bolton, was: utter chaos. 'The most complete confusion now prevails,' he wrote, only a few days into the conference. The 'monstrous monkeyhouse' Keynes had prophesied was in full swing.

Within only a few hours of the delegates' arrival, the building appeared to be falling apart at the seams. 'Boards laid through the doorways kept unwary feet off wet varnish, paint buckets were still sitting around, and the two large swimming pools were still glistening with fresh, bright blue paint.'[3] With the hotel manager having drunk himself out of a job, the Treasury had appointed its own replacement.[4]

'It's a great spot for a murder,' remarked one US newspaper editor as the world's press made its way up to the hotel.[5] He had a point: more than twenty miles from the nearest town, with telephones and electricity on the blink, here were the great and the good, converging on an enormous, decrepit building in the middle of nowhere. A host of delegates, many of them harbouring grudges built up over decades, would be locked up together for almost three weeks with (in economic terms at least) plenty to win and as much to lose. You could have been forgiven for drawing comparisons with Agatha Christie's murder mystery play *Ten Little Indians*, which had just opened on Broadway.*

Of course, that was mostly wishful thinking on the part of the journalists. A murder or two would at least have helped them break on to the front pages, which were dominated by news of a less abstruse variety: riots in Paris as the Germans started to lose their hold on France; Allied troops pushing further into Normandy; the American flag flying in conquered Rome. The war was being won in Europe, though the flying bombs over London still made for the occasional troubling headline.

With attention largely directed elsewhere, whether on the war effort or the build-up to Roosevelt's Democratic Party Convention in Chicago, much of what happened at Bretton Woods would be confined to the business pages, deep inside the newspapers. The boldest single move in international monetary history was to

---

*The play, latterly renamed *And Then There Were None*, launched in the Broadhurst Theatre on Broadway on 27 June 1944. It would run for just over a year.

happen out of sight and earshot from most of the world's population. This suited Harry Dexter White, who wanted the conference to look as uncontroversial, technical and boring as possible. And he had a counterintuitive solution: give the journalists everything they could possibly want.

In an abrupt departure from most summits before (and since), White announced on the first Monday of Bretton Woods that over the course of the following nineteen days the press would be given unprecedented access. They would be bombarded with more than five hundred notices, documents and press releases. They would be allowed to observe every event save for small committees and private meetings. They would be permitted to talk to anyone.

White's plan, which horrified Keynes and many of the other delegates, was partly a response to the hostile media reception of 1943's Hot Springs conference, where journalists had been kept largely in the dark. He figured 'that the press, by being informed, will be able to handle the material much more intelligently and will bother the delegates much less. Just how that will work out, we don't know. I understand from our press relations man that this is a novel attempt.'[6]

As a result, coverage of the conference was remarkably well informed. Every clause under discussion, every turn the public negotiations took, was covered in minute detail. And, given that many of the histrionics would take place in private, it meant the real drama of the event was kept quiet, until it bubbled over in the final days.

It also meant that on top of the 730 attendees, the hotel had to contend with 500 journalists. More often than not they were to be found snoozing in chairs on the terrace, or gorging on meals and drinks in the restaurant and bars. Their own hotel, the Twin Mountain, was six miles down the road – and it hadn't yet managed to put on running water or food.[7] For the VIPs this made it impossible to leave their rooms without being cornered either by a fellow delegate with a bone to pick or a curious journalist with copy to file.

Lydia wrote of her husband: 'Whenever Maynard passes from one place to another he is always caught for a chat.'[8]

On top of the delegates and journalists, four hundred or so permanent hotel staff, from maids and cooks to painters, plumbers and electricians, swarmed around, hoping to pick up a tip from one of the more generous delegates. Keynes, who had somehow earned a reputation as a mean tipper, gave away a cigar holder to one employee.[9]* There were even one or two parties of German prisoners of war who had been co-opted to carry out general repairs. The fortunate had to double up in their bedrooms. The American secretariat had to sleep in the loose boxes and empty garages.

'This country forfeits any right it may have claimed for itself as being the natural centre for post-war conferences, simply on the grounds of the incompetence of its hotel arrangements,' wrote one member of the British delegation.

Still, after the heat of Atlantic City, the temperate climate of New Hampshire was a blessed relief – 'cool and pleasant, a quiet green and soothing garden of the gods, circled by mountain ramparts', according to one correspondent.[10] 'It is cool and crisp,' wrote American delegate Oscar Cox in his diary. 'Sleeping in this kind of climate is superb. Even with only one day's solid rest we all feel like a new crew.'[11]

Since the first few days were preoccupied mainly with 'pompous opening sessions' rather than any serious work,[12] many of the delegates took a well-earned break. Some lazed by the swimming pools in the sun and played golf on one of the two courses. Others hiked in the woods and followed the local trails. One day Jimmie, the hermit-like caretaker in the lodge on Mount Washington, spotted a group of foreign-looking men walking down from the

---

*Skidelsky tells of how, on holiday in Algiers in the 1920s, Keynes 'apparently refused to increase a tip he had given to a shoe-shine boy, remarking "I will not be party to debasing the currency."' Robert Skidelsky, *The Life of John Maynard Keynes*, London, 2000, p. 304.

summit. Thinking they were Japanese spies, he bore down on them with his shotgun. 'I didn't know, at first, whether to shoot and then ask questions or to ask questions before I shot,' he said. 'But it's a good thing I decided to ask questions – because they turned out to be a party from the Chinese delegation, returning from a hike!'[13]

The Ammonoosuc River, which ran down beneath the hotel, had been dammed to create a fishing pool in which you could see trout gliding around. Much to the bemusement of the other delegates, Lydia would walk down there each morning, divest herself of her clothes and bathe in the frigid water. Shocking though such behaviour might have been for puritan New Englanders, it was par for the course for Lady Keynes, who, even in middle and old age, used to sunbathe naked at home in Tilton, only yards from a public footpath. As Keynes noted: 'a passer-by simply couldn't believe his eyes.'

Lydia's eccentricities weren't limited to her early morning ablutions. Over the course of the conference she was to become one of the most talked-about guests. An entranced reporter from the *Philadelphia Inquirer* wrote: 'Long-haired, Russian-born Lady Keynes is small and darkly vivid and intense ... she drifted about in neo-Hellenic dresses, carefully seeing to it that her husband was properly taken care of.'[14] If you couldn't identify her by her hair or clothes, the other stand-out clue was the woven straw shopping bag she took everywhere with her, prominently marked 'Sennet, Fishmonger, Cambridge'.[15] 'She and her bag attracted much more notice than many of the big-shot delegates,' wrote another reporter.[16]

The British delegates' wives were less charmed. For them, Lydia's eccentric clothing choices and wild behaviour were unbefitting a lady of the realm – not to speak of the way she managed her domestic affairs. Kathleen Lee, present with her husband, Treasury delegate Frank Lee, recalled that one day, invited up to the Keyneses' suite, the wives were greeted by the sight of sodden socks and underwear hanging all over the radiator, having been washed by Lydia in the basin.[17]

Nor did she ingratiate herself with the wives of other delegates. Her evening routine, while many of the delegates were still in late-night meetings, was to practise her ballet exercises in her bedroom, much to the frustration of Morgenthau's wife Elinor, who was in the suite directly underneath.

Also staying in Morgenthau's suite was his daughter Joan, a history student at Vasser. The Treasury Secretary had decided to bring her along to give her a lasting first-person impression of what would undoubtedly be an historic moment. Some years later, when asked about Bretton Woods, she confessed she didn't remember anything about the conference at all.[18]

With the foreign delegates still finding their feet (and some yet to arrive), Morgenthau and White called a meeting of the US team. Even at this late stage, most of them were none the wiser about the fine details of the American position. That, of course, had been White's intention all along – it was how he would maintain control. But it now threatened to leave the group exposed.

During most of the meetings – particularly in the sub-committees where the nuts and bolts of the deal were to be negotiated – the delegates would be on their own. Success or failure would be determined by whether the entire team could present a common front. The big risk was that one ill-informed delegate would blurt out something compromising or, worse still, unwittingly sign up to a clause that undermined the American position. It was not enough for the more clueless members of the delegation to defer to White's well-briefed technicians from Atlantic City: everyone was a target.

Like a football coach ahead of a big tournament, White ran his team through the opposition's strengths and weaknesses. When it came to the Fund, he emphasised the most controversial issue, the one that would probably dominate the debates and cause the most aggravation: quotas.

In the first place, all countries want larger quotas, but the countries that will give us the most trouble ... are as follows: China
insists that she shall have fourth place. They don't care whether
that fourth place is much above the third or much below the
fifth, but it has to be the fourth place. France is insisting on fifth
place and India is insisting on fifth place ... The smaller countries
all want larger quotas. The most troublesome will be Australia
who is participating to an extent far beyond the proper role of a
country of her size and importance ... The South American
countries would like a larger quota. Now, it is the South
American countries who in this are going to be important to us
for reasons that we will discuss later ...[19]

Latin America, it turned out, was to be an essential bulwark to
the American delegation throughout the conference. Alone, the US
might conceivably find itself outnumbered and overpowered – in
diplomatic if not economic terms – by the combined force of the
British Empire. In the strategy that White was mapping out for the
coming weeks, the Latin Americans would play a key role backing
up his squad. The only problem was their obsession – the Mexicans'
in particular – with giving silver the same kind of economic recognition as gold in the international monetary system. That issue
would have to be handled delicately – meaning no slap-downs in
public.

The official US squad was twelve-strong. Morgenthau and his
deputy, the gruff tobacco-chewing Fred Vinson, would float in and
out of the meetings over the course of the conference. White was
backed up by his second-in-command Eddie Bernstein, who,
though not an official delegate, would step into his boss's shoes as
US representative when White was chairing sessions on the Fund.
Dean Acheson, immaculately turned out in a brass-buttoned blazer
with the coat of arms of Davenport College on its badge, would
represent the State Department.[20] His role would be to charm his

way out of the diplomatic messes White and Bernstein tended to leave in their wake – though despite the suave exterior, behind the scenes he was capable of as much vulgarity as the rest of them. 'Don't fuck it up, Eddie,' he warned Bernstein as the economist began to draft an important document on the Bank.[21] Leo Crowley, the man in charge of Lend-Lease, was there, as was Marriner Eccles, Roosevelt's Federal Reserve chairman. A self-made Mormon millionaire from Utah, who had later become Roosevelt's point man in overhauling the banking sector during the Depression, Eccles' CV was considerably more interesting than his oratorical perform-ances. He would give New Zealand's dreary Walter Nash a run for his money as the most self-important and tedious delegate.

More quixotic was the sole representative of the banking indus-try, Edward Eagle Brown – Ned to his friends. A mountain of a man, Brown was president of the First National Bank of Chicago and one of the few bankers that Roosevelt trusted. 'He is a great big fellow who flaps his lips in a way that makes you think it is impos-sible to understand him,' said one of his colleagues, the Federal Reserve's learned old economist Emanuel Goldenweiser.[22] 'US Treasury people describe him as a typical middle westerner,' reported the Bank of England's George Bolton. 'He is careless in his appearance, weighs over 250 pounds and has not seen his feet for years. Close cropped white hair, perpetually smoking a pipe, a deep asthmatic voice and a laugh like a bellow from an angry bull.'[23] Adding further to the caricature was the fact that Brown spent most of the conference wearing the same rumpled blue serge suit, which gradually became more and more stained with tobacco, food and drink.

But notwithstanding his gruff appearance and predilection for dirty jokes and gossip, Brown had one of the key roles at Bretton Woods. As the sole financier within the US delegation – indeed one of the few practising bankers at the entire conference – it was his job to represent the financial sector. What was to be laid down at the Mount Washington over the coming weeks would represent one of the biggest structural challenges to international finance in modern history. Happily for White, Brown was so focused on plotting the downfall of his New York rivals that he would put up little meaningful resistance.

Mabel Newcomer, an economics professor from Vasser, had the distinction of being the only female delegate among the Western delegations (there was also one other female delegate in the Russian team). Rumour had it that Eleanor Roosevelt herself had passed down word that the American delegation must have at least one woman on board. Conveniently for her, Newcomer was a neighbour, living on a two-acre plot where she had, according to the *New York Times*, 'a large garden which, she says as an economist, makes her kitchen entirely self-sufficient'.[24] She had also taught Morgenthau's daughter at Vasser.

A woman of few words, except when it came to the wellbeing of her students, Newcomer's biggest fear was another Great Depression. In the 1930s she had seen even her most gifted pupils leave college and fail to find any kind of employment. She couldn't forget spotting one promising former student walking the streets looking for a job. 'You don't have to remind the mothers of America of unemployment and bread-lines and bank-failures,' she said. 'They remember only too well – and they want this conference to see that it doesn't happen again.'[25] Though Newcomer kept beneath the radar for much of the summit, she did surface briefly to complain that what with all the work she hadn't had time to indulge her real passion: mountain-climbing.

Then there were the politicians – one congressman and one senator from each party: Congressman Brent Spence represented the Democrats in Kentucky, and Republican Jesse Wolcott served on the House Committee on Banking and Currency. From the Senate came Republican Charles Tobey, the local man who would make the conference's inspiring opening speech, and New York Democrat

Robert F. Wagner. A campaigning politician responsible for pioneering workers' rights in the US, the latter's main contribution to the meetings was a relentless stream of alcohol-related wisecracks.

When one included all the technicians and secretaries, the entire US team came to forty-five. White had briefed most of the technical team in Atlantic City, so now it was time for the pre-match briefing for the main delegates. Having assessed the threats posed by the opposition – quotas, voting rights, the exchange clause controversy with the British, the Mexicans and silver – White got to the point. Bretton Woods was about creating a structure to stabilise and correct imbalances in the international monetary system – to prevent a repeat of the Great Depression, where some parts of the world had become so indebted and reliant on imports that they were left vulnerable to sovereign debt crises.

He reminded his colleagues of perhaps the main sticking point between his and the British plan: Keynes wanted creditor nations to face charges for nursing large current account surpluses. The United States was the world's largest creditor nation. Economically sensible though it might be, the notion that it should be penalised for exporting a lot of goods and capital would never fly. And while White had largely extinguished this element of the Keynes plan in the preceding year's negotiations, the last thing he wanted was for it to be smuggled back into the articles here at Bretton Woods. So he drummed it into his colleagues' minds yet again. 'We have been perfectly adamant on that point. We have taken the position of absolutely no, on that. And that has created a good deal of discussion and will continue to create some.'[26]

Think of the gold in Fort Knox, he said. 'That is why the United States is in an enviable position; that is why we are in a powerful position at this Conference; that is why we dominate practically the financial world, because we have the where-with-all to buy any currency we want. If only England was in that position, or any of the other countries, it would be a very different story.'[27]

It all came back to the fundamental difference in the way the two men had conceived of what would become the International Monetary Fund. Both wanted an international institution that would keep the global economic system stable, but whereas White's Fund was there for emergency use, with money doled out only when specifically approved, Keynes's version was rather more like a permanent and unregulated credit line – an overdraft.

What might have sounded to the untrained ears of some of the delegates like a small nuance was, as far as White was concerned, a vital difference. If there was the merest suspicion on Capitol Hill that the Fund would channel American cash, with no questions asked, to the US's impecunious counterparts across the Atlantic, there was no way the deal would ever pass Congress. As a result, White added, 'we have surrounded this thing with protective devices at every point. That doesn't mean it is without risk. [But o]ur lawyers have done a job.'[28]

What the British and the Americans had in common, however, was the notion that the Fund and the Bank existed to try to prevent another Depression. No one could reasonably claim that the Fund was perfect in design or intent. In a press conference a few days later Keynes was to acknowledge that when it came to the kinds of balance of payments crises the world had faced in the 1930s, 'the Fund can't solve continuing problems of this sort ... On the other hand, if you do run into this situation then you are given an organisation to find a rational approach, a friendly way out of it and a little time to think it over.' The Fund was, he admitted, 'quite a different thing in many respects from how it started and that is the result of a tremendous clash of brains of many, many countries.' But, he said, what was the alternative? 'I think if I was to set myself to criticise this Fund I should do quite a good job of it, but ... I could make a better job of criticising anything else, and that is what one must depend on.'[29]

But perhaps the most powerful argument in favour of the Fund, White told his colleagues, was the degree to which it would protect capitalism. 'People are not going to stand for prolonged unemployment in Europe,' he said. 'They will kick over the traces for Communism, or some other "-ism".'[30] The Fund, in other words, was designed specifically to attempt to fight the spread of Communism – not to perpetuate it, as those convinced of White's own Communism have occasionally claimed.

With the US delegation now a little more familiar with the lie of the land, a team photograph of most of the principals was taken before Morgenthau rounded the meeting up: 'So again, if we play this as a team, if we have any differences, let's have them here in the room and over the bar.'

Wagner interrupted: 'Where is the bar?'[31]

There were, as it happened, a number of bars dotted around the hotel – from the Prohibition-era Cave to the biggest and by far the most popular: the Moon Room, a large semi-circular room in the basement of the hotel, with French windows looking out towards the summit of Mount Washington. 'Commission IV', delegates nicknamed it – an economist's in-joke equivalent of the nineteenth hole in golf, since Commissions I, II and III were the main components of the conference's Articles of Agreement. It welcomed a more or less permanent stream of delegates, journalists and visitors 'with a small orchestra and drinks at $1 a throw'.[32]

For those who chose not to drink, or found the alcoholic fug downstairs too much to bear, there was also the so-called 'Sterling Area Club' – a drug store where the Britons, Indians and Egyptians gathered. It was the only place in the vicinity to serve decent tea.[33] As a teetotaller, Morgenthau was among those who found the constant stream of cocktail parties and receptions a challenge. The very first day, not long after the American team talk, the US delegation itself held a welcome drinks reception in the Hemicycle Room overlooking the golf course and the Presidential Mountain Range. The waiters were given strict orders to fill Morgenthau's martini glass surreptitiously with water.

Immediately preceding this reception was the very first of those 'pompous opening ceremonies'. Morgenthau was officially elected as conference president; the inaugural statement from President Roosevelt was read. It said:

It is fitting that even while the war for liberation is at its peak, the representatives of free men should gather to take counsel with one another respecting the shape of the future which we are to win.

The program you are to discuss constitutes, of course, only one phase of the arrangements which must be made between nations to ensure an orderly, harmonious world. But it is a vital phase, affecting ordinary men and women everywhere. For it concerns the basis upon which they will be able to exchange with one another the natural riches of the earth and the products of their own industry and ingenuity. Commerce is the life-blood of a free society. We must see to it that the arteries which carry that blood stream are not clogged again, as they have been in the past, by artificial barriers created through senseless economic rivalries.[34]

There followed a 'long series of banal or inaudible speeches'[35] from the Chinese, Czechoslovakian, Mexican, Brazilian, Canadian and Russian delegates before, finally, Morgenthau's speech, which would mark the official opening of the conference. The original plan had been to hold this event later, perhaps even the following day, to give the delegates time to acclimatise, but the American delegation moved it with an eye to getting Morgenthau maximum exposure in the Sunday papers. His speech was long on powerful rhetoric and as short as possible on the specific details of the negotiations, which he knew newspaper readers would find as unappealing as he did.

[T]he world is a community. On battlefronts the world over, the young men of all our united countries have been dying together –

dying for a common purpose. It is not beyond our powers to enable the young men of all our countries to live together – to pour their energies, their skills, their aspirations into mutual enrichment and peaceful progress. Our final responsibility is to them. As they prosper or perish, the work which we do here will be judged. The opportunity before us has been bought with blood. Let us meet it with faith in one another, with faith in our common future, which these men fought to make free.'[36]

Having been starved of anything substantial to write about – save the commotion at the hotel and the gossip about the competing Keynes and White plans – the press swarmed on to the news. Robbins wrote home: 'Our unfortunate Chairman was photographed from at least 50 different angles – Lord Keynes conversing earnestly with the Chairman of the Russian Delegation (neither of them know each other's language); Lord Keynes warmly clasping Dr Kung, the Chinese Banker, by the hand; Lord Keynes sitting down; Lord Keynes standing up; Lord Keynes in plan; Lord Keynes in elevation; and so on and so forth.'[37]

The opening ceremonies over, the conference was finally, officially, under way.

'I do not think I have ever worked so continuously hard in all my life,' said Keynes. With the conference only a few days old, the burden of work was already becoming overwhelming.

The typical working day began at 7.30 a.m., with a working breakfast at which each country's delegates would meet to discuss their respective battle plans, keeping an eagle eye out for eavesdroppers ('The only difficulty to talking at breakfast is that you find a Chinaman who understands English perfectly well sitting a half foot behind you,' reported Ned Brown one morning).[38]

After breakfast and a brief moment of calm, the demands of the day would rapidly ratchet up to almost unbearable levels: a succession of committee meetings held one after the other until darkness fell. Following dinner, and perhaps a quick fortifier at the bar, the committees and sub-committees would resume, often until around 3.30 a.m. The next morning, the whole process would start all over again. Many of the delegates had to subsist on, at best, four hours of sleep a night.

It wasn't merely the delegates who were overworked. After the negotiators went to bed many of the technical staff were left trying to finish documenting the day's proceedings. Even when there was a break from committees, the delegates would find themselves consumed by preparatory work. Although Lydia barred him from the late-night drafting sessions, Keynes had to read through nearly a thousand documents over the course of the conference, as well as composing a hundred long telegrams to the Treasury, asking advice and gradually drip-feeding the unsavoury reality back to London – that it was losing on almost every major policy battle.[39]

To make matters worse, in the first ten days, the White Mountains experienced unseasonably hot weather. The committee rooms became stuffy with sweat and cigarette smoke. Over at the Rosewood Inn the women of the Russian delegation took the opportunity to sunbathe on the terrace.[40] One of the boy scouts on duty, Charlie Ricardi, later recalled, 'A sixteen-year-old notices things like that.'[41]

Others took a rather more elevated view. For Indian delegate B.K. Madan, 'the total setting had at least something of the air of a papal election. The delegates worked toward the final outcome … goaded by a certain sense of compulsion in events that did not seem to brook failure.'[42]

In an effort to try to cover the mountain of material necessary over the course of the following two and a half weeks (the conference was set to finish on Wednesday 19 July, with new arrivals due at the hotel the following day), White split the conference into two main parts. Commission I was the more important, dealing with the International Monetary Fund; not surprisingly, White would chair it himself. Beneath this would be four committees dealing with the specifics: quotas, how the Fund would operate, how it would be managed and its legal status and form. Each committee would in turn end up creating sub-committees to deal with particularly sticky issues.

There was also a special standing committee whose job it was to mop up the issues no one else could resolve. This committee had consequently to meet late at night, by which stage many of the members were not merely exhausted but powered mainly by after-dinner brandy. Its chairman, Louis Rasminsky, made sure each evening to declare a fifteen-minute recess at 1.30 a.m. 'to enable the members of the Drafting Committee (including the Chairman) to join the unofficial Commission IV downstairs in the Moon Room and observe the titillating gyrations of Conchita the Peruvian Bombshell. Thus refreshed and reinvigorated, we were able to carry on with renewed vigour for another hour or more.'[43]

Commission II was to focus on the Bank. Chaired by Keynes, it, like its bigger brother, would have multiple committees and sub-committees, although, tellingly, few minutes remain of their decisions and deliberations: there were only so many stenographers and only so much time. There was also a Commission III, whose formal title was 'Other Means of International Financial Cooperation' but was more bluntly described by Robbins as 'a sort of residual rag bag for the whole Conference'.[44] Essentially a toxic waste dump into which White and Keynes could jettison some of the summit's trickier issues, this was where delegates would try to hammer out issues such as the role of silver and the fate of the Bank for International Settlements.

The plan was to devote the first week to the Fund and the second to the Bank, using the following few days to wrap things up. In the event this proved wildly optimistic, with the result that at various points all three commissions, sub-committees and all, were meeting at the same time, further adding to the sensation of chaos. By week two Bolton was reporting: 'The confusion here is becoming so great that one has the feeling we are living in a mad-house.'[45]

The objective was to try to turn the Statement of Principles published by the Americans a couple of months previously and signed up to (reluctantly) by the British before heading out to the United States into something all forty-four nations present in the hotel could assent to. As in Atlantic City, a variety of different drafts were circulating at any given moment, although the main template from which the conference worked was the original American draft.

In an effort to efface the impression that the outcome of the conference was preordained, White insisted that each committee be chaired by a non-American or British delegate. Though this made diplomatic sense, handing the gavel to delegates from Russia, China, Peru and so on had the unfortunate side-effect of adding to the sense of disorganisation. The debates, said Keynes, were 'carried on in committees and commissions numbering anything up to 200 persons in rooms with bad acoustics, shouting through microphones, many of those present, often including the Chairman, with an imperfect knowledge of English, each wanting to get something on the record which would look well in the Press down at home, and one of the most important Delegations, namely the Russians, only understanding what was afoot with the utmost difficulty and expense of time ...'[46]

Goldenweiser of the Federal Reserve was similarly frustrated by the 'great many varieties of unintelligible English spoken ... The Russians didn't speak English; neither did their interpreters. The French spoke English but always had trouble in being satisfied that their exact meaning was properly translated by their interpreters. The French spoke excellent French,' he added, a touch unnecessarily.[47]

Not only did the French insist on speaking in their mother tongue during the formal sessions, at one point Pierre Mendès

France even launched a bid to have the conference's resolutions printed in French as well as English on 'sentimental and psychological grounds'. The proposal was quickly snuffed out by the British, though it was a sign of things to come.[48] Even today, at the IMF's executive board meetings, while most other directors speak English, the French director will insist on addressing the board in his own language.

Keynes and the rest of the UK delegation would spend much of the conference fighting an increasingly desperate battle on two fronts. First, and most obviously, they tried to incorporate something – anything – broadly equivalent to the Keynes plan in the Final Act – though by now it was clear that the only feasible victories would be small ones. Second, they needed to fight off attempts by the Dominion economies to use the Fund as a tool for freeing up their mountain of sterling debts for use in international trade.

The 'blocked sterling balances' issue – a proxy battle signifying the final creaking moments of Empire – cropped up continually throughout the first week. The Indian and Egyptian delegations launched repeated assaults on the UK position, insisting that they should be allowed to convert their sterling balances so as to be able to spend them somewhere that wasn't devoting its entire economic effort to building tanks and guns. Such conversations had hitherto happened in private. At Bretton Woods they exploded into the auditorium at the Mount Washington.

In one early committee meeting, to the horror of Britain's representative, Lionel Robbins, the Egyptian and Indian delegates asked for the blocked balances issue to be put before Commission III. This was, to the British at least, inconceivable – it would bring the issue one step closer to becoming an official summit resolution. Young Manuel Noriega Morales, a graduate student from Harvard and the sole Guatemalan delegate, stood up and argued nobly in the Indians' favour. Then, according to one delegate present:

Professor Robbins immediately raised his hand and rose to speak. As I recall it, he peered over his spectacles – for the delegate from Guatemala was at the other end of a long conference room – and in a rather aloof and slightly condescending fashion, he said something like this: 'May I remind the distinguished delegate from ... er ... Ecuador that the question of sterling balances is strictly a matter of concern only to His Majesty's government and the governments of the countries directly involved', and sat down. Poor Mr Noriega-Morales, feeling literally squashed, *never* opened his mouth during the whole of the rest of the Bretton Woods conference!*[49]

However, Noriega Morales, who would later go on to become Minister of Economy and president of the Banco de Guatemala, had a point. After all, Bretton Woods was supposed to be an opportunity to create a new system for dealing with international economic imbalances: so wasn't it a little odd for the conference to ignore the enormous imbalances between creditor and debtor countries built up before and during the war? He was unaware that the Britons had rejected earlier in the negotiations White's (in retrospect) generous offer to tackle the issue at the conference. As far as London was concerned, such issues were too intensely political to be fought out explicitly at Bretton Woods, though that would not prevent the Indians trying. And in a sense, their struggle was analogous to the one between the US and Britain: a large, populous creditor nation attempting to ensure that its smaller, indebted counterpart would actually pay it back.

Happily for Robbins, the following day he bumped into another member of the Indian delegation, Ardeshir Darabshaw Shroff, and

---

*Mr Noriega Morales had other reasons to be preoccupied: the Guatemalan dictator, Jorge Ubico, had just resigned in the face of mass strikes across the country. His brother, also an economist, phoned him with the news on the first day of Bretton Woods.

the pair realised they had studied together at the London School of Economics between the wars. 'This has made all the difference,' said Robbins. 'Shroff and I converged as one old LSE man to another ... everything was very friendly.' And while the issue of blocked balances would resurface in the coming days, the Indians' outrage started to die down following these behind-the-scenes conversations; their campaign was eventually quashed a week later. Negotiations on debt to the Indians would have to wait until after the summit.

Nonetheless, this was a watershed moment. For the first time, the Indians had stood up on the global stage and threatened to strike an economic blow against their colonial masters. It was a clear signal of the shift in power that would culminate in Indian independence three years later.*

The conference wore on, the hours of interminable committee meetings punctuated by occasional moments of leisure. On Tuesday night, shortly after Robbins' blunt destruction of the Guatemalan delegate, the British were invited to a dinner held by the Chinese delegate, 'Daddy' Kung, ostensibly in an attempt to outdo Keynes's five-hundredth-anniversary celebration of the Oxford–Cambridge Concordat on Saturday.

The scion of one of the 'four families' who had dominated Chinese politics for decades, Kung was an odd cross between a member of the landed gentry, a Chinese technocrat and a slightly crass self-publicist. The jolly sixty-four-year-old would allow no photo opportunity to pass without diving into frame alongside whichever other delegation happened to be in the snappers' crosshairs. 'As my venerable ancestor, Confucius, put it a very long time ago,' he was heard to say more than once, before reciting a long Chinese aphorism, to the bafflement of those present.

*Shroff, then a director of the Tata Group, now one of the world's industrial giants, would make his name as one of the authors of the Bombay Plan – a set of proposals on how to develop the post-independence Indian economy.

Kung's party trick, according to *Time* magazine, was 'a stamping, lurching, conga-like version of a 14th-Century Ming dynasty dragon dance'.[50] He had reason to be cheerful. The millionaire, whose fortune derived from shopping stores, cotton mills, mining and finance, had now secured his position as one of the most influential players in China. For years he had played second fiddle to his brother-in-law T.V. Soong as they vied for the affections of Chinese leader Chiang Kai-shek. However, he now appeared to be the chosen one – and his appearance at the head of the Chinese delegation at Bretton Woods was, according to a cable from the Foreign Office in London, 'a clear indication that TV Soong is definitely out'.[51] What few at the conference realised was that not all was proceeding sweetly for Kung; in fact, so far had his popularity fallen that many in China suspected he had been sent to the conference to keep him out of the public eye.

Although some feted him as an economic genius, responsible for the diplomatic manoeuvring which helped rescue China from economic collapse after Japan annexed its salt mines and blockaded the coast, Kung was no technical economist. Like many of the delegates, he had little time for the detail of the negotiations – save for the question of how large China's ultimate quota would be. After all, national pride had to be served, and for China that meant being an official member of the so-called Big Four. It meant behaving like one of the great, wealthy economies, even though the country's economic star had waned since the days when it was the most advanced of all nations.

Kung ordered his enormous delegation to behave with as much extravagance as possible. Every member was issued with a roll of quarters as tips for the hotel staff. And that Tuesday night he laid on the most lavish of all Bretton Woods' parties. He summoned up a truly overwhelming spread, including a beef filet 'at least 3 inches thick and 6 inches square'.[52]

The Britons, who had endured five years of rationing back home, were speechless. They tended to regard China with the disdain they reserved for far-flung nations that remained outside the Commonwealth. Referring to Kung behind his back as 'the old Mandarin', Keynes would shoot him complex monetary questions at sessions in an effort to show him up.[53] Robbins would declare that 'the Chinese position at the conference is, of course, largely bogus, and the high place they are assigned to generally by American diplomacy rests on illusion – at any rate as regards our day, whatever may be the case in fifty years' time.'[54]

Nonetheless, the US had decided early on, and without much in the way of deep economic analysis, that China should be one of the primary countries at the table. Roosevelt had insisted on having China alongside the US, UK and Russia in the Big Four; when the United Nations was founded the following year, these countries, plus France, would become permanent members of its Security Council.

For some delegates, it was all evidence of 'the romantic attitude towards China which still exists in the United States':[55] an unwritten assumption that although this venerable nation was no longer the world economic superpower it had been a century earlier, it would at some point rise again from its slumber. Nonetheless, its pre-eminence was a cause of immense frustration for India, which was being asked to settle for a quota half the size of China's, despite the two countries having economies of rather more equal proportions.

For its own part, China's ire was reserved primarily for Russia. Diplomatic relations between Moscow and Beijing, which was already attempting to suppress the Communist movement in its own country, were dismal. The two nations had refused to sit at the same table when in Washington shortly before Bretton Woods. Now they were determined not to interact with each other. 'I don't know what the trouble is between the two countries,' Morgenthau said to Acheson, 'but there evidently is ... something which is burning in there.'[56]

The wretched battle over quotas was to bubble along, both publicly in the conference rooms and privately in the hotel corridors, until the very end of proceedings. While everyone wanted a bigger quota at the IMF, most countries were quite happy to keep their separate quota to the Bank as small as possible, viewing money there as a sunk cost contributing to reconstructing other countries.

From the very start, the Americans had insisted on a ceiling of around $10 billion – preferably with $8 billion going to the Allied nations. After the initial skirmishes before the conference, it was firmly established that America's share had to be the biggest, exceeding not merely that of any other country but also the combined share of the British Commonwealth (White spotted that loophole coming a long way off). In the event, no one would end up particularly happy.

The quotas themselves had originally been worked out in the US Treasury the previous year. Harry White had called thirty-year-old Treasury official Ray Mikesell into his office and asked him for an economic formula that fitted a few key criteria. First, America's quota had to be around $2.9 billion. That just so happened to be the same size as the country's existing Exchange Stabilization Fund – a Depression-era mechanism designed to protect the country from international shocks, and which could conveniently be transferred to the IMF without Congressional approval.

The United Kingdom's share was to be about half that of America and the Soviet Union's a touch less still, after which would come China. Provided the Big Four were in that order, White added, the rest of the ranking was up to Mikesell and his formula. 'He said he did not care where France ranked, and its ranking did not need to be an objective in the exercise,' Mikesell recalled some years later. 'As was typical, White wanted something on his desk in a couple of days – it took me four, including a weekend. A modern computer would have saved several days of work on my state-of-the-art calculator and might have produced a more credible result.'

Part of the problem was that this was an era before reliable, comparable figures for gross domestic product – the modern yard-stick of the size of an economy. Instead, Mikesell concocted a witches' brew of different statistics in an effort to calculate some approximation of relative economic size. He was perhaps fortunate that the appropriate numbers didn't exist. Russia's economy was about three times that of China, which was a minnow in compar-ison with most European nations. In an epic feat of statistical contortionism, Mikesell nevertheless devised a formula which gave White his favoured ranking (the most 'serious problem' was getting France's quota below China's, which involved having to add layer upon layer of complexity in order to efface economic reality).

Although White had hinted at the quotas occasionally over the past year, Bretton Woods was the first time the final rankings were made public. Predictably, they provoked volcanic outbursts of indig-nation. Russia was furious that it had been placed below Britain – and that its eventual quota was lower than the figure White had mentioned the previous year. France was devastated to be below China, as was India. The Mexicans wanted silver production to count towards the quota, while China and India wanted population to play a greater role.

The delegates' fury was intensified by the secrecy with which the Americans guarded the initial formula, which gave rise to angry speculation and rumours over how it was constructed. To add to the frustration of the almost entirely male population of the Mount Washington Hotel, a rumour went round that it had all been worked out by, of all things, a woman in the US Treasury and that the 'figures have never been checked'.*

The American response was to blind the delegates with a flood

---

*The woman named in the rumour was Dorothy Richardson, who was also pres-ent at the conference. Although her part in the construction of the quotas remains unclear, it transpired that her husband, British-born Treasury employee Solomon Adler, was accused of espionage several years later. Bank of England Archives, OV38/9.

of detail. Fred Vinson, whose lot it was to chair the committee meeting dealing with quotas, wheeled out Mikesell to explain all to the seething delegates. Right on cue, he launched into a 'rambling twenty-minute seminar on the factors taken into account in calculating the quotas', crucially omitting the cubist approach to mathematics that resulted in the formula. 'I tried to make the process appear as scientific as possible,' he said, 'but the delegates were intelligent enough to know that the process was more political than scientific.'[57]

After his litany there followed a blank silence from the baffled delegates. For the time being, their political resistance died away in the face of Mikesell's equations. But the bafflement did little to dull the pain of those smaller countries who figured they were being consigned to economic and political irrelevance for generations. Had they realised that an adapted version of the formula would later be used to calculate contributions and control at the United Nations, they might have fought even harder.[58]

And while many better-off countries could afford to be more relaxed about their quotas, for others a low number implied lasting economic vulnerability. The war-ravaged economies of Europe were well aware that those quotas would, under the terms of Bretton Woods, determine just how much each country was able to borrow from the Fund. Everyone knew that nations on the front line would hardly be able to stand on their own feet for some years. This was not, in other words, merely about pride. It was also a matter of economic survival.

When the quotas were finally brought before the official Commission I meeting on the second Saturday of the conference, Vinson attempted to reason with the disappointed nations. But, sorry as he was, he said, he suspected not everyone would ever be happy. '[I]t was impossible, I repeat, impossible, to put a slide rule on the economy of forty-four nations and come up and say that "this is it",' he said, before launching into soaring rhetoric:

We are met here in Bretton Woods in an experimental test, probably the first time in the history of the world, that forty-four nations have convened seeking to solve difficult economic problems. We fight together on sodden battlefields. We sail together on the majestic blue. We fly together in the ethereal sky.

The test of this conference is whether we can walk together, solve our economic problems, down the road to peace as we today march to victory. Sometimes problems seem to be most important on a particular day.

Some folks think that the problems of the world were made to be solved in a day or in one conference. That can't be.

We must have cooperation, collaboration; utilize the machinery, the instrumentalities, that have been set up to provide succor to those who are hungry and ill; to set up, establish instrumentalities that will stabilize or tend toward stabilization of economies of our world.

Maybe then some of the germs will be attacked either by serum or friendship and destroyed; maybe wars may be deferred or postponed indefinitely. I know it is our hope, our objective, to reach that.

The delegation of the United States submits that in respect of certain amounts, they may not be just exactly what the delegates from that particular country desire. If there be any irritation or unhappiness, we certainly regret it, because any error on our part is of the head and not of the heart.[59]

For a moment after he sat down, it looked as though Vinson had silenced the crowd and brought an end to the petty politicking. And then the objections began: Iran, China, Greece, the Netherlands, Australia, India, Yugoslavia, New Zealand (in a ten-minute sermon from the country's dreary lead negotiator, the Hon. Walter Nash) and France.

Mendès France had more reason than most to complain: not

only was the French quota smaller than the country's economy should have merited, it had (unbeknownst to him) actually shrunk since it was first calculated by Mikesell. However, the French delegate did not help his country's cause with a series of increasingly clumsy and emotional protests, his opening comment being to tell the meeting that he would 'have to reconsider the entire participation of this delegation at this conference if the question could not be reconsidered'.[60] But the impact of his intervention was undermined when his French was misunderstood by the translator, who had to interrupt proceedings to issue a correction a minute or so later.

Either way, Harry Dexter White was outraged. In one of the few public rebukes issued by the chairman during the entire conference, he said France's threats to withdraw 'strike me as being something less than befits the nation or any of the nations that are represented here'.

After the formal meeting was over, a fuming Mendès France buttonholed young Mikesell in the lobby of the hotel. How, he demanded to know, could France conceivably have a quota that was lower than China's and only a third of Britain's?* Mikesell trotted out his long-winded explanation and showed Mendès France some of the data – but, for obvious reasons, refrained from revealing the formula.

'He was not prepared to dispute my data but became increasingly agitated over the process that could give France such a low quota,' said Mikesell. 'I believe that Mendès France regarded the decision on the French quota as a deliberate insult. Because I also believed the French quota was too low, I was greatly embarrassed during the confrontation and wished some senior member of the American delegation would come along to rescue me.'

***

*France's was to be $450 million, compared with China's $550 million and Britain's $1300 million.

His wish was granted. Eventually the shouting drew the attention of Morgenthau, who stopped by to ask what the problem was. Mendès France launched into a tirade about France's 'disgracefully low quota', whereupon Morgenthau told him straightforwardly that President Roosevelt had promised China its quota would rank fourth. Suddenly the French delegate 'went into a rage, speaking unintelligibly, half in French, half in English' until Morgenthau promised him a private meeting later that evening. Mikesell had to go out for a walk on the lawn to try to calm himself; he was left shaking for the rest of the day.[61]

Mendès France was in an invidious position. Not only was France's political stock close to non-existent, he had also been effectively neutered by Charles de Gaulle. The general, who was that week in Washington meeting Roosevelt, had ordered Mendès France not to negotiate with Morgenthau 'at any cost'. There were major issues over how France's economy and currency would be reordered after the war but they should be handled over the 'diplomatic channel', de Gaulle said. That was 'the only one that allows us to operate with care, reserve, and without surprises'.[62]

Set against this, Mendès France, an intellectual prodigy and the brightest politician of his generation, realised the importance of fighting the quota formula. Under the proposed scheme, not only would France be less powerful within the IMF than Britain or China, it would also have a smaller quota in total than the Benelux countries – Holland, Belgium and Luxembourg. That would be nothing short of a national humiliation.

Unfortunately many of the delegates – particularly within the American delegation – regarded the French as something of a laughing stock. The diplomatic in-joke of the day involved referring to the country's exiled Algiers-based administration as a liberation movement or, as Secretary of State Cordell Hull called them, the 'so-called Free French' – a turn of phrase that provoked howls of outrage from de Gaulle. Technically speaking at least, Mendès

France was not representing a country but a people: a small distinction for everybody but the French, who were indignant when anyone corrected the name of their delegation.*

Mendès France also had a habit of turning up late. His tardy arrival at Bretton Woods was a source of irritation to the fastidious and punctual Treasury Secretary. He was late too for the private meeting that Thursday evening at which they were supposed to be hammering out their differences on the quota issue. He arrived, together with his colleague André Istel, just as Morgenthau was about to dismiss the rest of his delegation.

Nor did the clear-the-air session start very well. The Americans were furious that the French chairman had threatened to walk out of the meeting that afternoon. Mendès France, for his part, was annoyed not merely about the quota but also about the fact that countries facing war devastation (by which he meant mainly France) would receive no significant discount on their contribution to the Fund – not to mention the fact that it looked as if only the top three countries would be given permanent seats on the IMF's executive board. Unfortunately he had immense trouble being taken seriously by the room of Americans.

'I must tell you frankly I have not an easy position in Algiers,' he said, his faltering English apparently provoking titters from the US delegates. 'I understand why you are laughing now,' he continued, trying to silence the guffaws. 'When I go back to Algiers and have to explain all these things, [de Gaulle] will say: "You have lost on

---

*Leroy Stinebower, a secretary in the American delegation, would later say: 'if they would behave themselves and not insist on calling themselves the "Delegation of France", we would not insist on calling them the "Free French Liberation Movement." Actually at Bretton Woods, nobody noticed this except Mendès France himself. I played a little game with him ... Every time, in enthusiasm, Mendès France or any of his other people would get off their reservation in making a speech and talk about what the "delegation of France" says, I put it down as the "Free French delegation said this," in the minutes. Every time he referred to them properly I put it down properly, as the French delegation. That was their official title.' Leroy Stinebower, oral history interview, Harry S. Truman Library.

the quota, you have lost on the devastated countries, you have lost on these, and these, and these – then what do you bring back to us? What is the good news you bring back?'"

As it happened, there had yet been no firm decision on whether to have three or five permanent seats on the IMF board. 'I don't know who is handling this thing, but let's throw our weight to five directors,' said Morgenthau. Mendès France was finally satisfied – the fact that he was the most likely Frenchman to scoop up the available directorship (and its tax-free salary) sweetening the pill.

Morgenthau had earlier promised not to retire to bed until he had corrected the impression that the Americans were in some way prejudiced against the French. 'Now you say you have not got that impression and I can go to bed,' he said.[63]

In this way was the future leadership of the International Monetary Fund, the most important multilateral institution in global economics, determined – through a series of backroom deals that paid less attention to economic reality than to political horse-trading. Some countries, upon discovering that when their national income was passed through Mikesell's mysterious formula it resulted in a low quota, attempted to rectify the position by rustling up a new, magically improved figure. In the IMF archives in Washington you can still, even today, find handwritten scraps of paper from various countries addressed to Mikesell containing scribbles which supposedly justified a higher quota. Others pleaded politics or, occasionally, ignorance. New Zealand's Sir Walter Nash protested that he had failed to realise his quota number was in dollars rather than sterling. 'Throughout the conference [Nash] has shown a tendency to be about three bars behind the band,' remarked Robbins.[64]

Morgenthau entertained an almost constant stream of guests to his suite: the Czechoslovakians, Beyen from the Netherlands, Iran's rambunctious delegation head Abul Hassan Ibtehaj ('vain, obstinate and arbitrary', according to the Foreign Office's man in

The Mount Washington Hotel.

Keynes's 1925 marriage to Russian ballet dancer Lydia Lopokova was front-page news.

Harry Dexter White at work in the Treasury.

Keynes and Lydia checking in at the Mount Washington Hotel. Lydia is holding her famous carrier bag from a Cambridge fishmonger.

Abol H. Ebtehaj, governor of the National Bank of Iran, and Alexander Argyropulos (right) of the Greek delegation, arriving in New York on their way to the conference. Argyropulos had just escaped from a Nazi prisoner-of-war camp.

entlemen, we must
t, we cannot, we dare
t fail.' Senator Charles
bey (right) puts the
ishing touches to
s speech delivered
ar the opening of the
nference. He is assisted
his son.

me of the leading members of the American delegation at Bretton Woods. Standing
, from left, Harry Dexter White, Fred Vinson, Dean Acheson, Ned Brown, Marriner
cles and Jesse Wolcott. Seated are, from left, Robert Wagner, Brent Spence, Henry
orgenthau and Charles Tobey.

The American and Russian delegations pose for a photo. Alleged NKVD agent Nikolai Chechulin is standing fifth from the right. Harry Dexter White is two places to his righ Stepanov and Morgenthau sit in the centre. Mabel Newcomer sits on the far left.

The Russian and American delegations take a rare break from negotiations. Harry Dext White can be seen chatting with Mikael Stepanov (at centre, on chairs).

Keynes and China's Kung. The pair got along famously in public, though in private Keynes would refer to Kung as 'the old Mandarin'.

dia Lopokova shares a joke with Mikael Stepanov (second from right) and other embers of the Russian delegation. At one point she stepped into the conference oceedings to help translate.

Fred Vinson (left)
discusses matters with
Ned Brown, the US
delegation's token bank◦
between meetings in th◦
hotel lobby.

Harry White (centre) with two of the leading lights from the British delegation, Lione◦
Robbins (left) and Dennis Robertson (right).

he Indian delegation that proved so troublesome for the British. From left to right: B.K. Iadan, A.D. Shroff, Sir Jeremy Raisman, Sir Shanmukhan Shetty, Sir Theodore Gregory, ir Chintaman Desmukh.

red Vinson (left) discusses atters with Harold Fleming f the *Christian Science Monitor*. he conference allowed urnalists 'unprecedented' ccess to the delegates.

The big group photo of delegation heads: Keynes is seated, third from the left. Morgenthau sits in the centre, wearing a white suit..

hough by the time of Bretton Woods they were getting along better, relations between
1orgenthau (left) and Keynes were often strained.

merican delegates and technicians hard at work in one of the late-night technical
ommittees.

Federal Reserve chairman Marriner Eccles takes some time away from negotiations on the golf course.

There were a surprising number of glamorous women at the conference – most of them secretaries and assistants. Here is Mignon MacLean the dance instructor having her bracelet fixed by a member of the Ecuadorian delegation.

The swimming pool at the Mount Washington Hotel. Despite the amount of work being done indoors, it was rarely empty.

Members of the inscrutable Russian delegation take time out to read the American papers, proving that they could at least understand some English. Nikolai Chechulin makes a rare appearance on the far right.

Pierre Mendes-France at Bretton Woods. A highly intelligent man, he was hampered by the fact that few at the conference took the French seriously.

Lord Halifax formally signs the Bretton Woods Agreement in Washington in December 1945. The mood in the room was sombre, and Halifax was still exhausted from the Anglo-American loan negotiations.

Protesters outside Parliament demonstrate against Bretton Woods. There was uproar in the UK that there was no formal political debate over the agreement, or the post-war loan.

One of the pamphlets issued by the US government to persuade the American people of the merits of Bretton Woods.

John Maynard Keynes
and Harry Dexter White
talk beneath the palms at
Savannah.

White and Keynes share a
joke at Savannah in 1946.
By then, only a few weeks
before Keynes's death, the
pair had put aside most of
their differences.

Lydia relaxing at the Savannah conference in 1946. At home in Sussex she was known to sunbathe with rather less clothing.

Harry Dexter White playing volleyball at Savannah. He captained an American team against the Russians at Bretton Woods. The Russians won.

eynes delivers his final speech at Savannah.

The IMF's first ever board meeting, held in a makeshift room at the Washington Hotel 1946, two weeks after Keynes's death.

'My creed is the American creed.' Harry Dexter White testifies to Congress's Un-American Activiti Committee in 1948. Three days later, he was dead.

Tehran[65]). South Africa gave up $50 million, to be shared between Poland and Czechoslovakia; countries regarded to have put up a plucky fight in the war (Yugoslavia, Greece) were promised extra quota portions from the $800 million White had set aside as a sweetener to sprinkle on those disaffected with their allocation.* As the diplomatic conveyor belt rolled on, the feats of mental arithmetic required to keep the total quota figure unchanged became more and more challenging.

'See,' Morgenthau joked, 'that is why I am Secretary of the Treasury. I can add and subtract.'[66]

And the power structure of the Fund would remain broadly unchanged, save for a few nips and tucks, well into the twenty-first century – such that even on the eve of Bretton Woods' seventieth anniversary, Belgium would have a bigger quota than Brazil, despite its economy being a fraction of the size.

But of all the quota battles, none was so fierce, nor so drawn out, as that between the Americans and the Russians. It would continue all the way to the very final banquet, long after everything else had been settled. The initial plan – at least the one that had been agreed at Atlantic City – was that the Soviets would be awarded a quota of $800 million at both the Fund and the Bank. This was far more than Russia's national income justified but, as with the Chinese, a little economic leap of faith would be worth it to ensure all of the 'Big Four' were involved. After all, Bretton Woods was not merely about economic logic – it was also about laying down a precedent for the bold new world of multilateral dialogue.

However, the Russians had spied weakness. In a press conference the previous year, when asked about possible quota levels, Harry Dexter White had thought out loud: 'maybe for the Russians we'll have $1 billion ...' It was supposed to be an illustration, and was

---

*South Africa realised that in the event of economic disaster in the future it would be able to fall back on its gold reserves rather than the Fund's reserves. Its delegates appeared unusually relaxed about the political implications.

taken as such everywhere except Moscow. The Russians brought it up again at Bretton Woods. It was clear that they were treating $1 billion as a starting point for negotiations, with $1.2 billion the aspiration – preferably higher even than the British quota.[67] Then there was the question of how much of the quota would have to be submitted in the form of gold (Russia wanted its gold contribution to be lower than the rest).

It was a style of negotiation the Russians would perfect – and with which the Americans would become wearily familiar – over the coming years. They would refuse to compromise in any way, insist that Moscow was not prepared to move, even if this was not the case, and then, in the evening, they would try to toast their rivals under the table in the bar.* Eventually, late in the second week and following hours of private negotiations, White managed to scrape together the necessary quota portions to bring the Russian quota up to $1.2 billion. The Russians would nonetheless drop a further bombshell that threatened to upend the entire conference.

As this soap opera went on, some of the other delegates started to worry that it would mean that by the time the Fund was finally set up, it would be rendered economically irrelevant. After all, it looked to most of the economists at Bretton Woods as if Russia and China had every intention of drawing down on their quotas as soon as possible. If they did so, given the mammoth size of those quotas, it would mean very little was left for anyone else.

For others the episode raised yet more worrying questions. The conference was aimed not merely at setting up an economic system but also at instilling the same kind of solidarity in the international economy as had flourished on the battlefield. But as the Americans

---

*Indeed, reports from the US Embassy in Moscow suggested that even when Stepanov had been given instructions he would frequently declare that he was still waiting for orders from home. This is borne out by closer examination of contemporary records from the Russian finance and foreign ministries, which show that the Russian delegates enjoyed considerable autonomy.

were rapidly discovering, when it came to the Russians, solidarity was a one-way street.

This was not yet the Cold War: for many within the US administration Bretton Woods was intended to be a template for peaceful co-operation between the United States and their Communist allies in the coming decades. The Europeans were less optimistic. 'I confess that the 'Russians fill me with apprehension,' wrote Robbins. 'There is something morally impressive about such monumental selfishness. But I cannot think it augurs well for the future of the world.'[68]

As George Bolton had observed, by the first Thursday the conference was already descending into 'complete confusion'. You could hardly walk through the hotel lobby without bumping into one or another disaffected delegate desperate to vent their frustration. Occasionally the gripe was about an obscure matter like exchange controls or rules on looted artwork, but more often it was about those confounded quotas.

In a rare effort to escape the madhouse, that evening Redvers Opie, the Treasury man in Washington, took some of the British delegation, including Keynes and Robbins, for a ride in his car around the hotel grounds. To the east was the ever-present summit of Mount Washington, 'looming up over this upland basin'.[69] They rode 'among peaks, dales, streams and mountains with beautiful tints beyond,' wrote Lydia. 'And a feeling of grandeur & rest spreads in one's bosom.'[70]

But it was hard to enjoy the scenery, so all-consuming was the conference. The long days, the sleepless nights and the threat that two years of preparation would be for nothing ... it was all taking its toll. Keynes was suffering more than anyone else. Hard as everyone had tried to take the load off him (Lydia, in particular, had rationed his time and attempted to maintain silence in their rooms), he was difficult to control: 'it is intolerable for him to go slow', wrote Robbins. Everyone knew how fragile the great man's health had been, he added. 'Keynes is showing obvious signs of exhaustion and we are all very worried about him.'[71] It was an early portent of the collapse that would happen in little over a week's time.

CHAPTER ELEVEN

Week Two

The World's Worst Chairman

He is, of course, one of the brightest lights of mankind in both thinking and expression and in his ability to influence people, and he shone also by being the world's worst chairman.

Emanuel Goldenweiser on John Maynard Keynes[1]

And when I die don't bury me at all,
Just cover my bones with alcohol.
Put a bottle of booze at my head and feet,
And pray the Lord my soul to keep.

'The Bretton Woods Song'

An attempt to distil the Bretton Woods agreement into a single core principle would probably look like this: that, rather than having all the world's currencies tied directly to a physical element (as in the gold standard) or allowed to float (as in the fiat money system which began in 1971), they would all be pegged to the US dollar. There were other facets, among them that the peg would be more flexible than the gold standard, but in essence what was signed at the Mount Washington Hotel in 1944 established a dollar standard. The dollar, in turn, was tied to gold at a value of $35 an ounce. The US currency had been at the very centre of the economic constellation for decades, but this role would finally be legally cemented at Bretton Woods.

However, this took place not in the steady glare of public scrutiny but almost by stealth, without most participants in the summit even noticing it. More unexpectedly still, the decision to place the dollar at the very centre of the system was triggered not by an American but, of all people, by a member of the *British* delegation.

Needless to say, the delegate in question was not Keynes. By the second week, the British chairman was so exhausted he had taken to receiving guests to his suite lying on his couch. From this horizontal position he dealt with an almost constant stream of visitors: there were other Britons looking for guidance, rival delegations seeking a behind-the-scenes deal and one or two who simply wanted a moment with a celebrity. After a period, Lydia would gently (and occasionally not so gently) usher them away.*

'Sometimes I get out of temper, waiting while everybody else asks me where is he to be found,' she wrote home. It was Wednesday 12 July, 'our second week here, and in spite of [the] beautiful surroundings it becomes more and more like a mad-house, with most people assembled here working more than humanly possible.'

The previous day the British delegation had taken a second drive to see the Old Man of the Mountain – a granite ledge overlooking the valley which looked not unlike President Roosevelt.† As the Keyneses and the rest of the Britons stared up at the enigmatic stone face, they could hear the sound of bullfrogs croaking from the river. The men picked flowers – tiger lilies, water lilies and arum lilies.[2] It was possible, for a moment, to forget the world was still at war – that Bob Brand's son was, at that very moment, fighting through the battlefields of Normandy.

*If we took too much time, however, Lady Keynes would tiptoe over to protect him from becoming too tired.' Mikesell, *Foreign Adventures of an Economist*, Eugene, 2000, p. 58.
†The rock formation, which was a short drive from Mount Washington, collapsed in 2003.

But it was to be the last time the entire delegation had a moment to itself. Over the following week and a half the demands of the conference would escalate yet further – beyond even the intolerable levels of the first week. It would put unprecedented strain on the entire delegation – none more so than their chairman.

For in spite of his exhaustion, Keynes's workload had multiplied. Having focused mainly in its first week on the International Monetary Fund, in the second week the conference began to deal with the creation of the World Bank. The committees concerned swung into action, with chairman Keynes in possession of the gavel. 'Now, as regards our procedure today,' Keynes announced as he opened the debate that second Tuesday, 'I think you will all be of the mind that we want to make as rapid progress as we can. Time is running short.'

As a result, 'desperate measures' were called for, wrote his fellow UK delegate George Bolton. Keynes therefore 'began a system of taking a meeting so quickly that no-one could understand either what he was saying or to which clause he happened to be referring and by this means about half the clauses were referred to a Drafting Commission. The fun began after this process had been completed.'[3]

For the Americans, who thought it could get no worse than Harry White's style of chairmanship (once described as 'like a man directing the movements of a ship without a rudder in a hurricane'), his Lordship's technique was disconcerting to say the least.[4] Emanuel Goldenweiser of the Federal Reserve said that while Keynes may well have been 'the outstanding personality at Bretton Woods ... the General blazing the way both for the Fund and the Bank ... he shone also by being the world's worst chairman.'*

---

*Goldenweiser went on: 'He presided over meetings of the Bank in a way that was entirely intolerable because he had his own documents all fixed up so he could go through in a hurry.' Goldenweiser Papers Library of Congress, 'Bretton Woods Conference', Box 4.

With Keynes rattling so fast through the various clauses setting up the World Bank (including, it appears from the minutes, some which may not have even been available to the other delegates*), everyone found themselves left behind, Dean Acheson reported back to Morgenthau. 'Keynes is under great pressure,' said the Assistant Secretary of State. 'He knows this thing inside out so that when anybody says Section 15C he knows what it is. Nobody else in the room knows. So before you have an opportunity to turn to Section 15C and see what he is talking about, he says, "I hear no objection to that", and it is passed. Well, everybody is trying to find Section 15C. He then says, we are now talking about Section 26D. Then they begin fiddling around with their papers, and before you find that, it is passed.'[5]

Watching the great man of twentieth-century economics operate at full speed was quite a spectacle – though he did have a tendency to talk and talk, according to Senator Wagner. 'Harry,' said Wagner to White at one of the regular American meetings, 'Lord Keynes – is he *the* Lord?' 'Yes,' was White's deadpan reply. 'He talked longer than you did,' said Wagner. 'Well, he is a better man,' said White.[6]

Keynes certainly knew the details of the Bank documents inside out, having redrafted them himself on the voyage from Britain. The Americans still did not expect to make complete progress on the Bank at Bretton Woods – anyway, it was a very low priority compared with the Fund. But Keynes was a man on a mission. Having realised that few of his suggestions would end up being incorporated into the Fund, he was determined to leave his mark on the Bank. After all, while the Fund was designed to deal with the economic hereafter, the Bank was intended to ease the transition for war-ravaged economies like Britain. Because White and his team

---

*Schuler and Rosenberg (2012, p. 297) note that Keynes refers to an Article XI which does not appear in the relevant documents by this stage.

had paid less attention to the Bank in the previous two and a half years, he had been unusually open to his British counterpart's suggestions after Keynes turned up in Atlantic City with his proposals. White's original plan envisaged an institution with a cache of around $10 billion (he had considered as much as $20 billion – a staggering $270 billion at 2014 prices) to lend out to poorer, more unfortunate countries. Whereas the Fund was to provide the discipline in the newly stabilised world economy, the Bank was designed to lure countries in – particularly the Europeans and Latin Americans.

Keynes's brainwave was to treat the Bank not as a simple pot of cash but as a fund to guarantee private sector investments. About four-fifths of the money put forward by the countries at Bretton Woods was to sit in the Bank for use only when a loan went bad; that way, each dollar put up by the Bank could secure multiple dollars of private funds. The draft Keynes brandished in front of White in Atlantic City had entailed governments putting up a mere $5 billion to gain even more financial firepower than White's initial scheme. Or so the theory went: in practice, rather than the Bank using its pot of money to guarantee others' loans, most of the Bank's loans have been backed by money raised from world financial markets.[7]

Of course, this once again raised the question of why the institution was called a 'Bank' in the first place. It did not behave much like a bank; it did not take in deposits and use them to lend out. However, the minutes of the meeting show that when Keynes attempted to raise the prospect of changing the name to 'corporation' or 'association' he was opposed first by Dean Acheson and then by the Russian delegate, who said: 'This bank is not a corporation or association, therefore the Soviet delegation does not see any reason for substituting "bank" for any other word.' Keynes shot back: 'I don't know what may be the case in other languages. This performs none of the functions of an English bank, none whatever, and therefore it is terribly misleading.' However, by then it was clear that his resistance to the name would be futile.[8]

Consigned as they were to their own committees, Keynes and White by this stage had little face-to-face contact. Only occasionally did they bump into each other in the corridors and lobbies of the hotel, and when they did there was barely time for more than small talk, which usually entailed complaints about the volume of work. 'At one moment Harry White told me that at last even he was all in, not having been in bed for more than five hours a night for four consecutive weeks,' Keynes recounted.[9]

As a result, most of their battles amounted to shadow boxing – a stream of letters back and forth within the internal hotel mail, and arguments carried out on behalf of the pair by their colleagues. Both would hand down advice to those colleagues on how to handle their respective opponent. 'Just because Keynes is an autocrat doesn't mean that you have to take it,' White told Acheson. 'You stand up and you say you don't like the way things are running.'[10]

Acheson, for his part, found Keynes on the whole to be absolutely charming. It was a similar story in the British camp, whose members had been warned about White's prickly personality, but, according to Bolton, found him 'genial and good-tempered', showing 'the utmost patience'.[11] The more you appealed to his pity, Robbins found, the more compassionate White would become. At one point, with the Britons still waiting in vain for official advice from the Treasury on how to respond to American proposals to locate the Fund and Bank's headquarters in the US rather than Europe, Robbins had a quiet word. 'We know we will be beaten and we hope to avoid being humiliated,' he said, urging that at the very least the Americans hold back from a public debate on the issue for a few days. 'We can wait,' said White.[12]

As the Bank started to take shape in the meeting rooms at one end of the hotel, the Fund – and the articles that would determine the foundations of the world economy – was coalescing at the other end. The critical meeting – the one 'where we either fish or cut bait on most of these things', in White's words[13] – came on Thursday 13 July. The hot weather of the first week had been replaced by rain showers, routing the Russian secretaries from the outside pool. There had been thunderstorms and it was chilly enough that Lydia Keynes started to wear her furs. The summit of Mount Washington, which had for the first week loomed over the hotel as the delegates began their negotiations, was now obscured by a wreath of clouds.

While Keynes was occupied with the Bank meetings, Britain was represented by Dennis Robertson, the man who had nearly eaten his gherkin-shaped lapel pin in Atlantic City. Quiet, undemonstrative and quite brilliant, Robertson went even further back with Keynes than any of the other delegates. The pair of Old Etonians had been at Cambridge together – Robertson at Trinity College while Keynes was at King's – and Keynes had selected Robertson as a protégé from an early stage.

'There is a good deal in his favour, but a little pudding headed perhaps,'[14] was how the twenty-five-year-old Keynes had described Robertson – a great compliment in the Keynesian lexicon. Over the following years they would become companions of such intellectual intimacy that, as Robertson put it, in many of their formative papers 'neither of us now knows how much of the ideas therein contained is his and how much is mine'.[15]

Keynes paid Robertson the highest honour, electing him to the Apostles, the prestigious intellectual secret society; Robertson, himself a confirmed bachelor, helped facilitate Keynes's courtship of Lydia, inviting her up to Cambridge; and when Keynes came in the 1930s to draft the various papers aimed at uprooting the classical economics they had studied together in Cambridge, it was to Robertson that he turned for advice. Indeed, it was Robertson rather than Keynes who had been one of the first to postulate that during economic slumps it was conceivable that even interest rates of just 1 per cent could fail to simulate investment, something Keynes would later address in his *General Theory*.[16]

However, it was at this point that the fertile, harmonious relationship had started to fracture. As far as Keynes was concerned, the two simply had 'pathological' differences when it came to economics. When Keynes sent some of the early drafts of the *General Theory* to Robertson the result was a series of 'painful' letters which revealed a gaping and possibly unbridgeable intellectual void between the two men, covering a whole series of elements – Keynes's attacks on the traditional economic models of Alfred Marshall, definitions of demand, income, user cost and quasi-rent – but most of all their understanding of how interest rates functioned.

Robertson wrote, 'a large part of your theoretical structure is still to me almost complete mumbo-jumbo!'[17] To which Keynes responded curtly that 'Everything turns on the mumbo-jumbo and so long as it is obscure to you our minds have not really met.'[18] In the event, he did not even acknowledge Robertson in the book.

The war had forced the two back together, and by the time of Bretton Woods they were friendly once again – although the intellectual wounds had not entirely healed. Little differences kept cropping up during the preparations for the conference. Robertson, along with Lionel Robbins and a few of the other younger Britons, was concerned about the level of protectionism inherent in Keynes's conception of the Fund. They were more sympathetic, too, to American demands that Britain should abide by the Fund's rigid rules on exchange rate levels; Keynes was determined to fight the exchange clause, giving Britain the right to devalue the pound by a hefty chunk if need be.

These internal differences were to be exposed that Thursday as Robertson sat down to represent Britain at the fourth big meeting of Commission I, which tackled one of the most controversial phrases in the draft document.

The question of what kind of unit the world's currencies were to be hitched to had been lurking throughout the preceding two years' debates and discussions. That, after all, had been what prompted Henry Morgenthau to ask White to come up with a scheme for a new international currency; it was what Keynes had been intending to answer with his proposal for the creation of bancor/Unitas. However, that element of his plan had withered away some time previously, with nothing surfacing in its absence.

White had been clear from the earliest drafts of his plan that 'only the dollar has any chance of serving [as a unit of account]', though he conceded that officially anointing the dollar as the official measure of international bookkeeping would be politically unpalatable for most other countries.[19] By 1944, with the international currency scheme having dissolved away, even Keynes had accepted the primacy of the dollar in practice if not in principle, telling colleagues that the Fund would use the dollar for its bookkeeping, though he expected an international unit to emerge in due course.*

But even as the delegates arrived at the Mount Washington, the issue still hung in the air. In an effort to avoid what he realised would be a painful battle, not merely with Keynes but with all other countries, White had decided that spring to defer the decision until the conference, hence the insertion of that benighted phrase 'gold and gold-convertible exchange' into the initial drafts whenever it referred to a particular unit of account. Although Keynes had dismissed this phraseology as 'idiocy', in reality it was a kind of euphemism: the only currency around the world which could conceivably be exchanged with gold was the US dollar (America

---

*Keynes was ahead of his time here. It was not until the late 1960s, just ahead of the demise of the Bretton Woods system, that the Fund would create an international unit of account, Special Drawing Rights (SDRs).

having the world's biggest gold reserves), but saying so would only serve to inflame matters.[20]

Perhaps appropriately, it was neither a Briton nor an American who raised the matter in the meeting that Thursday. Shroff of the Indian delegation stood up and finally asked the question: 'I think it is high time that the USA delegation give us a definition of "gold and gold-convertible exchange".'

It was Robertson, rather than the Americans White or Bernstein, who volunteered the answer: 'I would like to propose an amendment to the text which is before us, according to which the criteria of payment of official gold subscription should be expressed as official holdings of gold and United States dollars.'[21] If there were any doubt as to his intent, the following day he double-checked that the phrase 'gold and US dollars' had been inserted into the Articles of Agreement. In between, White had referred the issue to a special committee which, overnight, had integrated the change into what would become the Final Act of the conference.

Quite what sparked Robertson's intervention remains something of a mystery – though he appears to have done it off his own back. What with the madness of the past week, the British delegation had yet to agree what formulation it wanted in the articles – they had hardly had a single opportunity to confer, let alone on a matter of phraseology. However, while some have attempted to paint the insertion of the dollar into the articles as evidence of a rearguard action by White and the Americans to displace the pound as the world's reserve currency, the evidence suggests otherwise.*

Most likely, Robertson was merely putting into black and white what was already considered by almost everyone to be the

---

*Remember, too, that at this stage Britain's main concern as regards the Indians related to blocked sterling balances. In light of this, Robertson's amendment might be seen as reinforcing the notion that whereas some currencies were perhaps convertible into dollars, sterling was pointedly not.

conventional wisdom: in 1944 the dollar *was* the only currency one could freely convert into gold. Though it had fully arrived on the international scene only a couple of decades before, it was by now the world's dominant unit of exchange.*

As with almost every conventional wisdom, however, Keynes took a different view. Just the previous week he had circulated a letter he had written to his old sparring partner Ralph Hawtrey, in which he insisted that 'there [is] no gold convertible exchange in the world ... The United States now admit it. This admission may pave the way to something very much more suitable from our point of view. Anyhow, I think you may take it that the term "gold convertible exchange" will disappear.'[22]

Keynes preferred something vaguer – 'convertible exchange' – that would further muddy the waters about what was and wasn't tied inextricably to gold. After all, linking the value of the US dollar to gold, as that phrase did, would mean a return to a system that was at least partially similar to the gold standard of old. This in turn went back to a recurrent theme throughout the Bretton Woods debates. There was no doubt gold was at the centre of the new blueprint: the dollar would have a direct value in gold, other currencies would then be priced in either gold or dollars; so what was the difference between this and the disastrous gold exchange standard of the 1920s?

From Keynes's perspective it was all a question of rigidity: the new system would still have a link to gold, but it would be far more flexible. Members would be allowed (expected, in Keynes's mind) to devalue their currencies whenever their economies became

---

*Technically speaking, more pounds than dollars were held in reserve by central banks and other countries around the world. However, while this would normally be the measure of a currency's prevalence or influence, in this case it was not, because sterling balances were effectively blocked from being converted into other currencies or gold. Barry Eichengreen, *Exorbitant Privilege: The Rise and Fall of the Dollar and the Future of the International Monetary System*, New York, 2011, p. 39.

uncompetitive. That way, countries would not be obliged to slash wages on a regular basis purely to remain within the club – as had been the case in the 1920s and 1930s.*

The problem was that by equating the dollar with gold, the agreement set in place a kind of mini-gold standard for one currency. The dollar was formally enshrined as being directly convertible into gold, which contributed both to its dominance over other currencies and to the ultimate collapse of the Bretton Woods system in the 1970s.

Whether Keynes would have objected to this amendment we shall never know. He was elsewhere, rattling through the clauses establishing the Bank, and so left everything in Robertson's hands. He trusted Robertson implicitly. 'If anyone is picked out I think it would have to be Dennis, whose help has been absolutely indispensable,' he wrote. 'He alone had the intellectual subtlety and patience of mind and tenacity of character to grasp and hold on to all details and fight them through Bernstein (who adores Dennis), so that I, frequently occupied otherwise, could feel completely happy about the situation.'[23]

This was, in retrospect, almost impossibly naïve. Robertson and Keynes had disagreed on so many occasions in the past that it was almost inevitable that they would differ on some of the key terminology of the new international monetary system. Although Robertson was almost certainly aware of Keynes's position when it came to the dollar clause, he appeared to have staged a last act of defiance against his old sparring partner.

Either that or he simply blundered. After all, as far as some

---

*In a joint press conference ahead of the Bretton Woods conference, Keynes put it thus: 'One of the signal purposes of this Fund is to return to good order and discipline, to bring back gold as the fundamental reserve money and make it clear that we are all going to trade together, and not indulge in arbitrary or unreasonable changes, and in any case in conjunction. So that the only confusion, I think, arises between these two senses, the rigid gold standard and a currency standard based on gold without the rigidity.' IMF Archives, Bretton Woods Collection.

onlookers were concerned, Robertson was off the boil at Bretton Woods. Ragnar Nurkse, the Estonian economist, present observing the conference for the League of Nations, jotted in his notes that Robertson had 'made a mess at least twice'.[24]

Though some historians have attempted to depict what happened as part of a clever plot by White and the Americans to displace the pound as the world's reserve currency, it looks far more like a well-intentioned error by Robertson. Although the Americans were in no doubt that they expected the dollar to remain the de facto global currency of choice in the coming decades, they showed little inclination either in public or behind the scenes to formalise this in law. Newly published transcripts of the meeting confirm that the crucial amendment was made, twice, by a British delegate in response to an Indian intervention. British delegates, moreover, also attended the crucial late-night special committee sessions where the amendments were inserted into the official Articles of Agreement.

By the time the conference ended, none of the delegates would have time to read the full text of the agreement. It was only in the following weeks that Keynes discovered some of the changes his colleague had inserted. This triggered a blazing row which would persist into the following year, bringing him to the brink of threatening to pull out of the Fund entirely. However, Keynes's real concern was not that the dollar had been given special status, but that the same convertibility might soon be imposed on the pound. The drafting change drove another wedge between Keynes and his intellectual sparring partner, Robertson – one that in this case would persist until death.

For when it came to the question of convertibility, Britain's immediate concern was not so much the distant future of currencies as the immediate question of how to salvage Britain's hideously indebted economy. One solution to this was to persuade the Americans to modify the articles so that countries could devalue their currencies by up to 10 per cent without permission from the Fund, and by even more if authorisation was sought. The British had scored a victory over the weekend by getting this so-called exchange clause incorporated into the Fund articles. Neither Robertson nor Robbins had had much appetite for the change, which as far as they were concerned undermined the very purpose of the Fund, but they had fought for it all the same.

However, there was no question of the pound being freely convertible into gold, or indeed any other major currency, any time soon. As the British would learn to their cost three years later, allowing investors to shift money into other currencies would open the floodgates and provoke a flight of money out of the country. So all the British efforts were devoted towards prolonging the period the UK would have to allow those with sterling to convert it, which came back to that quandary of blocked balances Lionel Robbins had shamefacedly fought the Indians over the previous week.*

And, for the time being at least, the British were successful, negotiating a generous five-year transitional period before they had to abide by the rules of the Fund and allow sterling to be freely convertible into other currencies. They also succeeded that second week in giving themselves a certain amount of freedom to devalue their exchange rate without the Fund's permission – another of the stipulations insisted on by the Bank of England.†

The problem, however, was that watering down the Fund's

---

*Robbins would later recall, 'I have always felt, in a way, ashamed at having to lead on that.' LSE Archives, Robbins 112, transcript of Economists' Dinner at the Reform Club, 5 March 1973.
†This (and the gold/dollar clause) would form part of Article IV of the Fund's Articles of Agreement, which dealt with the extent to which the Fund could intervene in domestic policies. Though the Bretton Woods system came to an end in 1971, Article IV was subsequently rewritten and now entitles the IMF to survey each member state's economy every year. These are called Article IV Consultations.

fundamental rules (remember, this was an institution designed specifically to control exchange rates) would undermine its ability to maintain control of its more errant members. As Will Brown of the US delegation whispered to one of his British counterparts, 'It is all very well for you Britishers to claim greater liberty ... But the net effect is that we have nothing left to control the Latin Americans and this fact may make the whole scheme suspect in the eyes of Congress.'

In any case, the controversy was further proof that by this halfway stage, it was impossible for those on the ground to have any conception of the coherence of what they were negotiating into law. 'No one has the faintest idea what this document will look like when it is eventually turned out,' declared the Bank of England's Bolton. 'The few of us here who are familiar with the shape and scope of the Fund have completely lost touch with the various developments, and I am more convinced than ever that an unworkable hodge-podge will result from this Conference.'[25]

Nikolai Fyodorovich Chechulin wasn't like the rest of the delegates at Bretton Woods. Younger, taller and more handsome than most of the academic economists who surrounded him at the Mount Washington, he stares confidently into the lens in the one official photo of him that survives from the conference, in the middle of a group of delegates, only a couple of places along from Harry Dexter White.

As the vice-chairman of Gosbank, the country's central bank, he also understood finance. Unlike most of the Russian delegation, moreover, he spoke fluent English, and was unafraid to switch on the charm when it was required – and as one of the delegation's few English speakers he played an important behind-the-scenes role at Bretton Woods. He captained the Russian volleyball team in an impromptu match against the Americans. The US team, captained by White, lost.

He was also, the FBI later concluded, a Russian spy, an agent from the NKVD.* A couple of weeks after the conference he would travel together with his fellow delegate Ivan Zlobin to White's country house outside Washington DC. This was, it was later alleged, White's first direct contact with a Russian agent.

Over the course of the conference, White would spend much of his time in private meetings with the Russians – so much so that other delegates would later remark how odd it was that the head of the US delegation would hole himself up for so long with the Soviets. Not that anyone at the time suspected Chechulin of having Soviet intelligence links. As far as they were concerned, the most striking thing about the Soviet delegation – aside from the fact that they seemed duty-bound to defer any major decisions back to Moscow – was how much fun they were having.

While Keynes's prediction ahead of the conference that 'acute alcoholic poisoning would set in before the end' was meant as a warning, the Russians seemed to take it as an invitation.[26] In the opening days of the conference, they were already to be found plying fellow guests with vodka and caviar. Keynes himself indulged in the delicacy, taking the opportunity to try to persuade the chair of the delegation, Stepanov, to arrange for the Bolshoi Ballet to tour London. The request had to be relayed via a baffled translator.[27]

As the conference progressed, the hierarchy in economic power between nations was complemented with a taxonomy of cocktail parties. The American parties were big but a little drab, with no one out for much in the way of fun; the Chinese were the most decadent; the English receptions were the stiffest and most exclusive (if you were lucky enough to get an invite).

---

*The disclosure of the identification was originally made by R. Bruce Craig in his book *Treasonable Doubt* (2004). Others, for instance Svetlana Chervonnaya, contend that he was a so-called 'co-optee' (*privlechennyi*) – 'a common practice with diplomats and other bona fide officials co-opted for making contacts in their official capacity, which is a far shot from being an agent.'

The Russian parties, meanwhile, were free-for-alls. 'The Russians have the reputation here,' wrote one reporter, 'of being very democratic because, unlike some of the other countries, when they give a party they invite everyone down to the lowliest stenographer and messenger boy.'[28] Their bashes were also by far and away the most alcoholic.

As Lionel Robbins would later recall, the British nightcap with the Soviets descended into 'a bibulous party, in which we vied with one another in demonstrating friendship by excessive consumption of liquor'.[29] Another witness simply recalled that 'immense quantities of strong liquor were consumed.'[30] Happily, the vast intake of booze probably added to rather than detracted from the quality of inter-delegation communication, since scarcely anyone could understand the other delegation's language anyway. Stepanov, who had the luxury of an interpreter, roamed at will, telling 'atrocity stories, and [congratulating] each other on the feats of our respective armies'.[31]

The Bank of England's George Bolton was cornered by Chechulin, who not only spoke English but, Bolton reported home, 'appears to have the most profound admiration for the Bank of England'. In his diary Bolton wrote: 'In our cups we have sworn eternal friendship and promised to exchange visits in the near future ... While it would obviously be unwise to pay too much attention to private conversations of this nature, more closer personal relationships may have some profitable results.'[32]

Had the man from the Bank of England realised that he was talking to an alleged Soviet spy, he might perhaps have been less friendly and rather more guarded. As it was, his unpublished diaries reveal that there was contact between the Bank and the very man with NKVD links whose association with White would later come to light so brutally.

In the following years, despite the falling of the Iron Curtain, Gosbank would enjoy a relaxed, co-operative relationship with its

British counterpart, partly thanks to Bolton's encouragement. A decade later its officials, including another delegate, Chechulin's State Bank colleague F.P. Bystrov, would be welcomed as friends to the UK as guests of the Bank of England and given lunch with the governor, although the police attempted to arrest them on their way there.*

Not that there was any shame among the Westerners in admitting their affection for Communism. Keynes's secretary, Miss Macey, was a self-confessed 'Bolshie' who took the opportunity to ask the Russians if they had come across Harry Pollitt, the general secretary of the Communist Party of Great Britain. They had never even heard of him.

They listened, rapt, to her all the same. According to Lydia, 'the girls made a hit with their men' – particularly Miss Macey, who Lydia had affectionately nicknamed 'cutie'.[33] There was, in fact, a preponderance of beautiful women at Bretton Woods; contemporary reports remark at the stream of glamorous 'secretaries' and 'typists' attached to each delegation – some of whose roles seemed to be enigmatic, to say the least. Certainly, they did little to counteract the stenographic shortage throughout the weeks at the Mount Washington.

A large proportion of these women were to be found in the Russian delegation, where they were occasionally employed as strategic devices. One day Canadian delegate Louis Rasminsky, the chair of the Fund's drafting committee, received a call from Stepanov. He wanted to discuss one of Russia's pet projects – to try to reduce the amount of gold it was obliged to deposit with the Fund. Rasminsky told him to come up to his room.

---

*Bank of England Archives, OV111/19, recounts a September 1955 visit from two Gosbank officials, Bystrov and V.S. Geraschenko, who had succeeded Chechulin as vice-chairman. The notes say: 'The occasion was slightly marred by the fact that the car which brought the Russian party from Oxford was stopped by the police outside Oxford, who said they had received instructions to arrest this car and examine the passengers' documents etc. However, not much was made of the incident and we had a very friendly discussion lasting about two hours.'

'After a few minutes there was a knock on the door and I opened it and there was a fairly statuesque and good-looking Russian blonde,' Rasminsky would later recall. 'She said that she had come to discuss the wording of the articles of agreement. I said that I preferred to discuss it with Mr Stepanov.' The Russian lady left, and a few moments later Stepanov called Rasminsky again and asked him to come downstairs. The encounter then became even more surreal as Stepanov confided in Rasminsky that Harry White had told him that the Canadian was the only man who had the authority to change the draft text. It turned out White had told this to Stepanov in a bid to get the Soviets 'off his back'.[34]

Like many other delegations, the Soviets had mixed feelings about their very presence at the conference. It was already clear that they would have few direct economic links with the Western world, and yet they were reluctant to miss the beginning of the post-war settlement. Moreover, the return to a reimagined gold standard would be excellent news for the Soviet gold-mining industry. Relations with the Americans were, for the time being, extremely positive – indeed, the Fed's Marriner Eccles remarked in one of the US delegation meetings that public sentiment was 'more sympathetic toward Russia at the moment than toward [the] UK'.[35]

The public had largely accepted the Russians as allies; it was only in the following years that relations would sour. For the time being, the Soviets were to be treated courteously and as colleagues rather than enemies – even if they did seem to be taking advantage of it. 'They're doing such a magnificent job in the war,' remarked Morgenthau, 'that I've got a weak spot for them.' He added, 'Lord Keynes said that every time they win a battle they want fifty million dollars more.' 'Well, it's worth it,' said Fred Vinson.[36]

The Russians' main problem – aside from the difficulty of reconciling Moscow's demands with the realities of the conference – was in trying to make themselves understood. So short were they of translators that at one point Russian-born Lydia Keynes stepped in as an unofficial translator to try to ease the burden. The Russians also co-opted six students from the Academy of Foreign Trade for interpretation assistance. In their debrief to Moscow, the delegation would later complain that its membership had been 'quite inadequate, particularly due to the limited command of English'.[37]

Communication issues tended to dissolve away when the delegates went downstairs to the bar and nightclub. Late at night, delegates from all sides would toast each other and attempt to sing each other's songs. According to a colleague, the first to lead off was usually White himself with an adaptation of a popular American drinking song which, for the delegates, would forever be known as 'the Bretton Woods Song':

> And when I die don't bury me at all,
> Just cover my bones with alcohol.
> Put a bottle of booze at my head and feet,
> And pray the Lord my soul to keep.[38]

White was not the only prominent delegate to lead the rest of the conference in song. One night in the lounge upstairs Lord and Lady Keynes sang 'The Blue Danube' to the assembled guests, with Brooks of the British delegation on the piano. It was a rare social appearance: for the most part, the pair of them would eat in their rooms.

Nonetheless, they could all enjoy food unlike anything most of them had seen for years. For those who had grown accustomed to wartime rationing, the sight of so much fresh meat and fruit would leave an indelible memory. Decades later Lionel Robbins would reminisce: 'how wonderful American food was in those days! Chicken Maryland, I remember, and enormous ice creams.'[39]

Stoneman, the hotel owner, had spared no expense, hiring the former chef of the King of Siam, Edmond M. Legendre, together with a staff of sixty, including 'pastry cooks, bakers and salad experts'. While Paris in 1919 had been an occasionally lavish affair, this was in another league in terms of scale and extravagance. Every night the kitchen would serve up a banquet for the thousand-plus guests, who would have to eat in shifts in order to find places in the dining room. The vastness of the hotel meant that at any one time, there would be hordes of delegates in the meeting rooms upstairs, hundreds having dinner in the ground floor restaurant, watching the sun set over the White Mountains, and others downstairs in the Moon Room, perhaps taking a dance lesson with Mignon MacLean, the blond instructor from the renowned Arthur Murray dance studios. MacLean managed to persuade twenty delegates to sign up, and even managed to slip into one of the private meetings in an upstairs suite, until she was asked which delegation she belonged to. 'None,' she answered defiantly. 'I am the Arthur Murray instructor.'[40]

For most delegates, the economic negotiations continued over dinner and then, later, over drinks in the nightclub downstairs. But those with minor roles, or from countries at the periphery of the negotiations, could afford to take it easier, and enjoy a welcome break from the hardships of war. One Soviet delegate would recall: 'We could only feel envious of the representatives of some of the smaller countries ... They relaxed in the "Moon Room", where there is a bar, went for walks in the woods, swam in the swimming pool, played tennis, golf, volleyball.'[41]

Indeed, one meeting between Keynes and his British colleagues and the representatives of the Dominions had to be cut short 'because the South Africans had an appointment for golf'.[42] Over the course of the meeting, the course record was captured by Federal Reserve chairman Marriner Eccles, who managed to break 100 in a round with Colonel Charles Dyson, one of the secretariat and a 'top-notch golfer'.[43]

The renowned illusionist Cardini had been whisked up to the

conference to provide a magic show for the delegates every night. Appropriately enough the most popular trick was one where he would make money mysteriously appear out of thin air.

For some delegates, alcohol consumption remained the only reliable coping mechanism for the chaos and pressure. Ansel Luxford, the legal adviser to the American delegation, would later recall long, late nights spent in a suite with White, Bernstein and Fred Vinson, discussing tactics and taking stock of the world economy: 'Nobody could see that [Vinson] was the man that was coming in as Secretary of the Treasury, but he liked to drink bourbon, we liked to drink bourbon, and this would start at one or two in the morning when we got through work and go through to the wee hours of the night. We spent that time educating that man on the problems of world economics.'

And Vinson was a fast learner. 'He had an excellent mind,' according to Bernstein. 'He was one of the men that I knew with the quickest capacity to learn.'[44] A rough-and-tumble Southern lawyer with a gruff manner and a roving eye, Vinson would distinguish himself as probably the only man ever to have been a professional baseball player, Treasury Secretary and later Chief Justice of the Supreme Court. At Bretton Woods, when he wasn't occupied with the quotas battle or knocking back bourbon with his colleagues, he was chasing after the ladies.

Morgenthau's loyal secretary Henrietta Klotz recalled being pursued 'all over the lot' by Judge Vinson. 'No matter where I sat, he sat next to me ... Just before we left, Vinson asked me to come up to his room and I wouldn't go. He came down and said he very much wanted to get to know me ... He was a low cheap nothing ... a dirty filthy dog.'[45]

Cheap sexism of the 1940s variety was rife at Bretton Woods, where the majority of women were secretaries or wives. The crowning accomplishment on this front was a rather dubious document produced by the American delegates on the final night of the conference. Having spent the past weeks producing articles setting up the International Monetary Fund, the demob-happy Americans drew up in the early hours of the morning a series of mock articles for the creation of something else – the 'International Ballyhoo Fun' (*sic*).

The document is a rather odd combination of Bretton Woods-style economic legalese and Vaudeville innuendo. The institution, it says, is to be set up to 'contribute to the promotion of international intercourse and collaboration', to 'lessen resistance and facilitate better understanding and closer relations of all members' and 'to assist in the resurrection of the reproductive facilities of the members devastated by hostilities'. Rather than providing quotas of gold and bonds, each country would be obliged to hand over 'gold blondes or their equivalents', with the rest of the quota payable in 'brunettes'.

'Members shall refrain,' the document adds, 'from maintaining relations with non-members. Preliminary explorations however shall be permitted, provided they are for the purposes of fun.'

For anyone wondering about the level of intoxication of the authors, there is a clue in clause XIV which refers to 'ad hic committees'. The three-page document was marked as a 'Confidential and Personal' report of Commission IV. Excruciatingly for the drafters, it later appears to have been mistaken for an official document and has been lodged among the thousands of other papers of the Roosevelt administration.[46]

Of all the journalists at Bretton Woods, few were as well informed as Carl McCardle of the *Philadelphia Evening Bulletin*. Whenever there was a twist or turn in the negotiations, it was certain that among the first to hear of it would be McCardle, who would go on to win awards for his reportage at the conference. This raised one or two eyebrows among his fellow reporters; in person as opposed to in print, he seemed as clueless as the rest of them.

However, McCardle had what the rest of them couldn't compete

with – a friend at the very top. At the end of the first day of negotiations he crept up to Dean Acheson's hotel room and levelled with
him: 'I've got to write a story for my paper, and I don't understand
a thing that was said today. This was way over my head. What went
on?'

So Acheson explained it all – the differences between the
American and British positions; where the Latin Americans stood;
what the Russians were holding out for. And over the course of the
next three weeks those journalists following the ups and downs of
Bretton Woods would repeatedly find themselves one step behind
the *Philadelphia Evening Bulletin*.[47]

Acheson wasn't the only delegate making efforts to brief the
media. George Bolton of the British delegation also went out of his
way to address what had thus far been almost relentlessly negative
coverage of their work. The overarching theme in the press was that
Britain was attempting to dupe the world's largest creditor nation
out of its savings. It hadn't helped that Keynes had begun the conference by revealing that the scale of the UK's war debts had
climbed to £3 billion, leaving the country essentially broke – nor
that his Lordship liked to sustain the impression of having the US
delegates wrapped around his finger.

So Bolton took it upon himself to try to rebuild bridges. Down
in the hotel bar he acquainted himself with the men and women of
the American media. 'It has meant quite a considerable amount of
hard drinking and late nights,' he reported, but he had become close
to a number of the scribblers, among them the *New York Evening
Post*'s Sylvia Porter, who had written a number of 'scurrilous' articles about the Bank of England's former governor, Montagu
Norman. 'I thought it my duty to make much of her and succeeded
fairly well,' he wrote. But shortly afterwards, he added, he 'got a
note from the *New York Times* man warning me that in the trade
she is known as "Sylvia Hot-Pants" since when I have been
attempting to exercise reasonable discretion.'[48]

Every day Harry White or one of his deputies would give a press conference ('seminars', the journalists waggishly, and more accurately, called them), remarking flatteringly at one stage that the intelligence of the press contingent exceeded that of 'some other groups' at the conference.[49] In an effort to stage manage the US–UK relationship, he also forbade Keynes from giving solo press conferences, insisting that when he appeared he would do so alongside his American colleagues.

Even among the journalists, a pecking order established itself. Predictably, those from the wealthiest economies were comfortably at the top, expressing particular irritation with the 'presence here of unnecessary foreigners'.[50] The richer press barons spared no expense in getting news out of the conference. Indeed, a rumour went around that one newspaper was chartering a plane to land on the golf course and fly photos out each day.

Notwithstanding the money their companies were splashing around, most of the journalists still had to take a communal bus each day from their hotel, the Twin Mountain, to the Mount Washington. One exception was Cecelia Wyckoff, the so-called Prima Donna of Wall Street, who had wrestled control of the *Magazine of Wall Street* from her ex-husband following their famed divorce some years earlier. She joined the pack in the second week, bringing with her her chauffeur and limousine from New York to ferry her and a lady friend between the two hotels, much to everyone else's envy.[51]

Across the Atlantic, *The Economist* was less amused by the tittle-tattle emerging from the conference. 'It is no good relying, in these matters, on the American journalists, whose telegrams read, to an Englishman, more like crime reports than serious accounts of what is going on,' the editorial sniffed. 'What should have been done at Bretton Woods was to see that at least one competent British financial journalist was present who, without being given any special facilities, would at least have known the difference between an exchange rate and a balance of payments.'[52] One might very well have said the same about some of the delegates. According to one of his colleagues, Sir Wilfred Eady, nominally the most senior member of the British delegation, 'used to get very muddled about whether the exchange rate went up or down, exports up or down.'[53]

However, the one place one could rely on for a relentless stream of negative publicity about the conference was Nazi Germany and her allies, where perfectly reasonable criticisms – that the Bretton Woods system would be dominated by the United States, and might open the door to future devaluations – mingled with the ridiculous. One article criticised the conference on the basis that Morgenthau and Stepanov were Jewish, misreporting the *New York Times* as claiming that it would lead to 'a great world inflation' and, ultimately, full-blown economic collapse. Japan's *Nippon Times* predicted that the conference's achievements would be 'hollow', and that it would ultimately be undermined by the 'selfish refusal of the United States to tear down her tariff walls and Britain's equally selfish determination to resort to her sterling bloc arrangements to regain her lost power in the field of international finance'.[54]

A week into the conference, the journalists in the American press pack realised there was an imposter at large in the Mount Washington Hotel. Quite how this man had made it past the sandbags, guards and security barriers was a mystery – although the conference identification cards were hardly very stringent: they didn't even include a photograph. However, the journalists recognised the fellow, who had been passing freely through the hotel over the past couple of days, not as a government official but as a private sector lobbyist.

His name was David Hinshaw, and he was a prominent public relations executive with connections to the American Smelting and Refining Company. It didn't take many guesses to work out why he had infiltrated the proceedings. He had been 'going round the

Conference for two days organising the silver bloc', wrote Lionel Robbins.[55]

For, while the campaign to ensure that silver was given a prominent role in the Bretton Woods agreements was waged mainly by the Latin American countries – led by the dashing Cuban Luis Machado (when he wasn't leading the downstairs nightclub in song) and Mexican Eduardo Suarez – it had powerful support in the US. Some twenty-five senators (mainly of silver-mining states) had signed a letter to Roosevelt urging him to find a role for silver in the new agreement. The Chinese delegation chair, Kung, with his long-held fascination for silver (and odd business interest in it) quietly lent his behind-the-scenes support.*

The Mexicans' insistence that they be allowed to contribute silver rather than gold towards their quota at the Fund would 'render the whole agreement derisory'.[56] Given, however, that the US was relying on Latin American support if it needed to force through other parts of the agreement, White found himself in the awkward position of trying to calm down the rebellion without dismissing the idea entirely.

No one at the conference seriously expected it to endorse bimetallism (incorporating both gold and silver into the currency system): to do so would go against the grain of more than fifty years of American economic policy. So for the most part, the rival gold lobby, led by South Africa, could relax and maximise its time on the golf course. But the very fact that a silver lobbyist had managed to infiltrate the hotel was a reminder of the lengths to which private

---

*A Foreign Office cable from E.L. Hall Patch to Nigel Ronald ahead of the meetings had said: 'There are ... distinct possibilities that Kung may produce wild schemes unless he is held in check. One of his pet fancies is silver, for which he has always had the sneaking admiration of the Shansi pawnbroker (which he is by profession), in spite of his lip service to modern ideas of managed currency. I do not know what weight to place upon the Mexican delegate's agitation for silver, but if he and Kung join forces on the silver question, you may have trouble.' National Archives, Kew, FO317/40916.

interest groups would go to try to bend the Bretton Woods conference in their favour.

In the event, Hinshaw was confronted at one of Morgenthau's
press conferences by Rodney Crowther of the *Baltimore Sun*, and
was ushered off the premises soon afterwards. On his way out he
remonstrated that he had merely been staying 'at a nearby resort
hotel for a rest' and had innocently wandered into the grounds by
bus that morning. He added that he 'was never so humiliated in my
life'.[57]

Ultimately White was to do with silver what he did with all
other tricky topics, shunting it off into Commission III, where a
compromise was found. So silver never found its way into the official agreement, but a so-called 'Coconut clause' was added which
allowed the Fund, at its discretion, to accept as collateral various
other commodities – be they coconuts or silver. Needless to say, it
has never been activated, but it did allow Suarez to save face, returning to Mexico proclaiming that 'after some stormy discussions [the
Fund] had agreed to Mexico's proposal to accept silver on the same
footing as gold, for contributions to the Fund.'*

However, the biggest Latin American legacy of Bretton Woods
is to be found not in the articles concerning the International
Monetary Fund but those regarding the World Bank. While, for
most of the major players at the conference, the Bank was intended
as a vehicle for repairing and reconstructing the war-torn
economies of Europe, the Latin Americans saw it from the start as
a permanent redevelopment bank, and attempted to insist on a
clause stipulating that its disbursements should be spent equally on
both reconstruction and development. In the event, it was the

---

*A UK Treasury official has underlined this sentence, which appears in a Mexican
press statement of 18 August 1944, and added: 'I have seldom seen anything more
disingenuous ... but on close reading I observe that the Mexicans may, if they like,
coin silver and turn it in as their local currency. What help this will be to them
I am not at all sure.' Bank of England Archives, OV 38/10.

Marshall Plan that provided much of the necessary cash for reconstruction of war-torn economies, and aside from some early loans in Europe, the majority of the Bank's work since the 1940s has been devoted to projects in developing economies.

Over the course of the three weeks, the Latin Americans managed to secure extra voting power and places on the boards of both institutions, as well as shifting their focus further towards development. Indeed, in many accounts of the conference, the efforts of smaller, younger economies such as those of the Latin American nations, India and China are often unfairly overlooked.

CHAPTER TWELVE

Week Three

The Final Act

This is some poker game – we keep raising our bets.

Henry Morgenthau Jr[1]

How much better that our projects should begin in disillusion
than that they should end in it!

John Maynard Keynes

By the beginning of the third week it was clear to the members of
the British delegation, if not to the rest of the delegates, that all was
not well with Keynes's health. In Atlantic City, he had been taken
ill once and had to escape to his rooms, where he was tended to by
Lydia. In the first week of Bretton Woods there were two such
episodes, and three in the second week. Robbins spoke for many
when he wrote: 'throughout the conference we have all felt that as
regards Keynes's health we were on the edge of a precipice.'[2]

Keynes had been given strict orders by 'The Ogre', Dr Plesch, to
rest whenever possible, and to take the lift rather than the stairs.
However, in the Mount Washington, where there was only one lift
and hundreds of yards of corridors, that rendered getting from one
meeting to another a long-winded process that was at odds with
Keynes's impatient and impulsive temperament.

Photos of Keynes taken towards the end of the conference show a pallid man, stooping slightly, his face pinched, wrapped up in a greatcoat while the rest of the delegates wore summer suits. In that final week, his health would once again come to the fore, delivering an almighty shock to the conference.

As Monday 17 July dawned it was clear that the conference was not going to finish on time. That morning one of the all-night negotiation sessions had broken down 'amid mutual insults and recriminations', with one of the technical experts 'seeking out Judge Vinson and asking him to see for himself that flesh and blood could not stand the strain any longer'.[3] It was obvious that there was little prospect of wrapping up negotiations on both the Fund and the Bank by Wednesday, the intended finish date.

Progress had been made, especially on the Fund. Indeed, only that morning Morgenthau had been able to issue a press release trumpeting that 'The International Monetary Fund has been born.'[4] The quota crisis had been laid to rest late the previous week. The Russians were to get a quota of $1200 million – a little less than Britain's $1300 million, but enough to satisfy Stepanov, or whoever was pulling the strings back home. Moreover, the Russians would have the right to reduce the amount of gold they were to put in. Running into Russian delegate Alexey Smirnov at yet another party (this one put on by the Canadians), Robbins teased him: '"Professor Smirnov, when you return to Moscow, Field Marshal Stalin will order in your honour a salvo of two hundred and forty guns!" He blushed to the roots of his hair,' Robbins reported.

He had good reason. Newly uncovered documents in the Russian State Archive of Economics reveal that even the Russians were taken aback by how willingly the Americans acceded to so many of their demands. One particular demand – that Russia should be entitled to control its own exchange rate, given its paucity of economic contact with the wider world – was forced through the special committee after the Russians suggested it. 'The Commission

Chairman, White, railroaded our wording so quickly and without any discussion, that the majority of the delegations that took part in the meeting of the Commission on the Monetary Fund were not aware of the substance of this change,' according to the Russian account of the conference.[5] The Russian text remains in the articles of the Fund today.

The negotiations over quota sizes went less smoothly. While the Fund was essentially finished, the Russians were making ominous noises about disputing their quota for the Bank, the articles for which were – despite Keynes's best efforts to speed them through the commission meetings with the minimum of debate – still unfinished. And although the stickiest issues had for the most part been decided, the poor technicians charged with writing up the articles were clearly suffering burnout. Holed up in their offices which, on account of the heinous conditions and relentless hours of labour, had been nicknamed the 'salt-mines',[6] the British technicians were close to full-blown mental breakdown, said Keynes.

'The pressure of strain and overwork was beginning to produce serious effects all round,' he reported back home. 'There are members of both staffs who have been working as much as 18 hours a day for two or three weeks ... The procedure of this conference is enormously complicated, the subjects under discussion are difficult and intricate, we are constantly sitting under chairmen who barely understand English and opportunities for the minor powers to waste time are unlimited.'[7]

The hotel was rapidly transforming into an economic vipers' nest where rival delegates would tear strips off each other in order to make their point. Watching from the sidelines, Ragnar Nurkse of the League of Nations jotted down notes on the histrionics playing out in front of him. 'Go away you nasty man,' someone is reported as saying to Edward Twentyman, a delegate from the United National Relief and Rehabilitation Administration. Brand of the British delegation is described as 'too old, cold, slow'. The entire French delegation is labelled as 'arrogant'.[8]

The pressure of work was by now impossible to ignore. As Fred Vinson put it, 'Lord Keynes's men last night – Sir Wilfrid Eady and Mr Robertson were just fagged.'[9] Ned Brown – the American banker 'of 20 stone who lives exclusively on beef, beginning with beef-steak at breakfast, and nods his big head like a bull in a stall'[10] – was struggling, smoking continuously in an effort to stay awake.[11] At one point he had burst into tears in full view of the rest of the delegates. Even White confessed he was 'cracking up', exploding in fury at his own team and, one evening, forcing himself to take an early night – ten o'clock.[12]

There was no hope of the Final Act being finished by Wednesday, when other guests were due to arrive. But given the arrivals were set to pay $96 per day as opposed to the heavily subsidised rate of $11 for the delegates, hotel owner David Stoneman was aghast at the prospect of having to cancel their reservations. Nonetheless, in an emergency meeting of the steering committee, Morgenthau said: 'We may have to get the President to get an order to seize the hotel as of Wednesday night, and put troops in here to run it … we may have to carry the manager of the hotel out with two soldiers!'[13]

Stoneman, who had no intention of being manhandled out of his establishment – as Sewell Avery of retail store Montgomery Ward & Co had famously been earlier that year after refusing to stamp down a strike by his workers – gave way almost immediately.[14] Later that day he sent a telegram to the impending arrivals, saying, 'we are obliged to ask our guests to postpone their arrival at Mount Washington until Monday, July 24. We are prompted to do this by patriotic motives and we are sure that all our guests will feel likewise and will cooperate with us by postponing or even sacrificing a few days of their vacation to help promote the war effort and the most important work of the forty-four nations composing this Conference.'[15]

Morgenthau declared that the rest of the day would be a holiday. That would at least prevent some of the delegates from completely losing their sanity. But they could only afford a single day's rest: the conference would be thrown out of the hotel on the 24th, and this time the deadline was final.

That Monday was also the deadline for a decision on the issue that most divided the British and American delegations: the locations for the headquarters of the Fund and Bank. Having surfaced as a bone of contention in the very earliest stages of negotiations, the issue had never really gone away.

As far as the Americans were concerned, it was inconceivable that the institutions could be based anywhere other than in their country, preferably in Washington, just out of reach of the New York bankers, who were determined to bring them down. Well before Bretton Woods, Harry Dexter White had made this effectively official, by stipulating, in the draft Articles of Agreement, that 'the principal office of the Fund shall be located in the member having the largest quota.'[16]

However, back in the UK, the governor of the Bank of England had warned, according to a Treasury memorandum, that locating the institutions (particularly the Fund) in the US 'would be a direct threat to the financial position of London, already weakened by the financial conditions brought about by the war'. The memo added: 'if these two new and powerful structures are to be located in Washington, then he could not answer for the consequential effects on the position of London as an international financial centre. The Treasury feel that much weight must be attached to the Governor's view, and that the point is one of great importance.'[17]

For years, London had been the de facto hub for international finance, but New York was catching up. It was to America that investors now flocked as the economy boomed, to American banks that companies went, and Wall Street was already rivalling London. At the very least, the Treasury asked Keynes, could we not locate the Fund in Britain and the Bank in the US? Or failing that, put the Fund in Amsterdam or somewhere else in Europe?[18]

However, as with so much else at the conference, there was never any doubt that the United States would get its way. The best Keynes could try to negotiate was a delay in the decision until the institutions were actually established and had their first board meeting. After all, why not wait until it was clearer where other post-war institutions such as the United Nations were to be located?

But even this was asking too much. As far as the politicians were concerned, putting the question in any doubt would threaten the passage of the legislation through Congress. Ever the diplomat, Dean Acheson tried to remonstrate: this was a matter for governments, he said, and did not need to be decided at the conference. Morgenthau, sensing that this would mean giving up the decision to his rivals in the State Department, was having none of it. 'Are you through? May I simply say this, Dean, that whether it is done between governments or whether it is done here, this thing is a matter of postponing the day of reckoning … the financial center of the world is going to be New York and we don't want to postpone this thing until another day where we may not be in as advantageous a position and maybe have then to get in a horse-trading position and maybe end up by having it in London. Now the advantage is ours here, and I personally think we should take it.'

'If the advantage was theirs, they would take it,' added White.[19]

A rather sheepish Acheson attempted to soften the blow, taking Robbins from the British delegation aside for a tête-à-tête. 'You fellows will have to give way on this matter if there is to be any hope of the Fund getting through,' he told him. 'If there were any doubt about the situation of the Fund's headquarters, it would not stand a chance in Congress.' When Robbins started to remonstrate, he added: 'I know, our attitude is perfectly illogical, and I can well believe that sometimes you think that you are dealing with a set of people who are perfectly crazy. I am simply telling you what the situation is. I do not apologise for it.'[20]

And so, with the Americans threatening to put the issue to a vote, using the Latin Americans to help swing a majority, Keynes officially withdrew his objections that Tuesday. It was yet another humiliation for the British, and the experience was clearly weighing on the head of their delegation.

For the following day Keynes would suffer his worst collapse of the conference after becoming embroiled in yet another row with the Americans. This one concerned the Bank for International Settlements. White and Morgenthau had been gunning for the Swiss-based central bankers' club ever since the scandal over the transfer of Czech gold to the Nazis in 1939. The Treasury Secretary had launched frequent verbal attacks at the Bank's American head, Thomas McKittrick, which caused a few awkward moments at home, since their daughters were at Vasser together, and were good friends.

No one had seriously intended to use the conference to bring about the demise of the BIS until a certain Norwegian delegate called Wilhelm Keilhau tabled the following proposal: 'Be it Resolved that the United Nations Monetary and Financial Conference recommends the liquidation of the Bank for International Settlements at Basel. It is suggested that the liquidation shall begin at the earliest possible date, and that the Governments of the United Nations now at war with Germany, appoint a Commission of Investigation, in order to examine the management and transactions of the bank during the present war.'[21]

The proposal was awkward for a number of reasons, chief among them the fact that the president of the BIS at the time of the Czech gold transfer was none other than Wim Beyen, head of the Dutch delegation. Moreover, Ned Brown of the American delegation had, through his bank, been instrumental in setting up the BIS the previous decade. So the expectation was that, despite having garnered support from France and Belgium, the motion would wither away. The issue was shunted off to Commission III, where everyone expected it to meet the same fate as the silver proposals. However, White then took it up, for political as much as moral reasons, with a recommendation that the conference make membership of the IMF and the BIS incompatible – a far more aggressive sanction that would effectively destroy the BIS.

For one thing, he told Morgenthau, it would probably take down McKittrick, no friend of the Roosevelt administration. It would also be a sideways blow for one of Bretton Woods' biggest US critics, Leon Fraser, president of New York's First National Bank, who had been in charge of the BIS some years earlier.

'The Americans are preparing the ground,' wrote Keynes, 'for alleging that the opposition in New York is due to a group of bankers with international associations and erstwhile Nazi sympathies who still think they can reconstitute the BIS and therefore object to the Monetary Fund as an obvious rival and successor. Pure politics, of course, and pretty bad politics at that.'[22] He didn't much care whether the BIS lived or died – but these noises-off were yet another example of the Americans steamrollering through their plans without even consulting the British. Plus, keeping the BIS intact would at least pacify the Bank of England (former governor Montagu Norman had been one of its chief architects), which had seen so many of its demands ignored at Bretton Woods.

So, when his colleague Nigel Ronald told him about the US motion, which White had proposed in person (a sign that he really meant it), Keynes was furious. This really was the final straw. He stormed out of the room, determined to see Morgenthau at once. Rather than walking all the way down the corridor and taking the lift, he instead bounded up a service staircase. 'He was noticeably "puffed" when we got to Mr Morgenthau's room,' recalled Ronald – not to mention in a furious rage. When Keynes burst into the room, Morgenthau was there, alone with his wife. 'The man was livid,' the Treasury Secretary would later report to his colleagues. 'He really was very much disturbed, and I don't think he was putting on an act.' 'You are not at all exaggerating,' said Elinor. 'The man was quivering, he was so excited about it.'[23] This was, he said, the most serious breakdown in the talks yet. He was considering pulling Britain out of Bretton Woods.

Morgenthau agreed to revisit the decision with the full delegation the following day, but that was by now the least of British concerns. Keynes was in some trouble – that much was obvious within minutes. 'When Lord Keynes got back to his own room, it was alarmingly clear that the stairs and the agitation had been too much for him and he at once lay down on his bed,' reported Ronald. 'I fetched Lady Keynes. She in her incomparable way did all that could be done, but the attack was a sharp one and during the night the rumour got about, and was actually cabled to London, that Lord Keynes was dying.'[24]

The reports were exaggerated. Lydia had confided in a lady friend present at Bretton Woods about what had happened. The friend had told her son, who happened to be a Reuters journalist. 'By the time it reached Germany,' Keynes later wrote, 'the rumour said that I was dead and I am told I received most satisfactory obituaries!'[25]*

But while Keynes played down the incident, there is no doubt that it was serious. Although he had recovered sufficiently to rise from his bed the next day, he was not well enough to take part

*The British delegation would receive numerous telegrams from worried colleagues back in London, including the following from the Bank of England's governor, Lord Catto, on 21 July: 'Very concerned at report in papers here that you have had heart attack. Hope you are all right but please rest. Love to you both. Catto'. National Archives, Kew, FO317/40918. Coincidentally, the reports came on the same day as erroneous reports of Adolf Hitler's death at the hands of Colonel Claus von Stauffenberg's assassination attempt, Operation Valkyrie.

himself in negotiations again. He relied on Ronald to present Britain's case against the BIS amendment in front of the US delegation that morning. They eventually agreed to remove the stipulation about membership of both institutions being incompatible, but kept a clause in the Articles of Agreement calling for 'The liquidation of the Bank for International Settlements at the earliest possible moment'.[26]

As Keynes would joke at the time, what that meant in practice was 'Not very early!'[27] Not only is the BIS still in existence today, it has become steadily more powerful, metamorphosing from a regulator of reparations payments into a secretive yet influential group of central bankers from around the world, responsible, in part, for laying down some of the international banking regulations which came under fire in the financial crisis of 2008. Various efforts have been made to shut it down since, all of which have fallen foul of the central bankers who run it.

In the meantime, the Russians had thrown yet another spanner in the works. Having won their battle to increase their quota at the Fund to $1200 million, they were now refusing to contribute the same quota to the Bank. Every other country had seen fit to provide identical quotas for each institution, but not Russia.

It came back to the conflicting attitude most countries had towards the two institutions: so far as those countries were concerned, the Fund was a possible source of future economic support while the Bank was merely a drain on their resources. Moscow, Stepanov said, was adamant on this point. On top of this, Russia was insisting on the insertion of a clause in the Bank's articles that any country which suffered enemy occupation (e.g. Russia itself) should be allowed to hold back 0.5 per cent of its contribution to the Bank.

The latter was relatively easily done. This clause is still in the Bank's articles today – one of the many fossilised remains of the late-night arguments in the committee rooms at Bretton Woods. However, if the Russian quota were reduced to the $900 million they were demanding, it would mean other countries having to make up the difference.

The Soviet delegation 'have pursued an unbroken policy of contracting into all benefits but out of all duties and obligations', the British delegation cabled back home as the final week began. By this stage, the apparent friendliness during the plenary negotiations belied the growing tensions beneath the surface. Stepanov still routinely sent flowers to Morgenthau's room. His statuesque blonde 'officials' were to be seen in and around the hotel at crucial points during the negotiations. At one point one of the American delegates, Will Brown, accidentally walked into one of the Russian delegates' rooms on the third floor, thinking it belonged to his colleague, John Parke Young. 'When he was in the room looking for the document Russians walked in from an adjoining room. They wanted to know what he was doing going through their papers. Will was very upset by this episode and thought he had created an international incident. Nothing happened. I am sure the Russians did not believe his explanations.'[28]

The tension and discomfort was plain for all to see. During the conference one columnist had described the administration as being 'in abject terror of Russian post-war power', bowing to Russian demands.[29] Harry White was by this stage alternating between long behind-the-scenes discussions with Stepanov and trying to avoid him entirely and palm him off to others. By the morning of the final Friday, 21 July, the matter had still not been resolved, so Fred Vinson called a crisis meeting of the biggest delegations at the conference.

As the Russian delegate looked on silently, a number of countries, including the United States, Poland, China, Canada and even some of the smaller Latin American countries, volunteered to raise their contributions to the Bank in order to prevent the conference from ending in disaster. Keynes said what was on most of the delegates' minds: 'I do urge, most sincerely, that it is scarcely consistent with the honour and dignity of a great country to remain so uncompromising at this stage.'

Compelling as the act was, Stepanov was privately unconvinced. It smacked of a plot to entrap him. 'The presentations of some delegations (Canada, China) ... were apparently imposed on them by the Americans ... to influence our position,' the delegation would later write in their account of the conference. He told the room he was 'deeply moved by the willingness of other delegations to reach the goal which was mentioned', but added that he still had no authorisation from Moscow to provide more funds. It was $900 million or nothing. That was how the position would remain throughout the day, and by the afternoon it was confirmed: those other countries would make up the $300 million gap.

This behaviour infuriated many of the Europeans, who believed they were being deceived by their unreliable ally. George Theunis, the aged Belgian who was, alongside Keynes, the only Bretton Woods delegate who had been at Versailles twenty-five years earlier, buttonholed Lionel Robbins. 'It is a disgrace,' he shouted. 'The Americans give way to the Russians every time. And you too, you British, are just as bad. You are on your knees to them. You wait. You'll see what a harvest you'll reap at the peace conference.'

What would you do about it? Robbins asked. 'The aged statesman was taken aback, but after a moment's hesitation he gathered his forces: "*ne pas avoir des illusions*" he said very solemnly.'[30]

Moreover, it might be asked with perfect validity whether there was any point in co-opting Russia into an agreement on exchange rates which could be incompatible with its closed command economy. 'Why not set up [the Fund and Bank] without USSR?' asked Ragnar Nurkse. As he was an observer, rather than a delegate, the question went no further than his own private notes.

Throughout the conference, the Soviet delegation had played a largely disruptive role, frequently objecting to minor changes in the text, and employing their typical *modus operandi* – blankly repeating their demands, and ignoring any entreaties to reconsider until they were implemented. Typical was one intervention by Bystrov, the man who a decade later would find himself nearly arrested on his visit to London, as described by Robbins: "'The Union", said he, spacing his words out with singsong monotony. "The Union (pause) of Soviet (pause) Socialist (pause) Republics (long pause) eenseest on Alternative E.'" Alternative E, needless to say, was entirely irrelevant to the debate in question.[31]

More often than not, the problems were those of translation; then, after something was misunderstood, the entire Russian delegation was to be seen 'hissing at one another like a nest of disturbed serpents'.[32] On another occasion the Soviet delegate kicked up a fuss when Bernstein, in an effort to cut down the verbiage in the articles, attempted to strike out part of the phrase 'reconstruction and rehabilitation' since the two words were synonymous.

'The Russian got up,' one American delegate would later remember, 'and made his little speech about the Russian devastated areas, and that they wanted those two words inserted. Everybody sort of smiled and it was again pointed out that they hadn't lost anything, that there was nothing to be gained by having those two words in there. He made his speech a second time, and a third time; and finally Eddie Bernstein smiled and said, "Well, what difference does it make, if he wants it in let's leave it in," so it's in there.'[33]

Had the rest of the conference realised that, although the Russian delegate did indeed defer to Moscow on crucial points, rather more discretion was available to Stepanov than he made out, they would have been even more disturbed. For one thing, his superiors had, from an early point, permitted him to provide $1 billion to the Bank. The decision to insist on a quota of $900 million was the delegation's alone.

Throughout the three weeks of the conference, the Russians bossed the debates and negotiations like no other country. They confronted every challenge with blank faces and unsmiling, only occasionally apologetic stubbornness. As their own report on the conference rightly concluded, it was 'an important diplomatic success for the USSR'.[34]

If the Russians had last-minute reservations about Bretton Woods, they were not alone: in the final meeting on the Fund a host of nations insisted that due to a variety of minor objections (which mostly came back to quotas) they could not give the Final Act their full approval. Australia's Leslie Melville, who had been hoping that Bretton Woods would incorporate a pledge towards full employment, went one step further and threatened to withdraw from the meeting entirely. The conference appeared to be ending in precisely the kind of discord Harry Dexter White had spent the past three weeks trying desperately to avoid.

By the time of the final plenary session and dinner, that Saturday night, the mood was lukewarm. After three weeks of non-stop negotiating and debating, most of the delegates were thoroughly exhausted – these last-minute Soviet histrionics only reinforcing the sense that the net product of Bretton Woods would be disharmony and disappointment rather than economic stability.

Whereas many of the meals at the hotel thus far had been fraught affairs, with negotiations still taking place from table to table, this final dinner was a more formal affair – 'like the Captain's Dinner on a pre-war ocean liner'.[35] As the delegates filed in for the lavish banquet at seven o'clock, they noted that Keynes's chair was empty. Outside, the clouds that had hung over the summit of Mount Washington had suddenly lifted, flooding the room with light. For the first time in days they could look up through the great windows to the glistening peak.

Eventually, after all the other guests had taken their places, Keynes finally appeared. A hush fell upon the room. Wilfred Eady would later recall: 'as he moved slowly towards the high table, stooping a little more than usual, white with tiredness, but not unpleased at what had been done, the whole meeting spontaneously stood up and waited, silent, until he had taken his place. Someone of more than ordinary stature had entered the room.'[36]

Keynes's health was at least starting to return – but he had been worn down again by the drama with the Russians. 'Good chaps' though they were, they had 'lost prestige and dignity in front of all the Delegations', he had written earlier that day to Catto at the Bank of England. They had secured everything they wanted, he added:

> 1. Too large a quota in the Fund. 2. Too small a contribution to the Bank. 3. Reduced gold subscriptions. 4. Provisions by which even gold they put up can probably never leave Moscow. 5. Virtually contracting out of the exchange fixing clauses and so forth.
>
> Nearly all the concessions, however, have been at the Americans' expense. It has been the concern of the American policy to appease the Russians and get them in. For my own part, I think this was wise. And I do not think the Russians have done themselves any good by their stonewalling tactics and hard horse-dealing. In a good many cases they were snatching for chicken feed and demanding concessions which were not really material.[37]

The good news was that, at the very last minute, Melville of Australia had received a cable from home giving him authorisation to sign up to the Final Act.

Keynes took his seat and the silence dissolved, replaced by the delegates' chatter. With no fixed places for most of them, the teams were jumbled up on various tables. The food was less extravagant than had been most of the meals provided by the hotel over the course of the past three weeks – the Mount Washington's version of chicken with green beans, followed by a fruit cup.

Halfway through the meal, Morgenthau rose to his feet and tapped on his glass to bring the room to silence. 'I have just received word,' he said, 'that the Soviet Union has decided to increase its subscription to the International Bank for Reconstruction and Development from $900,000,000 originally agreed upon to the amount of $1,200,000,000.'

The room erupted into applause. The eleventh-hour turnaround was a complete surprise. The elation seemed to transcend the barriers of culture, language and stoicism that had prevailed through-out Bretton Woods. Delegates stood up and cheered. As they cele-brated, at least one member of the Russian delegation burst into tears of joy.[38]

Perhaps predictably, it was only the British who raised their eye-brows and added a sardonic note. Dennis Robertson leant across to his colleague and quoted Luke 15:7: 'joy shall be in Heaven over one sinner that repenteth, more than over ninety nine just persons, which need no repentance'.[39]

As the diners began to eat, news spread around the room of the circumstances of the remarkable U-turn. With only an hour to go until dinner, Stepanov had burst into Morgenthau's room with the news that he had received Moscow's blessing to sign up to the extra quota.* The Treasury Secretary had asked the Russian to repeat himself three times to be absolutely sure. 'Mr. Molotov agrees to that?' he asked, referring to the Russian Finance Minister.

'He said that he agrees with Mr. Morgenthau,' said Stepanov.

'Well, you tell Mr. Molotov that I want to thank him from the bottom of my heart,' said Morgenthau, later adding: 'This confirms the long time respect and confidence that I have in the Union of Soviet and Socialist Republics.'

---

*According to the official Russian account of the conference he had actually received notice from the Kremlin in the morning, but had sat on it for some hours before notifying Morgenthau. Former Soviet archives references, *passim*.

'Mr Stepanov says that he will telegraph what you told him just as it was said by yourself,' said the Russian translator.

'Well, this makes me very, very happy,' said Morgenthau. 'The Conference was almost a success and now it is a complete success.'[40]

With Morgenthau's announcement of the news, all that was left were the closing speeches. There was a message to the delegates from President Roosevelt giving them his 'heartiest congratulations': 'They have prepared two further foundation stones for the structure of lasting peace and security. They have shown that the people of the United Nations can work together to plan the peace as well as fight the war.'[41]

As he was often wont to do, Keynes summoned up Shakespeare in his closing speech. He likened the boy scouts who ferried the microphones around to 'Puck coming to the aid of Bottom, to undo all the mischief first wrought in the Tower of Babel.' He referred to the strain and overwork of the past three weeks: 'We have had to perform at one and the same time the tasks appropriate to the economist, to the financier, to the politician, to the journalist, to the propagandist, to the lawyer, to the statesman – even, I think, to the prophet and to the soothsayer.'

It is worth quoting the remainder of the speech at length:

International conferences have not a good record. I am certain that no similar conference within memory has achieved such a bulk of lucid, solid construction. We owe this not least to the indomitable will and energy, always governed by good temper and humour, of Harry White.

But this has been as far removed as can be imagined from a one-man or two-man or three-man conference. It has been teamwork, teamwork such as I have seldom experienced. And for my own part, I should like to pay a particular tribute to our lawyers. All the more so because I have to confess that, generally speaking, I do not like lawyers. I have been known to complain that, to judge from results in this lawyer-ridden land, the *Mayflower*, when she sailed from Plymouth, must have been entirely filled with lawyers. When I first visited Mr Morgenthau in Washington some three years ago accompanied only by my secretary, the boys in your Treasury curiously enquired of him – where is your lawyer? When it was explained that I had none, – 'Who then does your thinking for you?' was the rejoinder ...

Mr President, we have reached this evening a decisive point. But it is only a beginning. We have to go out from here as missionaries, inspired by zeal and faith. We have sold all this to ourselves. But the world at large still needs to be persuaded.

I am greatly encouraged, I confess, by the critical, sceptical and even carping spirit in which our proceedings have been watched and welcomed in the outside world. How much better that our projects should begin in disillusion than that they should end in it! We perhaps are too near to our own work to see its outlines clearly. But I am hopeful that when the critics and the sceptics look more closely, the plans will turn out to be so much better than they expected, that the very criticism and scepticism which we have suffered will turn things in our favour.

Finally, we have perhaps accomplished here in Bretton Woods something more significant than what is embodied in this Final Act. We have shown that a concourse of 44 nations are actually able to work together at a constructive task in amity and unbroken concord. Few believed it possible. If we can continue in a larger task as we have begun in this limited task, there is hope for the world. At any rate we shall now disperse to our several homes with new friendships sealed and new intimacies formed. We have been learning to work together. If we can so continue, this nightmare, in which most of us here present have spent too much of our lives, will be over. The brotherhood of man will have become more than a phrase.

Mr President, I move to accept the Final Act.[42]

As he sat down the delegates 'rose to their feet and cheered for what seemed like several minutes'.[43] Predictably, this was followed by another long series of mind-numbing speeches, during which the delegates drank more and more, and became increasingly rowdy. There were addresses from Stepanov of Russia (or, to be precise, his translator), and from the French and Canadian delegates. The Norwegian delegate, Keilhau, pointed out that

> a great number of the disasters of the postwar period after 1918 had their beginnings in the field of international exchanges ... because the politicians of each country in those years tried to promote national interests, and national interests only, disregarding the interdependence of the exchanges, disregarding the interdependence of national economies. The result was mistakes and failures, new mistakes and new failures ...
>
> I feel certain that if we do not succeed in creating something new and unique, the next post-war period will bring us back to that economic chaos which we experienced in the early 1920s, and I have no doubt that it would inspire my world-famous friend Lord Keynes to a second brilliant volume of *The Economic Consequences of the Peace*.

He closed by adding that as the representative of one of the world's great paper-exporting nations, he had to congratulate the conference for being 'such a great consumer of paper', getting through two million sheets of it over the course of the three weeks.[44] The conference would later save all its waste paper – ten tons in all – and use it in the war effort.[45]

Morgenthau's closing speech, strategically delayed until the proceedings were broadcast live over the radio, underlined the ultimate objectives of Bretton Woods: 'after this war is ended no people ... will again tolerate prolonged and widespread unemployment.' In order to achieve this, he added, there would have to be both stable exchange rates and long-term financial aid for 'those countries whose industry and agriculture have been destroyed by the ruthless torch of an invader or by the heroic scorched-earth policy of their defenders'. He then rounded on the Fund's critics:

> Objections to this Bank have been raised by some bankers and a few economists. The institutions proposed by the Bretton Woods Conference would indeed limit the control which certain private bankers have in the past exercised over international finance. It would by no means restrict the investment sphere in which bankers could engage. On the contrary, it would greatly expand this sphere by enlarging the volume of international investment and would act as an enormously effective stabilizer and guarantor of loans which they might make.

The reality, however, was that the International Monetary Fund and the system it was set up to preside over would represent an 'epoch-making' challenge to the interests of international banks, in large part down to the controls it would impose on movements of capital from one part of the world to the other.*

Although Ned Brown of the US delegation pledged that same day to 'do what I can to sell it to the bankers of the country', he could do little to market the scheme to the financiers of Wall Street. But then, that was fine by him. He was, let us not forget, the head of a Chicago bank. He had approached the negotiations with the interests of his own city's banks in mind – and they were far more focused on commodity trade than international finance. He had been quite sanguine about the elements of the deal that would stem the flows of capital around the world: that, after all, was the concern of his rivals on Wall Street. Bretton Woods threatened to be

---

*The phrase was Bolton's. See Bank of England Archives, OV38/11, 'The International Monetary Fund'.

disastrous for the bankers of New York, who, in the following months, would do everything in their power to destroy it.[46]

As Morgenthau wound up his speech, he added a final thought: 'I like to think that in this enormous amount of words that has gone over the air through short wave, that the German people will realize that what we have done here at Bretton Woods on the economic front must make them realize that to continue to fight us on the battlefields is useless.'

The war was indeed turning the Allies' way. Their troops were pushing deeper into Normandy, capitalising on chaotic and under-strength German defences. The Nazi propaganda machine would dismiss the Bretton Woods agreements as wrong-headed and futile, the head of the Reichsbank, Walther Funk, declaring: 'Germany will never tolerate that the value of her currency shall be determined by foreign Governments or Wall Street bankers.'[47] In the event, West Germany would join the IMF less than a decade later; after the collapse of Bretton Woods, she would submit to various schemes, including the Exchange Rate Mechanism and, ultimately, the euro, all of which would in some way compromise her currency independence.

After Morgenthau brought his speech to an end, the orchestra played 'The Star-Spangled Banner'. Morgenthau was handed a bouquet, which he passed to White. White, in turn, gave it to Bernstein, who stood up and took a bow.

As Keynes struggled to his feet, there was a final round of applause, and the rest of the delegates stood up and spontaneously sang 'For He's a Jolly Good Fellow'. 'In a way, this is one of the greatest triumphs of his life,' reflected Robbins. 'Scrupulously obedient to his instructions, battling against fatigue and weakness, he has throughout dominated the Conference; and, although this is only the beginning of the struggle, I think he may well feel that with all the faults of the agreement which has emerged, something has been accomplished in the way of constructive internationalism which, despite the vagaries of Parliaments and Congresses, will not easily be brushed on one side.'[48]

There was a final comic note, which underlined the occasionally farcical tone of proceedings, when Morgenthau praised the Australians' military prowess at El Alamein. For some reason (presumably mistranslation), the Russian chairman Stepanov 'took the bow for the cheers which followed and then the whole audience rose to their feet and stood to attention to the strains of the only Australian tune known by the band, viz "Waltzing Matilda".'[49]

It was an appropriately surreal note on which to end an exhausting three-week spell of miscommunication, negotiation and, somehow, agreement. The delegates trooped along the corridor, through the hotel lobby and into a smallish side room, where, one by one, they signed the Final Act of Bretton Woods. The hotel's smartest table – round, made of rock maple and used by Caroline Stickney, the wife of its founder, as her private dining table – was wheeled in for the occasion.

The room which witnessed this historic moment – the Gold Room – has been preserved by the hotel's current management as it was back in 1944, with one small exception. The table on which Keynes, Morgenthau and the forty-two other delegations signed the agreement is missing four of its nine original legs. They were snapped off and disappeared some years ago when some guests at the hotel attempted to wheel the table out of the room during a wedding party.

PART IV

THE LIFE AND DEATH OF BRETTON WOODS

CHAPTER THIRTEEN

Unmitigated Evil

1944–1945

How long are we going to stand playing pay-off Uncle to the whole world, which plainly seems incompetent to manage its own affairs?

New York Daily Mirror, 8 July 1944

If we allow the same conditions to prevail again, they will surely lead us down the road to World War III. One thing the people don't want ever again is war. If we are to banish war, we must banish the causes of war.

'Bretton Woods Is No Mystery'

No sooner had the delegates woken on Sunday morning, barely conscious after the previous night's bar-room celebrations, than they were unceremoniously thrown out of the hotel. The well of patriotism from which its owner, David Stoneman, had drawn when asked to extend the conference was finally exhausted: it was time for everyone to leave.

It meant, Keynes wrote later – predictably making a reference to Shakespeare's *Hamlet* – that he and many others would end up signing the Final Act 'before we had had a chance of reading through a clean and consecutive copy of the document. All we had seen of it was the dotted line. Our only excuse is the knowledge that our hosts had made final arrangements to throw us out of the hotel, unhouselled, disappointed, unannealed, within a few hours.'[1] It was only when they got home and had time to read the full ninety-six-page document that they would realise the full extent of what they had agreed to.

Specifically, after spotting one or two clauses concerning Britain's obligation to convert its currency, Keynes embarked on a full-scale row with Dennis Robertson, who had been in the special committee doing the negotiating. The issue would soon be superseded by far more important problems – but Keynes had a habit of fixating on small details. He shot off a series of accusatory letters to his old colleague who, sensitive fellow that he was, 'carried the wound with him to the grave'.[2]

The circumstances of the hurried departure would spark further arguments in the coming months as the delegates arrived home. Even White would later admit that he had not had time to inspect every page of the agreement. However, quibbles over the small print were not the only obstacle. Bretton Woods had yet to be ratified by either Congress or Parliament: there was still every chance it could fall at this hurdle – precisely as the League of Nations had a quarter of a century earlier. This was hardly ancient history: were President Wilson's travails with Congress not already at the top of the Americans' minds, they need only have passed by the nearest cinema, where Darryl F. Zanuck's hagiographical film *Wilson* was playing that summer. 'Artistically negligible, but much powerful propaganda', Lionel Robbins concluded generously.[3] Ominously, perhaps, it was a huge flop at the box office.

Already the campaign to destroy the agreement was gathering steam. As the delegates packed up their offices and prepared to leave the Mount Washington, they were unaware that the very reason they were being kicked out so quickly was that the hotel was about to play host to a rival conference held by the American

Bankers' Association (ABA). The main item on its agenda: how to kill the Bretton Woods agreement.[4]

While Harry White and most of the delegates travelled straight down to Washington to begin their campaign to persuade Congress to put the agreement into law, Keynes headed north. There was no hope, now, that Bretton Woods would provide the kind of post-war financial support he had envisaged as part of his Clearing Union, so it was more important than ever that Britain secure other sources of cash. Canada had been extremely generous, providing Britain with a series of aid programmes throughout the war; Keynes now embarked on a mission to persuade it to give even more. It threatened, on the face of it, to be another nightmare mission; in the event, after the exertions of Bretton Woods, it ended up feeling, he said, like 'the nearest thing I have had to a holiday for years'.[5]

Britain's High Commissioner, Malcolm MacDonald, sent his car to the hotel to drive the Keyneses 'in great style and comfort' to Montreal. There they stayed in a suite at the Windsor Hotel, which, wrote Keynes, was 'so large that it is quite difficult to find one's way from my room to Lydia's!'

For the first time since arriving in North America, he had time to write to his mother. 'We are so thankful that Cambridge is out of range of the flying bombs, but are worrying greatly about London,' he wrote. 'It is very difficult to judge from here just how bad it is. But very bad indeed is what we think.'

He was right: Allied troops were at that moment pushing further into Normandy, squeezing Nazi troops back from the coast, attempting to target the V1 launch stations. But results were far from immediate. The bombs were still falling on London, each one causing ripples of fear when it was spotted in the sky, and outright terror when its engine suddenly stopped.

Life in Canada, on the other hand, could hardly have been more blissful. The weather was hot, rationing was hardly heard of, and there were 'Beef steaks every day as big as your plate and ice cream

and anything you have a mind for,' wrote Keynes. 'On this continent the war is a time of immense prosperity for everyone ... They
had never before felt their growing wealth and strength so
confidently.'[6]

Finally free of the retail wasteland that was Bretton Woods,
Lydia was able to hit the shops. Keynes sent her off with 'pocket
money', with the result that she bought 'a seersucker dress and a
pair of shoes every day'.[7]

Lady Keynes made quite an impression when the couple arrived
in Ottawa after their brief stay in Montreal. High Commissioner
MacDonald was nervous and excited at the front of the ranks of
besuited officials waiting at the airport to greet the couple. He had
watched from the gallery, entranced, as Lydia danced *The Sleeping
Princess* in London decades ago. When he stepped forward to
introduce himself, she 'ran with out-stretched arms towards me,
flung her arms round me in a warm embrace when we came
together, and before I could say a word exclaimed aloud with a
slightly Russian accent, "Oh, my dear High Commissar, how are
you? Last night I dreamed zat I was lying in bed, and zat you were
lying in my arms."

'No doubt the Canadian Minister of Finance and our teams of
advisers were rather startled by this unorthodox meeting; but with
impeccable official decorum they betrayed no hint that they had
noticed it,' wrote MacDonald.[8]

If that quickened the pulse, it was as nothing compared with
what would happen a few hours later, once they reached their hotel.
Maynard and Lydia had been put up in one of the most lavish
hotels in the city – the Chateau Laurier – where they occupied a
suite of about nine rooms, 'a sort of Moorish Palace'.[9]

Keynes mislaid the key to his red box containing details of the
British negotiation strategy, which prompted Lydia to scurry from
room to room looking for it. Eventually, with the key presumed lost,
the men sat down to discuss strategy together, leaving Lydia next

door to have a bath. A breathless MacDonald recounted what happened a moment later:

> The door opened, and into the room slipped Lydia Lopokova. She was no longer wrapped in furs; nor did she wear even a dress. For a moment I thought some whim had made her put on a ballet costume, for her long, shapely legs were as exposed as if she wore tights. Then I realised that they were naked, and also that the dramatic skirt of a ballerina's outfit was missing. In fact she wore nothing but a short white chemise (presumably with a pair of brief drawers below) which hung flimsily around her otherwise bare body. In that state of near nudity she stood in apologetic manner casting a half-guilty, half-mischievous look at Keynes as she said, 'Oh Maynard darling, I am so sorry. You did give me ze key; and I forgot zat I hid it for safety between my little bosoms.' At that she clutched in her hands a ribbon hanging round her neck, and as she lifted it over her head raised from between her breasts – which so far as we could detect were not quite so small as she suggested – the lost article.
>
> Keynes chuckled with laughter, remarked that he had said the treasure would turn up somewhere, and accepted the key from her. She blew him a kiss, turned in a ballerina's pirouette on her toes, glided through the door, and closed it behind her.[10]

Ottawa and much of the eastern seaboard were, at that time, experiencing a heatwave of stifling proportions. So hot and humid was it in New York, where some of the British delegation had travelled from Bretton Woods, that most of them were left feeling 'like wet rags'. As they attempted to write home, reporting on the conference, every letter was left smeared with ink marks. 'Please excuse this typing,' wrote one of the delegates, Gamble, 'the machine has got all gummed up and sticks occasionally.'[11]

So intense was the heat that, down in Washington, where a few

Britons had travelled, it was all but impossible to get any work done. That was, however, in itself something of a relief after the ordeals of New Hampshire. At night Robbins, Robertson and Frank Lee 'went and laid on the grass in Lafayette Square, talking till far into the night on all the usual shop topics: the intolerable complications of the post-armistice period; the longing of temporary civil servants to get back to their normal occupations; the position of the Treasury in the Whitehall hierarchy; the Congressional system; the vanity of human wishes ...'[12]

In Ottawa, the heat, which was well over 100 degrees Fahrenheit, became so intolerable during the evenings that, at one point, Keynes found Lydia escaping into the kitchen of their suite and then 'opening the lid of a large ice-box, squeezing her body into the freezing interior and shutting the lid "like Alice in Wonderland disappearing down the White Rabbit's tunnel."'[13]

The loan negotiations themselves went comparatively smoothly. Over the course of a fortnight, Keynes and Sir Wilfred Eady, who joined him soon after his arrival, managed to raise $655 million from the Canadians. It was a helpful boost for Britain's finances, though it would hardly last long. The real question was whether the Americans would be as amenable. Keynes was due to discuss the next stage of assistance with Morgenthau shortly, and the early noises were far from promising.

In the meantime, though, Keynes could bask in the glory of Bretton Woods, in the success of the Ottawa negotiations and in the Canadian sunshine. 'We are decidedly enjoying ourselves here,' he told his mother. 'Tell father we confirm his opinion that Canada is a place of infinite promise. We like the people, and if one were to emigrate, this should be the destination, not USA. The hills, lakes and forests make it a proper holiday place. Apart from its wild fruitfulness, they also have the effect of making it a place of peace and repose of mind, as one never finds in the USA.'[14]

Once the negotiations were over, Keynes and Lydia returned to

London, which, in a matter of weeks, had grown increasingly confident about the outcome of the war. With Hitler penned in by a
resurgent Soviet army on his eastern front and by the approaching
British and Allied forces to the west, it suddenly looked feasible
that the war in Europe might be over before the end of the year.
However, this prompted another question: what would happen to
Lend-Lease, and the rest of Britain's extraordinary support from its
allies? What would happen to the billions of pounds of sterling
debts incurred to India and Egypt, and what would happen to
Britain's economy after the war? The short answer, Keynes knew,
was that if nothing was done, the United Kingdom would soon be
bankrupt. The final act of his life would be devoted to trying to prevent the worst from happening.

'The Battle of Bretton Woods', as the newspapers soon took to calling it, was not only waged between White and Keynes. If anything,
the fiercest battle was fought by the Wall Street banks, which were
desperate to prevent the agreement from becoming law. The ABA,
lobby group for the investment firms of New York, had been
attempting to discredit both the White and Keynes plans with equal
aggression ever since they were first published the previous April.

The first accusation, made by prominent economist Benjamin
Anderson (formerly of Chase Bank), was that international monetary co-operation 'prolongs unsound tendencies'[15] – in other words
it encouraged governments to generate unnecessary inflation.
Keynes's Clearing Union was particularly worrisome on this front;
but even when it transpired that the White plan was the one to be
implemented, the sniping continued.

Advocates of the gold standard such as Edwin Kemmerer, the
man who had toured the world preaching the benefits of gold back
in the 1920s, soon piled in, to be followed by characters such as
Leon Fraser, the BIS man White and Morgenthau had wanted to
discredit. He told the House Committee on Banking and Currency

that the Fund was a scheme designed to squeeze money out of America. 'They put in lei, lits, lats, and rubles, and they take out dollars,' he said.[16]

The international banking community's horror was hardly surprising. White's Fund would partially obliterate the very foundations of the Wall Street business model. In the interwar years, as the international monetary system imploded and governments of every hue faced economic collapse, the investment banks had stepped into the vacuum, providing private loans to stricken nations. Britain had become wholly reliant on J.P. Morgan and its loans – indeed, the disastrous austerity round of 1931 had been partly carried out on the bank's recommendation. So dependent was Nicaragua on loans from its New York bank that it became known throughout Wall Street as the Republic of Brown Brothers and Company.[17] It was a heady time for American financiers; what White was proposing would bring it to an abrupt end.

His scheme would make the International Monetary Fund, not J.P. Morgan, Chase or Brown Brothers, the central port of call when a country faced an economic crisis. On top of that, it transpired that he was proposing to police flows of both international investment and foreign exchange, two of Wall Street's other profitable sidelines.

The bankers had been hoping that, just as had happened in 1933 and, indeed, at most international economic conferences in recent memory, the summit would end in recrimination and disarray. Indeed, in an effort to tip the proceedings over the edge, the bankers, together with anti-Bretton Woods Republican Presidential candidate Thomas Dewey, had made an audacious move to derail the negotiations. A few months before the conference, the bankers contacted Redvers Opie, Britain's Treasury representative in Washington, with a mischievous offer: they would loan Britain $3 billion on generous terms provided it agreed to ditch the monetary plan entirely. It was tempting – particularly since the

United States had as yet given no hint or indication that it would help out after the war. The proposal might well have been acted upon had Keynes not stamped it down, warning that there would be 'a great many' strings attached to the loan, and that 'the wise and prudent course is to run with the US Treasury rather than with its disgruntled critics'.[18]

Few were more disturbed that the meetings had, somehow, come to an agreement (and that Britain had not taken the bait) than Winthrop Aldrich, president of Chase Bank. Aldrich, a slight fellow keen on three-piece suits and panama hats, liked to see himself as a man of reason – he had visited Hitler at Berchtesgaden in 1933 to express his concern about Nazi policies (and the $35 million of Chase loans extended to Germany). If the technicians of Bretton Woods could not understand the folly of what they were doing, then perhaps the President and Congress would think differently?

He informed Morgenthau curtly that 'It doesn't look to me as though you can actually get my support,' and promptly embarked on a campaign to persuade Congress and the American public not to allow Bretton Woods to go ahead. The ABA published a long, weighty report on the matter. The main point was that, at the very least, the Fund should be abandoned, it said, though the new International Bank for Reconstruction and Development could be retained and given some powers to stabilise markets. In this, the ABA agreed with the Federal Reserve Bank of New York, one of the twelve regional branches of the central bank, which put its position thus: 'the plans for an International Monetary Fund, which have culminated in the Bretton Woods Agreement, are not only based on mistaken principles but risk eventual failure which would bring further discredit upon the cause of internationalism.'[19]

Perhaps they needn't have bothered. Few had read the conclusions of the ABA or the Fed – or, for that matter, those of the proponents of Bretton Woods. They all met with a wall of apathy when they tried to appeal to Main Street.

The fact was, the Office of War Information reported, 'There is virtually no public opinion about the Bretton Woods conference.' In a bid to try to take the public's temperature about the conference, it had sent out correspondents to ask the people. The responses were not encouraging: 'Great majority do not even know conference is in session', said one correspondent. Another reported: 'Not one in a thousand even knows there was a Bretton Woods conference. Most of them think it had something to do with fuel question. Sorry but that's facts.' For those who had heard of it, the conference 'and its swank environment has an aura of mystery, it has sinister implications with a dime novel drop curtain'.[20]

The respondents could hardly be blamed. Even the participants found the whole thing gave them a headache. Few of them had actually read the whole text of the agreement, and most remained unclear what exactly it represented. Was it a gold standard? Not entirely – but then again, it wasn't a system of floating exchange rates. That lack of clarity, of course, was precisely the point: it suited White, whose main objective was to blind the opposition with a flood of figures and then hope a credulous Congress would pass it. 'Harry,' said Marriner Eccles at one point, 'your plan is so darned complicated I asked our people to put down briefly in layman's language so I could understand the darned thing, just what it means.'[21]

The level of comprehension even within the administration was illustrated by one of the audience questions when Dean Acheson attempted to explain the scheme to officials in the State Department: 'I understand the Hitler organisation created a thing called the Reichsbank to carry out banking operations for them in Germany. Is it the object of the Bretton Woods plan to replace the Reichsbank by the new Bank?'[22] There was clearly a lot of educative work to be done.

So began what the *Herald Tribune* described as 'the most high-powered propaganda campaign in the history of the country'.[23]

Morgenthau and White were dispatched on tours around the country; newspaper columnists were invited into the Treasury for chats; friendly economists and businessmen were encouraged to speak out. Mabel Newcomer was charged with explaining the importance of the deal to women's groups from around the country. Clergymen were invited to Washington in the hope that they might recommend the deal in their sermons. The Treasury churned out booklets and illustrated pamphlets explaining the deal. 'As a matter of fact,' said one passage from 'Bretton Woods Is No Mystery', a pamphlet with cartoons by *New Yorker* cartoonist Syd Hoff, 'anyone who has troubled to read the objectives and general principles of Bretton Woods knows that they are much easier to understand than a recipe for apple-pie or the rules of gin-rummy.'[24]

Given that the eventual Bretton Woods legislation was the size of a small novel, with 45,000 words and 31 chapters, covering more than 100 subjects, it is unclear precisely what kind of apple-pie recipe the pamphlet had in mind. The complexity of the agreement was an inevitable consequence of the difficulty of drafting a catch-all document on the shape and function of the world's economic system while keeping every country onside. If it was ambiguous, then so had been the gold standard and the monetary mess of the interwar period. The more inflexible the agreement, the more likely that it would be wrenched apart as soon as one country or another faced a balance of payments crisis.

Financial correspondents in America could therefore, with relative confidence, warn that the new system was not sufficiently like the gold standard, and their counterparts in Britain could complain that it was too much like the gold standard. Paul Einzig of the *Financial News* – the man who had leaked the news of the plans the previous year – wrote: 'Is it really conceivable that Parliament could pass such a suicidal measure ... [It constituted a] return to the gold standard ... an unmitigated evil, spelling ruin and misery.'[25]

This confusion was not limited to the press. While White him-self could happily liken the plan to a gold standard in order to persuade his Russian colleagues to sign up to it, Keynes insisted in his House of Lords speech on behalf of the agreement that it was nothing of the sort: 'If I have any authority to pronounce on what is and what is not the essence and meaning of a gold standard, I should say that this plan is the exact opposite of it.'[26]

After a gruelling series of hearings, where the only provocative question that seemed to trouble White was the suggestion that his plan was copied from Keynes's, the agreement was approved by the House Committee on Banking and Currency. However, the biggest opponent on Capitol Hill was to be found in the Senate. Robert Taft, a Republican senator who had long ago decided that joining the Fund would be 'like pouring money down a sewer',[27] was determined that Bretton Woods would not be passed into law. He had little understanding of the minutiae of the agreement (not that anyone else did) and spent most of the sessions in the Senate committee warning that America's econ-omy would only be safe if its gold remained in Fort Knox rather than at the Fund.

White's – and for that matter the Treasury's – response to all critics remained the same: that if America rejected the Bretton Woods agreement, it would be guilty of sending the country back towards a prospective third world war. At the House hearing he summoned up the memory of the League of Nations, saying: 'I think history will look back and indict those who fail to vote the approval of the Bretton Woods proposals in the same way that we now look back and indict certain groups in 1921 who prevented our adherence to an international organization designed for the purpose of preventing wars.'[28] It was a powerful statement, and, in the end, far easier to understand than any single page of the Bretton Woods legislation itself. The New York bankers, the only effective oppo-nents of the bill, were repeatedly lambasted as wanting, for their own immoral reasons, to drive the world towards another war. Soon enough, the bill was passed by an enormous majority of 345 to 18 in the House and by 61 to 16 in the Senate. By July 1945, Bretton Woods was officially law in the United States.

By the time Keynes and Lydia arrived back from their long North American stay on 20 August 1944, France was in the final stages of liberation. Within a week, Allied troops would march triumphantly into Paris. The Vichy regime was driven into exile in Germany. It was a glorious watershed for Europe: the most symbolic indication that the continent's war was coming to an end. With Hitler facing defeat – perhaps within months – attention had started to switch to the question of what to do about Germany itself.

Earlier that month, Morgenthau and White had flown to London. The official purpose of the visit was French post-war aid, but the Treasury Secretary had another idea up his sleeve. On the flight over, White had handed him a copy of the State Department's proposals on reparations. Lessons had been learned from the post-Great War experience: the amount Germany was to pay to its victors was to be limited to what the country could feasibly afford. However, one aspect of the State Department memo stuck in Morgenthau's throat: it seemed to assume that Germany would be reintegrated into the world's economic system once the conflict was over. The upshot of the plan, White warned him, was that Germany could reindustrialise, and soon enough would once again be a dominant economy, capable of financing war operations. Morgenthau had helped create the War Refugee Board after the full horrors of the treatment of Jews in the Nazi concentration camps started to trickle out of the country. The notion that Germany would not be suitably emasculated after the war was disturbing. He asked White to come up with an alternative.

What became known as the Morgenthau Plan was, in retrospect, one of the most shameful experiments the Allies would embark on over the course of the war. A draconian scheme aimed at turning Germany into a pastoral economy, it envisaged the wholesale destruction of the country's industrial base. Germany was to be split into northern, southern and international sectors, and factory equipment was to be dismantled. The industrial heartlands of the Ruhr and Silesia were to become international territory, or sub-sumed into neighbouring countries. Germany, the plan proposed, would be converted 'into a country primarily agricultural and pas-toral in its character'.

To anyone who studies this era of history it remains, frankly, bizarre that, having spent years negotiating a deal designed to ensure that the mistakes of Versailles and the 1919 post-war settle-ment would never happen to the international economy again, White and Morgenthau sought to brutalise Germany with such a socially and economically illiterate scheme. Even if one took the view that the world wars were the result not of circumstance but of something inherently warmongering about the German people, this was a decidedly medieval remedy – the equivalent of treating a mentally ill patient by drilling deep into their skull.

It also overlooked a fundamental problem: Germany had estab-lished itself as Europe's factory; destroying its industrial capability would be as disastrous for the continent's economy as for the coun-try itself. While Britain and France could mop up some of the excess demand, the more likely prospect was that Russia would become even more dominant throughout Europe.

This may well have been White's intention. He called the Morgenthau Plan a 'Program to Prevent Germany from Starting World War III' – but then, as he wrote elsewhere, clement Soviet–American relations were precisely what would prevent such an outcome. Like Morgenthau and, for that matter, Roosevelt, he envisaged the post-war years being dominated by a United

States–Soviet axis; pastoralising Germany might not much appeal to Churchill, but it might be advantageous for the Soviet Union, which had repeatedly fallen victim to German aggression. For some historians, White's involvement here is yet more evidence of where his sympathies lay. The Americans, moreover, had little interest in trying to squeeze reparations out of the country – unlike Britain, which was desperate for whatever recompense it could get. But to presuppose a strategic, diplomatic aim is perhaps to assume too much sophistication of thought. The reality was that Roosevelt and Morgenthau were desperate to punish Germany – aggressively. 'We have got to be tough with Germany and I mean the German people not just the Nazis,' the President told his Treasury Secretary. 'We either have to castrate the German people or you have got to treat them in such a manner so they can't just go on reproducing people who want to continue the way they have in the past.'[29]

Even though it implied that Britain would inherit a portion of the market for German goods, Churchill was nonetheless disgusted by the plan. When he met Morgenthau at Quebec later that year, where the Allied leaders were discussing the post-war settlement, the British Prime Minister attacked the plan as 'cruel and un-Christian'.[30] After sleeping on it, however, he later signed up to the plan all the same. As Hitler's prospects of survival diminished, so too did any leverage Britain had over the Americans. Any post-war financial support would depend on Roosevelt's generosity (or, as it turned out, that of his successor as President, Harry Truman). When the issue of whether the Americans would extend Lend-Lease after the end of the war in Europe was raised at Quebec, Churchill found himself in an increasingly humiliating position. 'What do you want me to do,' he asked the President at one point, gesturing towards the President's obedient Scottish terrier, 'stand up and beg like Fala?'[31]

Whatever the reason, while both Churchill and Keynes had deep misgivings about the scheme, neither put up much resistance;

indeed, when White first told Keynes of it, he came away with the impression that the British economist was 'wholly in our corner'. In fact, Keynes was privately horrified. The best he could do was maintain an 'uncomfortable reticence' as White explained that there would have to be queues for food in the country's industrial heartland as the factories were shuttered. 'So whilst the hills are being turned into a sheep run, the valleys will be filled for some years to come with a closely packed bread line ... How I am to keep a straight face ... I cannot imagine.'

He nonetheless had little choice but to do precisely that. Morgenthau's prospective goodwill towards Britain was, he realised, 'strongly bound up in his attitude to Germany'.[32] And no sooner had he and Lydia unpacked after they arrived back from the United States than they were dispatched back to Washington to negotiate the future of Lend-Lease.

In late September they sailed to Canada on the French liner *Ile de France*. As in their previous voyage earlier that summer, the boat was packed with several thousand German prisoners behind barbed wire below decks, all of them apparently convinced that they were about to be thrown overboard. The exhaustion and strain of the past few months had turned Keynes into a near-invalid: he could hardly climb the stairs to the deck, taking a rest every two steps. Lydia continued, with difficulty, to try to ration his time and keep him in bed. After docking in Halifax they travelled down to Washington in a private railway car courtesy of the president of the Canadian Railway, complete with a bedroom and dining room, and a private chef named Romeo.

For Lydia, the return to the beltway proved another opportunity to confound American high society with her behaviour. At one dinner party given by Secretary of State Cordell Hull, the subject of lesbianism must have come up, for she was overheard saying loudly to her neighbour: 'Two men – yes – I can see they've got something to take hold of. But two women – that's impossible. You can't have two insides having an affair!'[33]

The negotiations threatened to be as difficult, if not more so, than those at Bretton Woods: Keynes had been instructed to persuade the Americans to maintain three-quarters of the Lend-Lease supplies they had been funnelling to the UK during the war. On top of that, it would prove difficult to say anything positive about the Morgenthau Plan, which had caused a shockwave of revulsion both inside and outside the administration since details of it had leaked out. The only way to get through unscathed, Keynes said, was 'by repeating every night the three vows which I always make before a visit to America, namely, one that I will drink no cocktails, two that I will obey my wife, and three that I will never allow myself to be betrayed into speaking the truth'.[34]

There were one or two uncomfortable moments in the negotiations. When, at one point, Morgenthau reacted with fury after Keynes suggested that the United States provide extra civilian supplies, Lydia intervened on behalf of her frail husband. She confronted Morgenthau in his office, pleading with him: 'Mr Morgenthau, *Maynar'* cannot sleep at night. He says he wants sixpence from you: only sixpence more. Why Mr Morgenthau why cannot you give *Maynar'* sixpence?' The Treasury Secretary said she could have her way, adding that she was 'one of the most skilled negotiators with whom he had ever to deal'.[35]

For the most part, however, the negotiations went well. This was, it has to be said, down less to the brilliance of the British negotiators than to the lack of interest among the Americans. According to Keynes, 'Morgy and Harry ... were both of them much more interested in their proposals for de-industrialising Germany, which for me is a highly embarrassing topic.' However, he added in a letter to Eady at the Treasury, 'our manic-depressive friend' – it is not clear whether he was referring to White or Morgenthau, probably the latter – was 'charming and easy to get on with'.[36]

The reality was that the officials' attention was everywhere but these comparatively minor negotiations. There was the ongoing lobbying effort for Bretton Woods; there was the Morgenthau Plan; and, above all else, there was a Presidential election. Dewey, the Republican candidate, was sailing comfortably towards defeat. He had not been taken seriously since he was spotted using two telephone directories to prop him up on his chair behind his desk. 'Apparently,' reported one of the British delegation at Bretton Woods, 'if Dewey doesn't sit on a high chair his head hardly appears above the level of the table.'[37] But the battle was nonetheless sapping most of the Americans' energy. They kept disappearing from the negotiating table; Frank Coe, who was taking the minutes, fell asleep more than once, and had to be woken by the chairman.[38]

Watching this activity all around him was a further education for Keynes, who would never really come to understand the nuances and intricacies of the American political system:

> Everything you are told, even with the greatest appearance of authority and decision, is provisional, without commitment, 'thinking out loud', a kit, a trial balloon ... All this is a process, unfamiliar to us, of discovering by open trial and error what will go and what will not. I liken them to bees who for weeks will fly round in all directions with no ascertainable destination, providing both the menace of stings and the hope of honey; and at last, perhaps because the queen in the White Hive has emitted some faint, indistinguishable odour, suddenly swarm to a single spot in a compact impenetrable bunch.[39]

The upshot was that against all expectations Keynes managed, for the most part, to get his way. He had come to Washington charged with finding $3 billion worth of extra military aid; he got just over $2.8 billion. He had sought $3 billion of civilian aid and been given $2.6 billion, with Morgenthau promising to add on a little extra in due course. The only disappointment was the British failure to persuade the Americans to allow them to start exporting before the end of the German war. However, given that many in London expected the war to be over by Christmas, this was hardly a disaster.

For a brief moment it felt as if all the awkwardness, difficulty and tension between the two sides had dissolved away. Even Harry Dexter White was all smiles and friendliness – though only when he encountered Keynes. 'It seems impossible to get Harry White to accept hospitality except to meet you,' Bob Brand told Keynes.[40] British delegate Frank Lee reported that White's 'difficult nature unfolds like a flower when Maynard is there, and he is quite different to deal with when under the spell than he is in our normal day to day relations with him'.[41]

Perhaps it was the success of Bretton Woods; perhaps the (false) impression that Keynes approved of the Morgenthau Plan. Either way, relations had never been better. It gave the seductive impression that negotiating post-war financial aid for Britain would be a painless experience. This could hardly have been more wrong.

The British plans were built on a series of expectations, none of which would be fulfilled. The first was that the war in Europe would end within months; in the event it went on not only to the end of 1944 but all the way through to May 1945. That meant Britain would continue to spend money on waging the conflict, would continue being reliant on American support without being able to get its own exports back into shape. The second was that the Japanese war would continue until at least the end of 1945 – if not even later. After all, Keynes failed to secure agreement that Lend-Lease would be continued after Japan's surrender. In the event, the atomic bombs dropped on Hiroshima and Nagasaki would end the Pacific war unexpectedly early in August 1945. It meant that this so-called Stage II assistance – the medicine London had hoped would give it time to bring its economy back towards partial health – would last for only three months. Within days of the

Japanese defeat, Lend-Lease would be abruptly cancelled, leaving Britain facing what Keynes called a 'financial Dunkirk' – an ignominious defeat comparable to the retreat from France in 1940. The third expectation was that in the wake of Bretton Woods the Americans would remain on friendly terms. They had not reckoned on the death of Roosevelt, Morgenthau's resignation, and a decidedly anti-British turn within the administration.

These three factors meant that the next time Keynes returned to America, it would be to a very difficult reception – and with very difficult expectations. In the 1945 general election, Clement Attlee won a landslide victory against Churchill. The arrival of Labour in Downing Street, on the back of its manifesto, *Let Us Face the Future*, marked a substantial change in British economic policy. Plans under way since the early 1940s for the creation of a welfare state had begun coming to fruition with the publication of the Beveridge Report in 1942. This had been followed in 1944 by the publication of White Papers and bills proposing the creation of its main elements: a national health service, social insurance, education and full employment. Now, it was clear that Britons wanted that change at once: they expected recompense of some sort for the suffering they had endured during the war. The welfare state Attlee promised would transform Britain's economy. It was also destined to be immensely expensive. The hitch was that Britain was, by most yardsticks, already bankrupt.

On the face of it, the country had, together with its allies, secured the greatest victory in history. Hitler had been vanquished. The forces of democracy had overcome those of tyranny. And the world's financial system was ready to be reshaped in the mould White and Keynes had designed at Bretton Woods. However, Britain's own economic fate was now hanging in the balance. Once again, it was Keynes to whom its people and politicians turned for help. Little did they realise he had only months left to live.

CHAPTER FOURTEEN

Starvation Corner

1945

The pity of it all is that he negotiated the US Loan, this is what killed him, and he did it with great brilliance, but badly, overcomplicating and finessing against London and against himself.

Richard 'Otto' Clarke[1]

Dictatorship is a mushroom on the dungheap of national despair.

Ambassador Alexander Kirk

What struck Emanuel Goldenweiser as he toured Europe in the summer of 1945 was not the scale of destruction. Yes, if you looked in the right places you could find the hallmarks of war: whole forests reduced to stubble outside Leningrad; bullet marks on every other building in Helsinki; blocks of Milan entirely destroyed. And that was before one considered the worst scenes of Allied firebombing – Le Havre, Cologne, Dresden. But, even allowing for all that, the thought that first occurred to 'Goldy', the wise old Federal Reserve economist, veteran of Bretton Woods, was how untouched it all looked. 'A farmer could travel all over Europe and, by avoiding a few of the cities, would never know that there had been a war,' he wrote.

It was a mirage, of course. You did not have to be an economist to realise how much invisible damage had been wrought. 'Nature quickly heals the scars on what is close to nature,' he wrote, 'but it cannot restore destroyed industrial plant or disrupted monetary systems.'

Even as the grass sprouted again in the fields of Normandy, a crisis of yet greater proportions than the aftermath of the First World War was bubbling beneath the surface. Food was not merely in short supply: parts of Europe were in famine. The average Italian was having to subsist on around 800 calories a day – less than half the recommended intake of 2200; in Finland food was terrifyingly scarce. Everything was running short: Denmark and Italy had coal shortages; France and Norway lacked raw materials.

Appalling as war had been, the economic conditions now that peace had broken out felt considerably worse. 'Under the Germans, who supposedly took all from France, the people had something left,' one Frenchman told Goldenweiser on the train to Switzerland. 'Under the Allies, who supposedly take nothing, there is nothing left.'

Though the ruined cities were the most vivid evidence of the conflict, it was the destruction wrought on the continent's infra-structure and communications network that caused most difficulties in those first few months. Roads had been destroyed, bridges blown up. Of 12,000 railway locomotives in pre-war France, just 2800 were still in service by the summer of 1945.[2] In Paris, you had to queue up for twenty-four hours simply to buy a train ticket. Getting goods, people, or indeed information from one part of Europe to another had become almost impossible. A month on from VJ Day, Goldenweiser's driver in Leningrad did not even know that the war with Japan was over.

It wasn't merely that whole communities had been wiped out – the scale of human catastrophe went far beyond that. Of the thirty-six million Europeans killed during the war more than half were civilians. The country-by-country statistics are even more disturbing: one in five of the entire Polish population was killed; one in eleven of the Russian population; one in fourteen Greeks; one in fifteen Germans; one in seventy-seven French; one in 125 Britons. In those countries occupied by the Nazis, the fatalities were often disproportionately among the educated population.

With each single statistic a family was ripped apart. Bob Brand's only son Jim, having taken part in Operation Overlord while his father negotiated Bretton Woods, and having survived both D-Day and the push into Nazi territory, was killed in France in March 1945.

Everywhere there was a shortage of men. The war left the Soviet Union with a surplus of twenty million women and a generational population crisis – though Goldenweiser noted that one by-product was greater equality. 'I saw two shines [shoe-shiners] on the streets of Moscow; one was a girl shining a soldier's big boots and chatting while doing it, and another a man shining a girl's big military boots also chatting in a friendly manner.'

Money had become next to useless. What the people needed was not pieces of paper, or indeed gold, but the food and goods that the continent was so desperately short of. In Amsterdam local barbers and waiters refused tips because 'money was no use to them. They were extremely grateful for a few cigarettes, which are selling in the black market at $3 apiece.' In Helsinki the central bank was heated by 'burning money in the furnaces'.

Worst affected of all were the countries which had never really recovered from the last war. France, in particular, had faced a succession of economic crises throughout the 1920s and 1930s, allowing corrupt politicians and demoralised administrators to undermine the rule of law. It was fine for countries which could pick up the pieces; in France, and for that matter Italy, there were few, if any, pieces left to pick up. Nor had Hitler's allies been treated any better: Italy had suffered the indignity of having to transfer the majority of its gold reserves to Germany.

The risk, said Alexander Kirk, US ambassador in Rome, was that something more maleficent would crawl into the vacuum. 'Dictatorship is a mushroom on the dungheap of national despair,' he told Goldenweiser. Leave the people to suffer for much longer, restricting your exports, imposing harsh conditions on any loans, and the chances were they would turn elsewhere for support – be it a local tyrant, the Soviet Union, or perhaps both. The International Monetary Fund or World Bank should help – but they could not do everything.

So difficult was it to travel from one country to another that Goldenweiser found himself stranded for days on end in Rome. Eventually he took a tour of the city, jotting down his thoughts on the Sistine Chapel and Vatican for his fellow economists back in Washington. 'Man is not intended to look at high ceilings; his neck is not built that way,' he wrote. 'The flat over-decorated ceilings and the bright lights seem to remove the religious atmosphere from the churches. They are more like gay concourses. St Peters is an absolutely first-class railroad station – in general effect.'

In London, where the trip began and ended, the mood was as gloomy as elsewhere in Europe. The Savoy and Simpsons in the Strand were still open, but the food was 'outstandingly poor', even by British standards. Whole districts of the city had been destroyed during the Blitz and later, in 1944, by the V1 buzz-bombs. George Bolton, Goldenweiser's old friend from the Bank of England, said that had the Normandy landings not succeeded, 'London would have had to be abandoned. The flying bombs coming from the French coast were too much ... The end did not come any too soon.'

It was yet to dawn on the British population that normal life was not about to resume. Many expected a return not merely to economic growth but to British dominance overseas. Only a few, of whom Bolton was one, realised that those days were well and truly over: the war had set in motion the final creaking disintegration of the Empire. Britain would have to work out its problems within three or four years or it would have to 'close up shop', Bolton said.

'I asked what that meant,' Goldenweiser wrote. 'He said it meant turn the Empire over to us and be a little country. I asked "and be hungry?" and he said "very hungry." He is against England going on relief. He is the stuff that England is made of.'

Keynes, when Goldenweiser visited him for tea, was similarly depressed, if a touch less despondent. Demobilisation was going badly, he said – though matters were worse still on the continent. So tight were the government's finances that the day Goldy visited, to Lydia's utter horror, Keynes took the train, rather than his official car, to Eton.[3]

By this stage, Keynes was having to spend a disproportionate amount of time in bed. A decade or so ago, this would have been quite welcome: as a young man, he had liked to spend as much time as possible under the sheets. It was from his mattress that he had made the investment decisions, dictated the letters and written some of the memoranda and pamphlets that would change economic history. Once, in the 1920s, when a group of Liberal friends had compared how many hours they spent in bed, Keynes was declared the clear winner. 'I snuff the candle,' he joked, 'at both ends!'[4]

By 1945, however, he was consigned to bed because he simply did not have the strength to get up. Despite the medications of The Ogre, Dr Plesch, Keynes's health had continued to deteriorate in the final months of the war. In March he admitted that 'my heart is very deficient in strength (lungs, liver and kidneys beyond reproach fortunately) and I cannot walk. I find it profitable to spend 12 hours in every 24 in a horizontal position in bed.'[5]

A bed had to be installed near his rooms in the Treasury so he could take occasional breaks, and Lydia was now almost permanently on hand to nurse him. Every day had to be carefully choreographed to ensure he would not drop from exhaustion again, as he had done at Bretton Woods. By now, the sixty-one-year-old's hair and moustache had turned white and even his eyebrows were flecked with grey. His eyes, once 'piercing, brilliant and dark', were now obscured by thick-lensed reading glasses.[6] He was fast approaching retirement age – but then again, so were many of the Cabinet.

In fact, the remarkable aspect of this era, in comparison with our own, was how frequently age and ailments intruded on the lives of the politicians attempting to rebuild the world. Harry Dexter White was plagued throughout the period by heart problems, which were exacerbated by his run-ins with Keynes. Though he did his best to keep them secret, he would disappear from the public stage for months at a time. Frederick Phillips, the Treasury's inimitably silent man in Washington, and the previous Chancellor, Kingsley Wood, had both passed away while still in their posts. Sir Richard Hopkins, Keynes's dear Hoppy, who ran the Treasury, was now semi-retired after suffering illness of his own. Keynes's old guard was dying out.

Then there was the newly elected Labour government. It might have come to office with an imposing list of proposals and an energetic mandate to reform the country, but Attlee and most of his top lieutenants, Ernest Bevin included, were in their sixties. Many of them were dogged by ill-health and needed sporadic breaks away from work. 'The cabinet is a poor, weak thing,' wrote Keynes.[7] Even Hugh Dalton, the Chancellor and perhaps the fittest of them all, suffered periodic health crises, and sustained himself throughout much of this period on a cocktail of drugs including Benzedrine, a type of amphetamine which, he boasted proudly, 'the German soldiers took before going into battle'.[8]

The change in government was unsettling, both for Keynes and for the Americans. Though Dalton had been a former pupil at Cambridge, Keynes neither rated his mind nor particularly trusted him. A narcissist and an intensely political animal, Dalton relied more on bullying than charm in his attempts to get his point across. His reputation for brutality had been sealed by one incident a few years earlier when, as Minister of Economic Warfare, he sent a peremptory order for Sir Frederick Leith-Ross, his director general, to come and see him immediately. 'Leethers' was eventually tracked down to a lavatory where the messenger passed a note under the door. 'Tell him that I can only deal with one shit at a time,' came the response.[9]

The Americans were nervous about dealing with this unpredictable, untested government – so nervous that Attlee was forced, when in Washington that year, to give a humiliating speech insisting that while he was not Churchill, his party was not opposed to freedom of the press or religion. With the question of post-war monetary support looming, Republicans in Congress were wary of financing a socialist government – particularly since two-thirds of Americans didn't want to give another loan to Britain anyway.

But support there would have to be. Long before the Bretton Woods negotiations, it had become inevitable that when the war drew to a close, Britain would have to squeeze some sort of financial help out of Washington. It was Keynes's hard luck that when that moment came it would coincide not merely with his moment of weakest health but with a change in personnel on both sides of the Atlantic.

President Roosevelt, another of those politicians dogged by ill health, had died on 12 April 1945. The Britons knew next to nothing about his vice-president, Harry Truman; neither, for that matter, did the American people. He had remained in the background during the previous year's Presidential campaign. But from the moment he came into office, the mood music changed. It was not long before Morgenthau, who had skidded into office on the back of Roosevelt's coat-tails, was out. Truman was no great admirer of the Treasury Secretary, or, for that matter, his plan to disembowel

Germany's post-war economy. Morgy resigned in July and was replaced by Fred Vinson, the tobacco-chewing former baseball star who had imbibed his way through Bretton Woods. One of Vinson's first acts after his appointment was to marginalise Morgenthau's greatest lieutenant: Harry White was about to fall from influence even more quickly than he had risen to it. The new President and his Treasury Secretary gathered around them a small cabal of trusted advisers, few of whom were particularly sympathetic to Keynes, or indeed to Britain.

Then again, Attlee and his new Cabinet were far less inclined than Churchill to turn to the United States. Various members of the Labour Party had made noises about forging closer links with Russia. Though this was an era before the Cold War (Churchill had not yet coined the phrase 'Iron Curtain'; George Kennan had not yet dispatched his 'Long Telegram' from Moscow, explaining the irreconcilable differences between the US and Russia), such overtures left a distinctly sour aftertaste in the White House. It didn't take long for them to get Britain's attention.

Within days of the Japanese surrender, the White House issued an abrupt press release. It read: 'The President has directed the Foreign Economic Administrator to take steps immediately to discontinue all Lend-Lease operations and to notify foreign governments receiving Lend-Lease of this action.' Though no one had expected Lend-Lease to last for ever (indeed, Keynes had failed in his Stage II negotiations the previous autumn to secure a post-war continuation), few anticipated it would be so brought to an end in what Churchill described as a 'rough and harsh' fashion. At the very least, Keynes had expected the Americans to reduce support gradually rather than cut it off at once. Vinson, it transpired, had advised precisely such a reduction; but Leo Crowley, the administrator of the scheme, took the decision to terminate it.

It was as much of a surprise to those in the administration who had worked on the international economy as it was to Britain. This 'stupid announcement', said Ansel Luxford, American legal adviser at Bretton Woods, 'fell like a ton of bricks on everyone ... This was one of the problems of an unanticipated change in government. Roosevelt's death permitted people who had previously had nothing to do, in terms of working in this field, to move in and express their own particular views on an opportunistic basis.'[10] Not only would it leave a lasting scar on the Anglo-American relationship, it would cause similar resentment in Moscow, at precisely the wrong moment for the Truman administration.

However, the fact that many in Washington were furious with Crowley, who was largely regarded as a mouthpiece for Congress and was, anyway, in his political death throes, was little solace to the British public. Truman may only have been following the letter of the law, but it felt like betrayal. A cartoon published soon afterwards in weekly magazine *Tribune* featured a British boy asking a GI: 'Any gum, chum, on a strictly long-term, interest-free, dollar-loan basis?'[11]

The move exacerbated what was already a grim outlook for the British economy. Roosevelt's initial conception of Lend-Lease had been that no member of the United Nations should end the war in debt to one of its allies. However, by 1945 Britain was the most indebted country in the world.

Since Churchill's decision to wage total war in 1940 the country had devoted almost all its resources to the fight – a full fifth of the working population was in the armed forces, with a further third working in war production. Exports were now at a mere 29 per cent of their pre-war level. The endless need to suck in extra imports (both of weapons and supplies) had left it with a cumulative current account deficit of £5.9 billion. Under half of this had been covered by Lend-Lease and Canadian Mutual Aid; the rest had been financed by gold sales and the enormous pile of sterling debts owed to its Dominions.[12] With the collapse of Lend-Lease, issues which had been bubbling away throughout the Bretton Woods negotiations exploded suddenly into the foreground.

The country's plight had been neatly summarised by Keynes himself a few months before Lend-Lease was cancelled. Unless Britain dramatically expanded its exports, cut its overseas spending and received 'substantial aid from the United States on terms which we can accept', it would face its 'financial Dunkirk'. He continued:

> What does one mean in this context by 'a financial Dunkirk'? What would happen in the event of insufficient success? That is not easily foreseen. Abroad it would require a sudden and humiliating withdrawal from our onerous responsibilities with great loss of prestige and an acceptance for the time being of the position of a second-class power, rather like the present position of France. From the Dominions and elsewhere we should seek what charity we could obtain. At home a greater degree of austerity would be necessary than we have experienced at any time during the war. And there would have to be an indefinite postponement of the realisation of the best hopes of the new Government.[13]

The pain, he added, would last for about five years – and it was no coincidence that this was the average length of a parliamentary term. For Labour, the message was clear. Much as it disliked the prospect, it would have to go cap-in-hand to Washington. After that, it would have to secure some kind of deal with India, Egypt and the other countries holding sterling debt. At least on that front, it was in a slightly better position. 'The very size of these sterling debts is itself a protection,' said Keynes. 'The old saying holds. Owe your banker £1,000 and you are at his mercy; owe him £1 million and the position is reversed.'[14]

*

As Goldenweiser discovered when he stopped by in London, imperial aspirations were dying hard in spite of Britain's lamentable economic prospects. The country having poured all its efforts into fighting the war, its post-war domestic policy amounted, in Keynes's words, to 'It will all come right on the day'.[15] Economists could now see, even if their political masters could not, that Britain's life as 'Lady Bountiful', ruling benignly over an Empire stretching across the world, was over (not that the 'benign' element had ever been entirely applicable).

But the notion that Britain might continue on its pre-First World War path of economic pre-eminence lingered on – nowhere more so than in the debate over Bretton Woods. The main complaint, after the inevitable one that the agreement too closely resembled the gold standard, was that it would result in the end of the sterling area and Imperial Preference. That seemed to be an inescapable consequence of freeing the pound to make it convertible into dollars: it would cause a flood of cash out of Britain as the Indians understandably decided to put their money to better use elsewhere.

As ever, it was the Bank of England that made objections behind the scenes, with Lord Beaverbrook, the newspaper baron and now Lord Privy Seal, repeating them in public. The former Max Aitken had already conquered the business world, owning a string of industrial firms and banks in Canada; he had conquered Fleet Street, owning the *Daily Express*, then the world's biggest-selling newspaper; he had conquered London high society, conducting affairs with half of the city's eligible women, married or otherwise. Now the charming pint-sized imperialist took it upon himself to destroy Bretton Woods.

Keynes attempted to tackle the Beaver head-on. 'Twice in my life I have seen the Bank blindly advocating policies which I expected to lead to the greatest misfortunes and a frightful smash,' he wrote in response to a Beaverbrook critique. 'Twice I have predicted it;

twice I have been disbelieved; twice it has happened ... The Bank is engaged in a desperate gamble in the interests of old arrangements and old-fashioned ideas, which there is no possibility of sustaining. Their plan, or rather their lack of plan, would, in my firm belief, lead us into yet another smash. Why, why, why should you be found, on this occasion, on their side?'

The Bank's own plan – namely to ditch Bretton Woods and maintain the sterling area, forcing India and Egypt to spend their sterling debts in Britain – would also involve a period of almost unprecedented austerity, he added. 'We are not going to win the war and then put on a hair shirt. But the Bank's plan is even more impracticable than this, for their idea is that the rest of the sterling area, which will emerge from the war much richer in overseas resources than they entered it, would be prepared to imitate us in austerity. The whole thing is sheer rubbish from beginning to end. For God's sake have nothing to do with it!'[16]

While the debate continued in private and in the newspapers, it was lamentably absent from the House of Commons. This was not merely because the newly elected Labour government had such an enormous majority that it could essentially pass into law anything it wanted; it was also clear that Britain's support or otherwise of Bretton Woods was one of the only pawns the country would have in its possession when it came to negotiating post-war financial aid. In the wake of the termination of Lend-Lease, Dalton decided to tie the passage of Bretton Woods through Parliament to the forthcoming financial support negotiations with the Americans. The upshot was that Parliament would hardly debate the biggest single monetary reform ever to be imposed on the country, and the world.

Instead, the Treasury focused almost all its efforts on trying to persuade the Americans to hand over some cash. After cancelling Lend-Lease, a mildly repentant State Department invited London to send over a delegation for negotiations. As Keynes saw it there were three potential paths Britain could follow: Austerity, Temptation or Justice. 'Austerity', which Keynes nicknamed 'Starvation Corner', involved eschewing any American loan or aid, maintaining the sterling area and attempting to tough out the next few years alone. Rationing would continue into the foreseeable future, living standards would continue to fall, and any dreams of a new, generous welfare state would have to be abandoned. 'Temptation' entailed taking on a large-scale loan from the United States, which would only be repaid with great difficulty and over an extended period of time. The third, and in retrospect the most unrealistic, path was precisely the one Keynes recommended. 'Justice' would entail the United States giving Britain $3 billion in exchange for what it had spent on American supplies before Lend-Lease began – plus a further $5 billion of credit at a token interest rate. Canada and parts of the sterling area would voluntarily write off chunks of the debts the British owed them. In return, Britain would implement Bretton Woods ahead of schedule. Under the terms of the agreement, all currencies would have to be freely convertible after a five-year transitional period; Keynes proposed cutting that down to one year.

The notion that the Americans would simply hand over money in return for Britain's speedy adoption of Bretton Woods was staggeringly ambitious – and even that is perhaps euphemistic – but, said Keynes, Britain had suffered disproportionately during the war. This represented a fair settlement for her suffering – one imbued with the 'sweet breath of Justice between partners'.[17]

It was a characteristically poetic piece of economics from Keynes. However, it was based almost entirely in fantasy. He seemed, for one thing, to have forgotten how much it irritated the Americans when anyone attempted to imply that they had in some way profited from the war – or that others had suffered more on their behalf. Nor was there any evidence, either from his previous missions to Washington or indeed from communication with the Americans, that they would be interested in extending anything other than a loan (and that was precisely what Washington was envisaging). A straightforward grant, or indeed debt forgiveness, had never been on the table. And yet that is precisely what Keynes persuaded the Cabinet to adopt as a strategy.

By the summer of 1945 Britain's aspirations had become policy. Keynes would be dispatched to Washington in search of an American grant of $5 billion. In return, Britain would agree to make sterling convertible by the end of 1946. A loan, he added in his discussions with Dalton, would not do – unless it was a grant camouflaged as a loan. He insisted that he should not be allowed to agree 'anything except an out-and-out grant'.

Somewhere along the way, the Cabinet, under the influence of the Bank, had ruled out the middle option, Temptation: it was to be Justice, or, if Keynes failed, 'Starvation Corner'. The question of commercial policy – trade rules and the competition clauses dredged up by Article VII of Lend-Lease – was unlikely to be raised, he added.

It was an intoxicating prospect, even for a Cabinet whose members were already heavily medicated. It was also almost entirely bogus. The British Treasury representative in Washington, Bob Brand, had repeatedly warned Whitehall that there would be no free gift from Truman. He added, ominously: 'The US is the worst country to owe huge sums to whether for political or financial reasons, the most difficult to repay, and the most likely to yell and scream about repayment. That other countries should repay every dollar and cent is indeed almost not one but all the Ten Commandments of their religion. Therefore we should, insofar as it is possible, limit our demands here as much as we can.'[18]

As had been the case ahead of Bretton Woods, however, Keynes allowed his optimism to get the better of him. Though he admitted privately to a friend that the mission had 'very moderate hopes indeed of sufficient success', he sowed deeply unrealistic expectations in the minds of ministers.[19] Whereas the previous year the complexity of the monetary negotiations – and the indulgence of his Chancellor – had given him enough leeway to brand the outcome as success, this time there would be no such flexibility. It was to be very clear: either Britain would get its way, or it would not.

Various members of the Cabinet would privately express doubts about Keynes's optimism. Dalton wrote that Keynes had been 'almost starry-eyed' before setting off for Washington. Ernest Bevin was reported to say: 'When I listen to Lord Keynes talking I seem to hear the coins jingling in my pocket; but I cannot see that they are really there.'[20] But none would stop him. In retrospect it looks suspiciously likely that Dalton knew precisely what he was doing. The mission was unlikely to yield a positive outcome; it needed a scapegoat. Dalton ought to have headed the mission himself, rather than sending his ailing adviser. But would any politically astute Chancellor have elected to spend his first months going cap-in-hand to Washington when he could just as easily stay in Britain and take credit for the implementation of the Beveridge Report?

And perhaps they were, to some extent, seduced by Keynes. Despite his age and infirmity, the economist could still summon up moments of oratorical magic. That summer a young Canadian official, Douglas LePan, recalled hearing Keynes hold forth about his scheme: the most memorable moment by far came when he mentioned the 'sweet breath of justice'. 'There was something cherubic, almost seraphic, about his smile. And there was something else that is difficult to speak about, the word has been so debased. His charm.'[21]

As the British technicians left for Washington once again that September, it was painful to compare this depressing mission with their previous transatlantic voyages. For Lionel Robbins the contrast with 1943, when they set out at the very dawn of the Bretton Woods negotiations, was particularly acute. 'Then we had a constructive case to argue, an initiative to take, a cause to forward,' he wrote in his diary, 'and despite the scepticism of cynics at home we won right through and brought back a series of drafts which if they had been followed up, could have been made the basis for a general settlement in the economic sphere considerably superior to anything which we can now possibly hope for. Now our case is defensive, initiative is denied us, there is no question of a cause to be vindicated, only a possible grudging acquiescence in a settlement, acceptable only for extraneous reasons.' Moreover, he added, there were personal differences within their ranks 'precipitated by the wayward impulse and intransigence of one whom we all admire and love and the complete failure of his immediate associates to exercise corrective influence'.[22] Anyone even barely close to the negotiations would have been able to identify this troublesome character as Keynes.

They arrived to find the United States hot, suffocating and, in stark contrast to desolate London, 'throbbing with vitality'. In New York, wrote Robbins, one found 'the shops full of goods, the streets full of people, the breath of helterskelter reconversion in the air'.[23]

Keynes and Lydia travelled separately via some brief negotiations in Canada, again occupying the palatial Moorish suite at the Chateau Laurier in Ottawa; once in Washington, they stayed in the Statler Hotel and Lydia once more did her 'wartime duty' by hitting the shops. 'In the last five weeks,' Keynes wrote to his mother a month and a half into the visit, there had been 'some two hundred objects purchased, including eighteen pairs of shoes, forty pairs of stockings, between twelve and twenty costumes, a new suit and a tie for me (the suit costing a thousand times as much as the tie), a new raincoat for me, a large trunkful of food, five safety razors, ten ferocious jewels, half a dozen headgear and in addition enough odds and ends to fix up a shop ... But from tomorrow, having had a satisfactory birthday present, she proposes to shop seriously.'[24]

The negotiations went less well. Each day the British team, led by the demure old Lord Halifax, with Keynes a step behind, trooped into the Federal Reserve or the Treasury and attempted to make their case. From the very beginning it was clear something was wrong.

As ever, it came down in some measure to personality clashes. It was difficult not to get on with Will Clayton, the disarmingly charming Texan cotton millionaire who led most of the discussions, but Keynes somehow found a way. In particular he could not stomach Clayton's fixation on free trade, which was extreme, even by State Department standards. 'Why do you persecute us like this?' he exclaimed at one point, when Clayton argued that Britain's imperial strength had been built on free trade. 'At one time I had come to believe that the Mayflower came over to this country filled with lawyers. I am now inclined to go back to my original belief that it was filled with theologians.'[25]

Vinson he found even more difficult. Beneath his easy-going Southern demeanour, beneath the quips about sport and booze, the Treasury Secretary was extraordinarily prickly. He could not escape the suspicion that every one of Lord Keynes's jokes was meant as a slight against him. For the most part, he was right. 'Please try to remember,' one colleague advised the British delegation, 'that you are dealing with Kentucky.' 'Well,' replied Keynes, 'Kentucky will have to like it.'

On one occasion, when the pair discussed payment provisions, Vinson suggested that Britain's capacity to repay money would be improved 'if suddenly, tomorrow, you found currency in a cave'. 'Why, of course,' Keynes exclaimed. '"Any currency found in caves" – we'll have that in the agreement!' According to one observer, 'There was a roar of laughter at this *riposte*. Vinson turned black with rage. He did not quickly forget the incident.'[26]

Another time, he ribbed the Treasury Secretary (and lawyer), saying, 'Isn't our scheme intended to get things done, whereas yours will merely provide a living for a large number of lawyers?' What followed was 'like a bedroom scene in a Noel Coward play', according to Robbins. 'Vinson, who is a very emotional creature, completely lost control of himself', shouting at the top of his voice: 'That is just the kind of statement you would make.'[27]

Keynes found the rest of the American contingent similarly tricky. Federal Reserve chairman Marriner Eccles would drone on at interminable length at any opportunity. 'No wonder that man is a Mormon,' quipped Keynes. 'No single woman could stand him.'[28] Henry Wallace, vice-president under Roosevelt and now Secretary of Commerce, was 'completely gaga', falling asleep in almost every meeting he attended – though Washington insiders joked that that was frequently a sign he was listening most intently.[29]

Then there was Leo Crowley, the man who had cancelled Lend-Lease. Keynes had once described him as a 'Tammany Polonius', but this time he upped the ante, declaring that Crowley's face was reminiscent of 'the buttocks of a baboon'.[30] In recognition, the Treasury used the codename BABOON for the cables it sent over from Washington. The replies from the mission were codenamed NABOB – the term for a corrupt Indian servant (and, coincidentally, the codename by which Russian intelligence officers referred to Morgenthau).[31] In the event, Crowley would resign halfway through the negotiations.

From the Americans' perspective, Keynes was similarly objectionable. The insolence of his jokes paled in comparison with his initial proposals. The 'Justice' strategy he and the Cabinet had alighted upon presumed that the Americans would recognise that they owed Britain a moral debt for their part in the war. The British delegation circulated a letter claiming its losses were three and a half times greater than those on the American side; this only served to infuriate the American negotiators and press, to whom it was swiftly leaked. Keynes spent hours detailing the country's current economic straits, its debts to India and the rest of the Dominions, expecting the Americans to open their wallets. Instead, Henry Wallace, who had been dozing again, woke up and, to the utter horror of Keynes and British ambassador Halifax, suggested that

Britain give the Indians independence in return for a write-down of the debt.[32]

Still labouring under the delusion that Clayton would offer a grant, Keynes foolishly showed his entire hand, spelling out precisely what Britain would give in return: it would allow sterling to be freely convertible, sign up to Bretton Woods and agree to a future multilateral trade deal. It was a monumental mistake. At no point had America even contemplated the financial gift Keynes seemed to have promised the Cabinet back home. 'Justice' was not on the cards. The Americans, it rapidly and painfully transpired, had only one offer to make: a loan, with interest, over a long period. In other words, the 'Temptation' option the Cabinet had ruled out long ago. Robbins realised what this meant. 'I perceive that we shall have great difficulty in dehypnotising London,'[33] he wrote in his diary.

Sure enough, when Keynes raised the prospect of a loan rather than a grant, the 'Baboon' that came back from Dalton dismissed it out of hand. In what was to become a recurrent theme, the Chancellor parroted Keynes's previous assurances back at him. 'My present inclination is to decline any loan which carries interest, however it is dressed up,' he said, 'because I do not believe that that principle is appropriate to the circumstances.'[34]

The Americans eventually offered a $5 billion loan at a low interest rate. However, rather than explaining that it was the only option on the table, Keynes's cables home hinted blithely that something better might turn up. Dalton continued to ask for a grant – leaving Keynes trapped in a vicious circle between the two sides.

When Keynes pushed harder, recommending that Dalton consider the American loan, the Chancellor refused. The proposal, he added icily, did not have the 'sweet breath of justice' about it. Keynes's earlier pledge not to be allowed to leave Washington with anything other than a straightforward grant had come back to haunt him.

It didn't help that for much of September and early October, Washington was trapped in a heatwave. So hot was Robbins at one cocktail party that as he moved 'from group to group I felt that I must be leaving everywhere puddles of perspiration on the carpet behind me'.[35] The rooms in the Treasury in which negotiations took place were habitually sweltering, with Venetian blinds drawn throughout the day, even when the sun shone outside.

The heat made managing Keynes's condition even more difficult. Each night Lydia would pick out ice crystals from their salads to fill the icebag compress for his chest. But, oppressed by the temperature and distraught by the negotiations with London as much as by those with Washington, Keynes's health failed him again. Each confrontation caused another jab in his heart. The symptoms began to abate only when he started to take sodium amytal, a barbiturate prescribed by The Ogre. The choice of drug may help explain the disastrous slippage of his poker face during the negotiations: in strong enough doses, sodium amytal has the additional effect of being a 'truth serum'.

The negotiations were complicated by the walk-on part played by Harry Dexter White. The architect of Bretton Woods was now a marginal figure at the Treasury, cast aside by Vinson and biding his time offstage until the inauguration of the International Monetary Fund and World Bank the following year. He moped about at the negotiation hearings, at one stage causing an immense racket by knocking over a large tripod ashtray, and confused matters by suggesting an alternative solution for Britain's sterling debts problem. While Keynes was desperately trying to persuade Dalton to consider the Americans' offer of a $5 billion loan, White was busy trying to persuade Vinson and Clayton that $5 billion was too much. By the time Keynes returned to the table and declared Britain was ready to talk terms, the United States had dropped its offer to $3.5 billion.

It was another tremendous blow for Keynes, who promptly

exploded with anger at the Americans and threatened to walk out on the negotiations altogether. The crisis was worsened by the fact that, over in London, Dalton was busy preparing his Budget, and so did not have time to consider the new offer. Over the following weeks rival bids came and went between London and Washington, with Keynes consigned to the role of frustrated messenger boy. He was tired and desperate to return home, his health continuing to deteriorate. By the time the Americans' final offer arrived midway through November, he was despondent. His colleague Freddie Harmer found him 'in bed looking very shaken and white; and all he could say was that we had better pack up and go home'. The Americans had seen fit to insert 'every kind of silly and insulting technicality ... into the draft: together with several major new points which would have caused an explosion of fury if sent home'. When White phoned Keynes offering technical advice, 'M was appallingly rude to him on the telephone – just what we wanted to avoid.'[36]

Fearing for his health and for the fate of the negotiations, Keynes's colleagues staged a minor mutiny and attempted to shift the lead role in the talks on to Halifax – though by this stage the damage had been done. What leverage might have been available to Britain had entirely dissipated. Towards the end of November London's faith in the team dissolved almost entirely. Dalton wrote in his diary that Keynes had 'completely spun out' while Robbins had become 'hysterical', and sent the Cabinet secretary, Sir Edward Bridges, to the US to take charge.[37] Not for the first time, Keynes threatened to resign.

At no point during the previous years – even during the depths of the Bretton Woods talks – had morale sunk so low. 'As you may have surmised,' Keynes wrote to Eady, 'life here for the past three weeks or longer has been absolute hell; though I doubt if you can have guessed quite how bad it has been.'

The final crisis came when it dawned on the Cabinet back home just how significant a move it would be to allow sterling to be freely converted into other currencies. Dalton attempted to insert a clause refusing any formal commitment along those lines. It was clear he could not quite believe what the Americans were insisting upon. Full sterling convertibility would probably trigger a sudden, dangerous exodus of cash out of Britain. Handled badly, it would be a financial disaster.

However, save for some minor amendments (most notably delaying the date of sterling conversion from the end of 1946 to mid-1947), the Americans would not budge. At this stage Dalton came close to calling off the negotiations altogether – and taking the path towards Starvation Corner. However, Keynes and his fellow delegates warned that to do so would be disastrous.

Just when it all seemed to be over, with the British ready to sign, a final cable came from the Cabinet asking the team to remonstrate one last time with Vinson. Eventually, the Treasury Secretary was tracked down to the nightclub of the Willard Hotel, the head-quarters of the British delegation. Even when cornered in this inebriated state, he still could not be persuaded to budge one inch.

There was no disguising the fact that the final agreement, signed on 6 December 1945, was a humiliation. Keynes had travelled to Washington in search of a gift of money; he came back with a loan (with interest), tied to a particularly poisonous condition that, according to Wilfred Eady at the Treasury, 'came as a shock'.[38] In contrast with the Bretton Woods negotiations, during which White and Morgenthau had at least moved a small distance towards the British position, Clayton and Vinson simply would not shift. 'We have all done our level best to move the Americans,' Lord Halifax cabled to the Prime Minister. 'I am sorry we have failed.'[39]

With Keynes still on his voyage home, the agreement was rapidly forced through the House of Commons, together with the Bretton Woods agreement. There were a few squeaks of protest – indeed, twenty-nine Labour MPs voted against their government's motion. Conservative MP Robert Boothby declared: 'This is our economic Munich ... Lord Keynes once described Mr. Lloyd George as "a witch flying through the murky streets of Paris from the hag-ridden bogs of antiquity." My description of Lord Keynes is, "A siren, beckoning us to our doom from the murkier depths of Bretton Woods." That is the danger. He is a siren, with his persuasive tongue.'

After brushing aside the rhetorical flourishes, one could hardly deny that Boothby had a point – not just about the loan, but about Bretton Woods itself, under which the 'onus is put upon the debtor nations to re-establish equilibrium in the balance of trade; and there is no onus at all upon the creditor nations'.[40] He had pinpointed precisely Keynes's greatest failure – to ensure the incorporation of that element of his Clearing Union into White's plan.

As the *Queen Elizabeth* carried the disappointed delegation back across the Atlantic, Keynes sat 'grey with anxiety' in his cabin, wrote Robbins, reading 'with growing anger and contempt, the misrepresentations, as they came from the wireless operators, of *his* efforts and *his* loan, and polishing the periods of the defence which he was gathering all his remaining forces to make'.[41] When the ship docked on 17 December, he headed straight for the House of Lords, where the debate raged on.

Britain was to receive a loan of $3.75 billion – equivalent to $56 billion in 2014 money – at 2 per cent interest. In return, Britain would have to allow sterling to be freely convertible for current transactions one year after the loan was enacted, which worked out as 15 July 1947. The loan would not be fully paid off until 29 December 2006.

Though it was not in Keynes's nature to admit defeat, it was clear that he was ashamed of the disastrous loan. 'I shall never so long as I live cease to regret that this is not an interest-free loan,' he told the Lords. 'The charging of interest is out of tune with the underlying realities. It is based on a false analogy.'

However, he would not apologise for the element of the loan that had so disturbed the Cabinet – the enforced convertibility of the pound, and the opening of the financial dam walls around Britain. At Bretton Woods Britain had fought for and won a five-year grace period before any country faced the onslaught of the open market. Now, in one fell swoop, this buffer had been denied them. Sterling, the most exposed of all currencies to an exodus of investors, was to be put on the block in little more than a year.

The alternative, he told the Lords, was to shrivel the sterling area into a separate economic bloc and fade into insignificance, which seemed to the Bank of England to be preferable. 'The way to remain an international banker,' he said, 'is to allow cheques to be drawn upon you; the way to destroy the sterling area is to prey on it and try to live on it.' He concluded by reminding the House that it was he who had denounced the gold standard so many years ago. Now some were suggesting that, in the form of the Bretton Woods agreement, he was attempting 'to resurrect and re-erect the idols which [he] had played some part in throwing out of the market place. Not so.'[42]

In the 1920s and 1930s, Keynes's reputation had soared even as the Bank of England's had collapsed. The Bank had lost credibility after it encouraged Churchill to put Britain back on gold. Now, when it wailed that Keynes was making a mistake, no one would listen. However, in this case, the Bank was right and Keynes was wrong. Fatigued by his heart problems and by years of wartime negotiations, struggling to meet Dalton's unrealistic demands and dosed up on medication which may well have undermined his tactics, Keynes's performance in Washington was an abject failure.

The convertibility of sterling, which he volunteered the Americans freely, threatened to spark economic catastrophe within only a few years – though Keynes would not be around to witness the consequences. By the time he returned to London, he was a shadow of his former self; the ordeal had left a rotten taste in the mouth. Exhausted, sustained on drugs and hardly able to stand, Keynes took his leave of the Treasury shortly after returning from America.

He was uncharacteristically depressed for some time. His countrymen, he ranted in a letter to Bob Brand, had been 'living in a complete fool's paradise and have not begun to readjust themselves to the post-war world'. England, he added in a second letter, was 'sticky with self-pity and not prepared to accept peacefully and wisely the fact that her position and her resources are *not* what they once were. Psycho-analysis would, I think, show that that was the real background of the reception of the American loan and the associated proposals.'[43] Britain and its exhausted population would never have been able to endure the full horrors of Starvation Corner.

Now that the money was agreed, though, his fear was that in a desperate effort to 'cut a dash in the world' the Cabinet would waste it on sustaining the Empire – using it to maintain army numbers in Egypt, Greece and elsewhere.[44] He needn't have worried. Over the following years, Attlee would brutally strip down the military. Country by country, the Empire would be discarded, provoking howls of fury in the Commons, from Churchill and from Beaverbrook.

Had the Prime Minister wanted to cling on, perhaps he could have put some of the American loan to use postponing the inevitable denouement. Instead, Attlee spent it on his New Jerusalem. According to Edmund Dell, 'The welfare state, as it stood in 1951, could not have been created without the American loan.'[45] Though the loan was supposed to go towards shoring up Britain's balance of payments ahead of the introduction of Bretton Woods, in the event American money helped pay for social security, the National Health Service and widespread nationalisation of the British economy.

CHAPTER FIFTEEN

Onward Christian Soldiers

1946–1948

What we call the beginning is often the end
And to make an end is to make a beginning.
The end is where we start from.

T.S. Eliot, 'Little Gidding'

My creed is the American creed.

Harry Dexter White

The festive decorations were still hanging in the State Department when the guests arrived – a couple of dozen men, wrapped in thick coats and hats against the freezing Washington winter. In they came, down the corridors and through to the ornate old Navy Library, where on the table in front of the photographers and reporters was the document they had come to sign. It was four days short of the 31 December 1945 deadline; Bretton Woods was about to become international law.

Leading the ceremony was the formidable figure of Fred Vinson, Treasury Secretary. He sat hunched at the table, his jowly features clenched in a stony frown. To his side was Lord Halifax, who as British ambassador had had the dubious honour of signing the notorious Anglo-American loan agreement only a few weeks earlier. Around the room were representatives from France, China, India ... twenty-eight countries in total.

However, something wasn't quite right. This was supposed to be a moment of celebration, and yet one could hardly ignore the sombre mood of the evening. As each man stepped forward to sign the document, he did so with such a gloomy face that when at last one of them, the Indian agent general, let slip a brief smile, a hail of flash bulbs went off all at once. When the ceremony was done, Vinson declared, 'I am pleased to announce that the agreements are now in full force and effect.' There followed the merest ripple of applause.[1]

It was not only the misery of the past few months' negotiations over the Anglo-American loan that hung over the official signing of Bretton Woods – it was the fact that one of the most important participants had not shown up. Throughout the conference the American delegation – Harry Dexter White especially – had gone to extreme lengths to persuade the Russians to sign the initial agreement. In their quest to satisfy Moscow, they had crowbarred various clauses and protections into the Final Act, they had corralled other delegations to contribute more to the World Bank's reserves so the Russians would not have to overextend themselves, they had waited nervously until the very last minute for Stepanov, the head of the Soviet delegation, to get on board.

But since the conference barely a squeak had been heard from the Russians. Almost every other country had passed the necessary laws in their parliaments and assemblies, and those that hadn't (such as Australia, New Zealand and Denmark) had legitimate technical reasons for not doing so. But Moscow had been absolutely silent.

It might have been easier to dismiss one's concern were it not for the fact that relations with the Russians had clearly deteriorated since Roosevelt's death. Shortly after taking over as President, Harry Truman had lashed out at Russian Foreign Minister Molotov, accusing the Soviets of breaking agreements with the United States.* A stream of visits and, subsequently, formal letters to Molotov about Bretton Woods had failed to elicit any response.

In September, George Kennan, chargé d'affaires at the American Embassy in Moscow, wrote to Molotov's deputy that 'in view of the very short time left till the signing ... I would very much appreciate the urgent expression of the opinion of your government' about Bretton Woods.[2]

By November, the Treasury was assuming the worst. Russia was simply deleted from the planning notices. It was not until the very eve of the deadline, after the ceremony had already passed, that Molotov sent Kennan his terse reply: 'at present, the Soviet Government does not find it possible to sign the drafts of the Agreements made at Bretton Woods ... The Soviet Government finds it necessary to subject the issues touched upon in these projects to additional scrutiny in the light of the new terms of the international economic development, which have been emerging in the post war period.'[3]

What were those 'new terms'? Until the opening up of the archives in Moscow in recent years, Western scholars were only able to guess. What has emerged is that the Russians came closer than many assumed to joining the Fund, but as was the case in the United States, the will of politicians eventually trumped the advice of their economic advisers.

Even in December, weeks before the signing ceremony, technicians from the Finance Ministry in Moscow were still drawing up briefing notes which were broadly positive about the advantages of

---

*In remarks to Robert Sherwood, which remained classified for many decades afterwards, Anthony Eden claimed that Roosevelt's death was 'a calamity of immeasurable proportions' which was directly responsible for the breakdown in US–Soviet relations in 1945 and thereafter. He said that 'had Roosevelt lived and retained his health he would never have permitted the present situation to develop.' See Frank Costigliola, *Roosevelt's Lost Alliances: How Personal Politics Helped Start the Cold War*, Princeton, 2012.

IMF and World Bank membership: it would be a useful tool for borrowing money; it would give Russia access to extra information. What few of them realised was that neither Stalin nor Molotov had ever had much enthusiasm for the scheme. When the foreign commissar first agreed to send a delegation to the conference, he couched it in ominous terms – saying, Kennan wrote later, that 'if our Government felt it necessary to have Soviet assent for purposes of its propaganda effect on outside world [*sic*], the Soviet Government would be willing to have its experts participate in discussions along these lines.'[4] In other words, it was a show of friendliness to help their allies.

In fact, there was another, ulterior motive: Molotov and Stalin had hoped to procure a loan from the United States. Six months before Bretton Woods, Harry Dexter White had begun lobbying Morgenthau to open up an enormous credit line of $10 billion to the Soviets; he had, according to Russian secret cables from the period, made such encouraging noises to their agents that Moscow was convinced a loan was on the cards. In their internal analysis following the conference, the Soviet analysts concluded that although Russia might 'get some tangible economic gains from participation in the [World] Bank', the country's economic problems 'may be resolved only by large government long-term loans from the USA and partly from England'.[5]

However, as time passed, the prospect of a loan had become less and less realistic. Dean Acheson had met with the Soviets throughout the sticky summer of 1944 to try to knock a deal into shape, but they could not agree over rates and fine points. By the time Vinson came into office, the proposal had been abandoned.

Having failed to secure its loan, Moscow watched indignantly as the British and French got theirs. In the internal memorandum drafted for Molotov, Russian officials wrote: 'In dealing with the USSR the Americans do not show a wish to offer credit, even though from our side we have made appropriate submissions to the government of the USA. Our membership in the Fund and the Bank in this light seems pointless.'[6]

The war was over, the loan talks were kaput and relations were beginning to freeze over. But what really killed off the chances of the Soviet Union joining Bretton Woods was when Stalin handed control of the official assessment over membership to Nikolai Voznesensky in March 1945. Voznesensky, head of the state planning agency Gosplan, was a stalwart opponent of the scheme. Playing on Stalin's paranoia about the security of Russia's gold reserves and the threat to the hermetically sealed Russian economy, Voznesensky dismissed the advantages of IMF membership.[7] Stalin barely needed convincing – there promised to be little economic benefit, and Russia would have been forced to divulge sensitive economic data Stalin would far rather keep to his chest. It would also disrupt his plans to devalue the rouble.

The Soviet decision, according to Kennan, brought forth an 'anguished cry of bewilderment' from the Treasury. They had allowed themselves to believe that the Fund could be a truly international body, convinced by the apparent sincerity of Stepanov, Chechulin, Bystrov and their colleagues at the conference. But it seems likely that the Russian men and women who took part were as oblivious as the Americans to their leaders' probable lack of desire to sign up to Bretton Woods.

The decision may have concerned money rather than nuclear warheads, but this was nonetheless the first substantial diplomatic fissure between America and the Soviet Union. For many, Russia's refusal to sign marked the very beginning of the Cold War.[8] Relations with Moscow cooled rapidly in the following months as the American Embassy sought to squeeze an explanation out of the Kremlin. It was in an effort to explain the snub that, early the following year, Kennan would write a series of cables to Washington, culminating in his 'Long Telegram' – the seminal diplomatic cable that outlined the gulf in attitude, philosophy and economics that had opened up between the West and Communist Russia.

As relations cooled further and tensions spilled onto the streets of Berlin and other parts of occupied Europe, the Truman administration continued to back away from the pro-Soviet policies of the Roosevelt era. In their place was installed an alternative diplomatic strategy based on Kennan's philosophy: containment and threat rather than collaboration and alliance. By March 1946, when Winston Churchill stood up in Truman's home town of Fulton, Missouri, and warned of the 'iron curtain' that was being erected across Europe, the public mood was already shifting alongside the political. A poll found that 60 per cent of Americans thought the US was being 'too soft' on Russia; only 3 per cent thought it was being 'too tough'.[9]

For their part, by that stage the Soviets were deriding the organisation they had helped to set up, whose articles they (more than most member nations) had shaped in its internal analysis documents. The Fund was 'connected with the self-interest of American capital'; hopes that it could help increase employment 'cannot be realized and to get rid of the crisis, as teaches Comrade Stalin, it is necessary to destroy capitalism'.[10]

Bretton Woods had been intended to bring countries together in mutual economic co-operation; instead it had provided the opportunity for yet more brinksmanship between East and West. After Christmas 1945 the optimists in Washington would realise that the pessimists, such as the American man in Moscow, had been right. 'The year 1946,' wrote Dean Acheson, 'was for the most part a year of learning that minds in the Kremlin worked very much as George F. Kennan had predicted they would.'[11]

Few were more traumatised by this epiphany than White himself. As the delegates lined up to sign the Bretton Woods documents that December evening, he sat unobtrusively out of sight. Only when Vinson asked him stiffly to step forward for applause did he emerge briefly from the audience, before dropping back into the shadows again.

Since Morgenthau's departure from the White House, White had been stranded in the twilight between influence and irrelevance. No longer did he hold sway over Treasury policy; Vinson simply did not trust him. The trait Keynes found most attractive in him (that he was an 'international civil servant [with] little or no American patriotism') was precisely what was no longer in fashion in the post-Roosevelt world.[12] Nonetheless, there was still one job he coveted: managing director of the International Monetary Fund.

In January, a few weeks after the ambassadors signed the formal agreement, Truman called White into his office to tell him he was nominating him as the first American executive director of the IMF. White was approved for the position by Congress a week and a half later. Flattering though it was, it wasn't the job he wanted. He had hoped to be the head of the entire institution; instead he was merely being asked to become its American representative.

It was a blow, but not a fatal one: the top position was not due to be decided officially until the Fund's special inaugural session in Savannah, Georgia, in March. But the President's silence on the matter had been alarming. As the weeks ticked down, it was whispered that the United States would only put forward a candidate for one of the institutions, and that it would not be the Fund.

What White did not realise was that his connections with Soviet intelligence were finally catching up with him. He had been under full FBI surveillance since November 1945. That very month, Elizabeth Bentley had turned herself in to the Bureau, confessing her involvement in the Washington-based espionage ring of which, she claimed, White was one of the most prominent members. This had triggered a flurry of activity as the FBI scrambled for evidence.

By 8 November 1945 enough had been amassed for a preliminary note to be sent to Truman's FBI liaison, General Harry Vaughan. White's name was second in the list of suspected members. For whatever reason, Truman never saw this first report: he would only become aware of the FBI's suspicions in February 1946. Shortly after nominating White for the post of executive director at the IMF, however, he received a detailed note which explained that White was 'a valuable adjunct to an underground Soviet espionage organization operating in Washington DC'.[13]

There was panic behind the scenes at the White House as the administration, horrified at the potential consequences, tried to carry out damage limitation. Truman called up the Senate to see if it was possible to reverse White's nomination. It was too late: the nomination had been approved that very afternoon. Truman faced a dilemma. According to J. Edgar Hoover, White was 'unfit' to serve in a senior governmental position; but removing him now would create an unholy fuss. Eventually the Attorney General, Tom Clark, decided that the best thing to do was to allow him to continue in the job, but to surround him 'with persons who were specially selected and who were not security risks'.[14]

While White was unaware of these conversations, he realised in the following months that he was being tracked by the FBI. The phone bugs might have been subtle enough, but the agents following him around everywhere were so heavy-handed that by March he had taken to joking about them when he went for meetings. As the year went on, there were, for the first time, whispers in the press about White's Soviet links. The turning of the mood meant that suddenly all things Soviet took on a sinister complexion.

Whether White would have been appointed to lead the IMF had it not been for the FBI charges remains unclear. Testifying about the episode some years later, Truman said that White was 'separated from the Government service promptly when the necessity for secrecy concerning the intensive investigation by the FBI came to an end'.[15] However, when asked directly whether the allegations had damaged White's prospects, Vinson insisted 'That hasn't a thing to do with it.'[16]

Indeed, in retrospect, the notion that Vinson would ever seriously have considered White for the role – regardless of the FBI's allegations – seems faintly laughable. The Treasury Secretary was midway through the process of 'gutting' his department, with the old guard of New Dealers (among whom White was the most prominent) being 'expelled or cast into outer darkness'.[17] Anyway, Vinson had, under the influence of New York bankers, decided some time previously that the World Bank was likely to be the more important institution. It was the Bank which would have the power to issue bonds, to dole out money for struggling countries, whereas the Fund's support would be predicated far more on whether a given nation was facing a balance of payments crisis. In these pre-Marshall Plan days, it was the Bank which appeared to have the power to finance reconstruction in Europe and elsewhere after the war. If at that point one had to choose an institution which might conduct American policy internationally, it was the Bank rather than the Fund.

And while White might have been a shoo-in for the Fund job, there was little serious suggestion that he would become president of the World Bank – particularly given the enemies he had made in Wall Street. 'White was hated in the banking community as perhaps no other man in the United States has been hated,' his Bretton Woods colleague Ansel Luxford would later recall. 'He was equally hated by people within the departments of every part of the executive branch of the government who had to deal with him – I say, by some people; he was loved by others.'[18] So far had White's stock within the Treasury fallen that Vinson would routinely overrule him and undermine him. It was out of the question that he would ever back him for such a significant role.

Vinson had instead decided to withhold the World Bank presidency as a political bauble for one of his friends and colleagues. Few of them were qualified to run a major international institution. The most preposterous name to be mentioned was W.L. Hemingway, a one-time president of the American Bankers' Association who George Bolton of the Bank of England described as 'a fantastic museum piece, more like a character in Alice in Wonderland than a twentieth century banker'.[19] In the end, the top jobs at both institutions were decided by way of a compromise, leaving no one happy. Financier and *Washington Post* owner Eugene Mayer was appointed World Bank president, while the job of IMF managing director was left for a non-American, the Belgian Camille Gutt.

It was a devastating blow for White. As he reeled from the news, he contemplated launching an independent bid for the position, trying to drum up support from other countries around the world – but to no avail. Then, as now, what mattered were America's votes.

White was not one to sulk and as the inaugural meeting in Savannah approached, he tried to put on a brave face. But for those who had negotiated and fought with him at the Mount Washington Hotel two years earlier, there was no mistaking the sad transformation in the man. 'He is a pale shadow of the intense, fanatic, ruthless figure we saw at Bretton Woods and Atlantic City; the sharp deflation even seems to have brought about a physical shrinking of the man.'[20]

While Bretton Woods ended with an almighty party, the inaugural meeting of the IMF in Savannah, Georgia, began with one. Economists arriving on the special train from Washington had the shock of their lives when they were greeted by an enormous crowd of cheering well-wishers at the station. The mayor, who had been as desperate to host the event as the New Hampshire politicians who fought to hold Bretton Woods, had declared this a special day of celebration. Schools had been shut and thousands of children lined the streets as a police motorcade escorted the speechless technicians on their parade through the town to the Oglethorpe Hotel.

It was a surreal beginning to the event. Still, it was a reminder that the world really was a happier place. The last time most of the delegates had seen each other was two years previously at the Mount Washington, when Allied troops were still pushing through Normandy and V1 bombs were falling on London. As the drinks flowed and they were served up an enormous spread of Southern food, Savannah had the air of a lavish reunion. Even Professor Bystrov, one of the Russian delegation from Bretton Woods, had made the journey, though only as an observer. The Soviet Union was still, officially at least, reserving its judgement on Bretton Woods, and he would spend most of the conference watching proceedings in silence, along with his assistant, a young and rather glamorous-looking woman.

Once again, Keynes had sailed over on the *Queen Mary*. But whereas the majority of his fellow passengers in those previous voyages had been German PoWs, this time the ship was full to the brim with young women. Some 2252 war brides and their young babies were on board, coming to the United States to be reunited with the American soldiers who had stolen their hearts while stationed in Britain during the war.

Keynes was still weak. Shortly before the journey he had suffered yet another heart attack, this time at the gala post-war opening of the Covent Garden Opera House, where he had to lie down most of the way through Tchaikovsky's *Sleeping Beauty*. Keynes had masterminded the renovations and chose the ballet especially for Lydia, who had entranced him in the 1921 performance at the Alhambra. In the days that followed he had been in two minds as to whether to come to the United States at all, particularly after the ordeal of the loan negotiations. But now, sailing out on a ship full of young women travelling to meet the men they loved, it was hard not to feel caught up in the good humour. 'Keynes persists in regarding the trip as a holiday and refuses to believe that any serious or difficult questions can emerge,' wrote one of his colleagues.[21] Disembarking from the boat with Lydia, who was sporting a leopard-print coat, he was asked by a reporter about suggestions that the loan would make Britain an 'illegitimate forty-ninth State of the Union'.

'No such luck,' he replied with a grin.[22]

However, before he even arrived in Savannah, he discovered that the trip was not to be the stress-free holiday he had been expecting. One of the few remaining issues – other than some questions of personnel – was where in the United States the Fund and Bank would be headquartered. Britain had been pushing for New York, but when Keynes stopped off in Washington Vinson told him that he had decided the institutions should be in the capital.

Keynes exploded: 'in that case these bodies could not be regarded as international institutions but were being treated as an appendage of the American Administration, which was just what the critics had declared them to be.' But Vinson could not be moved: siting them anywhere near Wall Street, he said, would put them under the influence of 'international finance'. Anyway, he had the votes to force through what he wanted.[23] Unbeknownst to Keynes, White had been pushing to have the institutions in New York, but, in a sign of his newly straitened circumstances, had been peremptorily overruled.[24]

It did not take long, however, for Savannah to ease Keynes's temper. This was his first visit to the South, and he was instantly intoxicated. 'To come from the cold, grey damp of an English March to the balmy air and bright azalean colour of Savannah refreshens the body.' The city, he added, was like 'a beautiful woman, the mother of many hopefuls, but whose face was concealed behind a veil of delicate lace'.[25]

His opening speech at the conference was similarly poetic. Borrowing from the tale of *The Sleeping Beauty*, which he had just seen in London, he said he hoped that the fairy godmothers would bestow upon these twins, 'Master Fund and Miss Bank', a whole range of blessings – but he added that he hoped

> that there is no malicious fairy, no Carabosse, whom he has over-looked and forgotten to ask to the party. For if so the curses which that bad fairy will pronounce will, I feel sure, run as follows: 'You two brats shall grow up politicians; your every thought and act shall have an *arrière-pensée*; everything you determine shall not be for its own sake or on its own merits but because of something else.'
>
> If this should happen, then the best that could befall – and that is how it might turn out – would be for the children to fall into an eternal slumber, never to waken or be heard of again in the courts and markets of Mankind.[26]

It was intended as a subtle warning about the risk that, located in Washington, the institutions might become overly politicised. The subtlety, however, was lost on Vinson, who was overheard muttering: 'I don't mind being called malicious, but I do mind being called a fairy.'[27]

The Treasury Secretary's own speech was as bombastic as the ones he made at Bretton Woods itself, marred only slightly by his monotone delivery: 'We were, when we gathered at Bretton Woods and when the sacrificial altar of tyranny was being pushed backward across the Rhine, actually better people. For a short space of three weeks we were making a better world by being better people. I hope, I believe, we still are better people.'

Figuring that they could hardly be improved on, he also recycled the lines he had used twice before at Bretton Woods: 'We fight together on the sodden battlefields. We sail together on the majestic blue. We fly together in the ethereal sky. The test of this conference is whether we can walk together down the road to peace as today we march to victory.'[28]

To his frustration, the applause was polite rather than rapturous; Keynes received the loudest ovation. But Vinson would get his way in almost every other respect. Although there were only a few small items on the agenda at the conference over the coming days, Vinson bulldozed them through. The decision as to the location of the headquarters was passed, despite British concerns. The British point that the Fund's directors ought to be part time, so that they could remain engaged with their national administrations rather than being subsumed into Washington life, was also very quickly dismissed. 'It was perhaps the least satisfactory negotiation of all those I have taken part in – which may be saying a good deal,' wrote Brand.[29]

For Keynes, the final straw was the astonishing scale of the salaries. The managing director of the IMF was to receive $30,000 tax free, making him the second-highest-paid official in Washington after the President of the United States. The salaries of the executive directors would be similarly high – begging the question of what, precisely, they were expected to be doing all day. As far as Keynes was concerned – even before one contemplated how the Fund would afford to pay them all – there would simply not be enough work to keep them occupied.

One night, Canadian delegate Louis Rasminsky, who was to be elected as Canadian representative, asked Vinson precisely that question.

'My dear young fellow,' said Vinson in his Southern drawl. 'You'll be busy as a lap-dog, busy as a lap-dog.'

Rasminsky pressed him: 'Yes, Judge, but what will I actually be doing?'

'My dear young fellow, you'll be busy as a lap-dog, studyin' trends and votin' on 'em, studyin' trends and votin' on 'em.'[30]

This odd mantra fast became one of the in-jokes at the conference. One morning a Canadian delegate told a British friend that the previous night 'he had just had a nightmare in which he had been pursued by a trend – and in a vicious circle at that.'[31] All the same, it was difficult for Keynes to muster much support, given that, generally speaking, the representatives in Savannah were the very same people who would end up drawing the salaries.

His was the only vote against the section on salaries at Savannah. It was, in retrospect, a slightly churlish move, set against the extent of the reforms represented by Bretton Woods. However, the experience at Savannah had, unexpectedly, been so much more unpleasant, so much more bullying, that it was not in his nature to accept such treatment lying down. 'I went to Savannah to meet the world,' he said, 'and all I met was a tyrant.'[32]

Within a few days the British delegation were dubbing the conference 'The Reptile House'.[33] Even American journalists were disturbed by the spectacle. Wrote one: 'I have watched with amazement the bluntness with which the U.S. has declared its power and said, in effect, to the delegates here: "America is the superior financial and economic country of the world ... make no mistake about one thing. We're tops in this bank and fund and we want everybody to know it."'[34] Nor did Vinson's behaviour provoke much resistance from the other delegates, most of whom were focused on trying to snag one of the lucrative new positions at the Fund or Bank.

While Harry White may have been a pale imitation of his former self, he nonetheless could not resist the opportunity to have the final say at Savannah. Keynes's problem, he said, was not really about salaries: 'I believe that his views and those of his Government stem from something that goes very far back [to] the very first conversation that we had with our British friends several years ago, when early drafts were being considered.'

Keynes, he said, continued to believe that the Fund should be an automatic machine, programmed to dole out money when countries needed it – as was the case in the earliest conceptions of his Clearing Union. However, he himself had conceived of an institution where some of the world's brightest economists would have discretion to decide whether and how to help economies avoid crises, and recover from occasional problems. The difference in stance was reflected in the fact that while Keynes thought the IMF could make do with around thirty technicians, White envisaged the staff being closer to three hundred.

'The problem of salaries which is before us, whether a few thousand dollars more or less,' said White, 'is not the real problem. The real problem is, shall you have a Fund which is competent to meet these various problems which are before us or shall you have an automatic source of credit?'[35]

For those who watched, it was a reminder of the tension that still existed between the two men. Both had been increasingly sidelined from policymaking; both were now physically frail; but neither would give up on attempting to map out what they believed was the ideal system under which the world economy should be run. That said, the atmosphere had mellowed significantly since those early discussions during the war. Whereas Keynes and White both looked tense in the group photographs at the Mount Washington in 1944, the pictures of the pair at Savannah are quite different. There they are, sharing a private joke, laughing with each other, and, in another shot, sitting out on deckchairs together by the shore, underneath the shade of the palm trees.

White was so much at his ease with Keynes that at one point he did what he would not even do with most of his colleagues – confide in him about his problems with Vinson. So far had he fallen out of favour, he said, that he had entirely lost the confidence of the Treasury Secretary. He did not expect to last in his new position as American executive director 'for more than six months'.

Keynes, for his part, could hardly hide his disenchantment with what had become of Bretton Woods. 'Keynes is a bitterly disappointed man and finds it hard to believe that these wonderful plans have gone so far astray,' George Bolton wrote in his diary. 'He is therefore in a critical destructive mood and is swinging to the other violent extreme of saying that he washes his hands of these two brats and he will encourage the Americans to destroy them by their own folly.'[36]

Never before had the pair felt comfortable enough to confide so readily in each other. But it had taken two years of pain and disappointment to get there. Only now could these two ageing men – both of them exiles within their own governments, both embittered with what had become of their grand plans for the world economy – see eye-to-eye. 'My last memory,' Keynes wrote soon afterwards, 'is of Dr Harry White, with vine leaves (or were they cocktails?) in his hair, leading into the dining room a Bacchic rout of satyrs and Silenuses from Latin America, loudly chanting the strains of "Onward Christian Soldiers".'[37]

As Keynes walked out at the end of the final banquet, the assembled audience stood up and sang 'For He's a Jolly Good Fellow', as they had at Bretton Woods. This time around, though, it was not a spontaneous gesture: Eddie Bernstein, conscious of the drubbing Keynes had suffered at the hands of Vinson, had asked the orchestra to play it as a final gesture of goodwill.

Savannah glistened in the moonlight as Keynes, Lydia and the rest of the delegates left on the special overnight train to Washington. It was a 'lovely middle March evening, with a full moon over the rivers and lakes of this delta, and the sea, with a temperature of about 70 at 10 o'clock in the evening'.[38] The hard work was now over, but the past week had taken its toll on Keynes. The following morning, as the train wended its way north, he collapsed on his way from the dining car to his carriage. It was a severe heart attack. He was laid out on a bed, as Lydia tended to him and Harry White stood by, sick with concern. As word spread of his collapse, delegates lined up to pay their respects to the great man. 'Those of us who were privileged to shake his limp hand on the train from Savannah to Washington ... were left with the memory of saying farewell to a truly noble man,' said Ray Mikesell of the American delegation.[39]

He managed to recover enough to take the *Queen Mary* back to Southampton, but the voyage was rough, the ship was dirty, and many of the passengers, including Keynes, came down with a stomach bug.

By the time he was back in London he looked even more ill than on his previous return from Washington, only three months earlier. 'We were rather worried about Maynard when he came back from Savannah,' Wilfred Eady would write later. 'He was not only very white, but he slumped in his chair, and very gentle as though he found it very difficult to revive interest in all the many daily things on which he guided us.'[40] Keynes seemed to recover in the next couple of weeks, so much so that, on Easter weekend, he was able to walk all the way down Firle Beacon, a windswept hill on the South Downs near Tilton. His mother described watching him and Lydia ahead of her 'as they disappeared gradually below the brow of the hill – he, bending down to her in animated talk, she looking up in eager response'.[41]

The following morning, Easter Sunday, he suffered a massive heart attack as he lay in bed. Within minutes he was dead. He was sixty-two.

Keynes had been ill for some time, but his sudden death was nonetheless a shock of immense proportions. 'It is not possible even yet to realise the hole that is made in our lives here,' said Eady. Bob Brand, who had worked so closely with Keynes throughout the negotiations, said, 'I cannot myself think of anyone whose talents, unequalled in their brilliance, are more wanted at this juncture than his. In the course of a pretty long life I have never met anyone else whom I would be sure was what is called a "genius"; but as to Maynard, I am certain.'[42]

The Times, in its obituary, wrote that 'To find an economist of comparable influence one would have to go back to Adam Smith …

And finally there was the man himself – radiant, brilliant, effer-vescent, gay, full of impish jokes. His entry into the room invariably raised the spirits of the company.'[43]

Though she restrained herself from hysterics, composing herself throughout the funeral and the grand memorial service at Westminster Abbey, attended by the Prime Minister and most of the Cabinet, Lydia was utterly devastated. A week after Keynes's death she wrote to Lionel Robbins, with whom they had spent so much time over his final years. 'I feel so lost,' she said. 'He was my captain also. In that long struggle how splendid you were ... I was always anxious but lately here in England, the last 3 weeks, life seemed to re-blossom, it was easier, the great strain was over.

'Before he died he was happy at Tilton, watching the details of his farm, strolling down hill in brilliant sunshine, infecting every-thing with his radiance, till sudden end on Easter Sunday in his bed after breakfast. I cannot bear it.'[44]

Two weeks after the announcement of Keynes's death, the International Monetary Fund held its first ever executive board meeting, in a makeshift room in the Washington Hotel on Pennsylvania Avenue. 'The problems before us, as we all appreciate, are extremely complex,' said Harry White. 'They will demand all that we possess of wisdom, experience, goodwill and economic statesmanship. Our hope of helping lies in being able to pool these resources for the benefit of all countries.'[45]

It was to be White's first and last speech as the most senior figure at the Fund. His second act was to elect Camille Gutt as managing director. It was left to Gutt to pay tribute to Keynes and to begin the IMF's work in earnest. White had not given up hope of advancement. After the first meeting he put on a lavish lunch for the executive directors, who immediately grew suspicious. Within a few days the subtext emerged: White had persuaded Gutt to try to support his appointment as his deputy. The plan imploded soon afterwards, and White would have to content himself with driving on the Fund from behind the scenes: satisfaction came not from the grand affairs of state, but from the small victories. Later that summer he took great pleasure in evicting a floor of State Department workers from a building at 1818 H Street NW – the future headquarters of the Fund.

The peace was now one year old but Europe was still mired in economic depression. While output in the United States bubbled ever higher, the rest of the world suffered from a desperate shortage of dollars. This was a shock to White. In his final letter to Keynes he had said there was only a 'remote chance' of such a situation occurring. Now it loomed large, with disastrous consequences for Europe. Desperately short of both goods and the money with which to pay for them, the continent lurched back into depression. The very problems of want and desperation that dominated in the interwar period seemed to be as evident as ever – as did the threat of extremism. These were issues of a size and scale which the newly established Fund and Bank could scarcely confront.

Simultaneously, tensions between the United States and Russia continued to escalate. Though at Savannah the delegates had, as a final gesture of goodwill, extended the window for Russia to join the Bretton Woods institutions, it was increasingly clear that it had no intention of doing so. In February Stalin predicted that Communism would eventually triumph over capitalism. Justifying the Anglo-American loan to the House Banking and Currency Committee in May, Fred Vinson said of the US and Russia 'there is no way at this time to avoid two economic groups but we have got to take the world as it is.'[46]

The United Nations, created following the 1945 Yalta summit, seemed to have devolved almost immediately into a venue for tense battles between the United States and Russia, rather than a forum for peace. By May, White was privately warning of an 'inevitable' atomic war between the United States and Russia, according to

George Bolton, who was now Britain's representative at the Fund. 'I believe that the only reason the loan passed the Senate and will probably get through the House, is this unreasoning fear of Russia,' wrote Bolton. 'England and the Empire are, of course, entirely disregarded in any argument or summing up of the situation, and I have to accept the fact that we are perhaps of roughly the same importance in the world, either individually or as a group, as one of the Latin American countries. The recent decisions about India and Egypt are instances of indisputable proof of the approaching complete dissolution of the Commonwealth and the relegation of England to a level comparable with that of say Sweden or France.'[47]

By a stroke of misfortune, Europe's post-war economic crisis coincided with the coldest winter in more than half a century. Millions were still homeless after the destruction wrought on cities during the war. In Berlin, the morbidly efficient Germans dug thousands of graves before the ground froze for those who would starve to death, while tension in the city streets between Soviets and American soldiers was ratcheting higher. The Communist movements in France and Spain gathered strength. In January 1947 London was swept with the worst blizzards since 1881, and struggled to maintain heating and electricity. Rations dropped to lower levels than during the war.[48]

As Hugh Dalton's budgetary constraints started to tighten and the dreaded day of sterling convertibility approached, Britain started to allow its Empire to fray and fall apart. It could no longer afford to step in when Greece slid into civil war – nor could it take responsibility for Palestine. All the while it was seeking to re-negotiate its loans with India, Egypt and other Dominion nations – to default on the loans it had taken out during the war.

In China, the Nationalists were starting to lose their grip on power, with the Communists looking increasingly dominant on the battlefront in Manchuria. For those, like White, who had hoped that 1944 would usher in a new era of peace and unity, it was a horrifying period – and yet the Fund, which was barely fully established, did not yet have the resources or the wherewithal to do anything about it.

These troubled nations, Dean Acheson feared, would soon become a battleground of influence. There were now only two great powers remaining in the world, he warned Congress in February 1947:

> We had arrived at a situation unparalleled since ancient times. Not since Rome and Carthage had there been such a polarization of power on this earth. Moreover the two great powers were divided by an unbridgeable ideological chasm. For us, democracy and individual liberty were basic; for them, dictatorship and absolute conformity. And it was clear that the Soviet Union was aggressive and expanding. For the United States to take steps to strengthen countries threatened with Soviet aggression or Communist subversion was not to pull British chestnuts out of the fire; it was to protect the security of the United States – it was to protect freedom itself.[49]

In March, Congress announced it would provide military aid to Greece and Turkey to help them ward off the threat of Communism. It was the first step towards what would become known as the Truman Doctrine. Such interventions, in countries on the border between East and West, would become commonplace throughout the Cold War.

Soon enough it became clear that the Treasury and State Department intended to use the IMF and World Bank to support this American international political agenda. Under White's conception, the Bank should have been free to lend to needy countries whatever their political credo, but later that year the United States vetoed a prospective Bank loan to Poland. The institutions he and Keynes had conceived of as independent economic bodies had become deeply politicised from the very beginning. Nor were they particularly effective. Though the Fund officially became active in March 1947, almost every member invoked their right not to make their currencies fully convertible within the five-year transitional period. Rather like White, the institution was trapped in limbo somewhere between ineffectuality and influence, with only the vaguest whiff of power.

To make matters worse, after less than a full year of operation, it was also running out of money. Those enormous salaries were responsible for 65 per cent of its budget. 'Harry White,' wrote one of his British colleagues, 'has become a very diminished figure and normally has to preface any remark – which are few enough nowadays – by saying that he is not necessarily speaking for his Government. The wheel has turned a full circle and White has become the victim of his blind and ruthless policy.' He was even convinced that the American deputy director had been appointed 'solely for the purpose of spying on Harry and reporting back to some other group'.[50]

A few weeks after the official launch, White handed in his notice to President Truman. 'I have for some time cherished the idea of returning to private enterprise but did not want to leave the Government until the Bretton Woods organizations, in which I am so deeply interested, were well launched,' he said. 'The work of the Fund is now off to a good start. The period of active operations is just beginning, and this is an opportunity for my successor to take over.'[51]

White became an independent economic consultant. Despite his antipathy to Wall Street throughout his career, he set up shop in New York, even pledging to help the mayor create 'the biggest and the best international trade center in the world in New York City'.[52] In recognition of his service at Bretton Woods he was made an honorary adviser to the Fund – to the immense irritation of many of his colleagues, who had spent the past year being lectured and berated by the man. He left without even saying goodbye to the board of directors.

That summer, the Secretary of State, George Marshall, would use his Commencement Address at Harvard to unveil the economic scheme that would, finally, set right so many of these problems. The Marshall Plan was an extraordinary programme of aid devoted to shoring up Europe's economy. Between 1947 and 1951, the European Recovery Program it engendered would help drag the continent back from the depths of its post-war slump. The last remnants of the Morgenthau Plan, aimed at de-industrialising Germany, were abandoned and the country – or, to be specific, the capitalist west of the country – was given every support to rebuild its businesses.

Marshall aid would contribute a full third to Greece's economic output, more than a quarter to Austria's, and sizeable chunks to other countries including the United Kingdom, Italy and France. Though the means were economic – restoring growth in Europe, remedying the dollar shortage – the ends were patently political. It was a multibillion-dollar diplomatic gambit to seal American influence throughout Europe.

It would also render the IMF and the World Bank effectively irrelevant for the first half-decade of their lives. The Fund's main role in 1947 and 1948 was to forward $600 million to member countries as a stop-gap before their Marshall Plan aid arrived.

Harry White watched on from the sidelines as the structures he helped set up became caked in dust. Working as a consultant to various clients, including the Bank of Mexico, and advising the Council of Jewish Federations and Welfare Funds in his spare time, he started, for the first time in his life, to earn a decent amount of money. With the proceeds he bought a farmhouse, Blueberry Hill, in Fitzwilliam, New Hampshire, a couple of hours south of the Mount Washington Hotel where he had made his name. He remained under FBI surveillance.

In November 1947 he was called to give evidence to the Federal Grand Jury of Southern District of New York on Communist activities in the United States. His wife sent a note explaining that he could not testify – he was recovering from a severe heart attack. As White convalesced, the investigation petered out, but the following year, the House of Representatives Committee on Un-American Activities began another investigation – this one in public. Elizabeth Bentley testified publicly, naming White as someone who provided information to her Communist spy ring. Phoned by reporters, he declared that he was 'shocked' and pledged to refute these 'fantastic' charges.[53] Shortly afterwards Whittaker Chambers appeared before the committee and, again, mentioned White's name as being a key part of his earlier spy ring.

White appeared before the committee on Friday, 13 August 1948, suddenly in the full glare of the media once more. In the photographs he looks tanned but considerably thinner than in previous years. His three-piece suit hangs a little loosely around his frame as he holds up his hand and makes his oath.

Before taking questions he asked if he could make a statement. Pulling a scrap of paper from his pocket, he began to read to the hushed room:

> I should like to state at the start that I am not now and never have been a Communist, nor even close to becoming one … The principles in which I believe, and by which I live, make it impossible for me to ever do a disloyal act or anything against the interests of our country, and I have jotted down what my belief is for the committee's information.
>
> My creed is the American creed. I believe in freedom of religion, freedom of speech, freedom of thought, freedom of the press, freedom of criticism, and freedom of movement. I believe in the goal of equality of opportunity, and the right of each individual to follow the calling of his or her own choice, and the

right of every individual to an opportunity to develop his or her capacity to the fullest.

I believe in the right and duty of every citizen to work for, to expect and to obtain an increasing measure of political, economic and emotional security for all. I am opposed to discrimination in any form, whether on grounds of race, color, religions, political belief or economic status. I believe in the freedom of choice of one's representatives in Government, untrammelled by machine guns, secret police or a police state. I am opposed to arbitrary and unwarranted use of power or authority from whatever source or against any individual or group.

I believe in a government of law, not of men, where law is above any man, and not any man above law.

I consider these principles sacred. I regard them as the basic fabric of our American way of life, and I believe in them as living realities, and not as mere words on paper. That is my creed. Those are the principles I have worked for. Together those are the principles that I have been prepared in the past to fight for, and am prepared to defend at any time with my life if need be.[54]

With that, he invited questions from the committee, and the audience burst into applause. Far from being an inquisition, as the day went on his appearance turned into a bravura performance. Sitting casually in the witness chair, one arm draped over the back, White sparred with each of the questioners, throwing in so many wisecracks that there was laughter and further rounds of applause throughout.

The most hostile questioning came from thirty-five-year-old Republican Congressman Richard Nixon. As the other members of the committee asked vague questions with no particular line, Nixon kept drilling away: did White know Whittaker Chambers? Had he ever met him? Why was he being so evasive?

Newspaper verdicts the following day varied. For some, White was a hero, mastering the format, speaking truth to power, not to mention amusing his audience. Others considered him slippery. But on balance, it was a points victory.

He travelled by train up to New York immediately after his testimony. Feeling unwell and worried, he saw his doctor there the following day, before taking the train to his farmhouse in Fitzwilliam. On the journey he was taken ill with serious chest pains. It was a heart attack, much like the one Keynes had suffered on the train from Savannah. Once he arrived he saw the local doctor, but there was little to be done. The attacks continued until the following day. By Monday afternoon, three days after his Congressional testimony, Harry Dexter White was dead.

It was front page news. Immediately there were conspiracy theories: White had committed suicide; he had been poisoned; he had disappeared to South America. Many of the theories linger on today, though there is no meaningful evidence to support them. His doctor, who saw him enough times in his final days to know, insisted it was simply heart disease.

The funeral took place three days after White's death. The event contrasted starkly with Keynes's memorial service. While his British adversary had been honoured by the great and good of his country and beyond, who filled the aisles of Britain's most renowned place of worship, White's funeral was attended by only thirty-five friends and family. It took place at Waterman's Chapel in Boston, an unobtrusive place not far from the Beacon Hill neighbourhood where he had been born fifty-five years earlier.

Though Harry Dexter White was dead, speculation over his involvement with Soviet espionage lived on, thanks in large part to Richard Nixon. Having detected apparent inconsistency and evasion in White's testimony, the young representative continued to plug away at the case, as well as those of other government employees. In January 1950, Alger Hiss, an official who had been involved in the creation of the United Nations, was found guilty of two charges of perjury before the Grand Jury investigating Communism in the United States, and was sentenced to five years in prison. The following day, Nixon stood up on the floor of the House and revealed that since December 1948 he had had in his possession the documents White had allegedly passed to Whittaker Chambers. In the years that followed the posthumous case against the economist mounted.

Two years later, Herbert Brownell Jr, Eisenhower's Attorney General, accused President Truman of appointing White to the IMF despite allegedly knowing about his involvement with the Soviets. White, said Brownell, 'was a Russian spy. He smuggled secret documents to Russian agents for transmission to Moscow.'[55]

Not only did this most unequivocal accusation reignite the intrigue over White's activities, it sparked a parallel flurry in London. The Foreign Office immediately launched its own internal investigation: had Britain attempted to influence White's appointment? Perhaps unsurprisingly, the investigation concluded that Britain hardly had the capability to do so. The story provoked a flood of letters to Anthony Eden, by then the Prime Minister. One, from Waldron Smithers MP, asked: 'Did Mr Truman warn Lord Keynes that White was a Communist and, if not, is that why Keynes fell for the Communist policy of exchange control and abandoned the British plan to return to money of intrinsic value in the form of a gold coin to be called a Bancor?'[56] The fact that Keynes's original bancor plan was intended to do precisely the opposite of returning the world to a gold standard appeared to have escaped Mr Smithers.

The release of the Venona transcripts in the mid-1990s, and then, following the end of the Cold War, the publication of Russian intelligence cables shown to a former KGB agent, Alexander Vassiliev, sparked further interest in the case. A subsequent investigation by Democrat Senator Daniel Patrick Moynihan in 1997 concluded that White's complicity in espionage 'seems settled'.

Nonetheless, while historians have scoured White's private papers at Princeton University and his official documents at the National Archives, they have never found evidence that proves his guilt beyond reasonable doubt. Though his involvement with the Russians undoubtedly looks shady from certain angles, the reality is that we shall never know for certain whether White knowingly betrayed his country by passing information to the Soviets.

Just as intriguingly, however, the papers left behind at White's death show that he had soured on the very scheme that bore his name at the Bretton Woods conference. These documents, some of which have apparently been overlooked by White's historians, show that the author of the post-war international monetary system developed deep misgivings about the rules he fought so hard to implement in 1944.

At the very centre of the Bretton Woods system was the principle that the dollar would be convertible into gold at a rate of $35 an ounce. There was nothing particularly scientific about this figure – it had, after all, been plucked out of the air by President Roosevelt in the 1930s when he and Morgenthau sought to extricate the United States from the gold standard. But at the Mount Washington Hotel in 1944, Harry Dexter White effectively set it in stone. All other currencies would be tied to the dollar at certain rates, while the dollar, in turn, would be tied in value to gold, at that fixed rate. The notion that the United States should want to change the gold value of the dollar, White exclaimed at the time, was 'nonsense'.[57]

However, in a handwritten essay, jotted on a memo pad found in his home some time after his death, White confessed that setting the dollar at this gold value had been a mistake. 'The action I would commend for consideration by economists,' he wrote, 'is the return by the US to the pre-New Deal old gold value of the dollar – $20.67.'

The suggestion, he added, 'will doubtless seem startling to many'. Knowing as we do how rarely White admitted failure, it was certainly a turnaround. But he explained that appreciating the value of the dollar (so that an ounce of gold could be bought for fewer dollars) would help avert a looming international economic crisis. If the United States did not act soon, he warned that there would be 'an unending round of currency depreciation' elsewhere, with America sucking up practically all of the world's gold reserves and its neighbours becoming increasingly antagonistic towards it. He added that these possibilities 'add up to a terrific price to pay for failure to act'.[58]

It was not the only misgiving White faced in his final days. He was also becoming ever more disenchanted with what had become of Bretton Woods. In a separate document written that same year he gave a harsh assessment of the state of the international monetary system under the IMF and World Bank. Their achievements, it said, had 'been much less than anticipated'.

Part of the problem was the friction between the United States and the Soviet Union. 'I doubt that if any responsible official of the member governments in the spring of 1944 believed that by 1948 – only three years after the cessation of hostilities – the tensions between certain of the major powers would have been so pronounced and that the world, instead of drawing together during these years, would have moved so precipitously toward a split.'

The economic consequences were 'almost catastrophic', he added: 'One World' had been split 'into at least two'. His remedy again involved a U-turn on his previous position at Bretton Woods. He suggested an 'international medium of exchange' not dissimilar to Keynes's bancor plan, which he had ruled out in 1944. His point was that this new currency might help the IMF to increase its resources, so it could be a real force for economic support around the world, rather than sitting idly by in the shadows as the Marshall Plan continued.[59]

So far as we know, neither of these two late shifts in White's opinion about the Fund was publicised. They died with him in the summer of 1948. But the problems that White had diagnosed in his final months were to haunt the world economy over the following decades. The Fund would struggle for years to obtain the resources it needed to become effective. The United States would cling on to Roosevelt's $35-an-ounce dollar until the entire global monetary system reached breaking point, causing the successive devaluations White had warned of and, years later, the ultimate demise of Bretton Woods. And at the centre of events once again was the man who had led the case against Harry Dexter White in the economist's painful last days: Richard M. Nixon.

CHAPTER SIXTEEN

The Bretton Woods System
1947–1973

Foreigners are out to screw us. Our job is to screw them first.

John Connally, US Treasury Secretary 1971–2

If I had a tailor who, every time I bought a suit, lent me back the money I paid for it, I would be encouraged to buy far too many suits and might be led into habits of living above my means.

Jacques Rueff, French economist, on the US and its privilege of having the world's reserve currency[1]

Every so often there occurs within the world economy an event so dramatic that it changes our behaviour for a generation.

It happened in 2008, when the bankruptcy of Lehman Brothers left in its wake such financial devastation that policymakers refused to countenance allowing another investment bank to fail throughout the worst days of the ensuing crisis. It happened in the 1930s, when the Great Depression caused such horrific falls in incomes and employment that politicians and newly enfranchised voters vowed never again to allow 'hot money' to flow untrammelled from one country to another, but instead to create safety nets for the dispossessed that gave rise to the welfare state and the Bretton Woods system.

In 1947 Britain faced another such event. Though you could be forgiven at first for assuming this was distinctly parochial, the economic crisis of that year and the two that followed would scar the global economy for decades to come. They would change the functioning of the Bretton Woods system almost beyond recognition.

July and August 1947 were blissfully hot – a wonderful relief after the worst winter for sixty years. In the run-up to those months, it had looked as if the country was finally rousing itself from economic slumber. The $5 billion American loan had helped finance the very beginnings of the British welfare state. Though parts of the British Empire (Greece, India, Palestine) were being shed at a rapid rate, the Cabinet retained enough optimism and self-belief to commission Britain's own nuclear weapon. 'We've got to have the bloody Union Jack on top of it,'[2] as Ernest Bevin put it.

Hugh Dalton, the Chancellor, was merrily adding to the collection of newspaper cuttings that hailed him as the man responsible for the country's unexpected economic resurgence. In his crowning moment the previous year, he had masterminded the nationalisation of the Bank of England – belated punishment for its performance during the 1920s and 1930s.

Then came 15 July, and sterling convertibility. One year on from the ratification of the American loan, as stipulated in the deal, investors who had hitherto been forced to leave their pounds within the sterling zone could suddenly convert them into dollars and spend them elsewhere.

It was like pulling the plug from an enormous bath. At first the gush of cash out of Britain was only obvious in the City of London – the financial sinkhole through which the money escaped. Within a few days the Treasury and Bank managed to pull together some rough statistics; the scale of the outflow was horrifying. In the very first week, $106 million had escaped the country. Soon money was spurting out at a rate equivalent to $6 billion a year. Within a few weeks, the loan, which had been intended to last beyond the end of the decade, was effectively exhausted.

As the torrent of cash continued to flow, Dalton was to suffer one of the greatest falls from grace of any finance minister before or since. Exhausted, relying in his public appearances on ever heavier doses of Benzedrine, he escaped to his country house in Wiltshire. Precisely a month after the day of convertibility, his officials delivered the bad news. The outflow was now so rapid that there was nothing for it but to reverse the decision and cancel convertibility.

'Maybe I'll fly to Washington,' Dalton scribbled in his diary. 'Maybe I'll resign! I'll just give up the ghost!' Characteristically, after this outpouring of self-pity he did none of the above, returning sheepishly to London that weekend. In his desperation to avoid being spotted by the press, when the car arrived in Downing Street he ordered his two secretaries to get out first and then he laid low, alone and shamefaced inside the vehicle, until the coast was clear. Late on 20 August he made a short announcement suspending convertibility, insisting that the 'full and free convertibility of sterling was still a long-run objective'.[3]

It was a moment of utter humiliation – though worse was to come. In November Dalton was forced to table an emergency Budget, packed with an eye-watering catalogue of austerity measures. En route to the chamber he mentioned one or two of the tax changes to a journalist from London evening newspaper the *Star*. By the time the Chancellor delivered his speech, the details were already in print. Dalton resigned shortly afterwards, leaving the tax rises and spending cuts to be implemented by his successor, Sir Stafford Cripps (whose name is a byword for hair-shirt fiscal policies even today).

Though the humiliation was felt most keenly by the Labour Party, whose reputation for economic management would never fully recover, the impact would reverberate across Europe. Panicked investors began to pull money out of France, Italy and Germany, forcing the devaluation of the franc in early 1948.

The Marshall Plan came into effect that year, but the $13 billion of aid provided by the United States to Europe over the next four years could help alleviate the dollar shortage only to a certain extent. In 1949, the pressure finally proved too much. Britain was forced to devalue against the dollar, and was followed in short order by the rest of Europe. It was, according to Eddie Bernstein, 'a big change ... the readjustment of the international economic position of the rest of the world to the United States, as it had been affected by the Great Depression and the war'.[4]

Under the new IMF rules, the UK was duty-bound to give the Fund seventy-two hours' notice of a change in currency value. The Bank of England, paranoid then as it had been back in 1944, squealed that Britain 'might consider leaving the IMF' if it leaked the news. And though Britain warned the Fund that a parity change was on the way, it only provided the full, gory details – that it was going to reduce the value of sterling by a third – a mere twenty-four hours in advance.

The shock move was followed by similar reductions in currency values across the board. Only the US dollar, the Swiss franc, the Japanese yen and a few Latin American and Eastern European countries' currencies remained unchanged.

On the one hand the devaluation put right the inherent problem in the international monetary system: as after the Great War, Europe had wrong-headedly attempted to return its currencies to levels they never should have merited. However, the experience was hardly the ordered, managed process John Maynard Keynes and Harry Dexter White had assumed at Bretton Woods. The scar left by the economic ordeal would change the nature of their system for good.

There was no end of matters White and Keynes had disagreed on – everything from the smallest details of the Fund and the Bank to the very structure of the international monetary system. But when it came to the broad vision for Bretton Woods, the pair found themselves unusually aligned (at least when they had brought to an end their initial fights in 1943 and 1944).

As they saw it, Bretton Woods would do away with the worst effects of the gold standard and the interwar years of instability and depression. Fixing currencies against the dollar would ensure that international trade was protected from exchange rate risk. Nations would determine their own interest rates for purely domestic economic reasons, whereas under the gold standard, rates had been set primarily in order to keep the country's gold stocks at an acceptable level. Countries would be allowed to devalue their currencies if they became uncompetitive – but they would have to notify the International Monetary Fund in advance: this element of international co-ordination was intended to guard against a repeat of the 1930s spiral of competitive devaluation.

In return for such measures, most member countries would have to impose controls on the flow of investment capital moving across their borders (though Keynes and White differed on how long this would be necessary – White thought only for a few years; Keynes imagined it would be permanent).

They expected the Fund to be in operation within a few years, lending its members certain currencies when they ran short of them, keeping the system of fixed currencies running in lockstep with one another. They expected the Bank to use its loans and guarantees to help channel money to the parts of the world that most needed it – whether post-war Europe or the poorer parts of Latin America. It might take some time for the most beleaguered economies to submit their currencies to full convertibility, but five years – the adjustment period agreed at the conference – ought to be enough.

This was, it soon turned out, hopelessly optimistic. As an adviser to British Prime Minister Clement Attlee put it, by the end of the

1940s the Fund had 'more or less gone into voluntary retirement'.[5] It wasn't merely that almost all the countries needed that five-year grace period before becoming fully signed-up Fund members: it would take far longer.

Tempting as it was to blame everything on the Marshall Plan, which had rendered the Fund almost irrelevant, that was only the beginning of the explanation. The Fund's quotas, which at White's insistence had been whittled down from the large amounts Keynes initially proposed, were sorely inadequate for the needs of European countries facing balance of payments problems. An additional complication was that while the quotas (and for that matter the Anglo-American loan) were in specific amounts of dollars, US inflation suddenly jumped by 25 per cent in the second half of 1946, instantly diminishing their purchasing power.

Over the following two decades the Fund would engineer various fixes, but few were bold enough to set right this initial problem. With every dollar by which world trade flows increased, the Fund's firepower to protect countries against 'sudden stops', where investors ceased buying their debt, diminished. Quotas were raised by 50 per cent in 1950; however, by then the value of world trade had more than doubled – so the system was less generous even than the one White conceived of in 1944. A further quota increase in 1966 would be limited to 25 per cent in the face of Belgian, French, Italian and Dutch resistance. As at the Mount Washington Hotel itself, agreeing on quotas was about as pleasant as having one's fingernails pulled out. Fund lore has it that an economist charged with heading one of these quota revisions was so overwrought by the experience he took his own life.

As an alternative, in 1961 the rich nations set up a system called General Arrangements to Borrow – essentially a means of lending their own currencies to struggling countries through the Fund (rather than drawing on its quotas).

However, there was also a deeper problem facing the Bretton

Woods system, one which went back to the crises of 1947 and 1949. So much fear had those crises engendered over the consequences of both convertibility and devaluation that while Bretton Woods existed, members would do everything they could to avoid them. And if devaluation proved necessary, they would attempt to keep it a secret (even from the Fund) until the very last minute.

In an effort both to protect themselves from the threat of capital outflows and to maintain trade between themselves, the Western European members set up the European Payments Union in 1950. The system, which was supposed to last only two years, stayed in place for eight – a direct affront to what had been envisaged at Bretton Woods. Far from being removed, barriers to capital movements in and out of Europe were actually increased. However, the United States, its energies now directed at contesting the Cold War rather than at tearing down barriers to globalisation, encouraged the development. From the State Department's perspective, a stronger European economy would be a potent bulwark against the creeping threat of Communism in the East. It went further still, using the US Economic Cooperation Administration (ECA) and Organisation for European Economic Co-operation (OEEC), which supervised the implementation of the Marshall Plan, to encourage European governments to splash out on extravagant social welfare systems.*

Only in 1958 did European countries finally restore convertibility on their current accounts, ten rather than five years after the system officially came into being. It took until 1961 for the Fund to declare the countries fully in compliance with its Articles of Agreement. Nor did the parallel effort to liberalise trade proceed more successfully. The State Department had long intended to create an international agreement on free trade alongside Bretton

*Their descendant, the Organisation for Economic Co-operation and Development (OECD), still monitors the state and health of social welfare systems today.

Woods, but these talks, which had begun in the 1943 negotiations with the British, tailed off soon after the war. Congress rejected the creation of an International Trade Organisation. Although the General Agreement on Tariffs and Trade (GATT) began talks on reducing tariffs and subsidies, the absence of the US (officially, at least) was a difficulty. It was not until 1995 that the original conception of an international body with legal powers over trade policy was finally realised in the shape of the World Trade Organisation.

Nor was the Fund itself immune from political influence. Since it holds the majority of voting rights on the board, the United States has always had effective control over the IMF. This is rarely obvious on the surface: since Savannah the convention that a European should be the Fund's managing director has remained in place (just as the World Bank's president is an American). However, the United States has appointed a deputy managing director whose task it is to work behind the scenes and ensure that the Fund's activities remain in line with American interests.

The Bretton Woods system that came into being towards the end of the 1950s was therefore a very different organisation from the one its founders originally envisaged. The World Bank had been designed in large part to help finance European recovery; in the event Marshall Plan aid was twenty times greater than any of the Bank's loans to the beleaguered continent. The International Monetary Fund was designed to regulate a system of freely convertible, managed currencies; but the prospects of such an ordered scheme had been punctured by the British crisis of 1947–9. The dollar, which had implanted itself as the world's reserve currency between the wars, became even more central to the system. As had been explicitly written into the Bretton Woods articles in 1944 at Dennis Robertson's insistence, the dollar was as good as gold – at least for the time being.

Recognising that the system was hardly ideal, some countries flirted with the idea of floating their currencies – a notion hitherto considered to be economically beyond the pale, not to mention in breach of Bretton Woods rules. Canada unpegged its dollar temporarily with alarming success: it was able to become fully convertible at the end of 1951, long before almost anyone else. George Bolton of the Bank of England proposed doing something similar in the UK – the so-called ROBOT scheme (the B stood for Bolton). However, the plan was abandoned, in part because it would have represented an effective default on the billions of pounds' worth of sterling debt still owed to the Dominions, in part because it would have destroyed the European Payments Union. The fact that it was in direct contravention of the Bretton Woods system seemed to be the least of Bolton's concerns.

It was only with the end of the Marshall Plan that the Fund and the World Bank started to come into their own. The European Payments Union was wound down in 1958, though its legacy was a constellation of European institutions which would evolve into the system of economic and political linkages that are still developing even today. In 1957 the Treaty of Rome created the European Community. Britain remained characteristically detached, sniping from the sidelines rather than joining up.

The United Kingdom, weighed down by its wartime debts, soon distinguished itself as 'the most persistent troublemaker within the international monetary system', in one economic historian's words.[6] Its 1949 devaluation was followed by another in 1967, when Prime Minister Harold Wilson notoriously attempted to persuade the British public that the 'pound in your pocket' had not lost its spending power. This time the IMF was given only an hour's notice. There had also been a near-miss in the late 1950s, as Britain overextended itself in the Suez crisis and was forced to seek American approval for financial support (which, in this case, was not immediately forthcoming). The sterling debts to India and Egypt, which could have been dealt with in one fell swoop had the Treasury accepted

White's initial offer ahead of Bretton Woods, continued to haunt the once-great nation.

While Britain distinguished itself as the black sheep of the family, the United States was happy, for a period, to play the role of broadly benevolent father figure. As Europe and Japan started to recover, the perennial dollar shortage that everyone had been fearing came to an end. Those devaluations had made Europe a cheap destination for American investment. Helped by the very manufacturing base that Morgenthau had sought to castrate in 1945, Germany started to pump out enough exports that by the late 1950s its current account had swung into a strong surplus.

As the 1950s gave way to the 1960s the world economy started, against all expectations, to balance out. No longer was the United States the dominant exporter: other countries were catching up, and then overtook it. Soon enough, Germany began to fret over the long-term implications of its perennial trade surpluses. Haunted like everybody else, however, by the spectacle of Britain's traumatic 1949 devaluation, it was reluctant to change the value of the deutschmark.

All the same, for a moment at least, the system did seem to be working. The global economy was growing at a rapid rate, and although there were periodical exchange rate wobbles, these were as nothing compared to the interwar period. But there was a fatal flaw, which went back to that apparently innocuous clause inserted by Dennis Robertson at the conference in 1944.

Though the dollar had been the linchpin of the international monetary system since at least the 1920s, it now assumed a new degree of hegemony. Robertson's clause change had made it official: under Bretton Woods, the dollar was formally equivalent to gold. So when they sought to bolster their foreign exchange reserves to protect them from future crises, foreign governments built up large reserves of dollars.

The French, who had a history of railing against foreign

domination of any monetary system, found this particularly irritating. The dollar's position as the dominant global reserve currency gave the United States an 'exorbitant privilege', declared French Finance Minister Valéry Giscard d'Estaing. Unlike other central banks, the Federal Reserve could print as many dollars as it wanted and there would still be an almost limitless appetite for them around the world. It was up to other countries to adjust their policies accordingly. High interest rates in the United States ran the risk of drawing in investment from, for instance, Paris – so Paris would have to lift its own borrowing costs if it wanted to maintain financial and economic stability.

In one respect, this meant the United States had carte blanche to behave as it wanted, churning out an endless supply of dollars and keeping its economy in an almost permanent state of boom. However, there was an inherent problem with this system, as Belgian economist Robert Triffin pointed out soon after its conception: that limitless demand for dollars, which put the US under pressure to carry out expansionary policy, also carried with it a cost. The more dollars there were sloshing around the global economy, the more difficult the United States would find it to convert them back into gold at the specified rate of $35 an ounce. For those who had witnessed the dying days of the gold standard, this felt distinctly like history repeating itself all over again.

In his testimony to Congress after Bretton Woods, Harry White had insisted that he could not envisage the United States being unable to convert its dollars back into gold. However, by 1960, the total liabilities of the United States exceeded the amount of gold it held in repositories such as Fort Knox; over the following years those liabilities ballooned even higher. Rather like a weak bank facing a depositor run, the United States would face a crisis if its foreign counterparts demanded gold in exchange for their dollar reserves.

Which was precisely what French President Charles de Gaulle

now threatened. The price of gold quoted on private markets rose above $35 an ounce, reaching $40 in late 1960. The Vietnam War and the social pledges of the Kennedy–Johnson era meant that, far from pressing the brake pedal and imposing fiscal austerity, successive White House administrations simply kept on spending.

The problem came back to one of the first arguments between Keynes and White: the conflict between Keynes's desire to create bancor – a supranational currency at the centre of the international monetary system, safeguarding it from the risk of becoming too reliant on one country – and White's resistance to the idea (though he would recant shortly before his death). It was not that White wanted the system to be a straightforward gold standard, with every currency directly convertible into gold, but nor did he show much inclination towards formalising the dollar's central role – in the long run, he thought, it might sit alongside the Russian rouble. Robertson's intervention at the Mount Washington Hotel, however, changed the definition of the linchpin at the centre of Bretton Woods from 'gold-convertible exchange' (in other words, any currency considered financially credible enough to be converted into gold) into 'gold or US dollars'.

No one at the conference – White and Robertson included – could have conceived that this clause would end up skewering Bretton Woods. But as the 1960s wore on that is precisely what happened. With Congress unwilling to change the gold value of the dollar, this internal contradiction – the 'Triffin dilemma' – would end up destroying the system.

Realising the direction things were taking, in 1964 finance ministers agreed at the IMF's annual meeting to return to Keynes's idea and set up their own equivalent of an international currency. Initially the United States refused to countenance the idea, but a year later it relented, and thus was born the Special Drawing Right (SDR). This awfully named instrument (what, one wonders, happened to Keynes's 'unicorn' idea?) was an international currency unit which could be created by the Fund (with its members' approval, of course) and converted into any other currency. But SDRs would take years to come into being.

As the decade went on, American liabilities continued to mount. Though SDRs might have been a useful tool had they been deployed earlier, by now it was difficult to see a way out. The United States was determined not to devalue the dollar (the scars of 1947–9 again), so no one wanted to countenance that prospect until it was absolutely unavoidable.

Instead, the US Treasury imposed an increasingly preposterous series of constraints (taxes, regulations, surcharges and so on) on the movement of capital in and out of the country. At one stage John F. Kennedy threatened to cut off military aid to Europe unless the Europeans promised not to attack the dollar. As one economist put it, the 'array of devices to which the Kennedy and Johnson administrations resorted became positively embarrassing.'[7]

By the time Richard Nixon became President in 1969 the system was buckling so badly it seemed almost certain to collapse. Paul Volcker, who would later become one of the world's most feted economic policymakers, warned Nixon that he had only two years to save the dollar. While the US government held $10.5 billion of gold, foreign governments owned $40 billion worth of dollar reserves and foreign companies and individuals owned a further $30 billion. Once again, the world's monetary system had become an inverted pyramid of paper money perched on a static stack of gold.

Between 1950 and 1969, as Germany and Japan churned out cheaper and better-quality goods into international markets, the United States' share of world economic output dropped from 35 per cent to 27 per cent. Washington was nursing an ever-growing trade deficit and a ballooning budget deficit as the costs of the Vietnam War continued to mount. By the end of 1969, inflation exceeded 6 per cent for the first time since the Korean War. Only the most credulous could now claim, straight-faced, that the value of the dollar, in gold terms, was $35 an ounce. The adjustment was not going to come from anyone else: neither Germany nor Japan would allow their currencies to appreciate more than a small amount; this further exacerbated the imbalances. Controls on capital movements, which had been an integral part of the Bretton Woods system in its infancy, had largely been dismantled, thanks in part to the creation of new international money markets such as London's Eurodollar market. Money could flow freely to wherever investors thought it best placed – which at this point meant anywhere except the United States.

John Connally, Nixon's Treasury Secretary, took a hardline approach. This was, he told the President, 'an economic war ... The simple fact is that in many areas other nations are out-producing us, out-thinking us and out-trading us.'

'We'll fix those bastards,' said Nixon.[8]

Quite what that 'fix' would be remained a closely guarded secret – partly because any American plan to change its exchange rate or its relationship with gold would be explosive news for the market, partly because very few people in the administration understood precisely what was going on. Volcker, the adviser to the Treasury Secretary, was one of the few exceptions. At six foot seven inches (an inch or so taller than Keynes), Volcker was perhaps the only senior official aware that the US might have to destroy the system the great British economist had helped create.

A growing number of economists, including Milton Friedman, were arguing that the United States should ditch gold convertibility and simply allow the dollar to float. Others suggested it should devalue the US currency, pushing up the cost of gold from $35 an ounce to $40 or higher. Volcker's initial instinct was to avoid the former option: fixed exchange rates remained a far more familiar way of ordering the international monetary system. They also imposed extra discipline on countries, theoretically deterring them from printing more money than their economies could support. However, nothing could be ruled out; Volcker was charged with leading a working group to determine a solution to the problems with the monetary system.

Given that every other currency in the Western world was tied to the dollar, it was clear that whatever Volcker decided would have enormous consequences elsewhere. But, in contrast with 1944, when the future of the monetary system was decided in full sight of the world's press, the demise of Bretton Woods was to be decided in private, in a series of dimly lit, smoke-filled rooms. In one such room in Paris, a spooky basement filled with fermenting wine, Volcker was confronted by Cecil de Strycker of the Belgian central bank who shook his finger at him and said: 'If all this talk about flexible exchange rates brings down the system, the blood will be on your American head.'[9]

In the spring of 1971, Volcker wrote a memorandum warning of an imminent dollar crisis. He proposed devaluing the dollar by 15 per cent and suspending the convertibility of gold, meaning foreign central banks could no longer come to the US and demand the precious metal in exchange for their dollars. Money continued to flow out of the United States and towards the surplus nations. In May, having attempted to intervene in the markets to keep the deutschmark at its pre-agreed level, Germany gave up and allowed its currency to float. It was joined shortly afterwards by Switzerland, the Netherlands, Belgium and Austria. The *New York Times* described this as 'one of the gravest monetary disturbances since World War II'. American tourists at the Intercontinental Hotel in Geneva could not pay their bills as the desk refused to accept dollars.[10]

As the bad news streamed into Washington, it played havoc with Volcker's nerves – and his digestive system. He later recalled that a colleague whose office was directly below his 'could always tell when a crisis had reached the critical stage by the cascade of flushing he heard. The more I thought about that, of course, the more frequently I visited the john.'[11]

The final straw came in the second week of August, when newspapers reported that France and Britain were planning to convert further batches of dollars into gold. Nixon summoned a small band of his very closest advisers and took them to Camp David, the presidential retreat, over the weekend. Few of them knew precisely why they were going. Nixon's speechwriter Bill Safire was told not to tell his wife or secretary where he would be. When the car picked him up, Herbert Stein, a member of the Council of Economic Advisers, gave him the lowdown.

'This could be the most important weekend in the history of economics since March 4, 1933,' he said, referring to the day President Roosevelt was inaugurated and took steps to end American membership of the gold standard.

'[Are] we closing the banks?' Safire asked.

'Hardly,' said Stein. 'But I would not be surprised if the President were to close the gold window.'

Like most people in the White House, Safire hadn't a clue what that meant. 'How would you explain to a layman the significance of the gold window?' he asked.

'I wouldn't try,' said Stein. 'That's why you're along.'[12]

As weekend retreats went, this one was particularly odd. The men slept two to a cabin (the bed was too short for Volcker) and the dollar's fate was hammered out in the dining room.[13] Nixon insisted that everyone sign the guest book, and fussed around when there was a photocall, but other than that, he mainly stayed locked inside his cabin, the Aspen Lodge, calling occasionally for updates. He had handpicked the team, refusing to admit any 'foreign relations types' – something Volcker put down to his experiences dealing with the State Department when he sat on the House Un-American Activities Committee.[14]

Over the course of the weekend, to the complete ignorance of the world's media, or indeed the leaders of the world's other major economies, this small group of officials brought an end to the Bretton Woods system. Invoking a number of archaic laws, including the Trading with the Enemy Act of 1917 (the aim was to circumvent Congress for the time being), they imposed radical changes on the exchange rate system, most significantly suspending gold convertibility.

For the first time since the 1930s, the United States would not provide gold to official foreign holders of dollars at $35 an ounce – or indeed any other price. It was a major rupture with the past, the consequences of which are still being felt today.

Since the very beginning of international finance, policymakers – whether finance ministers or central bankers – had decided economic measures largely in order to keep the exchange rate stable. Only in times of war or extreme crisis had domestic economic conditions come first. Suddenly, in the space of a few days, international economic policy had been flipped on its head.

The move was coupled with aggressive new surcharges and taxes on imports intended to push other countries into revaluing their own currencies. By the time the International Monetary Fund was informed, the wheels were already in motion.

For Volcker, the move was particularly painful. 'I hate to do this,' he told his colleagues. 'All my life I have defended Bretton Woods, but I think it's needed ... we cannot continue this way. But let's not just close the gold window and sit. We need to negotiate a new set of exchange rates. This is an opportunity to repair a system that needs fixing.'[15]

Nor was everyone agreed on the move. Arthur Burns, the chairman of the Federal Reserve, was sidelined when he attempted to resist it. There were 'grave risks', he said; for one thing, the Soviet newspaper *Pravda* 'will headline this as a sign of the collapse of capitalism'.[16] As far as Nixon was concerned, however, what was more important than 'gobbly gook about crisis of international monetary affairs' was the political impact.[17]

On Sunday night, Nixon delivered the most significant television address in international monetary history:

> I have directed Secretary Connally to suspend temporarily the convertibility of the dollar into gold or other reserve assets, except in amounts and conditions determined to be in the interest of monetary stability and in the best interests of the United States. Now, what is this action – which is very technical – what does it mean for you?
>
> Let me lay to rest the bugaboo of what is called devaluation.
>
> If you want to buy a foreign car or take a trip abroad, market conditions may cause your dollar to buy slightly less. But if you are among the overwhelming majority of Americans who buy American-made products in America, your dollar will be worth just as much tomorrow as it is today.
>
> The effect of this action, in other words, will be to stabilize the dollar.

It was much the same rationale as Harold Wilson had used when insisting to Britons in 1967 that the 'pound in your pocket' would remain as strong as ever. But this time the reception was rapturous, on Wall Street at least. Share prices soared by more than 3 per cent the following morning, with exporters (who would benefit most from the cheaper dollars) particularly strong. The press was almost universally laudatory. The Nixon Shock, as it came to be known, was described at the time as one of the boldest moves in economic policymaking for a generation.

Burns, however, wrote in his diary: 'What a tragedy for mankind!'[18] For while the move was cast almost exclusively by Nixon as being designed for domestic economic purposes, behind the scenes it was regarded as an act of international aggression.

French President Georges Pompidou sent frantic messages to the White House urging them not to abandon the gold peg. Connally was characteristically combative, suggesting that Washington ditch its entire gold reserves on world markets and retire the precious metal from monetary duty once and for all. '[We should] tell Pompidou and his people, "You like gold? We're going to have plenty of it for you. Because we're going to unload it."'[19]

For as long as anyone could remember, the value of the dollar had been pegged to gold. Suddenly, overnight, that was over. The French declared, with some delight, that the era of dollar hegemony had now effectively come to an end. The Italians blamed the Vietnam War.

When a country abandons a particular exchange rate policy, the move is almost always described as temporary, but invariably it soon becomes permanent. From the moment Nixon cut the link with gold, there was little real prospect of putting Bretton Woods back together again. However, that did not stop finance ministers stringing together a series of international deals with their counterparts aimed at setting new exchange rates.

The talks were fractious, particularly when the French were involved. France's fixation with gold, which had somehow withstood the Great Depression, the collapse of the gold standard and the entire Bretton Woods era, was on full display. At one conference, held in the lavish Palazzo Corsini in Rome, French Finance Minister Giscard d'Estaing insisted that the French would only allow the Americans to appreciate the dollar against the franc if they could devalue it against gold by the same amount; in other words, if they could ensure the franc's gold value would remain unchanged. No one else cared very much.

At the Smithsonian Institution in Washington that December, the finance ministers signed up to the new set of exchange rates. The dollar was weakened against other major currencies, pushing down its gold value to $38 an ounce (not that you could convert dollars at the gold window, which remained closed). The rest of the world's currencies were to be fixed slightly less rigidly than hitherto, allowed to move by 2.25 per cent against their counterparts, rather than 1 per cent.

Nixon, who was deeply uninterested in international economics ('I don't give a shit about the lira,' he once snapped when an adviser attempted to brief him on the Italian currency), declared that this was 'the most significant monetary agreement in the history of the world'. This was rather like describing the launch of the *Titanic* as the most significant send-off in the history of shipbuilding. The President, busy on his re-election campaign, left most of the work to Connally and Volcker.[20]

The pair toured the world on an economic diplomacy mission – a good cop, bad cop double-act with Volcker eminently reasonable and the Treasury Secretary cheerfully abrasive. 'The dollar may be our currency but it's your problem,' Connally told one shocked European audience. Back home he put it even more crudely: 'Foreigners are out to screw us. Our job is to screw them first.'[21]

It was all a far cry from the days of the gold standard, when international monetary policy was decided privately in chummy meetings between the Federal Reserve's Benjamin Strong and the Bank of England's Montagu Norman. In 1972 it was Britain's turn to stick the knife in. Following a speculative attack on sterling, Prime Minister Edward Heath announced that he would allow the pound to float, rather than keep to the Smithsonian bands of values. The international economic system began to look increasingly shambolic. In an attempt to impose some kind of order, Volcker worked up a secret scheme called Plan X. It was a system of fixed and floating exchange rates in which those countries with large surpluses (such as Germany or Japan) would be compelled to increase the values of their currencies, and those countries with deficits would do the opposite. It was a good idea, one of his colleagues told him – so good that Keynes had come up with the same notion in his plan for Bretton Woods.

The United States, which under Harry White's direction had sought to prevent the levying of taxes or constraints on surplus nations, now argued that these were precisely what should be imposed on countries like Germany and Japan. It even considered attempting to enact Roy Harrod's beloved scarce currency clause which the British had once thought might need to be used against the United States. Months went by and the system continued to founder, with money continuing to escape from the US economy. Volcker was again sent off on a diplomatic mission to Tokyo and Bonn, but found it difficult to keep a low profile. 'At six foot seven inches and 240 pounds, Paul Adolph Volcker, the Under Secretary of the Treasury for Monetary Affairs, has certain obvious problems as a secret agent in foreign capitals,' wrote the *New York Times*.[22]

In February 1973, for the second time in fourteen months, the United States was forced to announce a devaluation, taking the dollar value of gold from $38 to $42.22 an ounce and reducing its value against the yen and deutschemark. However, it was not enough: the so-called Volcker Agreement lasted less than three weeks.

In March the Europeans, the last group of nations still tied to the US dollar, announced they would sever the link. The Bretton Woods system was over. In 1973 one economic era ended and another began. Richard Nixon had presided over the most significant economic shift since the era of Roosevelt – though, with the Watergate scandal now the dominant story in the international press, neither he nor the general public took much notice. The Bretton Woods system, which had begun with fanfare, an unprecedented series of conferences and the deepest investigation in history into the state of macro-economics, ended without almost anyone realising it.

Epilogue

1973–

From the summit of Mount Washington, the hotel looked much the same in April 2011 as it did in 1944. The only obvious difference was the dusting of snow all along the valley. In the twenty-first century as in the twentieth, spring came late to Bretton Woods.

The Mount Washington Hotel had long since left the hands of David Stoneman and his Boston syndicate, its owners at the time of the conference. In the decades that followed it passed from owner to owner – five of them coming and going and struggling to make much of a business of it. Air conditioning and mass-market air travel meant that by then the White Mountains were in direct competition with the Caribbean and Hawaii. Tourist revenues shrank, but the cost of maintaining the hotel against the elements continued to mount.

The lowest ebb came in the early 1990s when the hotel was auctioned off after its then-owners, a subsidiary of a Boston bank, fell victim to the collapse of the US savings and loan system. The building was in such a state of disrepair that some speculated it might soon collapse altogether.

Then, against all expectations, the hotel's fortunes started to improve. Tourists started returning. Some came for their holidays, seeking out a cheaper alternative to the Caribbean. Some came to ski. One or two even came to see the hotel where the famous Bretton Woods agreements had been hatched. By the spring of 2011 the Mount Washington had been wrestled back to something resembling its former glory. A new set of owners repaired the leaks, threw out most of the old, creaking furniture and reopened the doors to paying tourists. They even managed to remove most of the white paint the government workers had daubed over the priceless Tiffany windows in 1944.

The hotel was, by then, a year-round holiday resort: skiing in the winter, hiking in the summer. But in April of that year, it found itself occupied by a familiar-looking crowd. Some of the world's most renowned economists and financiers had come from around the globe to discuss the state of the economy.

For it wasn't merely the hotel that looked the same. The global economy, too, was in an eerily similar state to that of the 1940s. The world still reeled from a financial and economic crisis of historic proportions, vast parts of its population remaining unemployed. Elements of the international monetary system seemed on the brink of collapse. For a few days, the economists holed themselves up in the hotel for a conference thrown by the hedge-fund manager George Soros. They dined in the vast room overlooking the Presidential Mountain Range, where Keynes had appeared like a pale apparition at that final banquet. They drank in the Cave Bar (what used to be the Moon Room had been converted into a slightly drab steak joint). And, for at least some of the time, they discussed economics.

It was hard, in such a setting, not to become nostalgic for the world Keynes and White had established in the hotel all those decades before. The Bretton Woods system might have felt occasionally fraught, pockmarked with currency traumas as Europe recovered from its wartime debts, but by 2011 it looked like a positive Utopia.

A Bank of England study that year underlined why. Between 1948 and the early 1970s, the world enjoyed a period of economic growth and stability that has never been rivalled – before or since.[1] During that time, global gross domestic product expanded by 2.8 per cent – more than double the 1.3 per cent achieved during the gold standard and comfortably stronger than the 1.8 per cent between the early 1970s and the financial crisis of 2008. Remarkably, there was not a single global downturn – something, again, which one cannot say about any other period in economic history (particularly recent history).

Imbalances between different nations – the current account deficits and surpluses that can leave countries vulnerable to economic collapse – were three times smaller than during the era of the gold standard – not to mention smaller than in the couple of decades building up to the 2008 crisis. There were hardly any banking crises; countries defaulted less often on their debts than they had under the gold standard or during the modern era. Granted, inflation was higher during the Bretton Woods era – around 3.3 per cent on average across the world, compared with 0.6 per cent under the gold standard. But then prices rose even more between 1973 and 2008, by an average of 4.8 per cent.

That this economic performance was also coupled with significant social gains only added to the mystique. Across the Bretton Woods membership, life expectancy climbed swiftly higher, inequality fell, and social welfare systems were constructed which, for the time being at least, seemed eminently affordable. As households' incomes rose, so too did their access to the newest innovations. Products once considered the privilege of the wealthiest now became accessible to the middle classes: motor cars, air conditioning, refrigerators and dishwashers. Human innovation scaled unprecedented heights. In 1943, as he sailed out to Washington alongside Keynes to discuss the international economy, James Meade had wondered out loud whether, before the end of his lifetime or that of his son, 'men will be visiting the Moon'. In the event, Meade, who would live into the 1990s, would only have to wait until 1969.*

It is probably fair to assume that had either Keynes or White witnessed this golden era of economic performance, they would have rejoiced (though Keynes, who had in 1930 predicted that we would move towards a fifteen-hour working week, might have been perturbed by how long people stayed in the office[2]). However, had they inspected the reasons behind the performance they would have been more than a little alarmed. For while the world economy thrived, the way the international monetary system behaved bore little resemblance to the picture mapped out by Keynes and White at the end of the Second World War.

Bretton Woods was an economic success in spite of, rather than because of, the strictures laid down at the Mount Washington Hotel in July 1944. Europe was rebuilt with money not from the IMF or the World Bank but from the Marshall Plan. Contrary to the architects' hopes that countries might be able to alter their exchange rates as they saw fit, the stigma of devaluation remained as traumatic and painful as it had been in the interwar years. Member nations (Britain being a good example) did everything they could to avoid devaluing until a crisis pushed them into it.

Capital controls remained in place for the vast majority of the system's existence. The simple task of moving money from one part of the world to another was mired in red tape, in part because politicians and central bankers did not trust the international architecture to protect them in the event of a future crisis.

Behind the scenes, the same central bankers who had been widely discredited during the Depression and, supposedly, declawed

---

*Meade added that he hoped 'that we shall have a world government by the time that inter-planetary travel becomes frequent'. Howson and Moggridge (1990), p. 98.

by Bretton Woods kept the system going through their own informal arrangements. They set up so-called swap lines so that weaker
currencies were not shunned internationally, and further crises
were averted. The British, who continued to be haunted throughout by their wartime debts and those blocked sterling balances
of the Indians and Egyptians, received billions of dollars' worth of
invisible, informal aid through these back-door channels.[3] Such life-
saving measures were co-ordinated by the Bank for International
Settlements, the very institution White had attempted to kill for
ever at Bretton Woods.

The world's financial system became even more reliant on the
dollar – not on the varied array of 'gold-convertible' currencies
White envisaged in his original drafts, or indeed on Keynes's
bancor. The international currency established in the late 1960s –
the Fund's Special Drawing Rights (SDRs) – was available in too
small quantities and came too late to save the system. It remains a
marginal, largely unheard-of currency today. Dennis Robertson's
fateful suggestion to insert the word 'dollar' into the conference
agreement probably made little practical difference, but it nonetheless underlined the fact that the post-war West was entirely
dollar-centric.

The system functioned for as long as the United States was both
willing to extend finance to troubled nations (whether through the
Marshall Plan, other forms of aid or, eventually, the World Bank)
and prepared to keep its own finances under control. For as long as
that was the case, the notion that America could afford to exchange
$35 for an ounce of gold would not be challenged, and the system
would remain stable. And in the immediate post-war era this was
not a problem. Growth was strong, inflation was under control and
government debt was falling. Come the 1960s, however, the costs
of the Kennedy/Johnson social welfare reforms kicked in, while the
expense of the Cold War and the Vietnam conflict started to
mount. When, inevitably, markets lost faith in the US's capacity to

keep the value of the dollar unchanged, the demise of the Bretton Woods system became almost inevitable.

The arsenal of regulations and controls countries set up to try to protect their countries from sudden inflows and outflows of hot money were gradually worn down. Systems such as the Eurodollar market were set up to help companies and investors move dollars and other foreign currency around the world without falling foul of such restrictions. This new currency market proved an enormous boost for the City of London, contributing to a renaissance in its position as an international financial centre, in much the same way as the foreign exchange market had in the interwar period.

Moreover, attitudes changed. The notion that the movement of money between one country and another should be constrained began to be seen as distinctly old-fashioned. A long lobbying campaign by financial institutions, for whom the policing of global monetary flows was among the greatest challenges they faced during the twentieth century, helped reinforce the view that capital controls were prehistoric and outmoded.

It meant that over time these restrictions – upon which, in the absence of the ability to alter their exchange rates, finance ministers had become wholly reliant – became less and less effective. The breakdown of Bretton Woods was not merely a consequence of American budget mismanagement, but of a world where borders became increasingly porous to flows of money.

As is often the case, politicians were trying to have their cake and eat it. In an ideal world, they might have enjoyed all of the benefits of fixed exchange rates and domestic monetary policy along with the free movement of capital. However, as Canadian economist Robert Mundell pointed out in the 1960s, centuries of experience have shown that one can only ever have two of these three features at any one time.[4] This is often known as the 'trilemma' or the 'impossible trinity'.[5]

Under the gold standard exchange rates were fixed and cash could move freely from country to country – but domestic monetary policy was sacrificed. In practice, under Bretton Woods exchange rates were fixed and each member country set its own interest rates for domestic reasons. The system could survive only as long as flows of capital were restricted.

With the collapse of Bretton Woods in the early 1970s, the era of fixed exchange rates was over. It is hard to over-emphasise the significance of this rupture. For most of economic history one thing had come first: the stability of exchange rates. Yes, there had been evolutionary changes: under the gold standard currencies had revolved around gold; during Bretton Woods they revolved around the dollar, which in turn was linked to gold. But this was as if the entire cosmos had been upturned. The value of currencies was to be determined not in relation to a fixed system of exchange rates and an anchor commodity like gold or silver, but simply by what traders and investors thought they were worth. The only time anything similar had happened in history was after catastrophic wars or depressions, and there was always the will to put the system back together again. Not this time.

Countries reacted in different ways. The United States, the engine room of global growth since the war, had little inclination to return to a system of fixed currencies. Free market economists such as Milton Friedman had long argued for floating currencies as part of a broader shift from a highly regulated Keynesian world to one free of such restrictions. In the 1970s, as Keynesian spending policies continued, this time without the anti-inflationary anchor provided by the Bretton Woods system, prices leapt higher. The upshot was a decade of high inflation and stagnant economic output, giving rise to the term 'stagflation' and hammering the final nail into the coffin of Keynesian policies.

With central banks no longer constrained by a fixed exchange rate system to regulate the flow of money around their economies, there was little to stop them printing more money. The purchasing power of currencies around the world was dramatically eroded. Nowhere was this more evident than in the gold price, which rocketed from $35 an ounce (or a touch above if you took the market price) in the early 1970s to $600 in the early 1980s. The gold was not necessarily any more precious; but a dollar bill was certainly less valuable. Paul Volcker, the man who had, with gritted teeth, advised Nixon to close the gold window and bring Bretton Woods to an end, was eventually tasked, as Federal Reserve chairman, with bringing prices under control. That meant putting the country through a gruelling period of high interest rates, high unemployment and low growth until inflation was finally tamed in the early 1980s. This attempt to drain cash out of the economic system gave rise to a new economic orthodoxy (the twentieth century is dotted with numerous such intellectual crazes) that what mattered above all else was the 'money supply'. Monetarism, as it was called, became fashionable in the UK as well.

Europe reacted differently to the end of Bretton Woods. The continent had been building up its own internal system of economic linkages since the European Payments Union; there was little question of endorsing freely floating currencies. When the Smithsonian Agreement collapsed in 1973, European countries attempted to keep their currencies pegged against one another in the same tight bands. This arrangement, which came to be known as the 'snake in the tunnel' (the tunnel being those tight currency bands), evolved in the 1980s into the European Monetary System, which in turn evolved into the Exchange Rate Mechanism and, by 1999, into the euro – a single currency.

Britain, which had undergone more monetary trauma than most under Bretton Woods, found itself situated, in intellectual terms, somewhere in the mid-Atlantic and dabbled with both paths. Still haunted by the legacy of its wartime debts and by the fall of its Empire, the country continued to suffer periodic crises of confidence. In the post-Bretton Woods era they were accompanied by high inflation, low growth and, in the 1970s, an IMF bail-out. An increasingly desperate sequence of politicians sought out whatever sources of credibility they could lay their hands on.

They experimented by following the 'snake' for some years – with limited success. In the 1980s they attempted to 'shadow the deutschmark', essentially aping German interest rate policy in an effort to maintain stability and ward off inflation. This culminated, in 1990, with their ill-fated decision to join the Exchange Rate Mechanism (ERM).

The ERM was a system of fixed exchange rates akin to Bretton Woods, except that there were no bars on capital flows between European countries, and while members technically had independence to set their own interest rates, they were expected to follow the lead of the German Bundesbank. But investors were rightly sceptical about most member countries' willingness to abide by the rules, particularly when it meant imposing gruelling interest rate rises on their people if they were already facing a slump. Conservative MP Norman Tebbit dubbed it the 'Eternal Recession Mechanism'.

As Britain attempted to hitch its monetary policy to Germany's (which, to complicate matters, was going through the economically turbulent experience of reunification), it was forced to yank interest rates higher and higher. A recession soon followed, as mortgages became unaffordable and house prices tumbled. Investors, convinced Britain would soon abandon the strictures of membership, started to bet on a big fall in the pound. Eventually on 16 September 1992, after having had to raise interest rates to 12 per cent, and then 15 per cent, Britain abandoned its membership of the ERM. The decision made some of the hedge-fund managers who bet against the pound very wealthy, most notably George

Soros, who became known as 'the man who broke the Bank of England'. Italy left the ERM the same day, although it, and a number of other struggling European nations, would later rejoin.

While Europe attempted to piece its monetary system together again, creating the structures which would become the euro, Britain took an alternative path. Having failed to attain credibility by controlling its exchange rate, it tried to go straight to the source of its post-Bretton Woods problem: inflation. The Bank of England was ordered to use interest rates to target inflation itself, though rate decisions were still approved by the Chancellor. When Gordon Brown took charge of the Treasury in 1997, he gave the Bank independence to set interest rates itself.

Though the new regime Britain had introduced came along at a time of crisis, inflation targeting soon became the dominant monetary system among Western nations. Economists queued up to endorse it as a method of controlling one's economy. Using interest rates to control inflation seemed to represent the holy grail of modern economics. By accident, policymakers seemed to have alighted on a method which would maximise economic growth (the expansion of gross domestic product) while taming inflation – the bogeyman of the 1970s. Many central banks around the world followed suit and started targeting inflation, including the European Central Bank, when it was established in 1998. So too did the Bank of Japan. Tokyo also allowed itself occasional forays into the foreign exchange market where, by judiciously selling yen, it could push down the value of the currency whenever Japanese goods started to look a little pricey for international buyers. Many small countries with vulnerable economies opted for currency pegs, manipulating interest rates and flows of money in and out of their borders to keep their currencies fixed to another country's – almost always the dollar.

The replacement of Bretton Woods with a hodge-podge of other currency systems was coupled with the renaissance of the international financial sector, which had been stuck in a mini Ice Age since the 1940s. Its downfall had partly been due to the swingeing reforms introduced by Roosevelt and others in the 1930s which, among other things, split up regular banks and their investment bank wings. But equally important were the capital controls baked into the Bretton Woods system between 1940 and the late 1970s.

At about the time of the Wall Street Crash in 1929, the banking industry accounted for over 5 per cent of total national income in the United States. After the war this collapsed to about 2 per cent; even by 1970 it was still below 4 per cent.[6]

After the collapse of Bretton Woods in the 1970s, there was no longer so great a need for controls on international capital. In Britain, the Thatcher government lifted capital controls and shook up the corporate structure of British finance with the 'Big Bang' reforms of the early 1980s. The City of London, which had quietly thrived through the 1960s and 1970s thanks to the Eurodollar market, became bigger and more boisterous.

The sudden proliferation of radically different currency systems in the wake of Bretton Woods also created a whole new industry of international currency trading and arbitrage. Any company wanting to trade overseas was now confronted with the risk of currency-related losses if there were sudden fluctuations in exchange rates. Investment banks created vast new businesses to attempt to mitigate these risks for their clients. As time went on, the size of this market swelled to almost incomprehensible proportions. By late 2013, the global turnover in the foreign exchange markets had reached $5.3 trillion (that's $5,300,000,000,000) every single day. According to the BIS, the size of this lucrative market never stopped growing, even in the face of the 2008 financial crisis. The City of London was responsible for the biggest chunk of the business.[7]

In 1999 the United States repealed the 1933 Roosevelt legislation that split finance houses into risky investment banks and less risky deposit-taking banks. In this era of new, more open financial markets, such a restriction looked positively prehistoric. Many of the big American banks merged with investment banks. Some of the oldest finance houses ditched their unlimited liability partnership structures, under which their directors and owners would be liable for every penny of their losses. To those carrying out the reforms, such changes seemed like a natural modernisation of a hitherto archaic industry.

All the while, the size of the financial sector was growing. In the United States, by the turn of the millennium banks now accounted for around 8 per cent of the country's total economic output – more than double their size when the Bretton Woods system ended. In Britain, which never had much of a financial boom in the 1920s, the disparity was even greater. From the Victorian era until 1970, the size of the British banking system's combined balance sheet had never risen much above half of the country's total economic output. Starting in the 1970s, it rocketed higher. By 2006, Britain's banks had balance sheets more than five times the value of UK economic output.

To put it another way, this was a monumental shift in terms of bank profitability. Until 1970, an investor in a UK bank could expect to make about 7 per cent a year on his investment. After 1970, the return on equity roughly trebled to 20 per cent, a figure maintained without a break until the financial crisis of 2008.[8]

There is no single, simple explanation for this astonishing rise of the financial sector; however, there is no doubt that one important element is the sudden change in the international monetary architecture following the collapse of Bretton Woods. Almost immediately after the demise of Keynes and White's system in the early 1970s, every single measure of the size, profitability and leverage of the banking industry began to increase at unprecedented rates.

While the shift towards a more liberalised financial and economic system began in the 1970s, it accelerated after the fall of the

Berlin Wall in the 1990s. The demise of the Soviet Union was proof, it seemed, that planned systems and international regulations were the problem, not the solution. This was the 'End of History', to borrow Francis Fukuyama's phrase: the collapse of Communism seemed to have solved the conundrum as to which political and economic system was superior. In the following years, countries around the world opened up their economic systems to trade and capital flows in a manner that had not been witnessed since the early years of the twentieth century.

In this, they were egged on by the International Monetary Fund. Far from shrivelling into obscurity after the death of the system of fixed exchange rates it was originally set up to monitor, the Fund became still more influential. International economic organisations rarely expire: they simply find new ways to occupy themselves. So, like the BIS (originally set up to monitor German First World War reparations) and the OECD (set up to regulate the Marshall Plan), the IMF reinvented itself as an international economic consultant and adviser.

Its trump card was that it also retained the power to bail out stricken countries. And whenever it doled out money, it predicated its assistance on recipient countries reforming their economies. The conditions, which tended to include liberalising one's markets, opening one's borders to trade and cutting public spending, became known as the 'Washington Consensus'.

After the collapse of Communism, any question marks over the wisdom of following such advice evaporated. In the 1990s many developing countries did precisely what the Fund (and, for that matter, the World Bank) advised. This appeared to make sense until, towards the end of the decade, a number of Asian countries suffered financial crises and had to be bailed out by the IMF. The harsh conditions the Fund imposed during the bail-outs pushed unemployment and poverty levels still higher.

Neighbouring countries (even those that weren't affected) looked on and vowed never to put themselves in the same situation. As the Chinese economy grew and the country pumped out increasing amounts of exports, it began to put aside the dollars it earned as a cache of reserves so that it would not have to resort to IMF protection in the future. The fact that the country was also actively intervening in the currency markets to peg its currency at a low level and keep export demand high, and that its households tended to hoard cash, lifted its dollar stash higher still. As the years went by and China's economy grew stronger and stronger, its demand for dollars, usually in the form of US government debt, known as Treasuries, began to affect the global economic system.

At first, the effects seemed perfectly benign. Chinese demand for Treasuries from the late 1990s meant the US could issue enormous amounts of debt without facing an increase in interest rates (which tend to rise when the supply of bonds outstrips demand). Inflation in the developed world remained low, in part because China was pumping cheap goods around the world. Give or take a few years, growth was strong. Central bankers were lauded as superheroes for apparently locating the Goldilocks formula of high growth and low inflation.

The 'Great Moderation', as economists came to call it, was in fact something of an illusion. During this period, the imbalances between different countries were mounting to new, unprecedented levels. America's total external liabilities – the country's combined debts to the rest of the world – quadrupled in size between 1998 and 2008; it was a similar story in the UK. Given that one man's debt is another's savings, the total assets of China, Japan and Germany leapt by similar proportions during this period. Such imbalances were precisely what had contributed to the destruction of the gold standard during the interwar period; they were precisely what the Bretton Woods system set out to prevent. But because they were not accompanied by the warning signal of rising interest rates, central bankers assumed there was nothing fundamentally wrong with the global economic system. How wrong they were.

The combination of strong global growth and low interest rates during this period unleashed a torrent of cash that flowed around the world's financial system. Given how low interest rates on 'safe' investments such as government debt were, investors embarked on a 'search for yield', putting money into all sorts of instruments which were hitherto considered risky, whether that meant subprime US mortgage debt or Greek government bonds. That this coincided with a period of lax financial regulation, and with a widespread myopia about the frailties of the euro, was unfortunate. However, good sense is generally the first casualty in a bubble, and the bubble created by the malfunctioning of the world's monetary system was among the world's biggest.

The financial crisis which began in 2007 with the freezing of interbank lending markets, reached its height in 2008 with the collapse of Lehman Brothers, one of the world's oldest investment banks, and transmogrified into the euro crisis in 2009 and 2010, was at least partly a consequence of the chain of monetary events described above. As the world suffered a recession the like of which it had not experienced since the 1930s, economists, politicians and academics sought an explanation.

As with the Great Depression, the causes for which are the subject of debate even today, there was no single, simple answer. Economists made intellectual mistakes, financial regulators made misjudgements and investors took missteps. But shadowing the entire episode was the mangled state of the world's monetary system.

Look beyond the financial innovations blamed for much of the chaos and the problems governments were wrestling with were precisely those that had been under discussion at Bretton Woods. Simply: without some anchor or system to co-ordinate matters, some countries will have a tendency to borrow too much, others to lend too much. When the resultant balance of payments

surpluses and deficits become too large, they leave the global economy vulnerable to a crisis. Deficit nations may face a sudden buyers'
strike in the bond markets; surplus nations may face an abrupt fall
in demand for their exports.

The identities of the surplus and deficit nations may have
changed – the United States is the deficit nation today; in the
1930s it was the surplus nation – but the underlying problem is
no different. Under the gold standard, central bankers informally
agreed economic policy between themselves, conveniently ignoring
their non-voting populations when recession struck. Under Bretton
Woods, politicians constructed a system to constrain member states,
which worked passably well (if not in precisely the way its progenitors intended) for as long as it lasted, which was only a few
decades. Since 1971, the world's monetary system has been run on
an ad hoc basis, with no particular sense of the direction in which
it ought to travel.

Most of the experiments since 1971 – monetarism, currency
boards, exchange rate agreements and inflation targeting – have
been ill-fated. In the wake of the financial crisis, most of the world's
major central banks abandoned inflation targeting; at the time of
writing it was not yet clear what they intended to replace it with.
Occasionally, crises have brought politicians and central bankers
together in an effort to iron out the wrinkles in the system. At
the Plaza Hotel in New York in 1985, the Group of Five nations
(France, West Germany, Japan, the United States and the United
Kingdom), who saw themselves as the inheritors of the role played
by the main nations at Bretton Woods, agreed to intervene in
currency markets. At the IMF Annual Meetings in 2008, and then
again at the G20 summit in London the following year, politicians
committed to rescuing their banking systems and pumping cash
into their economies respectively.

However, by their very nature such crisis summits always come
too late, and the response itself is often misplaced. There have been

plenty of measures implemented to address the failings of the financial system since 2008, but few, if any, designed to improve the fundamental workings of the international monetary system. The challenges are too great; the will to confront them never came close to what the Bretton Woods participants summoned up in 1944. All the same, few doubt that there remains something wrong with the international monetary system today, and that it may well continue storing up problems for the future. According to Mervyn King, former governor of the Bank of England, 'what there was then was a plan to deal with this problem. What we've got today is everyone running away from the problem without any plan to deal with it. It's a bit harsh to compare Bretton Woods with where we are today, because where we are now is the problem, not a solution.

'Rather than let something awful go wrong down the road, why don't we deal with it now?'[9]

Part of the problem is that few people share a vision of what the international monetary system of the future might look like. One rare insight was provided by Zhou Xiaochuan, the chairman of the People's Bank of China. 'Back in the 1940s, Keynes had already proposed to introduce an international currency unit named "Bancor",' he said in 2009. 'Unfortunately, the proposal was not accepted. The collapse of the Bretton Woods system, which was based on the White approach, indicates that the Keynesian approach may have been more farsighted.'

What was needed in the post-crisis world, Zhou added, was a 'grand vision' of a new international monetary system, perhaps involving a global reserve currency to replace the dollar.[10] Inspiring as the speech was, it made little difference to the international debate. China continued to stack up Treasuries on top of an already towering pile. Those who sit at the summit tables say that despite their wise words, even the Chinese are unwilling to contemplate a drastic change to the existing order.

In part, this is because it would simply be too disruptive. The United States and China, the only nations with a realistic hope of reforming the system at present, are locked in an interdependent economic relationship that has paralysed any movement towards reform. The Chinese – and indeed many others – complain that with its enormous household debts and growing budget deficit, the US is living unsustainably. However, given that China owns a third of the US national debt – $17 trillion and climbing at the time of writing – it has little incentive to encourage an American default, whether through inflation, devaluation or simple repudiation of the debts.

As was the case in the 1970s, there are periodic calls for the United States to put its house in order – and occasional panics that its moment as the world's superpower is about to come to an end. Once the noise dies down, the existing order tends to reassert itself.

That said, while the United States once enjoyed undisputed authority, it may well have to share influence in the global economy in the future. As Paul Volcker says, 'Nobody else is saluting when we come into the room automatically the way they used to when I was in the Treasury in the 1960s. Now they are willing to go off and make their own system. It's a lot more difficult now but I don't think we can ignore the problem.'[11] If history is any guide, this may portend a prolonged period of instability, as the global economy has tended to face repeated crises when there has been a challenge to the existing hegemon.

Where this will leave the two children of Bretton Woods remains to be seen. At the time of writing, they remain more powerful and influential than ever. During the euro crisis the International Monetary Fund extended its biggest ever loans (far bigger than anything Keynes envisaged in 1944) to Greece, Portugal and Ireland. It may well be able to lay claim to having saved the euro – at least for the time being.

However, some suggest that during the crisis the institution squandered some of its independence. This was quite a contrast to the earliest decades of its life, when the Fund was regarded in many developing countries as a benign, liberating force – a useful counterpoint to the imperial powers which dominated the nineteenth century. The Bank of England could never countenance its former colonies establishing their own central banks; the IMF positively encouraged it. However, in the 1980s and 1990s the Fund and the Bank were accused of attempting to spread American economic policy worldwide. During the euro crisis, developing countries found themselves part-financing a rescue for a single currency whose members could quite easily have afforded to bail each other out.

According to Mervyn King, this may leave a lasting scar. 'I think it is a major problem as to how far the IMF is seen as being the instrument of the US and Europe – in which case other countries simply will not put up with it indefinitely,' he says. 'I'm not saying they'll withdraw from the IMF, but they will create, in terms of financial support, networks in their region and not bother to go to the IMF for support.'[12] For Paul Volcker, there is no point in attempting to devise a comprehensive international system of rules in the mould of Bretton Woods. The objective, instead, is to 'try as hard as you can to have a domestic financial system that people respect, and is compatible with their own needs. And you can then build on that and see if you can get some agreement – much looser than we dreamed about at Bretton Woods, and certainly much looser than we had in the Gold Standard – but nonetheless has enough discipline in it that people will respect.'[13]

Whether the Fund can survive in a more fractured world remains to be seen. For Olivier Blanchard, its chief economist throughout the crisis, the world economy needs an international lender of last resort, to provide 'liquidity' – short-term help for countries, provided they can pay it back.* The Fund only partially played this role during the euro crisis. Although it helped co-ordinate and finance loans to troubled countries, it was not involved in the countless 'swap lines'

---

*'There has to be at the international level some system of liquidity provision. You have very large herding-like movements in capital flows, and countries can get hit – I think it's important that there be facilities to supply the liquidity.' Olivier Blanchard, interview with author, July 2013.

set up between central banks to help keep them from running out of particular currencies. Here, as in so many other areas of international policy, the world is falling back upon bilateral, country-by-country support arrangements rather than the international deals that characterised the post-war years.

For Blanchard, another lesson of the crisis is the need for more capital controls. 'My faith in the financial system has substantially diminished. I'm quite open to the idea that capital flows don't always reflect good judgements on the part of investors. And some of the movements caused by those flows may be quite bad for economic welfare.'[14]

However, like many others who spent the crisis attempting to plug economic leaks and prevent sovereign bankruptcies, he believes that there is no realistic 'big vision' for the international monetary system. 'It's too complicated,' he says. 'Let's have a sense of a direction and proceed step-by-step.'[15]

One pragmatic lesson of the past decades is that the genie is well and truly out of the bottle when it comes to fixed exchange rates. Ever since Britain ended its membership of the gold standard in 1931, the notion that a country could yoke its exchange rate to someone else's, or indeed to a precious metal, has been undermined time and time again.

The European single currency has provided the world with the best example to date of what happens when one tries to reinstitute the gold standard in the modern world. The single currency may not have gold as an anchor, but it is akin to the gold standard in almost every other way, with member states unable to devalue or change their own interest rates, unable (except in direst emergency) to restrain money from flowing in and out of their borders and forced to suffer periods of deflation and recession in order to grind their competitiveness down to their neighbours' levels. For the United States and Britain in the late 1920s, read Germany and Greece in the early twenty-first century.

Blanchard says that while the euro helped protect some of its members in 2008, 'today things would be easier if some countries could float'.[16] However, getting there would be extremely painful. In the summer of 2012 Europe's politicians looked into the abyss and considered allowing Greece to leave the single currency. But they realised that any departure would create havoc, perhaps to an even greater degree than followed the collapse of the gold standard in 1931.

The easiest words to say in economics are 'we need a new Bretton Woods'. Politicians have been doing so for decades. In 1998 Bill Clinton complained to his advisers: 'How come Blair got to call for a new Bretton Woods when you wouldn't let me do it?'[17] But, seductive as it is to believe that the world could be strapped into an all-purpose monetary system, such hopes are unrealistic. The search for the ideal international monetary system is as old and as futile as the search for the legendary philosopher's stone, which would turn lead into gold.* Bretton Woods itself was imperfect, did not cover vast parts of the world, and was short-lived.

Moreover, no great shifts in the monetary system could happen without being preceded by a global war or an economic depression of even greater proportions than the recession that began in 2008. The authors of Bretton Woods recognised as much. They knew they had been handed a once-in-a-lifetime opportunity to install a global framework for exchange rates and capital controls – but that the window was a small one. As White himself told his fellow Americans as they sat in their hotel room at Bretton Woods, 'within a few years after the end of the war you won't be able to get an international arrangement of this kind any more than you could fly.'[18]

---

*Keynes, it so happened, suspected that such alchemy might in due course become possible. He was a keen collector of Newton's writings on alchemy and indicated in numerous analyses of the gold standard that it might prove possible to manufacture gold in the future.

Neither of them had any delusions that the system they were setting up was perfect. Both, in fact, died harbouring critical concerns
about a variety of its features. In his final speech at Savannah,
Keynes acknowledged as much, adding: 'There is scarcely any
enduringly successful experience yet of an international body which
has fulfilled the hopes of its progenitors.'[19]

The Bretton Woods system is no more. But while their influence
has ebbed and flowed, the two institutions Keynes and White set
up still exist today. As representatives of the world's leading
economies met in the face of the financial crisis of the 2000s, they
did so watched over by a couple of familiar faces. Seven decades on
from that meeting at Bretton Woods, there are still two cast bronze
busts in a prominent place in the IMF's boardroom: they depict
Keynes and White.

Like the institutions they created, the reputations of both men
have been scarred by disputes in the years since 1944. Keynes's ideas
on public spending were dismissed by many as invalid during the
1970s and 1980s. White's Soviet links were seen as so shameful
that, for a time, his bust was removed to the Fund's basement. It
languished there for some years before being returned to its place
in the boardroom.[20]

While there will always be significant question marks over
White's motives and actions in consorting with Russian intelligence, today the world looks more kindly on the two architects of
Bretton Woods. Perhaps it's the fact that so many of the financial
crises since the 1970s have, one way or another, come back to mal-
functions in the international monetary system. Perhaps it's because
we are still fighting the same demons they did.

In retrospect, the most remarkable thing about Bretton Woods
was that it happened at all. This was not the first attempt to put the
world back together again after the Depression. Nor were Keynes's
and White's ideas on how to do it in tune with conventional
wisdom, particularly in the United States. The banking industry

would almost certainly have squashed the proposals had it not been confronted with an extremely anti-finance White House. And the International Monetary Fund and World Bank were lucky enough to be born in an era when international organisations were an optimistic vision of the future, not a remnant of the past.

Life is messy – in international economics as much as in the everyday world most of us inhabit. But in this messy world, Bretton Woods has come to represent something hopeful, something closer to perfection. The most important mission facing the world's politicians and policymakers then, as now, was to repair the world's economic system and replace it with something better. For a time, they succeeded.

Acknowledgements

Though I suspect it was the last thing he intended, Dani Rodrik first planted the seed that eventually sprouted into this book. The idea came to me somewhere in the middle of a course I took with him at Harvard on international monetary systems a few years ago. As I waded through the economic analysis texts he had set me on the Bretton Woods system, I kept getting diverted by the 'noises off' at the conference: the Russians drinking in the bar, the Chinese desperate to put on the biggest parties, the stories about Harry Dexter White and the Soviets. Given that the conference was frequently depicted as a dull, dry affair, the existence of so much of this stuff in archives and libraries around the world came as something of a shock – not to mention the fact that so little of it had ever found a wider audience.

However, planting a seed is one thing – encouraging it to grow is another. I have two other professors at Harvard to thank for that: Richard Parker for convincing me that there was a book in it; and David King for telling me, kindly but sufficiently brutally, that it was a far better idea than the politics guidebook I had somehow convinced myself I should write when I got back home. When I joined Sky News, the idea might easily have gone into hibernation, but then the euro crisis happened – another international monetary disaster – and the echoes of 1944 kept coming back to haunt us. I got back to work.

It's of enormous credit to my bosses and colleagues at Sky that they have been so patient and supportive of this book, despite the fact that digging around on an economic conference from seventy years ago hardly generates many news stories. Thank you, especially, to John Ryley and Jonathan Levy, who have been not just encouraging but, frankly, indulgent all the way through.

The book is also a product of countless conversations with historians, economists and policymakers I've had the privilege of spending time with over the past decade. They really are too numerous to mention – but those who gave me some specific thoughts about the past and present of Bretton Woods included Mervyn King, Olivier Blanchard, Bernard Connolly and Adair Turner. James Boughton, Eric Rauchway, Eric Helleiner and R. Bruce Craig were kind enough to share research and material, some unpublished, about the conference and its participants. So, too, did Michael Rasminsky and his family, sharing some of the private memoirs of his father Louis Rasminsky. Kurt Schuler provided me with an early version of his transcripts from the conference, which proved enormously useful.

I've been fortunate enough in my travels researching this book to meet some extremely helpful archivists who have pointed me in the right direction and allowed me to pepper them with stupid questions. Thank you in particular to Premela Isaac at the International Monetary Fund, and, for that matter, to Bill Murray and Jennifer Beckman in the press office; to Holden Stoffel at the Bank of Canada; to the various archivists who helped me at the Bank of England Archives and at the FDR Library; to Peter Monteith and colleagues at the King's College, Cambridge, Archives; to Eric Kelsey at the Mount Washington Observatory, who kindly provided me with weather reports for the period. Thank you, especially, to Svetlana Chervonnaya, who spent days in the official archives in Moscow, digging out dusty, untouched documents that shed new light on the Soviet part in the conference.

My thanks, too, to those who have read the book in excerpt and in full, and who provided such useful commentary and constructive criticism. Some of them are mentioned above; others included Jonathan Portes, Jamie Martin, David Litterick, Philip Aldrick, Steve Field, Django Davidson, Alistair Bunkall, Fred Casella and Sara Mojtehedzadeh, the last of whom has had to put up not only with reading every single word in it, but with living with a man unhealthily fixated on this project. Thank you.

Enormous thanks to all at Little, Brown, who have embraced this project with an enthusiasm I never thought would have been elicited by a history of the international monetary architecture. It has been a privilege to be edited by Tim Whiting, who nurtured it with care and even excitement. Iain Hunt has helped turn my occasionally overwritten prose into something resembling a book. Steve Gove has done likewise, correcting my many mistakes in as gentle a way as one could have imagined. Thank you to Linda Silverman for helping provide the pictures, which really help you feel what it was like to be in the room back in July 1944. And to Emily Burns and Steve Dumughn who have helped project it for a wider audience, as well as to Lucy Ellison at Sky.

Finally, thanks to my agent and friend Jonathan Conway. We've been talking about books and book projects since we met at university more than a decade ago. I'm so delighted we can finally share this project, as well as a surname. Thank you for turning this idea into something real; we must do it again sometime.

It almost goes without saying that even with all the help I've received from this amazing array of talent, I will probably have managed to slip one or two errors into the book. For those I apologise, and offer up Keynes's great friend Lytton Strachey as my witness. Ignorance, he wrote, 'is the first requisite of the historian – ignorance, which simplifies and clarifies, which selects and omits, with a placid perfection unattainable by the highest art.'

Finally, it strikes me as inevitable that, given how much material on the conference had yet to see the light of day when I wrote this, there will be other fascinating nuggets stored away in archives. I would be forever grateful if anyone who encounters them passes them on. After all, Bretton Woods may have happened a full seven decades ago, but the story of the conference and its aftershocks live on today.

London, May 2014

Notes

The papers of John Maynard Keynes – both personal and economic – are kept at King's College, Cambridge. Those consulted in this book are referred to together with their box and folder numbers. There are in addition one or two references to Lydia Lopokova Keynes's papers, also at King's. Many of Keynes's economic writings were published in *The Collected Writings of John Maynard Keynes*, edited by Donald Moggridge, which comprises thirty volumes and was published by Macmillan and Cambridge University Press for the Royal Economic Society between 1971 and 1989. For ease, all references to this series are abbreviated as JMK, followed by the volume number. This is only the beginning, however: many of Keynes's Treasury files are today stored in the National Archives at Kew, along with a host of other documents related to Britain's part in the conference.

Harry Dexter White's personal papers are to be found in the Mudd Manuscript Library at Princeton University; his Treasury files are stored in the United States National Archives. Henry Morgenthau's own papers – particularly his diaries – have been useful in gleaning information about the United States delegation's strategy at the conference. Each reference to them includes the diary number.

Many of the files and papers associated specifically with the foundation of the Bretton Woods institutions are kept in the archives at the International Monetary Fund. In recent years, archivists have scanned the majority of these files and put them online – something which was of immense help in the course of researching this book. They can be found on the IMF website. The majority of material published at the time of the conference, including speeches made at the event and all the press releases issued, have been collated into a two-volume publication published by the United States Government Printing Office. This is referred to as 'Proceedings', followed by the volume number.

Other sources of primary material consulted in the course of research for this book include the following:

Bank of England Archives: Papers of George Bolton; Papers of Lucius
Thompson-MacCausland; Overseas files
Bodleian Library: Papers of Robert Brand
Franklin D. Roosevelt Presidential Library: Papers of Henry Morgenthau
Jr; Oscar Cox Papers
Harry S. Truman Library: Various oral histories, including John Parke
Young, Leroy Stinebower and Ivan B. White
Library of Congress: Averell Harriman Papers; Emanuel Goldenweiser Papers;
Leo Pasvolsky Papers; Katie Louchheim Papers; Philip Jessup Papers
Princeton University: Papers of Ragnar Nurkse
The Russian State Archive of Economics (RGAE), Moscow; The Archive
of the Foreign Policy of the Russian Federation (AVP RF), (courtesy
of Dr Svetlana Chervonnaya)
University of North Carolina: Edward Bernstein Oral History, Louis
Round Wilson Special Collections Library

I am also grateful to Dr Michael Rasminsky and his family for sharing his
father's personal reminiscences of Bretton Woods.

For anyone who has encountered the writings of Keynes and White
only through biography and other secondary sources (including, I suppose,
this book) and has the curiosity to find out more, I would strongly recommend reading some of those writings. Part of what made Keynes, in
particular, such a significant figure was not merely his economic analysis
but his capacity to explain it – whether in text or in person – in such
engaging fashion. Harry Dexter White was a touch more long-winded,
but was a skilled writer all the same.

PROLOGUE

1 Emanuel Goldenweiser, remarks made at a joint meeting of directors
of Federal Reserve Bank of Cleveland and branches, 2 November
1944, Goldenweiser Papers
2 JMK XXVI, p. 106, letter to Sir Richard Hopkins, 21 July 1944
3 Susan Howson and Donald Moggridge (eds), *The Wartime Diaries of
Lionel Robbins and James Meade, 1943–45*, New York, 1990, p. 191
4 J.K. Galbraith, *A Short History of Financial Euphoria*, Harmondsworth,
1994
5 Interview with the author, 31 May 2013

1 THE MOUNT WASHINGTON

1 Joel J. Bedor, *The Mount Washington Hotel & Resort – a Heritage of Optimism*, Newcomen Society Address, 2003

2 Ted Landphair and Carole M. Highsmith, *The Mount Washington: A Century of Grandeur*, Singapore, 2002

3 JMK XXVI, p. 28, Keynes to White, 24 May 1944

4 Robert Skidelsky, *John Maynard Keynes: Fighting for Britain, 1937–1946*, London, 2000, p. 339

5 *New York Mirror*, 31 August 1944. It added that 'Some Congressmen want to investigate the Bretton Woods scandal.'

6 Bettye H. Pruitt, *The Making of Harcourt General: A History of Growth Through Diversification 1922–1992*, Cambridge, Mass., 1994

7 'They're Burnishing up FDR's Mountain Profile for Big Conference', *Boston Globe*, 4 June 1944

8 Loyd MacNayr, oral history, Boston and Maine Railroad Historical Society

9 Shirley Boskey, 'Bretton Woods Recalled', IMF Archives

10 Interview with Mac McQueeney, historian, at Mount Washington Hotel, July 2012

11 'N. H. Boy Scouts to Be Pages at Parley', *Christian Science Monitor*, 28 June 1944

12 Proceedings II

13 Lydia Lopokova Papers, King's College Archives, LLK/5/122/9, letter to Milo Keynes, Thursday 6 July

14 *New Yorker*, 5 August 1944

15 Dean Acheson, *Present at the Creation: My Years in the State Department*, New York, 1969, p. 82

16 JMK XXIII, pp. 295ff, letter to Sir Wilfred Eady, 20 October 1943

17 Howson and Moggridge (1990), p. 167

18 Ibid.

19 Ibid., p. 178

20 Emanuel Goldenweiser, remarks made at a joint meeting of directors of Federal Reserve Bank of Cleveland and branches, 2 November 1944, IMF Archives

21 Howson and Moggridge (1990), p. 169

22 Morgenthau Diary 750, p. 148

23 Acheson (1969), p. 82

24 JMK XXVI, p. 73

2 THE BITTER PEACE

1 Keynes Papers, King's College Archives, letter to Vanessa Bell, 16 March 1919, cited in Robert Skidelsky, *John Maynard Keynes: Hopes Betrayed, 1883–1920*, London, 1983, p. 363

2 Milo Keynes (ed.), *Essays on John Maynard Keynes*, Cambridge, 1980, p. 64

3 JMK II, pp. 75–6

4 John Maynard Keynes, *The Economic Consequences of the Peace*, London, 1919, pp. 4–5

5 'The Bank and the Banks', speech by Andrew Haldane, Bank of England, 18 October 2012

6 David Rees, *Harry Dexter White: A Study in Paradox*, New York, 1973, p. 22

7 R. Bruce Craig, *Treasonable Doubt: The Harry Dexter White Spy Case*, Lawrence, 2004, p. 19

8 David Garnett, diary entry 28 May 1918, cited in Skidelsky (1983), p. 350

9 Robert Skidelsky, *John Maynard Keynes 1883–1946*, London, 2003, p. 259

10 Milo Keynes (1980), p. 71

11 E.M. Forster, *Two Cheers for Democracy*, London, 1965, p. 76

12 Michael Holroyd, *Lytton Strachey*, London, 1994, p. 343

13 David Lloyd George, *War Memoirs*, Vol. II, London, 1933, p. 684

14 Skidelsky (1983), p. 319

15 JMK XVI, p. 264, Basil Blackett to Hamilton, 1 January 1918

16 Spring-Rice Papers, Churchill College, Cambridge, cited in Skidelsky (1983), p. 342

17 Bertrand Russell, *Autobiography*, Vol. III, London, 1969, p. 69

18 Charleston Papers, King's College Archives, cited in Skidelsky (1983), p. 352

19 Keynes Papers, King's College Archives, PP/20A/3

20 Skidelsky (1983), p. 352

21 Ibid., pp. 352–3

22 Rees (1973), p. 23

23 Ibid., p. 26

24 Barry Eichengreen, *Exorbitant Privilege: The Rise and Fall of the Dollar and the Future of the International Monetary System*, New York, 2011, p. 32

25 Ibid.

26 Skidelsky (1983), p. 333

27 David Kynaston, *City of London: The History*, London, 2011, p. 274
28 Kynaston (2011), Kindle location 6995
29 Rees (1973), p. 27
30 Ibid., p. 28
31 Library of Congress, Baker notebooks, 9/6/19, cited in Margaret Macmillan, *Peacemakers: The Paris Peace Conference of 1919 and Its Attempt to End War*, London, 2001
32 Skidelsky (1983), p. 353
33 Keynes (1919), p. 62
34 Harold Nicolson, *Peacemaking*, London, 1933, pp. 44–5
35 Sylvia Nasar, *The Grand Pursuit: The Story of Economic Genius*, London, 2011, p. 251
36 National Archives, Kew, CAB 1/28
37 Macmillan (2001), p. 168
38 Keynes Papers, King's College Archives, Keynes to D. Grant, 14 May 1919
39 Herbert Hoover, *The Memoirs of Herbert Hoover*, Vol. 1, *Years of Adventure, 1874–1920*, New York, 1951, p. 462
40 Lloyd George Papers, Parliamentary Archives, 5 June 1919, cited in Skidelsky (1983), p. 375
41 Skidelsky (1983), p. 384
42 Keynes (1919), p. 20
43 Peter Rowland, *Lloyd George*, London, 1975, p. 480

3 A SHORT HISTORY OF GOLD

1 http://www.youtube.com/watch?v=CTtf5s2HFkA
2 Thomas Sargent and Francois Velde, *The Big Problem of Small Change*, Princeton, 2002
3 John Maynard Keynes, *A Treatise on Money*, New York, 1930, p. 26

4 ECONOMIC CONSEQUENCES

1 JMK XII, pp. 10–12
2 Skidelsky (1983), p. 349
3 Skidelsky (2003), p. 522
4 Ibid., p. 297
5 Malcolm MacDonald, *People and Places: Random Reminiscences of the Rt. Hon. Malcolm MacDonald*, London, 1969, p. 175
6 Polly Hill and Richard Keynes (eds), *Lydia and Maynard: The Letters of Lydia Lopokova and John Maynard Keynes*, London, 1989

7   Skidelsky (2000), p. 266
8   Virginia Woolf diary, 11 September 1923, quoted in Robert Skidelsky, *John Maynard Keynes: The Economist as Saviour, 1920–1937*, London, 1992, p. 145
9   John Maynard Keynes, *Tract on Monetary Reform*, London, 1923, p. 167
10 Ibid., p. 1
11 Ibid., pp. 198–9
12 Ibid., p. 172
13 Ibid., p. 4
14 Ibid., p. 80
15 Craig (2004), p. 289
16 Harry Dexter White, *The French International Accounts*, Cambridge, MA, 1933, p. 312
17 Interlocking Subversion in Government Departments Hearings, 30 August 1955, p. 2570
18 Henry Morgenthau III, *Mostly Morgenthaus: A Family History*, New York, 1991, p. 311
19 'One Man's Guilt', *Time*, 23 November 1953
20 Craig (2004), p. 292
21 Edward Bernstein, oral history, Southern Historical Collection, Louis Round Wilson Special Collections Library, UNC-Chapel Hill, 1983, p. 41
22 Samuel Rosenman (ed.), *The Public Papers and Addresses of Franklin D Roosevelt*, Vol. II, *The Year of Crisis 1933*, New York, 1938, p. 264
23 John Morton Blum, *From the Morgenthau Diaries*, Vol. I, *Years of Crisis, 1928–1938*, Boston, 1959, p. 70
24 Fred Block, *The Origins of International Economic Disorder: A Study of United States International Monetary Policy from World War II to the Present*, London, 1977
25 'From Keynes to Roosevelt: Our Recovery Plans Assayed', *New York Times*, 31 December 1933
26 JMK XXI, p. 438
27 Skidelsky (2003), p. 509
28 Roy Harrod, *The Life of John Maynard Keynes*, London, 1951, p. 20
29 Frances Perkins, *The Roosevelt I Knew*, London, 1947, p. 225
30 White Papers, Princeton, Bax 7/1, 'Summary of conversations with men interviewed in London', 13 June 1935
31 JMK IX, p. xvii
32 JMK XXVIII, p. 42
33 John Maynard Keynes, *The General Theory*, London, 1936, Book 3, Chapter 10, Section 6, p. 129

34 Nicholas Wapshott, *Keynes Hayek: The Clash That Defined Modern Economics*, London, 2011, p. 81

35 http://tmh.floonet.net/articles/foregt.html

36 JMK to Lydia, 15, 16 November 1936, cited in Skidelsky (1992), p. 628

37 Skidelsky (1992), p. 629

38 Skidelsky (2003), p. 562

39 Ibid., p. 578

40 Donald Moggridge, *Maynard Keynes: An Economist's Biography*, London, 2003, Kindle location 15577

41 MacDonald (1969), p. 181

42 Adam Lebor, *Tower of Basel*, New York, 2013, p. 69

43 Bank of England Archives, Bank of England unpublished War History, Part 3, Chapter 9, available at: http://www.bankofengland.co.uk/archive/Pages/digitalcontent/archivedocs/warhistoryww2.aspx

44 Lebor (2013), pp. 62, 59

45 White Papers, Princeton, Box 9/17, 'Speech post VJ day about problems in economies in Europe: "Monetary and Financial Problems Facing the World"'

5 LUNATIC PROPOSALS

1 JMK XXV, p. 20

2 Goldenweiser Papers, Library of Congress, Box 4, International Currency Stabilization, Statement by E.A. Goldenweiser, 28 June 1943

3 National Archives, Kew, FO371/28899

4 Ibid.

5 Hadley Cantrill (ed.), *Public Opinion 1935–1946*, Westport, CT, 1951, p. 973

6 Samuel L. Rosenman (ed.), *The Public Papers and Addresses of Franklin D. Roosevelt*, Vol. IX, New York, 1940, p. 517

7 William R. Rock, *Chamberlain and Roosevelt, British Foreign Policy and the United States, 1937–1940*, Columbus, OH, 1988, p. 48

8 Moggridge (2003), p. 949

9 Mark Harrison, *The Economics of World War II*, Cambridge, 1989, p. 94

10 Peter Acsay, *Planning for Postwar Economic Co-operation – US Treasury, Soviet Union and Bretton Woods*, 2000, available at: http://www.centerforfinancialstability.org/hfs/Acsay_Planning.pdf, p. 164

11 Ian Kershaw, *Fateful Choices: Ten Decisions That Changed the World, 1940–1941*, London, 2007, pp. 239, 232

12 Ibid., p. 233
13 National Archives, Kew, FO371/25209
14 Lionel Robbins, *Autobiography of an Economist*, London, 1971, p. 187
15 Keynes Papers, King's College, JMK/BE and JMK/PP/45/168
16 JMK X, p. 330
17 JMK XXIII, p. 106
18 National Archives, Kew, T175/121
19 Morgenthau Diary 410, p. 122
20 JMK XXIII, pp. 87–91
21 Morgenthau Diary 410, p. 123
22 Ibid., p. 188
23 Eleanor Lansing Dulles to R.H. Brand, cited in Moggridge (2003),
    p. 660
24 Department of State Foreign Relations Archives, 1941, Vol. III, p. 5
25 JMK XXIII, p. 155
26 Acheson (1969), p. 29
27 Harrod (1951), p. 512
28 Roosevelt Papers, Secretary's File, Box 78, cited in Armand van
    Dormael, *Bretton Woods: Birth of a Monetary System*, London, 1978,
    p. 25–6
29 Keynes Papers, King's College Archives, PP/80/9, JMK to P.A.S.
    Hadley, 10 September 1941, cited in Skidelsky (2000), p. 115

6 BEDLAM

1 Gardner (1956), p. xiii
2 Goldenweiser Papers, Library of Congress, International Currency
   Stabilization, Statement by E.A. Goldenweiser, 28 June 1943
3 Raymond Mikesell, 'The Bretton Woods Debates: A Memoir', *Essays
   in International Finance*, March 1994, p. 2; Morgenthau Diary 417,
   p. 16
4 Morgenthau Diary 470, pp. 82–3
5 Keynes Papers, King's College Archives, W/1, JMK to Dean
   Acheson, 17 October 1941
6 White Papers, Princeton, Box 1/3, 1936 paper on Chinese economic
   situation, pp. 40–1
7 Bank of England Archives, OV38/1, C.F. Cobbold to M. Norman,
   29 December 1941
8 National Archives, Kew, T247/121, 'Post-War Currency', 21
   September 1941
9 Ibid., undated

10 National Archives, Kew, T247/116, 'Postwar Currency Policy', 8 September 1941
11 National Archives, Kew, T247/121, 26 November 1941
12 JMK XXV, p. 66
13 Keith Horsefield, *International Monetary Fund*, Vol. III, Washington, 1969, p. 21
14 Brand Papers, Bodleian Library, File 198, Brand to JMK, 10 October 1941
15 Skidelsky (2000), p. 219
16 National Archives, Kew, T247/122, L.P. Thompson-McCausland to JMK, 25 October 1941; JMK to L.P. Thompson-McCausland, 12 November 1941
17 Robbins (1971), p. 184
18 White Papers, Princeton, Box 8/24
19 Ibid., Box 3/8
20 US Treasury Records, memorandum 29 December 1941
21 White Papers, Princeton, Box 8/24
22 Morgenthau Diary 545, p. 37
23 Howson and Moggridge (1990), p. 101
24 JMK XXV, p. 159
25 Skidelsky (2000), p. 247
26 Bernstein (1983), pp. 49–50
27 Ernest Penrose, *Economic Planning for the Peace*, Princeton, 1953, p. 48
28 Richard Gardner, *Sterling–Dollar Diplomacy: Anglo-American Collaboration in the Reconstruction of Multilateral Trade*, Oxford, 1956, p. 111
29 Bernstein (1983), p. 57
30 Penrose (1953), p. 49
31 Louis Rasminsky, 'A Very Personal Piece', Rasminsky Family
32 Moggridge (2003), p. 639
33 *New York Times*, 9 May 1943
34 National Archives, Kew, T160/1281/F18885/1, Keynes to Phillips, 16 December 1942
35 Van Dormael (1978), p. 67
36 National Archives, Kew, T160/1281/F18885/1, Keynes to Eady, 21 January 1943
37 National Archives, Kew, T160/1281/F18885/1, Waley to Chancellor, 19 February 1943
38 Morgenthau Diary 622, pp. 8–9
39 Paul Einzig, *In the Centre of Things*, London, 1960, pp. 241–51
40 National Archives, Kew, T160/1281/F18885/3, Keynes to Phillips, 16 April 1943

41　National Archives, Kew, T247/30a
42　National Archives, Kew, T247/34
43　White Papers, Princeton, Box 9/14
44　Howson and Moggridge (1990), p. 98
45　Ibid., p. 97
46　Ibid., p. 92
47　Ibid., p. 100
48　Ibid., p. 110
49　Ibid., p. 106
50　JMK XXV, pp. 353–4
51　Bernstein (1983), p. 66
52　Howson and Moggridge (1990), p. 141
53　Bank of England Archives, OV38/5, Thompson-McCausland to Cobbold, 18 September 1943
54　Howson and Moggridge (1990), p. 135
55　Raymond Mikesell, *Foreign Adventures of an Economist*, Eugene, 2000, p. 54
56　Van Dormael (1978), p. 105
57　Ibid., p. 101
58　JMK XXV, p. 364
59　Bernstein (1983), p. 54
60　JMK XXV, p. 356
61　Howson and Moggridge (1990), p. 133
62　Bernstein (1983), p. 54
63　JMK XXV, pp. 362–4
64　Howson and Moggridge (1990), p. 130
65　JMK XXV, p. 374
66　Acsay (2000), p. 269
67　Bernstein (1983), p. 60
68　Morgenthau Diary 723, pp. 1–7

7 THE WRONG HARRY WHITE

1　'The Right Mr White', *Time*, 8 January 1945
2　'National Affairs: The Record', *Time*, 23 November 1953
3　Ibid.
4　'INVESTIGATIONS: Basement in Chevy Chase', *Time*, 23 August 1948
5　FBI Silvermaster file, p. 81
6　Craig (2004), pp. 60–1
7　Whittaker Chambers, *Witness*, Washington, 2001, p. 384

8 Ibid., p. 442

9 Rees (1973), p. 381

10 The transcripts can be found at: http://www.nsa.gov/public_info/declass/venona/

11 Elizabeth Bentley, *Out of Bondage*, New York, 1951, p. 113

12 JMK XXVIII, p. 38

13 See, for instance, the extensive translations of the Vassilev notebooks by Svetlana Chervonnaya at: http://www.documentstalk.com/wp/harry-dexter-white-in-alexander-vassilievs-notes-on-kgb-foreign-intelligence-files

14 Letter from Julius Kobyakov to R.J. Sandilands, 22 December 2003, available at: http://www.documentstalk.com/wp/de-profundis-lauchlin-currie-and-harry-dexter-white-julius-kobyakov-evidence

15 Mikesell (2000), pp. 55–6

16 Allen Weinstein and Alexander Vassiliev, *The Haunted Wood*, New York, 1999, pp. 163–4

17 See, for instance, http://www.imf.org/external/pubs/ft/wp/2000/wp00149.pdf

18 Senator William Jenner's Interlocking Subversion in Government Departments Investigation by the Senate Internal Security Subcommittee

19 1997 Bipartisan Moynihan Commission on Government Secrecy

20 Winston Churchill, *Triumph and Tragedy*, London, 1954, pp. 227–8

21 Howson and Moggridge (1990), p. 120

22 Brand Papers, Bodleian Library, Oxford, Box 197, letter from Brand to Hugh Dalton, 23 April 1946

23 White Papers, Princeton, Box 6/5, 'Maintaining Peace', 30 November 1945

8 SNAKEBITE PARTY

1 JMK XXVI, p. 59

2 Johan Willem (Wim) Beyen, *Money in a Maelstrom*, London, 1951, p. 149

3 Keynes Papers, King's College Archives, PP/45/168/11, letter of 16 June 1944

4 Norman Longmate, *How We Lived Then: History of Everyday Life During the Second World War*, London, 2002, p. 110

5 Beyen (1951), p. 149

6 Horsefield (1969), p. 79

7 JMK XXVI, p. 71

8 Ibid., p. 41

9 Ibid., p. 16

10 Ibid., p. 10

11 Ibid., p. 17

12 Kynaston (2011), Kindle location 9281

13 Howson and Moggridge (1990), pp. 156–7

14 Wilfrid Eady, 'Maynard Keynes at the Treasury', *The Listener*, 7 June 1951

15 LSE Archives, Robbins 112, Transcript of Economists' Dinner at the Reform Club, 5 March 1973

16 Skidelsky (2000), p. 340

17 Beyen (1951), p. 150

18 Bernstein (1983), p. 95

19 James Bisset, *Commodore: War, Peace and Big Ships*, London, 1961

20 Wapshott (2011), p. 198

21 Bank of England Archives, OV38/8, Bolton diary

22 Ibid.

23 The 'Boat Draft' can be found in the IMF Archives, Box 1, File 15, 'Atlantic City Conference – Material Submitted by British on Fund and Bank', as well as in the Treasury files in the UK National Archives, Kew

24 Howson and Moggridge (1990), p. 156

25 Bank of England Archives, OV38/8, Bolton diary

9 BABEL ON WHEELS

1 Morgenthau Diary 746, p. 134

2 Ibid p. 128

3 'Has the Bretton Woods Conference Begun?', *Financial Chronicle*, 29 June 1944

4 J. Burke Knapp, oral history, Harry S. Truman Library

5 Bernstein (1983), pp. 4–11

6 Ibid., p. 55

7 Morgenthau Diary 746, pp. 133–9

8 IMF Archives, Box 1/7, Atlantic City Conference, 'Bourneuf Summary of Comments on Individual Bank Provisions'

9 IMF Archives, Harry White note to Morgenthau from Atlantic City

10 Dr John Parke Young, oral history, Harry S. Truman Library

11 Ibid.

12 Bank of England Archives, OV28/9

13 Bernstein (1983), p. 59

14 Bank of England Archives, OV28/8

15 JMK XXVI, p. 70

16 Beyen (1951), p. 150
17 'Notes on the Resorts', *New York Times*, 25 June 1944
18 Howson and Moggridge (1990), p. 159
19 JMK XXVI, p. 68
20 Dr John Parke Young, oral history, Harry S. Truman Library
21 Acheson (1969), p. 82
22 JMK XXVI, p. 123
23 Ibid., p. 67
24 'Has the Bretton Woods Conference Begun?', *Financial Chronicle*, 29 June 1944
25 Howson and Moggridge (1990), p. 163
26 JMK XXVI, p. 61
27 IMF Archives, Harry Dexter White, memorandum to Morgenthau, 25 June 1944
28 *Detroit News*, 14 August 1944
29 Kaity Argyropoulo, *From Peace to Chaos: A Forgotten Story*, New York, 1975
30 Craig (2004), p. 149

10 WEEK ONE

1 Bank of England Archives, OV38/9
2 Morgenthau Diary 755, p. 260
3 'Things at Monetary Parley Scene in Bit of a Dither', *Baltimore Sun*, 3 July 1944
4 National Archives, Kew, FO317/40918, letter from Richard Miles
5 '378 Envoys, 500 Newsmen Due at Monetary Parley', *Boston Globe*, 2 June 1944
6 Bretton Woods minutes, Commission I, International Monetary Fund first meeting
7 'Mt. Washington Hotel Awaits Opening of Fiscal Conference', *Christian Science Monitor*, 30 June 1944
8 Lydia Lopokova Papers, King's College Archives, LLK/5/122/9, 6 July
9 Ted Landphair and Carol Highsmith, *The Mount Washington: A Century of Grandeur*, Singapore, 2002, p. 97
10 *Banking*, 6 July 1944
11 Oscar Cox Diary, Franklin D. Roosevelt Library, 30 June 1944
12 Bank of England Archives, OV38/10, 'The International Monetary Conference'
13 'Pot Begins to Boil at Money Parley', *New York Post*, 14 July 1944
14 *Philadelphia Inquirer*, 3 September 1945

15 Milo Keynes (ed.), *Lydia Lopokova*, London, 1983, p. 185
16 *The Star*, 28 August 1944
17 Judith Mackrell, *Bloomsbury Ballerina: Lydia Lopokova, Imperial Dancer and Mrs John Maynard Keynes*, London, 2008, p. 386
18 Morgenthau (1991), pp. 344–5
19 Morgenthau Diary 749, pp. 2–3
20 'Seen and Heard at Bretton Woods Monetary Conference', *Banking*, 13 July 1944
21 Bernstein (1983), p. 104
22 Goldenweiser Papers, Library of Congress, Box 4
23 Bank of England Archives, OV38/10, note from George Bolton
24 *New York Times*, 4 July 1944
25 Morgenthau Diary 755, p. 260
26 Morgenthau Diary 749, p. 24
27 Ibid., p. 30
28 Ibid., p. 53
29 Transcript of Press Conference with White and Keynes, Bretton Woods Conference Collection, IMF Archives
30 Morgenthau Diary 749, p. 18
31 Ibid., p. 23
32 '1,300 Men with a Mission', *Time*, 17 July 1944
33 Susan Howson, *Lionel Robbins*, Toronto, 2012, p. 525
34 Proceedings I
35 Howson and Moggridge (1990), p. 167
36 Proceedings I
37 Howson and Moggridge (1990), p. 167
38 Morgenthau Diary 749, p. 219
39 Keynes Papers, King's College Archives, JMK/PP/45/168/11, letter to Florence Keynes, 25 July 1944
40 Goldenweiser remarks made at a joint meeting of directors of Federal Reserve Bank of Cleveland and branches, 2 November 1944
41 Landphair and Highsmith (2002), p. 97
42 B.K. Madan, 'Echoes of Bretton Woods', *Finance & Development*, June 1969
43 Louis Rasminsky, 'Private Reflections on Bretton Woods', courtesy of Dr Michael Rasminsky
44 Howson and Moggridge (1990), p. 171
45 Bank of England, OV38/9
46 JMK XXVI, p. 106
47 Goldenweiser Papers, Library of Congress, Box 4, 'Bretton Woods Conference'

48 National Archives, Kew, FO317/40917, 12 July 1944
49 Howson (2012), p. 526
50 'The Mission of Daddy Kung', *Time*, 3 July 1944
51 National Archives, Kew, FO317/40916
52 Howson and Moggridge (1990), p. 171
53 Acheson (1969), p. 83
54 Howson and Moggridge (1990), p. 171
55 National Archives, Kew, DO 35/1216
56 Morgenthau Diary 756, p. 6
57 Mikesell (1994), pp. 35–6
58 Mikesell (2000), pp. 34–5
59 Kurt Schuler and Andrew Rosenberg, *The Bretton Woods Transcripts*, New York, 2012, p. 123
60 Ibid., p. 128
61 Mikesell (1994), p. 37
62 Jean Lacoutre, *Pierre Mendès France*, trans. George Holoch. London, 1984, p. 153
63 Morgenthau Diary 754, pp. 164–79
64 Howson and Moggridge (1990), p. 186
65 National Archives, Kew, T247/29, cable 12 June 1944, Tehran to FO
66 Morgenthau Diary 754, p. 22
67 Bernstein (1983), pp. 61–2
68 Howson and Moggridge (1990), p. 172
69 Ibid., p. 173
70 King's College Archives, LLK/5/122/9, letter to Milo Keynes, 6 July 1944
71 Howson and Moggridge (1990), 6 July 1944

11 WEEK TWO

1 Goldenweiser Papers, Library of Congress, Box 4, 'Bretton Woods Conference'
2 Keynes Papers, King's College Archives, LLK/5/122/9, Lydia letter to Milo Keynes, 21 July 1944
3 Bank of England Archives, OV38/9, Bolton diary, 14 July
4 Howson and Moggridge (1990), p. 71
5 Morgenthau Diary 753, pp. 133–64
6 Morgenthau Diary 749, p. 224
7 Mikesell (2000)
8 Schuler and Rosenberg (2012), p. 308
9 JMK XXVI, p. 107

10 Morgenthau Diary 753, p. 138
11 Bank of England Archives, OV38/9
12 Van Dormael (1978), p. 209
13 Morgenthau Diary 753, p. 9
14 King's College Archives, JMK to Duncan Grant, 24 November 1908
15 *The Times*, 22 April 1963, p. 22
16 Peter Clarke, *The Keynesian Revolution in the Making*, Oxford, 1988, p. 171
17 JMK XIII, p. 506
18 Ibid., p. 520
19 White Papers, Princeton, Box 8/24a, from van Dormael (1978), p. 46
20 Van Dormael (1978), p. 113
21 Schuler and Rosenberg (2012), p. 63
22 National Archives, Kew, T247/38, Keynes to Hawtrey, 4 July
23 JMK XXVI, p. 109
24 Nurkse Papers, Princeton, Box 2, File 3
25 Bank of England Archives, OV38/9, Bolton diary, 14 July 1944
26 JMK XXVI, letter to Sir David Waley, 30 May 1944
27 Lydia Lopokova Papers, King's College Archives, LLK/5/122/9, letter from Lydia to Milo Keynes, 6 July 1944
28 I.F. Stone, 'Keynes, Once a Heretic, Seer of Money Parley', 17 July 1944, *PM*. From papers of Philip Jessup, Library of Congress, Box 3
29 Howson and Moggridge (1990), p. 178
30 Bank of England Archives, OV38/9, George Bolton diary
31 Howson and Moggridge (1990), p. 178
32 Bank of England Archives, OV38/9, 10 July
33 Keynes Papers, King's College Archives, LLK/5/122/9, letter from Lydia to Milo Keynes, 12 July 1944
34 Bruce Muirhead, *Against the Odds: The Public Life and Times of Louis Rasminsky*, Toronto, 1999, p. 325
35 Morgenthau Diary 751, p. 117
36 Morgenthau Diary 750, p. 238
37 Russian State Archive of Economics (RGAE), Fond 7733, op 29, File 1202, p.6
38 Mikesell (2000), p. 53
39 Robbins Papers, LSE Archives, Box 112, Transcript of Economists' Dinner at the Reform Club, 5 March 1973, p. 61
40 '1,300 Men with a Mission', *Time*, July 1944; Shirley Boskey, 'Bretton Woods Recalled', IMF Archives
41 http://evols.library.manoa.hawaii.edu/bitstream/handle/10524/32789/32-Volume8.pdf?sequence=1

42 National Archives, Kew, DO 35/1216

43 'At Bretton Woods', *Banking*, August 1944

44 Bernstein (1983), p. 101

45 Morgenthau (1991), pp. 344–5

46 George McJimsey (ed.), *Documentary History of the Franklin D. Roosevelt Presidency*, Vol. XL *The Bretton Woods Conference*, Bethesda, MD, 2008, pp. 428–30

47 Edwin McCammon Martin, oral history interview, Harry S. Truman Library, 1970

48 Bank of England Archives, OV38/9, Bolton diary, 6 July 1944

49 'Significant and Insignificant Happenings at Bretton Woods', *Banking*, 6 July 1944

50 Ibid.

51 'Seen and Heard at Bretton Woods', *Banking*, 13 July 1944

52 *The Economist*, 12 August 1944, p. 213

53 Robbins Papers, LSE Archives, Box 112

54 Oscar Cox Papers, FDR Library, Box 126, 'Extracts from Various German and Japanese Broadcasts ...'

55 Howson and Moggridge (1990), p. 179

56 Ibid., p. 174

57 'Publicity Man Causes Conference Flurry: Hinshaw Departs after Protest by Press', *New York Times*, 9 July 1944

12 WEEK THREE

1 Morgenthau Diary 756, p. 37

2 Howson and Moggridge (1990), p. 191

3 Bank of England Archives, OV38/10

4 *Financial News*, 17 July 1944

5 Russian State Archive of Economics, Fond 7733, op 29, File 1202, p.23

6 National Archives, Kew, T231/367, letter from Gamble to Haybittle, 8 July 1944

7 National Archives, Kew, FO317/40918, No. 76, Remac 17 July

8 Nurkse Papers, Princeton University, Box 2, File 3

9 Morgenthau Diary 755, p. 81

10 Keynes Papers, King's College Archives, letter from JMK to Catto, 22 July 1944

11 'Brown Opines World Bank Is OK, Also Rest', *Chicago News*, 25 July 1944

12 Morgenthau Diary 755, p. 78

13 Morgenthau Diary 755, p. 74
14 'Conference Adds Three Days to Talks', *New York Times*, 18 July 1944; *The New Yorker*, 5 August 1944
15 Proceedings II, p. 1185
16 Proceedings I, p. 790
17 National Archives, Kew, FO317/40919
18 National Archives, Kew, T231/366, Foreign Office to Bretton Woods, 2 July 1944
19 Morgenthau Diary 753, p. 162
20 Howson and Moggridge (1990), p. 184
21 Proceedings II, p. 1166
22 Keynes Papers, King's College Archives, letter from JMK to Lord Catto, 22 July 1944
23 Morgenthau Diary 756, pp. 54–7
24 LSE Archives, RES 9/8/2, letter from Nigel Ronald to unidentified newspaper
25 LSE Archives, RES 6/1/92, letter from JMK to Colin Clark of the Bureau of Industry, Australia
26 Proceedings 1, p. 939
27 Morgenthau Diary 756, p. 151
28 John Parke Young, oral history, Harry S. Truman Library
29 Samuel Crowthers in 'Journal American', in American press summary, 9 July 1944, in National Archives, Kew, FO317/40918
30 Howson and Moggridge (1990), p. 192
31 Ibid., p. 185
32 Ibid., p. 191
33 John Parke Young, oral history, Harry S. Truman Library
34 Russian State Archive of Economics, Fond 7733, op 29, File 1202, p.61
35 Morgenthau Diary 755, p. 83
36 Wilfred Eady, 'Maynard Keynes at the Treasury', *The Listener*, 7 June 1951
37 Keynes Papers, King's College Archives, letter from JMK to Lord Catto, 22 July 1944
38 John Parke Young, oral history, Harry S. Truman Library
39 Howson and Moggridge (1990), p. 193
40 Morgenthau Diary 757, pp. 13A–B
41 Proceedings II, p. 1234
42 JMK XXVI, pp. 101–3
43 King's College Archives, PP/45/168/11, 25 July 1944
44 Proceedings I, p. 1123

45 'Dumbells Odd Items from Everywhere', *Boston Globe*, 28 July 1944
46 Morgenthau Diary 757, pp. 1–13
47 'Funk Denounces Currency Parley', *New York Times*, 8 July 1944
48 Howson and Moggridge (1990), p. 193
49 Bank of England Archives, OV38/10, 'The International Monetary Conference'

13 UNMITIGATED EVIL

1   JMK XXVI, p. 149
2   Skidelsky (2000), p. 358
3   Howson and Moggridge (1990), p. 211
4   Louis Rasminsky private memoir, p. 24
5   Keynes Papers, King's College Archives, PP/45/168/11, JMK to Florence Keynes, 7 August 1944
6   Ibid.
7   Ibid.
8   MacDonald (1969), p. 176
9   Keynes Papers, King's College Archives, PP/45/168/11, JMK to Florence Keynes, 1 August 1944
10 MacDonald (1969), pp. 178–9
11 National Archives, Kew, T247/368
12 Howson and Moggridge (1990), p. 195
13 MacDonald (1969), p. 179
14 Keynes Papers, King's College Archives, PP/45/168/11, JMK to Florence Keynes, 8 August 1944
15 'The Battle of Bretton Woods', *Fortune Magazine*, July 1945
16 Hearings before Committee on Banking and Currency, House of Representatives, 79th Congress, 1st Session, HR 2211, pp. 405–73
17 John Parke Young, oral history Haarry S. Truman Library
18 National Archives, Kew, T160/1281/F18885/11, Keynes memorandum, 16 May 1944
19 Goldenweiser Papers, Library of Congress, Box 6, memorandum dated 21 December 1944
20 Morgenthau Diary 752, pp. 279–80
21 Morgenthau Diary 657, p. 22
22 Brand Papers, Bodleian Library, Box 197, Brand to Eady, 7 March 1945
23 Van Dormael (1978), p. 286
24 'Bretton Woods is No Mystery', IMF Archives
25 *Daily Express*, 10 August 1944
26 JMK XXVI, p. 17

27 John Morton Blum, *From the Morgenthau Diaries: Years of War, 1941–1945*, Boston, 1967, p. 252

28 Testimony before the US House Committee on Banking and Currency, in Gardner (1956), p. 141

29 John Morton Blum, *Roosevelt and Morgenthau, A Revision and Condensation of/From The Morgenthau Diaries*, Boston, 1970, p. 572

30 Morgenthau Diary 776, p. 33

31 Morgenthau Diary 783, pp. 23–9

32 JMK XXIV, pp. 134–5

33 Milo Keynes (1983), p. 184

34 JMK XXIV, p. 134

35 Milo Keynes (1983), pp. 172–3

36 Keynes Papers, King's College Archives, L/E, letter to Sir Wilfred Eady, 5 October 1944

37 Bank of England Archives, OV38/10

38 JMK XXIV, pp. 187, Frank Lee to F.E. Harmer, 6 December 1944

39 Ibid., pp. 214–15, JMK to Sir John Anderson, 12 December 1944

40 Brand Papers, Bodleian Library, Box 198, Brand to JMK, 24 October 1944

41 JMK XXIV, p. 188, Frank Lee to F.E. Harmer, 6 December 1944

14 STARVATION CORNER

1 Papers of Richard (Otto) Clarke, Churchill College, Cambridge, CLRK 4/4/4, 22 April 1946

2 Tony Judt, *Postwar*, London, 2005, Kindle location 593

3 Goldenweiser Papers, Library of Congress, 'Conversations and Reflections in Europe, Summer 1945'

4 David Hubback, *No Ordinary Press Baron: A Life of Walter Layton*, London, 1985, p. 77

5 Keynes Papers, King's College, Cambridge, PP/45, JMK to Marcel Labordere, 28 March 1945, cited in Skidelsky (2000), p. 378

6 Milo Keynes (1980), p. 64

7 Harrod (1951), p. 619

8 Ben Pimlott, *Hugh Dalton*, London, 1985, p. 509

9 Ibid., p. 284

10 Ansel F. Luxford, oral history, Columbia University, 13 July 1961, p. 12

11 *Time*, 17 September 1945

12 Moggridge (2003), pp. 756–7

13 JMK XXIV, *The Present Overseas Financial Position of the UK*, p. 410

14 JMK XXIV, p. 258

15 Ibid., p. 35
16 National Archives, Kew, T247/34, JMK to Beaverbrook, 8 March 1944
17 JMK XXIV, p. 279
18 Brand Papers, Bodleian Library, Box 196, Brand to JMK, 5 March 1945
19 Keynes Papers, King's College Archives, PP/45
20 Edmund Dell, *The Chancellors*, London, 1997, pp. 23–5
21 Skidelsky (2000), pp. 395–6
22 Howson and Moggridge (1990), p. 221
23 Ibid., p. 223
24 Skidelsky (2000), p. 419
25 Ibid., p. 432
26 Gardner (1956), p. 199
27 Howson and Moggridge (1990), p. 230; Skidelsky (2000), p. 416
28 Ibid., p. 435
29 JMK XXIV p. 510
30 Ibid., p. 218
31 Moggridge (2003), p. 798
32 Skidelsky (2000), p. 414
33 Howson and Moggridge (1990), p. 224
34 Roger Bullen and M.E. Pelly (eds), *Documents on British Policy Overseas*, Series 1, Vol. III, *Britain and America: Negotiation of the United States Loan 3 August–7 December 1945*, London, 1986, p. 169
35 Howson and Moggridge (1990), p. 224
36 Skidelsky (2000), p. 433
37 Dell (1997), pp. 31–2
38 Brand Papers, Bodleian Library, Box 197, Eady to Brand, 22 December 1945
39 Bullen and Pelly (1986), p. 431
40 http://www.theyworkforyou.com/debates/?id=1945-12-12a.421.7
41 Robbins (1971), p. 210
42 JMK XXIV, pp. 605–24
43 Brand Papers, Bodleian Library, Box 198, JMK to Brand, 6 January 1946; 29 January 1946
44 JMK XXVII, p. 467
45 Dell (1997), p. 61

15 ONWARD CHRISTIAN SOLDIERS

1 *New York Times*, 28 December 1945
2 Archive of the Foreign Ministry of the Russian Federation, The

Ministry of Foreign Relations, Fond 0129, op. 29, P. 166, File 3, 'Letters of the US Embassy in Moscow to the People's Commissar of Foreign Affairs and to the Assistant People's Commissars of Foreign Affairs, vol. 2, May 1–December 24 1945', pp. 166–8, George F. Kennan, Charge d'Affairs to His Excellency A.J. Vyshinsky, Assistant People's Commissar of Foreign Affairs, Moscow, 27 September 1945. Translated from Russian original

3 Archive of the Foreign Policy of the Russian Federation (AVP RF) (courtesy of Dr Svetlana Chervonnaya), The Ministry of Foreign Relations, Fond 0129, op. 29, P. 166, File 1, 'Letters from the NKID to the US Embassy in Moscow', 1945, p. 224, V. Molotov to G. Kennan, 29 December 1945. Translated from Russian original

4 Averell Harriman Papers, Library of Congress, Box 185, Folder 8, Kennan to Secretary of State, 2 January 1946

5 Russian State Archive of Economics, Fond 7733, op 29, File 1202, p.74

6 Harold James and Marzenna James, 'The Origins of the Cold War: Some New Documents', *The Historical Journal*, Vol. 37, No. 3 (September 1994), p. 619

7 V.I. Batjuk, *The Sources of the Cold War: Soviet–American Relations in 1945–1950*, Moscow, 1992

8 James and James (1994)

9 Walter Isaacson and Evan Thomas, *The Wise Men*, New York, 1986, p. 365

10 Batjuk (1992)

11 Isaacson and Thomas (1986), p. 362

12 Bank of England Archives, OV38/13, Bolton diary, 1 March 1946

13 Rees (1973), p. 381

14 Ibid., p. 387

15 *New York Times*, 17 November 1953

16 Luxford (1961), p. 28

17 Bank of England Archives, OV38/13, Bolton diary, 15 March 1946

18 Luxford (1961), pp. 21–2

19 Bank of England Archives, OV38/13, Bolton diary, 12 March 1946

20 Ibid., 15 March 1946

21 Ibid., 1 March 1946

22 *New York Times*, 2 March 1946

23 JMK XXVI, p. 211

24 Luxford (1961)

25 JMK XXVI, p. 214

26 Ibid., pp. 215–17

27 Gardner (1956), p. 266

28 IMF Archives, Box 2/5

29 Brand Papers, Bodleian Library, Box 197, Brand to Eady, 22 March 1946

30 Rasminsky memoirs

31 Van Dormael (1978), p. 297

32 Ibid., p. 302

33 Bank of England Archives, OV38/13, Bolton to Siepmann, 9 March 1946

34 Sylvia Porter, 'US Bossed Money Parley', *New York Post*, 18 March 1946

35 IMF Archives, Box 2/5

36 Bank of England Archives, OV38/13, Bolton diary, 15 March 1946

37 JMK XXVI, p. 232

38 Keynes Papers, King's College Archives, PP/45, JMK to Janos Plesch, 20 March 1946

39 Mikesell (2000), p. 58

40 Brand Papers, Bodleian Library, Box 197, Eady to Brand, 23 April 1946

41 Skidelsky (2000), p. 471

42 Brand Papers, Bodleian Library, Box 197, Eady to Brand, 23 April 1946; Brand to Eady, 22 April 1946

43 'John Maynard Keynes', *The Times Great Lives: A Century In Obituaries*, London, 2005

44 Robbins Papers, London School of Economics, Box 112, Lydia Keynes to Robbins, 29 April 1946

45 IMF Archives, Executive Board Minutes, 6 May 1946

46 *New York Times*, 16 May 1946

47 Bank of England Archives, OA11/1, 18–22 May 1946

48 Isaacson and Thomas (1986), pp. 385–6

49 Joseph M. Jones, *The Fifteen Weeks (February 21–June 5, 1947)*, New York, 1955, pp. 129–47

50 Bank of England Archives, OA11/1, 10 September 1946; 22–4 May 1946

51 Interlocking Subversion in Government Departments Hearings, Part 30, pp. 2415–816, Washington, 1956

52 Ibid.

53 Rees (1973), p. 410

54 HUAC Hearings, 13 August 1948

55 *New York Times*, 7 November 1953

56 National Archives, Kew, FO 317/103508

57 Morgenthau Diary 751, p. 93
58 White Papers, Princeton, Box 9/18, undated notepad
59 White Papers, Princeton, Box 9/16, 'Rough draft'

16 THE BRETTON WOODS SYSTEM

1 Cited in Paul Bareau, 'The Disorder in World Money, from Bretton Woods to SDRs', Wincott Lecture, 1981
2 David Kynaston, *Austerity Britain*, London, 2008, p. 140
3 Ben Pimlott (ed.), *The Political Diaries of Hugh Dalton, 1918–40, 1945–60*, London, 1986, pp. 409–10
4 Bernstein (1983), p. 120
5 Piercy Papers, LSE Archives, Box 8/9, 'International Financial Machinery'
6 Harold James, *International Monetary Cooperation since Bretton Woods*, Oxford, 1996, Kindle location 1543
7 Barry Eichengreen, *Globalizing Capital*, Oxford, 2008, p. 127
8 Richard Reeves, *President Nixon*, New York, 2001, Kindle location 6785
9 William L. Silber, *Volcker: The Triumph of Persistence*, London, 2012, p. 57
10 *New York Times*, 6 May 1971; 11 May 1971
11 Silber (2012), p. 80
12 Reeves (2001), Kindle location 7075
13 http://www.businessweek.com/magazine/the-nixon-shock-08042011.html
14 Silber (2012), p. 87
15 Ibid., p. 88
16 Ibid., p. 87
17 William Safire, *Before the Fall: An Inside View of the Pre-Watergate White House*, New York, 1975, p. 520
18 Robert H. Ferrell (ed.), *Inside the Nixon Administration: The Secret Diary of Arthur Burns, 1969–1974*, Kansas, 2010, 12 August 1971
19 Scott W. Ohlmacher, 'The Dissolution of the Bretton Woods System – Evidence from the Nixon Tapes, August–December 1971', p. 31, available at: http://udspace.udel.edu/handle/19716/4275
20 Silber (2012), p. 110
21 James (1996), Kindle location 4356
22 *New York Times*, 12 February 1973

EPILOGUE

1 Oliver Bush, Katie Farrant and Michelle Wright, 'Reform of the International Monetary and Financial System', Financial Stability Paper No. 13, December 2011. Many of these calculations are derived from original research by Bordo, M., Eichengreen, B., Klingebiel, D. and Martinez Peria, M. S. (2001), 'Is the Crisis Problem Growing More Severe?' *Economic Policy*, Vol. 16(32), pp.51–82

2 John Maynard Keynes, 'Economic Possibilities for our Grandchildren', 1930

3 Eichengreen (2008), p. 121

4 Robert Mundell, 'Capital Mobility and Stabilization Policy under Fixed and Flexible Exchange Rates', *Canadian Journal of Economic and Political Science*, Vol. 29(4)1963, pp. 475–85

5 The 'trilemma' in international monetary policy, which shows how a country can have two, but not three, of the following at any one time: fixed exchange rates, free movement of capital, and independent national monetary policy:

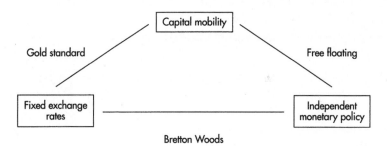

6 T. Philippon, 'The Evolution of the US Financial Industry from 1860 to 2007: Theory and Evidence', 2008, available at:http://economics. stanford.edu/files/Philippon5_20.pdf. Cited inAndrew Haldane, 'The Contribution of the Financial Sector –Miracle or Mirage?', 2010, available at: http://www.bankofenland.co.uk/publications/Documents/ speeches/2010/speech442.pdf

7 Bank for International Settlements Triennial Central Bank Survey, September 2013

8 Haldane (2010)

9 Mervyn King, interview with the author, May 2013

10 Zhou Xiaochuan, 'Reform the International Monetary System',

March 2009, available at: http://www.pbc.gov.cn/publish/english/ 956/2009/20091229104425550619706/20091229104425550619706 _.html

11 Speaking at event in Yale: 'The Future of the Global Financial System', 10 January 2014. http://som.yale.edu/our-approach/edward-p-evans-hall/opening-events/business-society-leadership-increasingly-complex-world/future-global-financial-system

12 Mervyn King, interview with the author, May 2013

13 Speaking at event in Yale: 'The Future of the Global Financial System', 10 January 2014: http://som.yale.edu/our-approach/edward-p-evans-hall/opening-events/business-society-leadership-increasingly-complex-world/future-global-financial-system

14 Olivier Blanchard, interview with the author, July 2013

15 Ibid.

16 Ibid.

17 Jeff Frankel, 'Restructuring the International Financial System: A New Bretton Woods', available at: http://belferfrankel.wordpress.com/ 2008/10/24/restructuring-the-international-financial-system-a-new-bretton-woods/

18 Morgenthau Diary 749, p. 161

19 JMK XXVI, pp. 215–16

20 http://weekly.ahram.org.eg/2003/656/ec4.htm

Index

About the Author

Ed Conway is the economics editor of Sky News. Previously he was economics editor of the *Daily Telegraph* and *Sunday Telegraph*. He is the author of *50 Economics Ideas You Really Need to Know*, which was an Amazon bestseller and has been translated into thirteen languages. He lives in London, where he was born in 1979.